And We Shall Shock Them

By the same author
ALANBROOKE

And We Shall Shock Them

The British Army in the Second World War

David Fraser

"Come the three corners of the world in arms,
And we shall shock them. Nought shall make us rue,
If England to itself do rest but true."

(W. Shakespeare, *King John*)

BOOK CLUB ASSOCIATES
LONDON

The author and publishers wish to thank the following for their kind permission to reproduce the illustrations: the US National Archives for the photograph of Von Bock; Camera Press for the photograph of Bradley; the US Foreign Histories Division for the photograph of Kimura; the Robert Hunt Picture Library for the photograph of Mutaguchi and the Imperial War Museum for all other photographs.

For my friends
who fell

Contents

Part V
Triumph at Last

Author's Preface

This book is not an essay on grand strategy. It is a book about the British Army's character, actions, failings and achievements in the most recent of great wars in which it has taken part, but, in dealing with particular aspects or with campaigns in the circumscribed span of one volume, treatment has to be impressionistic rather than analytical. The picture has to be painted without too much detail; and only certain features can be given prominence. This book is not, therefore, a comprehensive history of all the army did. Much is omitted. I have not discussed the mighty achievements of Anti-Aircraft Command; nor the heroic defence and defiance of Malta; nor expeditions sharp and bitter at the time until the tide of war washed over them, such as those to Madagascar, into Syria, to the Dodecanese Islands, to restore the internal situation in Greece. I have, instead, painted this impression of the British Army with colours drawn from some of its major struggles.

It is impossible to write about the British Army in the Second World War and to isolate that army from the actions of its comrades from different lands. In Greece, Crete, North and East Africa, Malaya, Burma, British units or formations were a minority in what was, nominally, a British Army. The majority were Australian, New Zealand, Indian, African and South African divisions, with a gallant mixture of Greeks, Poles and French fighting for a while beside the British flag. In describing operations I have made little distinction. In discussing character, composition and tactics my observations are upon the British. Difficult though it is to write in isolation about the British Army when its troops were fighting shoulder to shoulder and inter-mingled with men of other nations the attempt has to be made. This book, then, is not a history of any other Commonwealth nation's Army, nor of the Indian Army of the old British Empire. Still less is it about the armies of Allied Powers, intimately connected though their operations later were with those of the British Army, and often under the same Supreme Command: the war was an Allied war, victory an Allied victory. But this book is about the British Army.

Marshal of the Royal Air Force Lord Tedder made one of the wisest comments on British books about war.[1] The British, he observed,

[1] *Air Power in War*, Hodder & Stoughton, 1947.

ix

concentrate upon their successes, and thus draw lessons too much from the later stages of conflict when there are, very often, resources in abundance. "It is," Tedder wrote, "the problems of the early stages which we should study." I agree. At the beginning of a war resources are in short supply. Mental and physical condition has not been hardened by battle. Illusions abound. Unless arrangements have been far-sighted and loyalty to alliance nurtured in time of peace, Allied co-operation is defective, command systems ambiguous. The psychology and condition of the nation, the army and its commanders all reflect the mood of the period of peace preceding hostilities. That mood may have engendered realism, readiness, an even determination to see that all the resources and particularly the manpower of the nation are planned to play their part if the worst occurs. The mood may, on the other hand, have been escapist, indolent, apathetic or cowardly – often seeking excuse for inaction in glib assumptions about the course of future hostilities, assumptions often brutally disproved when it is too late to react. If ever we hear echoes in contemporary events of the wasted twenty years before 1939 we should recall with melancholy what followed, and the young lives lost which realism and preparedness might have saved. Early and avoidable calamities in war are the consequence of softness, myopia and unprofessionalism in peace.

The story of the early stages of the British Army in the Second World War is not a happy one, but it is important; hence the balance of this book reflects Tedder's view. I have devoted much more space to the early encounters where resources were inadequate, weapons defective, tactics and training faulty than to the glories of later years. The balance of the book does not, therefore, match the duration of particular operations, nor the comparative size of forces deployed. Indeed, in the early campaigns the scale of British operations in terms of troops employed was generally so small that the actions of single divisions, brigades or even battalions represented the military effort of the nation, and need description in order to comprehend the often disastrous outcome.

The first part of this book describes the appalling shocks suffered by the British Army in the beginning. The second and third parts tell something of the long learning period when the army was struggling towards reconstitution and competence and only the few, less than ready for their opponents and frequently mishandled, were engaged – in the Mediterranean, in Burma and in Malaya. Only in the fourth part is it possible to sense light breaking, as the British went forward from Alamein, cleared North Africa, invaded Italy, defeated the last Japanese offensive, and stood again upon the fields of France. In the last part the army's task came to culmination, the loop of its destiny completed, as the taking of Rangoon redeemed Singapore, as Dunkirk was avenged by the crossing of the Rhine, and as the army that had straggled back before Rommel at Gazala stood at last upon the Alpine passes. It is a story which moves from triumph to tragedy, and then upward again to triumph at the last.

Acknowledgments

I acknowledge with gratitude agreement of the Trustees of the Alan-brooke Settlement and Executors of the late Viscount Alanbrooke to my again using the Alanbrooke Papers in the writing of this book, and in that connection the unfailing helpfulness of the staff at the Liddell Hart Centre for Military Archives, King's College, London.

I am especially indebted to those who have read particular chapters and given me the benefit of their knowledge and advice; and in this connection wish especially to thank Dr Brian Bond, Field Marshal Lord Carver, Major Warren Freeman-Attwood, Colonel Lord Freyberg, General Sir John Gibbon, Major-General Desmond Gordon, Major-General Patrick Hobart, Mr Ronald Lewin and Brigadier Pollock. I am most grateful, too, to those who have agreed to quotation from letters, in particular Viscount Montgomery of Alamein and Earl Alexander of Tunis.

The authorities at a number of libraries have been as helpful and patient as usual: I must especially thank the librarians and their assistants at the Royal College of Defence Studies, the Royal United Services Institute and the Ministry of Defence Library.

The typescripts, frequently repeated, have been the work of several hands, but I must particularly mention Erica Vaux. Lastly my wife, as usual, has provided throughout practical support, and patient, perceptive advice.

List of Maps

Maps by W. F. N. Watson.

Part I

Triumph to Tragedy

1

The Rusting Sword

11th November 1918

Throughout the British Army in France and Flanders men rubbed
their eyes and stretched their wet and weary limbs. "One has been
feeling one's way through the dark for four and a half years," wrote a
Battalion Commander, whose time on the Western Front had been
unbroken save when wounded, "and now one has come out into the
sunlight, but one is blind, one cannot see the sun."[1] As companies
turned out in the early morning, to march towards the enemy, to parade
for training if in reserve, the message came through which had been
rumoured for the previous three days. The Armistice would be signed
at eleven o'clock.

There was some relief, little triumph, rather a bemused sense of
anticlimax mixed with exhaustion. Yet the army's achievement was on a
mighty and memorable scale. Sixty divisions formed the command of
Field Marshal Sir Douglas Haig. Behind this huge force, the greatest
by far ever put into the field by Britain, lay a vast administrative system
of transportation, ports, depots, field hospitals, repair and recreation
facilities, a great training organisation for the British Expeditionary
Force alone. The British Army was enormous and all-conquering.

It had not always been so. The Expeditionary Force of 1914 was
excellently trained and disciplined, entirely professional, described
even by its enemy as "a perfect thing, apart" – but tiny. A mere four
British infantry and one cavalry divisions faced the Germans at Mons
and Le Cateau. That little Regular Army largely perished at the First
Battle of Ypres, and a hastily improvised citizen army, drawing still on
the voluntary principle alone, formed the "New Armies" which fought
the battle of the Somme. Conscription was only introduced in 1916. It
was both the glory and shame of Britain that the army had been
manned entirely by volunteers in its greatest expansion, and throughout the first two years of the most demanding war in its history: glory to
the race and generation that volunteered, shame on society and

[1] Fraser Papers.

3

government that permitted such inequitable sacrifice of the bravest and the best.

Now, after all the suffering, the achievements of the army were phenomenal, the soldiers' spirits high, their victory assured. Since August 1918 the army had undertaken six major offensives, ended the long stalemate of the trenches, broken through the redoubtable Hindenburg Line, carried the campaign into enemy-held territory and played the major part in forcing upon Germany an historic capitulation. Fifty-nine British divisions fought and defeated ninety-nine German in the battles of those last months, taking nearly 200,000 prisoners and close on 3,000 guns. At Amiens, Courtrai, Le Cateau, Maubeuge, Mons the German Army was driven with terrible cost from the fields they had overrun. Their Emperor abdicated. Their emissaries sued for peace.

These triumphs, however, found little place in popular British mythology about the First World War. Triumphs they certainly were. German spirit, worn down by the attrition of the last four years, was beginning to fail; but this was no rounding up of a beaten enemy, rotted by internal subversion. Here and there the British took whole German units prisoner with few casualties – but in much of the great area of campaign, right up to November itself, British battalions were recording actions in language reminiscent of any time in the last four years:

23rd October 1918

The Companies got a good bit mixed up at the entry to the village but they got to their objectives pretty well. The village itself was being very heavily shelled all the time by the Boche. Have not seen his artillery fire so heavy in battle for a long time now . . .[1]

But the enemy was beaten – in open warfare, in fair fight and beyond hope of negotiation. "Haig," ran a German assessment, "is master of the field."[2]

This encomium was deserved. True, the British formed only part of a great Allied force. But the Americans, fresh and unwearied, were still few in numbers of divisions, having entered the war only in 1917; and the French were exhausted, bled white by the terrible casualties of Verdun in 1916 and the disastrous offensive of 1917 which followed. A great and disproportionate share of the fighting of the last glorious months was done by the British Army.

[1] Fraser Papers.
[2] British Official History, Vol. II.

That army had learned much. At the grim game of trench warfare it had become adept. It had shown itself – New Armies and conscript force alike – worthy successor to the old Regular Army of 1914. Its organisation was magnificent – it was a huge and well-designed machine. "The army," said Alfred de Vigny of other times, "is a machine – but a machine that can suffer." And this army had shown exemplary capacity to endure. Nearly 600,000 British soldiers had died, on all fronts. Now all the endurance seemed redeemed, all the suffering rewarded, all the terrible and costly attrition of the enemy justified. The Hindenburg Line was breached, clean open country was at last discovered behind the brown shell-torn landscape of the trenches. In muddy fields surrounded by bivouacs, in the squares of battered villages and looted towns, drums and fifes, pipes and drums, paraded to play the Regimental Marches to the cheers of French and Belgian inhabitants, dazed by it all. It was over. We had won. November 1918.

Twenty-one and a half years later, on the same ground and against the same enemy, another British Army suffered humiliating defeat. Once again, early in a war, it formed a small element of an Allied force; and whatever its skill it could hardly have averted disaster if the French Army collapsed as it did. But in fact skill was absent. The British Army at the beginning of the Second World War was unprepared for war, materially, tactically and – perhaps above all – psychologically. In less than a generation the hard-won heritage of victory had been dissipated. "If mortal catastrophe should overtake the British nation," declared Churchill, "historians a thousand years hence will never understand how it was that a victorious nation suffered themselves to cast away all that they had gained by measureless sacrifice." No reversal of military fortune has ever been more complete than that evoked by the two dates 1918 and 1940. In that fact lie the seeds of the tragedies and triumphs to come.

So great a victory as that of the First World War should have been followed by a determination to protect its fruits and to learn its lessons. Instead, the next twenty years were marked by neglect of every principle which the war had produced.

First, and by far the most important, was the very principle of participation by the British Army in Continental warfare. This had, before 1914, been contentious. There had been those who believed that our strategy should be solely maritime, relying upon our island situation and upon that sea-power which, it was argued, had played the ultimately decisive part in frustrating the ambitions of Napoleon, and in other historic struggles. The difficulty, as ever, was to reconcile this essentially national and protracted strategy with a policy of alliance. Some, like Lord Esher, had maintained that British naval power would be "the value of the Entente to France in war" – to find, as had always been manifest, that no Continental ally is interested in the attritional effects of sea-power unless the land frontiers are secure. A coalition only survives if there is some perception of equality of sacrifice. Britain's maritime contribution, however formidable, could never hold together a Continental alliance. The lesson had been clear from the first to the last day of the war – not only clear in political terms but militarily compulsive, since all could see that without the British Army France would have been beaten by Germany on land.

Yet, after 1918, there was revulsion from the terrible logic of these events. Because Britain, surrounded by sea, had once been able to "eat à la carte" in the matter of a Continental commitment for her army – to take as much or as little as desired – it was soon believed that this could again be so. Soon the experience of the war was to be described as "abnormal" for the British Army – not because of the tactical nature the war assumed but because of the scale of our participation on the Continent. This was irrational. The advent of air power had increased the significance of keeping an enemy as far as possible from our shores, and the resurgence of Germany in the 1930s made clear who that enemy might be. But the principal lesson of the First World War which the British decided to learn was that our casualties had been proportionately higher than in previous wars, and that these had been, in the main, suffered on land and on the Continent of Europe. It seemed reasonable to listen to those voices that preached the possibility for Britain, maritime power and possessor of a worldwide empire, to avoid Continental war. Even when under the pressure of international politics, and late in the day, it was recognised that an Expeditionary Force would once again need to be despatched, the commitment was hedged about by reservations. There must be no great national army raised for Continental warfare on the pattern of 1914–18. There must be limited liability. The respected "guru" of British military thinking, Captain Basil Liddell Hart, preached a "British way in warfare" which, when shorn of qualifications, eschewed the Continental commitment altogether.

Under the stimulus of Adolf Hitler all this changed – jerkily, tardily and reluctantly. Almost throughout the last twenty-one years, however, the British Army had no clear role to guide it towards preparedness for war. Instead it was absorbed by the many tasks of imperial policing which arose in the aftermath of 1918 and for which it was often inadequate in size; as well as by the minutiae of garrison and regimental life without clear military purpose. No army can produce quality in such circumstances. Many of the best had fallen in battle. Unsurprisingly, the army generally failed to attract the sort of minds it needed: its function provided inadequate stimulus, and its beggarly pay derisory reward. Idleness and intellectual sloth, besetting sins of armies, tended to prevail. It was all remarkably and sadly different from the years before 1914.

This lack of defined role and this determination to regard the experience of the First War as an aberration rather than a foundation had two other notable effects. The first was a half-hearted attitude toward technological and tactical development. This is not to say that there was not study and profound discussion, by particular officers, of the tactical lessons of the war and the way ahead. There was, and the professional periodicals of the day are full of it. Staff College courses hummed with argument. But in the absence of any coherent strategic philosophy on what sort of war the army might in future have to fight, there was failure to develop a clear line at the official level, to evolve and establish tactical doctrine and draw organisational deductions therefrom. Instead, policy in these matters drifted, subject to the pressure of interested lobbies or inertial forces. The oft-told story of the tank provides an example.

The tank, developed by the British in 1916, had first achieved great success at the Battle of Cambrai. No technical task could be more challenging than to develop the mechanical reliability of the tracked vehicle, able to move across country and obstacles, and to develop the protective power of armour and the penetrative power of anti-armour weapons. No tactical task could be more demanding than to study how the new weapon should be employed, how (if at all) it should be combined with other arms, and how mobility of the latter should be attained, so that a force might move at better pace than that of the slowest, and remain united for action. Its future and the whole concept of mechanised warfare were the most urgent matters to confront all armies during the period between 1918 and 1939. For the combination of the internal combustion engine, the caterpillar track and armoured plating had restored the possibility of manoeuvre to the battlefield, but to what models might these manoeuvres conform?

The British should have led the way, as pioneers of tank development; they had a cadre of officers well versed in its use, who had survived the war. A few were men of outstanding intellect, prolific writers. Nevertheless, these tended to be prophets without honour in their own country. There were many reasons for this. A certain intolerance and arrogance on the part of the prophets: military conservatism, always strong in time of peace: affection for the horse, as part of the combat arms, threatened, it appeared, by mechanisation: shortage of funds: while, of course, there was no shortage of simple prejudice between those regarded by their opponents as greasy mechanics on the one hand and as snobbish amateurs on the other. But the underlying reason was the same as the root cause of all the army's unpreparedness and neglect – that there was no strategic assumption that the army should participate in major warfare. There was, therefore, little stimulus to respond to the prophets, or intelligently to dispute with them: little motive to answer the great questions posed by mechanised operations, without a strategic background against which such operations could be conceived.

As a result the British Army entered the Second World War without a coherent doctrine of armoured operations, and with little general understanding of how those operations might change the whole pattern of warfare. The Expeditionary Force arrived in France with no properly constituted armoured formation. In such disorder did the victorious British of twenty-one years before come to encounter once again the defeated German Army – the latter restricted to 100,000 men and forbidden modern weapons until all was changed by the advent of Hitler in 1933, and yet fielding against the Western Powers seven years later ninety-three divisions, including no less than ten armoured divisions with some 2,500 tanks.

The British rejection of the experience of 1914–18 had a further consequence: perhaps the most paralysing malady which can afflict an army – the doctrine of the perpetual defensive. The huge and tragic casualty lists of the earlier war were associated in the political, the public – and the military – mind with the offensive. The most expensive attacks of that war had been, in the main, undertaken under political imperative. The French Army had had to be sustained, and the German Army stood on the soil of France and had to be dislodged. But these truths were brushed aside. The offensives were remembered as battles at great human cost for a few miles of ground won, no great strategic benefit, sacrifice for nothing. The victorious offensive battles of the closing months were quickly and perversely forgotten. Instead there was a popular picture of "The Offensive" which assumed, in Winston Churchill's memorable phrase, that it consisted of "fighting machine-gun bullets with the breasts of gallant men". There was some justice in this folk-memory, but it was selective. And it led, inevitably, to the conclusion that the strongest – the only sane – method of war was to entrench, fortify and wait for the enemy to expose his body and equipment to the power of the defender's direct fire and artillery.

Such an attitude, however understandable, was outdated and erroneous. It was also insidious in its effect upon morale. Of course the British could reasonably assume that in a future conflict they would be standing upon the *strategic* defensive – that they would not be the aggressors. But the operational and tactical offensive is not only consistent with the strategic defensive, but generally inseparable from it – and never more necessary than when outnumbered, as Napoleon and other great captains ceaselessly demonstrated. And an army which thinks *only* in defensive terms is doomed. It yields initiative and advantage in time and space to an enemy – even an enemy inferior in numbers. It loses the sense of the hunter, the opportunist. It settles down to observe, wait, endure and probably withdraw. No army, regardless of numerical balance, has won battles with so indifferent a spirit. Sensitivity over casualties, furthermore, can be self-defeating unless balanced by courageous judgment. A bold operation is often the most economical in lives, while a series of over-cautious moves can accumulate a distressing tally of losses for small gain.

Thus it was with the British in 1939, and a spirit of caution and hesitancy was never completely eradicated from all parts of the British Command. More significantly, the army of France was similarly afflicted. Great in numbers, reluctant and dispirited, it was soaked in the doctrine of the defensive, and sheltered behind the illusory safety of a great and expensive system of frontier fortifications. By a tragic paradox this loss of aggressive spirit, however comprehensible, came at exactly the moment when the evolution of land warfare and weaponry had restored mobility to the battlefield, enabled once more great manoeuvres to be undertaken, and made the offensive again the strongest form of war.

In this matter of offensive spirit the British Army was, at this time, strikingly inferior to the Royal Navy, whose general attitude was to hunt and destroy any enemy vessel wherever she might be if there was any chance to do so. Of course the navy's long traditions were consistent with this confident vigour. But in recent history the navy had no disillusioning – and misleading – experiences on which to draw; they had not been brought up to mutter "never again". They felt that they were inherently superior to any enemy; and that they could always win. They were right. Upon the army, by contrast, lay heavily the shadow of the barbed wire.

9

This instinctive rejection of a Continental commitment for the army, so soon after winning a great war by accepting such a commitment, did not represent a universal consensus; nor, of course, was it without its own rationale.

Soon after the Armistice, in July 1919, a War Office Committee reported on the post-war army. The committee drew clear lessons from the past and made proposals for the future. It was reckoned that for a minor war (by definition, outside Europe) a small, all-Regular Expeditionary Force could be improvised from the peace establishment, but that for a major war, inevitably, it would be necessary again to produce a great national army. Here the committee could draw on the experience – and chaos – of the massive expansion in and after 1914. It envisaged a peace establishment (perhaps manned by National Service) capable of expanding on mobilisation to an army of forty-one divisions. In 1920 the General Staff produced a sensible survey, ending with the words:

> One thing is certain, viz. that despite the temporary elimination of Germany the problem before us is not less menacing than that for which we had to prepare prior to the recent war. That emergency could only be met by mobilising the manpower of the nation in support of the fighting services, and we should be well advised to retain the machinery for a similar expansion in future.[1]

For more than a decade the response of successive British Governments to this line of argument was simple. They did not (or did not yet) challenge the proposition that a major war would require major effort on land by Britain. They simply ruled that the contingency would not arise. It was found convenient – and at the time by no means unconvincing – to dismiss the assumption that a major war, involving the United Kingdom, might again break out. Instead, as early as the autumn of 1919, the Cabinet first enunciated what came to be known as the Ten Year Rule. Its prime motive was economic. There was savage pressure on public spending. The Services, in a period of reaction from the demands and sacrifices of war, were easy targets for retrenchment: and the army, for the same basic reasons which led to rejection of a Continental commitment, was and remained the Cinderella of the Services. Far from attention being devoted to a peace establishment

[1] Quoted in Brian Bond, *British Military Policy between the Two World Wars*, Clarendon Press, 1980.

with machinery capable of expansion to a large national army in real emergency, twenty-two infantry battalions and eight cavalry regiments were amalgamated or disbanded; and the army had its Vote for funds reduced in every year between 1919 and 1932.

By the Ten Year Rule the Cabinet, in 1919, agreed that the next year's Service estimates should be prepared on the assumption that there would be no major war for ten years. The army was thus relieved of the necessity to plan for major war, and of much of the responsibility for its subsequent unpreparedness. In 1919 the guideline established by the Ten Year Rule was not unreasonable, although even so soon after the Armistice it was an imprudent assumption that there would be ten years' notice for preparation and recovery. But the Ten Year Rule was reaffirmed each year, producing a sort of rolling programme of inactivity and neglect. It was first seriously challenged in 1931, when the Chiefs of Staff united in suggesting that it had, in its effects, brought the British military establishment to a dangerous level of incapacity. But by then the harm had been done. The Ten Year Rule compounded every damaging outcome of policy already noted. It suggested that nobody need ever be ready, nor well-trained, nor progressive in mind, nor organised for emergency, since there would always be time to evolve these qualities and capabilities. Under such a stimulus, of course, it is impossible to act at all, let alone inspire action in others.

As far as the army was concerned the Ten Year Rule was emphasised by such further pronouncements of the government as that of 1922, when it was laid down that the army should be responsible for home security and imperial defence, but should *not* aim to be prepared for major war. Instead, such forces as existed at home (largely to find drafts for India) should be capable of being organised into an Expeditionary Force for a minor war outside Europe. Again, this was not initially unreasonable. The situation within an exhausted Europe seemed unlikely to produce, for a long time, a repetition of the tragedy of 1914. Hope was extended by some to the League of Nations as an effective mechanism for the peaceful resolution of international disputes. Outside Europe, on the other hand, imperial commitments (and, in the view of some, opportunities) were more likely to demand the military efforts of the nation. The war had left a host of worldwide problems for Britain, increased by her new responsibilities as a victor nation. There were small occupation forces in Turkey; newly mandated territories: Egypt, and its security: the recently created problems of Palestine; troubles in the Concession areas in China – all these raised demands for troops. And there was always unease at the political and industrial

11

situation at home, culminating in the need for troops in the General Strike of 1926.

Dominating all demands for troops was the question of India, where 60,000 British troops were stationed, in addition to the Indian Army, 190,000 strong. Ostensibly it existed for the defence of India – at that time conceived as probably threatened by Russian moves into Afghanistan. But as this great establishment was supported by Indian taxes alone, there were difficulties in the way of regarding it as employable elsewhere, on an imperial basis.

The British system was to find drafts from units in England for linked units in India, and thus to preserve a certain balance between the two establishments. The effect was to regard many units in England as little more than draft-finding sources and to commit a large part of the British Army to deal with a threat to India of decreasing credibility, supported by most of the rest of the British Army, whose effectiveness the system negated. But the "defence of India" and the "threat of decreasing credibility" were not the heart of the matter. The imperial forces in India were themselves largely dispersed on tasks of internal security. These tasks had to be done; but, as elsewhere, they had the effect of diminishing the capability of the Indian establishment, despite its size, to furnish a proper field army. The stimulus of a "real" threat did not lead the army in India to produce an effective force, modernised, mechanised, trained. That would at least have balanced Britain's unreadiness in Europe by an effective counterpoise for use in the East, and its hour might have come in 1941. Instead, the army in India was at least as starved of funds as its comrades elsewhere, was as dominated by outmoded theories of warfare and was subject to the lethargic influence of climate and tradition.

Britain spent the twenty-one years between 1918 and 1939 with an army in India and an army at home, neither seriously designed, trained, equipped or organised for major war and neither in the least ready for it.

In terms of size the army was reduced by demobilisation after the peace to something like its prewar strength. Three and a half million men were under arms in November 1918. By November 1920 there were 370,000 and by 1927 about 207,000. But numbers, dependent once more upon recruiting, can also mislead and give little picture of the effectiveness of the army as a fighting force.

Much of the army was dispersed in garrisons, often of one or two units, as opposed to fighting formations – brigades, divisions, corps.

This was inevitable overseas, where many stations required merely a few units for internal security duties. At home and in India, however, large numbers of units were stationed at all times, and although they were (nominally, and in most cases) organised in formations, this had little reality. These formations were in general so lacking in communications, in transport and logistic backup, in the appropriate support of artillery and engineers that they could seldom be assembled for the combined training of all arms, for the exercise of commanders and staffs. This amateur approach to preparing formations for war continued well into the Second World War itself. II Corps, one of only two in the British Expeditionary Force and composed of Regular units, sailed to France in September 1939 absolutely deficient in many of those equipments and all of that experience which make a formation a fighting organism rather than a list of units on paper. When a Regular brigade group sailed for Norway in 1940 to be landed (it was thought) and seize Narvik its battalions came straight from Public Duties in the West End of London and had never been seen by the Brigade Staff (itself assembled only days before) until boarding ship. These examples were symptomatic of an approach to the joint training of staffs and formations, which defied the whole experience of the First World War. Thus the overall numbers of the army give little indication of its effectiveness, because so few formations were organised as such – with all their component parts.

The largest number of units in the army were infantry battalions, and the infantry may be taken to illustrate the point. At that time it was usual for three battalions to constitute a brigade, and for three brigades to form an infantry division. In 1927, as an example, there were in the United Kingdom over sixty battalions of infantry. In that year the General Staff announced that an Expeditionary Force of five divisions might be formed of which *one* could be mobilised after two weeks and the rest after *six months*. Some units essential to a fighting formation in war would actually have to be raised from scratch. There was nothing surprising about this, but it demonstrated that the army in the United Kingdom was not designed as a field force: rather, a field force might be cobbled together from it.

The situation in India was comparable: 145 infantry battalions (45 of them British), and over 20 regiments of cavalry. From these a field army of a mere four divisions was envisaged. Yet even so small an army lacked modern weapons, anti-aircraft defence, and transport – to say nothing of mechanisation. Even in February 1939 the whole of India had only one anti-aircraft battery. Most units in India were committed to internal security. Whatever the British Army's overall numbers, therefore – whether in men or in count of units – its internal policies, deployment, lack of modern equipment, and subjection to financial constraint meant that its ability to place in the field an effective fighting force, whether on the Continent or on the frontiers of empire, shaded from the derisory to the non-existent. The explicit or unspoken assumption behind all planning was that there would always be time – time to change gear, probably introduce conscription, raise new units, assemble and give reality to formations existing on paper if at all. Time would be granted, and would solve all.

Time has to be used with energy. In 1933 Adolf Hitler came to power in Germany. In December that year he ordered that the German Army – limited by the Treaty of Versailles to 100,000 men – should be trebled in size. Ten months later a further expansion, establishing twenty-one infantry and three cavalry divisions was authorised.

In that year in England, where the Ten Year Rule had at last been successfully challenged, the Chiefs of Staff reviewed the situation. They opined that Germany would undoubtedly cause trouble a few years hence. Sir Archibald Montgomery-Massingberd, Chief of the Imperial General Staff (CIGS) and thus professional head of the army, told his colleagues that the British Army was worse off than the other Services in every respect, and could by now do nothing effective in the first six months of European war. The Cabinet gave its own direction on strategic priorities in November: first, the defence of our possessions in the Far East, second, any commitment we might undertake in Europe, third the defence of India. The Cabinet also established a Defence Requirements Committee to examine how the worst deficiencies in all three Services might be made good, and at what cost. Britain was stirring in its slumber.

In the Defence Requirements Committee the Chiefs of Staff exercised a moderating influence. They knew that to ask too much would be to price themselves out of the market – for this was before the international scene appeared as menacing as soon it would. None was more cautious than Montgomery-Massingberd. The CIGS maintained his view that no larger Expeditionary Force for the Continent could be considered than one of four infantry divisions, one cavalry division and one tank brigade. This was a small force – and he made clear that it would take a great deal of time and money to make even this fit for service from the Regular units in the country. But the Defence Requirements Committee was nevertheless convinced that a Continental commitment for the army was vital – as a token of our will to

14

fight, and as a contribution to the security of the Low Countries and thus of the United Kingdom from air attack. Ministers had yet to be convinced, but it was a turning point, a start.

The CIGS believed that this small force, deployed to the Continent at the start of war, would be effective for the limited role of protecting advanced air bases, a concept which necessarily assumed the main defensive battle being fought only by allies. But he appreciated that to equip even such a force – and to add to it a modernised and equipped Territorial Army, a further twelve divisions – would cost a total of £145 million. He knew that this was an impossible sum (the programme for all three Services, as eventually recommended, came out at £80 million) and was thankful for the committee's proposal that the army – admitted by all to be especially starved of funds – should receive £40 million. With this a start could be made on the Regular Expeditionary Force, and it was anyway thought unlikely that industrial capacity would have enabled the army to spend more.

The Cabinet was, however, unimpressed. In particular the Chancellor of the Exchequer, Mr Neville Chamberlain, argued that so small a force could surely make no strategic difference. In a phrase with a modern ring Chamberlain said that while the air force was a "deterrent", the army only came into action if the deterrent failed; a sufficient reason, it appeared to him, to deny it resources. He also argued (and felt, with personal emotion) that the whole concept of an Expeditionary Force was bound to be unpopular. "If we spend too much [on the army]," he said, "the government could be turned out and a successor might do nothing at all." It was therefore, he suggested, a wise calculation to "under-provide", in some circumstances.

Some Ministers found this line of debate persuasive – indeed they asked that in official documents the expression "Expeditionary Force" should not be used. The Chiefs of Staff united in their view that a commitment to the Continent was vital to British security, but the Cabinet, while accepting the point in principle, remained sceptical about its effectiveness in practice. In consequence the funds allotted to the army were cut to £20 million, of which only £12 million were to be spent on the Expeditionary Force, by whatever name.

The General Staff were by no means happy with receiving this commitment while deprived of the means to honour it, in a worsening situation. Some of the most gifted of British soldiers opposed the commitment of an Expeditionary Force to Europe at this time, although well aware of the importance to Britain of Continental defence. Their doubts were known to and used by Chamberlain and those who felt with him, but they were in reality very different from his.

My one and only reason for thinking as I did [wrote Sir John Burnett-Stuart, commanding Southern Command and probably the most intelligent General of his day] was the state of the army: whatever the political, strategical or ethical arguments for the despatch of an Expeditionary Force, they must give way when faced with the fact that we had no Expeditionary Force to send ... I continued to the end obsessed with the iniquity of a policy which accepted for the army a most exacting and hazardous commitment, and at the same time denied to it the means of making itself fit to meet it.[1]

This was no argument against the principle or strategic necessity of a Continental commitment but against its acceptance without resources; against willing the end without provision of the means. Indeed, had the Continental commitment been rejected with a whole heart and with absolute consistency, Britain would have had a coherent policy, and her army, rightly or wrongly, organised on a different basis, while the country rigorously avoided European alliances and, above all, avoided the hostility of Germany. But what was done was to become involved in the European turmoil (as was surely predictable given British standing after 1918) while entirely neglecting to face its implications. A note of despair was sounded in the Chiefs of Staff annual review in 1935. They reiterated that the integrity of the Low Countries demanded the deployment of a British force, but simultaneously protested that the force which existed was inadequate in size, composition and all else; and that its commitment to Europe could be a disaster. It would all depend on the use of time.

In Berlin, in March 1935, conscription was reintroduced for the German nation. Every German would serve twelve months. An expanded army of thirty-six divisions was ordered. This was but a beginning. By summer 1939 the German Army – a mere six years after its rearmament and expansion began – contained fifty-two active and fifty-one reserve divisions, and could mobilise over three and a half million men.

In its third report, in November 1935, the Defence Requirements Committee went further down the road of Continental commitment. It recommended that not only the Regular field force – still reckoned at five divisions – but also the whole of the Territorial Army of twelve

---

[1] Quoted in Brian Bond, *op. cit.*

divisions should be sent to France in war; but sent in three successive echelons during the first year of war, after lengthy periods of training. It was proposed that financial and equipment provision should be based on this strategic assumption. Ministers accepted this as a working premise as far as the Regular Army was concerned, but left the question of the Territorial divisions in abeyance. Argument about the role of the army, and how wholehearted should be the commitment to an Expeditionary Force, dragged on through 1936, and, in December, General Sir Cyril Deverell, now CIGS, said bluntly that the army was not in a position to intervene effectively to defend the Low Countries. It was too small and it could not arrive in time. Deverell regarded this as an argument for welcoming Belgian neutrality (since Belgium could not be effectively helped), and for endorsing a more positive attitude towards the Continental commitment so that our contribution to the defence of France should be on a sufficient scale. Others, however, took his well-founded scepticism as support for their belief that we should send few if any troops to the Continent, for fear of being once again drawn into disastrous involvement in the ambitious – and probably offensive – plans of France. Liddell Hart was vociferous in this view, suggesting (in a strange and unconvincing combination of his advocacy of mechanisation with his hostility to Continental commitment) that a small force of two mechanised divisions could make it possible to "limit" our effort: presumably because their mobility would make it easier for them to act independently, and be more influential upon Allied strategy – a peculiar argument.

None of this was helpful to the army. By now the General Staff believed, without enthusiasm, that they would, in the event, be required to send the largest force they could to France if war came; and that the best way to anticipate that requirement was to press ahead with the equipment of, first, the Regular field force, and, second, the Territorial force, while also accelerating progress on anti-aircraft defence (on which there was little dissent). But although they were perfectly correct in their expectations – and were ultimately to be pressed to do more and to do it quickly – in 1937 there was still disagreement in government about what the army should do if war came. Chamberlain, who had succeeded Baldwin as Prime Minister, appointed Mr Leslie Hore-Belisha as Secretary of State for War.

To the general irritation of the army, Hore-Belisha appointed Liddell Hart his personal adviser at the War Office. The Minister soon echoed his adviser's views not only on military matters (where they were sometimes sound) but on strategic questions where they were articulate and educated, but at root emotional. Liddell Hart opposed a

Continental commitment for the army (except in most limited form) because, despite his own claims to prophetic understanding of the nature of future hostilities, he thought of European war as likely to produce comparable conditions to those of the last war and he wished the British Army to have no part of it.

Hore-Belisha, therefore, thought likewise. In November 1937 he told the Prime Minister: "My view is that . . . our army should be organised to defend this country and the empire, that to organise it with a military prepossession in favour of a Continental commitment is wrong."[1] Chamberlain found this welcome. A month later the CIGS, Deverell, was dismissed. Whatever his shortcomings, he had fought for some recognition of the necessity to prepare the army for European war, since he was sure that in the end it would be ordered to take part. Once again, however, this view was almost completely out of fashion, and in December Ministers agreed a list of priorities for the army which placed anti-aircraft defence top and any commitment to operations in Europe bottom. A more likely area of deployment for the army's field force was thought to be Egypt, whose garrison had been strengthened in the aftermath of the Abyssinian crisis with Italy. The Italians had also reinforced their army in Libya, and a further British brigade was sent to Egypt in March 1938. These measures (which proved ultimately beneficial, through a run of events nobody foretold) were congenial to those whose main dread was involvement in Europe; but they did not represent a consistent policy of priorities.

The Cabinet was now obsessed with the air defence of Britain. Ministers did not, until the eleventh hour, accept the corollary that British defence was bound up with that of France, and that German bombers should be kept as far as possible from our shores by, if necessary, our own efforts. Instead, a wholly unrealistic (at that time) power was ascribed to the German bomber force, and feverish measures were half-undertaken to confront it. For the army a major expansion of searchlight and anti-aircraft units was planned. The demand was largely controlled by the Air Staff. The bill was inevitably paid by the army. Meanwhile expenditure on fitting the field force for modern war dwindled, and the idea of preparing the Territorial divisions for war was abandoned. In early 1938 it was proposed that planned army expenditure should be reduced by, in effect, fifty per cent in the next two years. This reduction was agreed by the House of Commons. On the same day, the German Army entered Austria, which henceforward was incorporated into the Reich.

[1] Quoted in Brian Bond, *op. cit.*

Throughout 1938 the Cabinet maintained an attitude towards a possible Continental commitment for the British Army which is best described as ambivalent hostility. As a result little money was available. An experimental mobile division, precursor of the armoured divisions of the future, was formed in Southern Command in 1937, and another, in wholly inadequate strength, was composed in Egypt in 1938. Certain measures to modernise the Regular units of the field force went ahead – but only on scales appropriate to an Eastern, not European theatre of war, and excluding the vital areas of armour and anti-aircraft support. Thus, although some urgency was shown over anti-aircraft defence at home, in the matter of preparing the army for war against Germany little was or could be done. Nor did the Munich Crisis of September 1938 give any immediate stimulus. On 1st November Chamberlain pledged the government not to introduce conscription in peacetime: "We are not now," the Prime Minister told the House of Commons, "contemplating the equipment of an army on a Continental scale." Meanwhile his agreement with Hitler had removed for Germany the threat from thirty-four Czech divisions if war should come.

Following Munich, however, the realities of European politics, the lessons of history, at last began to intrude. There was no formal alliance with France, and no commitment to join hands with her against Germany. But public and parliamentary opinion now began to turn. More and more people in Britain began to feel with the First Lord of the Admiralty, Duff Cooper, who had (in a minority of one among Ministers) declared in the Committee of Imperial Defence in April that, "It was impossible to contemplate France with her back to the wall, and three million young men in this country in plain clothes."[1] Now the French, deprived of the possibility of the Czech alliance and the cooperation of the Czech Army, began to look with urgency and scepticism at what Britain might do, if Britain were indeed to be an ally – and if not, there could be little sense for France, alone, to oppose the ambitions of Germany. From the British there was no question what France required: soldiers. "France does not intend to allow England to fight her battles with French soldiers,"[2] said the French Deputy Chief of General Staff, General Dentz, to the British Military Attaché. To the French, only British conscription, and evidence of a major effort intended by Britain on land, would be sufficient earnest of

[1] Quoted in Brian Bond, *op. cit.* Duff Cooper resigned over the Munich Settlement.
[2] Quoted in Brian Bond, *op. cit.*

good faith. The British Ambassador in Paris was unequivocal in the matter. "It was no use," he wrote to the Foreign Secretary, Lord Halifax, in January 1939, "pointing to the size of the British Navy or Air Force or talking of Britain's financial stability . . . rightly or wrongly French public opinion wanted large numbers of British troops in Europe."[1]

These sentiments took a little time to sink into the British political consciousness. In October 1938 Hore-Belisha, now a convert to the view of the General Staff in his own Ministry, again submitted proposals for the whole Regular field force and four of the Territorial divisions to be equipped to go to France. In December he pressed his case for more money for this purpose – and this time Halifax was on his side. The Chiefs of Staff were now unanimous for the Continental commitment of the field force – in maximum strength. Sir John Simon, Chancellor of the Exchequer, thought the proposed expenditure dangerously high, but Chamberlain came near agreement. Then on 22nd February 1939 *for the first time* the British Cabinet took an unequivocal decision about the role of the Regular Army in the United Kingdom. It should be equipped – four infantry divisions and the mobile division – for European war, as should four divisions of the Territorial Army.

At long last the British Army was again given the role which had been rejected for it so long; for which it had been starved of funds, equipment, training and encouragement; without which it had drifted without purpose, deteriorating in quality and inspiration; kept in being at derisory strength but denied a coherent task in which men could believe. It was February. On 15th March, Germany discarded the pretence of regarding the Munich Settlement as permanent satisfaction of her territorial ambitions. On news film throughout the Western world audiences watched the German Army marching into Prague.

Changes of direction in army policy now came ever faster. "Every man thinks meanly of himself for not having been a soldier," remarked Dr Johnson, and something of the same spirit now prevailed. But time and order are required, as well as men and general support, in the expansion and repair of a neglected army. Aware that public opinion was by now well ahead of the Cabinet in demanding some evidence of military preparedness, Hore-Belisha proposed to Chamberlain two measures for the army with which the General Staff did not agree, and on the first of which they were not even consulted. On 29th March 1939, following an impulsive conversation with the Prime Minister the

[1] Quoted in Brian Bond, *op. cit.*

20

day before, he announced that the Territorial Army would be doubled in size – regardless of the fact that no plans had been made for the expansion, while the equipment of even the existing force was totally inadequate. The measure did, however, win a headline. Then, in April, it was announced that conscription would be introduced, despite the Prime Minister's assurances. The justification for this measure was home defence, in particular to increase the rate of expansion of Anti-Aircraft Command. Everything was done to create the illusion of purpose and strength.

For the actions of government were now as immoderate as previously they had been supine. On 31st March a guarantee was given to Poland, a guarantee extended on 7th April to Rumania and to Greece (Italy had invaded Albania). Britain was now committed to war should Germany move in a direction where she had well-advertised (and not wholly unreasonable) claims. The glove was thrown down by a nation entirely unfitted for war, and absolutely incapable of doing anything to help Poland if attacked, except, perhaps, by an early essay in strategic bombing, which was disallowed and would have been most unlikely to affect the immediate outcome. The Chiefs of Staff were appalled. The die was cast.

In readiness for war, as in operations themselves, the attacker has the advantage of timing. Governments of peaceable nations, on the other hand, have to be armed against an event they trust will never occur, at a moment over which they have no control. They cannot sustain indefinitely an effective measure of defence against all contingencies. They have to wait until a threat looms large, yet if they seek to be prepared too early – or early enough – it is probable that they will lack popular support. If, as is usual, they are too late, their compatriots will at best blame them afterwards, at worst be crushed by the enemy.

By April 1939, few doubted what the future held. The British Government was now at last committed, with something like a whole heart, to a strategy of Continental engagement – to belated recognition that a hostile power dominating the Continent could pose deadly danger to Britain; and that for a policy of European alliance to work there must be clear evidence of major commitment on land. Policy towards the army, for what turned out to be the last five months of peace, became as feverish as that of the preceding twenty years had been equivocal. Plans were now agreed with the French. The Expeditionary Force of four infantry divisions (the mobile division was as yet inadequately equipped) would assemble in France and take position on

21

the left of the French Army, opposite Belgium. It would be followed by Territorial divisions as they became "ready". Save for the fact that there was no cavalry division it all appeared a re-enactment of 1914.

It was, in fact, very different and infinitely worse. The extraordinary measures with which Britain responded to the German occupation of Czechoslovakia – the doubling at a stroke of the Territorial Army, the introduction of conscription without systematic forethought, the creation (on paper) of an army of no fewer than thirty-two divisions, the demand for ever earlier readiness where before there had been torpor – all these created a situation in armaments manufacture of predictable chaos.[1] By mid-summer even the four Regular divisions of the field force had only about fifty per cent of their (totally inadequate) scales of anti-tank and anti-aircraft weapons, and about thirty per cent of their ammunition. As to armour, a number of reconnaissance regiments were armed with light tanks, not designed for tank-to-tank encounters: the Mark II tank, the first to be armed with a two pounder anti-tank gun, was only slowly coming into production, and the first tank battalion was not equipped with it until early 1940. A new (and excellent) close support artillery piece, the twenty-five pounder, was approved, but in the short term had to be mounted on older eighteen pounder carriages which limited range and ammunition type; and modernised medium artillery, with its greater range and power, would not be in production for a long time.

Thus the British Army, of inadequate size and deplorably under-equipped, was again propelled towards war. To maintain in peace a large military establishment is beyond the will and capacity of most nations, but at least a system can be evolved which trains the manpower of the country for emergency or – at least – plans how, quickly, to do so. Wars cannot be won without best use of every resource, particularly human. This had been deliberately neglected in a Britain lethargically confident that its army need play a minimal part. Now, at the last minute, a huge and unpremeditated expansion had begun and had upset such programmes as existed. The army had suffered from protracted equivocation over its purpose. It was largely untrained at the higher levels, for the upheavals and changes of policy of the preceding years had been accompanied by the holding of no major manoeuvres. The quality of tactical doctrine and thinking was outmoded and indifferent and too few officers, from top to bottom, had been stimulated

[1] As an example of disruption, between September and December 1939, 11,500 men, members of the Territorial Army, had to be withdrawn from the army to return to key posts in industry.

to study their profession. Study is not the only route to military proficiency, and some natural leaders are naturally indolent. There were, fortunately, many excellent officers despite the frustrations of their professional upbringing. But a small Regular Army also needs a cadre of officers who can fill posts in war well above their peacetime rank, and in 1939 there were too many who did not really know their own jobs, too many whose minds and characters were inadequate for the pace of modern war. In common with allies and in harmony with the country itself the army also suffered from a defensive mindedness which was in striking contrast to the enemy and which could bode nothing but ill.

Critics of policy between the wars have often and justly referred to the state of public opinion, as Ministers so frequently did themselves. It was indeed a major factor, although too often prayed in aid by those whose taste, anyway, was for inaction. For most of the period and in much but by no means all of the country, there existed an aversion to military preparedness and to European commitment, under the pathetic and recurrent delusion that preparedness makes war more likely, and that the nation could stand aside from history. Leaders, political and military, receive much blame and deserved some. The villains of the piece were the people of Britain. It was also they who paid the price.

On 1st September the German Army invaded Poland. Two days later Britain was at war.

2

The First Shock

It took a little more than five weeks for the first four divisions of the British Expeditionary Force,[1] under the Command-in-Chief of General Viscount Gort, to concentrate in France, and by 12th October 1939 they had taken over a sector of the front. The divisions, the 1st and 2nd of I Corps (Lieutenant-General Sir John Dill) and the 3rd and 4th of II Corps (Lieutenant-General Alan Brooke), were composed of Regular battalions – thirty-six of them.

Gort was a magnificent man, holder of the Victoria Cross won as a Battalion Commander in 1918, a soldiers' soldier, cheerful, unpretentious and brave. Since 1937 Gort had been CIGS, the professional head of the army, a position demanding continuity above all at the transition from peace to war. He was made Commander-in-Chief of the BEF on 3rd September, the day war was declared. Dill, commanding at Aldershot, had been expected by the army to become Commander-in-Chief in war, a post generally associated with the Aldershot Command in peace. Alternately, he was also widely regarded as the most suitable man for CIGS, a soldier of great tact, intelligence and resource. Instead of either, Dill was placed in command of I Corps. Brooke had just taken over Southern Command at Salisbury and had held the mobilisation appointment of Commander II Corps only since 31st August. At the head of the army, in place of Gort, was set General Sir Edmund Ironside, recently brought home from Gibraltar and given to understand he was Commander-in-Chief designate of a BEF. Whatever his qualifications for the latter post he had few for that of CIGS and knew it. It was a peculiar way to open a great war. Ironside was a massively built Artilleryman. He had a personality of the kind the Press enjoys – apparently made on the grand scale and indestructible. By an easy connection these qualities could be imagined as typifying the army. This was doubly misleading. The army was neither massive

[1] The divisions forming part of the British Army in the Second World War are listed in Appendix I.

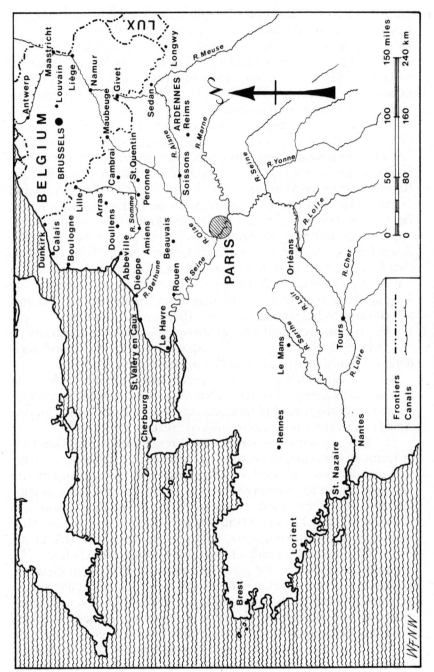

Northern France and Belgium

nor indestructible; and Ironside, with a fine record behind him, had neither the clarity of mind, nor the strength and articulacy to persuade politicians, which the post of CIGS demanded. He had never served in the War Office. He did not understand its ways, nor how to manage its machinery. His interventions in the first campaigns were inept. Like many others he was to be overcome by events which he, too belatedly and too dimly, perceived as disasters.

The move of the army to France went smoothly. From fear of German air attack, ports well to the west had been selected. The British line of communication therefore was extensive, running from Cherbourg, from Nantes and St. Nazaire on the Atlantic coast, through Rennes east to Le Mans and Rouen, and to Arras, the railhead and General Headquarters. Forward of Arras the BEF took station on the Belgian frontier between the French First Army (General Blanchard) on the right and Seventh Army (General Giraud) on its left. These three armies, and much of General Corap's Ninth Army on Blanchard's right, were deployed facing neutral Belgium, not Germany. It was confidently believed that rather than attempt a frontal attack on the Maginot Line the German onslaught would come with its principal weight through Belgium, as in 1914 – Belgium and, perhaps, Holland. For this reason the Allied left was strong; and there was much debate on what to do if and when the expected occurred. Beyond their defences British troops gazed at flat, neutral land.

No army can function effectively except with and within a clear and unequivocal Command system. That of the BEF was neither, and in consequence the force and its Commander-in-Chief – utterly loyal to Allied cooperation as he was – suffered greatly.

The BEF was deployed between two French Armies, and Gort had, in terms of the military chain of command, the status of an Army Commander, on the level of Blanchard and Giraud, and would normally expect to be responsible to an Army Group Commander – probably one of two or more on so long a front. But he was also Commander-in-Chief of all British troops in France, including those on the lines of communication, and as such was responsible to the British Government – a difficult dual role in battle, if not before.

Gort was, in fact, under the direct authority of General Georges, Commander of the "Armies of the North-East" – himself subordinate to General Gamelin, the Supreme Commander of the French Army, including the army in North Africa. Before the Germans attacked, Gamelin often sought to bypass the authority of Georges vis-à-vis the BEF, because Gort was a Commander-in-Chief of a national force with inevitable political implications in orders given to him. This was understandable on politico-military matters but reprehensible for operations, since Georges was the Commander of land forces facing Germany, that is north of the Swiss frontier. But Georges found the task of international coordination impossible when the Germans attacked; therefore an Army Group Commander, General Billotte, 1st Army Group, was directed to "coordinate" the actions of the two left-hand French Armies, the Belgian Army and the British Army. Before this belated and inadequate appointment, Billotte had no command responsibility for the BEF. There was, therefore, a confused and extempore arrangement made, to deal with a difficult situation in the middle of a chaotic battle – ambiguities from the start and changes on the day, a sure recipe for disaster. And the unfortunate Gort could expect to receive directions, if at all, from three different French levels of Command, none of which was effective.

French strategic thinking was entirely defensive. For a short while at the beginning of the war the main strength of the German Army was in the East: all its Panzer divisions, the cutting edge of its offensive capability, being wielded against Poland. In the West, the Germans were weak. But the experiences of 1914–18 had scarred the French mind even more than the British. There must be no offensive. There must be fortification, defensive preparation, a move into Belgium, if possible, so that a line could be established forward of the soil of France. Then the Germans would attack, as before, but this time be met by prepared troops, in position. Meanwhile it was a matter of waiting until the Germans decided to beat out their own brains upon an organised defence, the strongest form of war. This strategy, which gave every advantage of timing and initiative to the enemy, was inevitable. No French Government would have sanctioned an offensive, however timely. Nor was the French Army organised for it. The French had a mass of tanks, many of high quality. They were by no means seriously outnumbered, whether in men or material, by their enemies. But all was organised for the defensive, and upon predictable and traditional lines. The great majority of tanks were deployed in support of infantry divisions. There was no accent on mobility, concentration or offensive action. There was no central reserve, and in consequence little ability of the High Command to influence the battle except by exhortation. The country was divided and her soldiers apathetic. The flame of the French spirit of attack had been extinguished in Champagne in 1917. It had not yet been rekindled.

The British, even had they wished, could have done nothing to affect this. The size of the BEF was tiny compared with the eighty divisions mobilised by France. The influence of the British upon strategy was proportionate. They had, however, fully acquiesced in a purely defensive concept; and their capabilities were inconsistent with anything else. There were, for instance, only two British tank battalions in France. The 1st Armoured Division, which actually possessed some cruiser tanks armed with anti-tank guns, only started to arrive in France in the middle of May 1940. A strategic offensive was out of the question, and even a limited, tactical offensive was beyond the capacity of the BEF. "In September 1939," wrote Field Marshal Montgomery, at that time Major-General commanding 3rd Division, "the British Army was totally unfit to fight a first-class war on the Continent of Europe."[1]

The army was not called upon to fight. Instead, as month succeeded month and the Germans, having crushed Poland, forbore to attack, the British prepared defensive positions, dug anti-tank ditches, carried out at least some much needed training, and waited. There was prolonged debate on the action to be taken when the Germans attacked. Reinforcing divisions began to arrive. In December, 5th Division, largely composed of Regular units, joined II Corps. In January and February 1940 came the first three Territorial divisions – the 48th and 50th joined I and II Corps respectively, and the ill-fated 51st (Highland) Division in April became part of a third army corps, III Corps (Lieutenant-General Sir Ronald Adam). In April, too, seven months after the outbreak of war, two more Territorial divisions – the 42nd and 44th – reached France to join III Corps. This was not all. In April three more "Reserve" divisions, 12th, 23rd and 46th, with little equipment and almost completely untrained, were sent for labour duties and "to complete their training". All their artillery and most of their administrative units and communications were left behind. They were caught up in the maelstrom to come, and the first two of these divisions was disbanded in England in the summer of 1940.

The divisions of the BEF had only a small minority of Regulars. A few interchanges were made in France, to dilute the Regular divisions of the first echelon and, in theory, to stiffen the remainder. It should not, however, be assumed that the number of Regular units – or number of Regular officers and soldiers in a unit – was the sole index of performance. Indeed, as the war went on, the intelligent civilian, who became quickly dedicated and assimilated military training, was seen to be superior to all too many of his so-called professional comrades: the Regular Army had so suffered from the neglect and inertia of the preceding decades that its quality and leadership was often flabby and

[1] Montgomery of Alamein, *Memoirs*, Collins, 1958.

defective. Nevertheless Regular units possessed a basic discipline and standard of administration which Territorial units had in many cases had too little time to acquire, and too little experience to develop. Regular units had at least a tradition of a high standard of skill at arms, which the majority worthily maintained; and their tactical skill, although developed in a discouraging and ambivalent atmosphere in the past, was not wholly absent. The Regular divisions, too, had the months of what was soon called the "Phoney War" to grow into formations, rather than collections of units, and to train; the Territorial divisions had little such chance.

Though many units were now improving, and would soon give a noble account of themselves, the level of hardness and training was still inadequate throughout the BEF. To use even the months available to better effect would have demanded a stronger base of modernised, tactical doctrine and vigorous, intelligent leadership at all levels than the army possessed. In some formations much was done, in spite of a demanding programme on the defensive works. In others the standard was deplorable. Furthermore, as the French insisted on wireless silence, there could be no Command Post exercises to practise communication and control, of the kind vital to give cohesion to an army. Overall there was little running of the machine of war, such as modern operations absolutely demand. The atmosphere of "peace in war", the inevitability of waiting on the enemy's will rather than preparing for an initiative, was itself a subtle disincentive. The "Phoney War" ran counter to any sense of urgency or adventure.

In Britain armaments production was beginning to recover from the long sleep. Both immediately before the war and in its first few months considerable strides were made, and a good deal of energy and dexterity was shown by the War Office in making good the deficiencies. But those deficiencies were huge nevertheless. Much of the army was not equipped for modern war at all. This was unsurprising – it had only recently been decided that it should take part, and no power on earth can speed armaments production, from an inadequate industrial base, beyond a certain point. The Regular divisions themselves suffered a shortage of vital specialist weapons, of ammunition, of spare parts, of communications; but above all, of tanks. There was totally inadequate air support. The BEF was an infantry force, albeit with a great deal of motor transport.

From the declaration of war the strategic debate was conducted at all levels of French Command and continued throughout the winter. It was eventually decided that there would be a forward movement into Belgium by the BEF and the French First Army on their right, with Giraud's Seventh Army on the extreme left moving into Holland through which a German advance was also expected to come. Such a plan – to be carried out in vehicles, a move frequently practised in the winter months – was, however, hard to formulate since Belgium was strictly neutral. The ostensible background to the Allies' move would be Belgian appeals for help. Meanwhile only covert reconnaissance was possible, and coordination with Belgian plans had to be as circumspect as it proved inadequate. The Belgians had no desire to provoke Germany's hostility by detectable arrangements with the Allies, and their neutrality had been welcomed by the British as likely to buy time at the outset, which was probably true; but neutrality has to work both ways, at least when practised by a nation in so vulnerable a position as Belgium.

The final plan for the British Army – Plan D – was to advance to the River Dyle, a narrow stream a short way east of Brussels. Here they would adopt a defensive position between the French First Army, making a similar wheeling advance on their right or southern flank; and (it was presumed) the Belgian Army on their left, northern flank. It was also presumed that the movement would be covered by the action of Belgian forces on the frontier.

"I don't think the Germans have any intention of attacking us,"[1] Chamberlain remarked to Montgomery on a visit to France in December, and was met with sharp dissent. It was convenient, however, for the government to suppose that because the Western Front was inactive it was somehow stable. Now, to compound the BEF's problems, the British Government began to consider excursions elsewhere. The first of these was to Finland, which had been attacked without provocation, warning or excuse by the Soviet Union in November 1939. The Western Allies decided to help Finland – a popular and deserving cause – with an expedition, largely inspired by Winston Churchill, First Lord of the Admiralty. But the only arms available in Britain were those designed for the BEF, or for divisions being prepared to reinforce it. Mercifully for Britain, Churchill's scheme was overtaken in March 1940 by Finnish capitulation, which ended the "Winter War". Meanwhile two of the BEF's reinforcing Territorial divisions – 42nd and 44th, due to form Gort's III Corps in France – had been held back for possible operations in Northern Europe, and the possibility of those operations interrupted the flow of equipment to the BEF.

[1] Montgomery, *op. cit.*

Then, in early April, Gort was suddenly ordered to withdraw 5th Division from the line and place it in "War Office Reserve" – outside his control except with permission from London; one of that division's brigades was even shipped home from France. A new drama was beginning in which at last the British Army would have a brief but active part to play.

On 9th April the German Army occupied Denmark and began the invasion of Norway.

In any military exercise involving opposing forces, there is a well-established procedure for making credible a mock clash of arms between the two sides, and for ensuring that it happens on the day and at the point selected by the Directing Staff. A "general narrative" is given to both contestants, containing the overall background and focusing the attention of each on some issue and area which could lead to conflict. Then a special narrative is issued to each adversary, and concealed from his enemy. This produces an operational aim for each side, and, probably, explicit orders designed to get the troops moving in the right direction or establishing themselves on some ground which will culminate in an encounter as the enemy seeks to achieve a contrary aim by simulated force of arms. The troops taking part are often, it must be admitted, either ignorant or sceptical of these dignified preliminaries. The procedure is, and has to be, artificial and the timings harmonious; and the circumstances at the start of such exercises, methodical, synchronised and contrived, seldom resemble the brutal sequence, the shock, surprise and confusion with which campaigns in reality tend to begin. The Norwegian operations of 1940, untrue to form, recall nothing so much as a carefully planned exercise – until the fighting actually began. There was, as on exercises, a certain symmetry.

The Allies placed great importance on Norway. They were determined to cut off German supplies of Swedish iron ore, which were known to be exported to Germany via Luleå, at the northern end of the Baltic, or by rail via Narvik in Northern Norway. For the four winter months when Luleå was icebound Narvik was the sole route. And by taking advantage of Norwegian territorial waters German ships were able to move with impunity from near the Arctic to the Skagerrak, almost to home waters in fact. If the British were successfully to blockade the sea-lanes of Europe they could not allow Germany to use a seaway of such strategic importance.

For their part the Germans understood how vital it was that the

Norwegian coast should not fall into hostile hands. They went further. Should they themselves be able to obtain bases in Norway the British blockade could not be maintained nearer to Northern Europe than the general line Shetland – Faroes – Iceland, as compared to the close blockade of the waters between Shetland and Norway. And, in addition, the Germans placed almost – although, it appears, not quite – as much importance on the passage of Swedish iron ore as the Allies assumed.

The Norwegians, meanwhile, perfectly aware of the interest taken in their country by the combatant nations, were resolved to remain neutral and to interpret that neutrality strictly. Under no circumstances were they prepared to accept the unsolicited help of friends or the insinuation of "volunteers" on some pretext or other. They were ready to defend their own national integrity against attempts to infringe it, from whatever quarter.

In Britain the answer, as propounded by First Lord of the Admiralty, Churchill, was to mine Norwegian waters, to bottle up the route via the Norwegian coast to the Baltic approaches. The matter was soon, however, subsumed by helping Finland in her struggle against the Soviet Union.

The British and French decided that not only supplies but troops should be sent to Finland. There would, it was secretly hoped, be an important contingent benefit. The ports by which iron ore was shipped to Germany would be those used by Allied forces en route to Finland. These forces, moving to support the gallant Finns, would occupy points vital for the German war economy.

An expedition was planned. There was no reason to presume Norwegian and Swedish acquiescence, but since both were strongly opposed to Soviet aggression it was reckoned that somehow or other Scandinavian goodwill might be procured on the day. The British Army planned to provide forces from the two Territorial divisions held back from France, and a Guards brigade in England. The main force would land at Narvik, and other Norwegian ports would be seized. The object of operations (apart from helping the Finns) would be to exclude the Germans, and to control the ports and their traffic.

Meanwhile the Germans were also busy. The German Naval Commander-in-Chief, Grand Admiral Raeder, persuaded Hitler that the Norwegian ports and air bases could be a decisive factor in the sea war against England. He also convinced the Fuehrer that British control of Norway would be a grave threat to Germany. Studies were ordered, and at the end of January contingency planning began. The object of operations would be to occupy Norway and exclude the British. The

Germans had no more reason than the British to assume Norwegian goodwill. They had a "Fifth Column" party led by Vidkun Quisling but they were (rightly) sceptical of Quisling's influence. German plans were based on the hypothesis of invasion without the invitation, assistance or prior knowledge of the Norwegian Government.

The Allied plan was approved in February, the same month that the British destroyer *Cossack* entered Norwegian territorial waters to seize a German auxiliary vessel in which captured British merchant seamen were held prisoner. This seems to have convinced the Germans that the British were prepared to infringe Norwegian neutrality if it suited them, and they, too, decided to put their plan into operation.

In March the matter was complicated for the Allies by the Finnish capitulation. There could now be no excuse of moving across Norway to the aid of the Finns. Plans were recast. Instead, it was decided to revive Churchill's scheme and mine certain Norwegian waters, effectively blocking the Narvik route, and it was thought inevitably provoking a German reaction. Before this reaction could take the form of a landing, Allied forces would land at Norwegian ports, including Narvik, to protect the Norwegians from German action thus designedly (but covertly) provoked. All this required nice timing, and the soldiers were to be embarked immediately after the mine-laying by the Royal Navy. This plan was accepted on 28th March, with mine-laying ordered to start on 8th April. It was recognised that Norway (and Sweden) would protest vigorously and that the Norwegians might actually seek to sweep the mines. The latter were, therefore, to be laid under protection of strong maritime forces, also stationed to engage any German force directed to interfere. Had all gone well it was anticipated there would be Norwegian acquiescence, produced by the German offensive reaction; and this reaction would itself be met by Allied defence of Norwegian ports.

Unfortunately German plans followed all too similar a timing. On 2nd April Hitler approved the operation – WESERUBUNG[1] – and the date was fixed for 9th April, the day after the British mining operation was due to start, but coinciding with the planned landing of British troops. Unbeknown to the other, each side decided to enter Norway on the same day and forestall its occupation by the enemy. Whereas the Allies, however, had decided to go through a sequence which would, they hoped, obtain Norwegian acquiescence if not goodwill – the mining operation, the visible threat of German counter-measures – the Germans were prepared to go in on the appointed day without preliminaries, warning or manoeuvre.

[1] Codewords appearing in the text are listed in Appendix II.

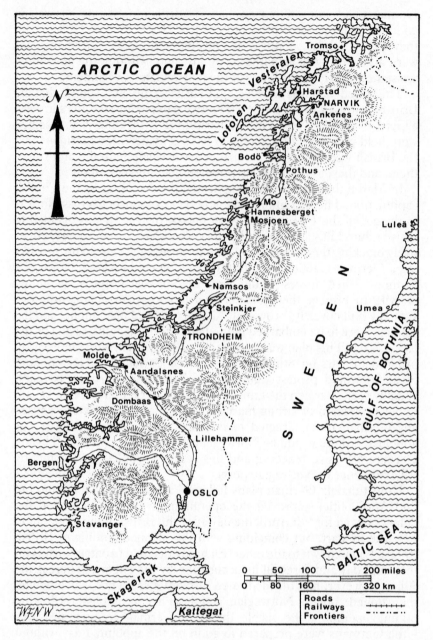

Norway

34

The German amphibious plan, which crammed many of the assault battalions into warships and made considerable use of deception, was brilliant. The invasion force, however, was detected on 8th April steaming northwards, and the British Admiralty decided that mine-laying must stop and all forces be concentrated for what appeared to be the chance of a major naval engagement. Although it was not known that the German warships were carrying or escorting a land force sufficient to occupy Norwegian ports and achieve a great strategic objective, had a naval encounter occurred and been won by the Royal Navy the Germans would not have invaded Norway.

In the event, the unconscious symmetry of each side's actions, as if planned by some remote and efficient directing authority, now yielded to the fog and chaos of war. In order to concentrate maximum naval forces Churchill personally ordered the disembarkation of forces in Scotland and the move of all available warships, unencumbered, towards the Norwegian sea. Thereafter the weather, some ineptitude, and sheer bad luck conspired to prevent a decisive naval engagement. The enemy's main forces were not found. Because of the sudden change of plan on the appearance of the German expedition the mines had not been laid. The German reaction which British mine-laying was designed to provoke, having been organised in ignorance of its role in Allied planning, arrived deadly ahead of cue. German forces seized Narvik, Trondheim, Bergen, and the capital, Oslo, simultaneously. They thus acquired ports and bases. They had overwhelming air superiority over Norwegian land and water. The German plan was audacious – its execution daring and efficient. WESERUBUNG was a triumphant success.

The Allies' strategy – to forestall the Germans in Norway – was not unsound; but their plans were complex and they changed them too lightly. They failed in execution. There was division of authority and miserable lack of communication. Now they had a new situation for which the previous arrangements were entirely unsuitable, and at this point Allied operational planning – and the British were leading in the Norwegian business – became deplorable. For the Allies had now to face the need to land forces from the sea in the presence of a numerous enemy already established on shore, albeit recently, and in the face of enemy air superiority. This was a very different matter from putting troops ashore without opposition, to forestall the enemy. Such an operation, if to be carried out at all, needed forces and staffs trained in combined operations, equipment suitable to conditions on land where they would have to fight, unequivocal channels of command, sufficient air support and an immoderate amount of luck. Little of this was vouchsafed.

The original Allied plan had covered landings at four points, Narvik, Trondheim, Bergen and Stavanger, with a brigade to Narvik, and battalions distributed over the other three. Many of these troops, embarked to sail for a pre-emptive move, were hurriedly disembarked in Scotland when it was decided to concentrate the fleet for action. That and their later re-embarkation led to some confusion and loss. Battalions were shipped without some of their weapons and ammunition. Vital signals equipment was left behind or loaded on a different ship. The force was ultimately fitted into warships and transports and put to sea. Prepared for a different sort of operation they had little of the necessities of modern war. They were woefully short of the means of anti-aircraft defence, and, with the exception of one battery which ultimately reached Narvik, they had no artillery. Other essential arms and stores were also in short supply.

The former landing plan was now completely inappropriate. On the evening of 9th April, as the scale and success of the German assault became clearer, it was decided to concentrate on Narvik, reckoned to be the most important, as it had been the original objective. It was also remote from Southern Norway where the Germans would presumably aim to establish their main base for the reinforcement of the captured west coast ports, and for the subjugation of the country. Landings would also be attempted to the north and south of Trondheim, at Namsos and Aandalsnes. At the same time a Regular infantry brigade – 15th Brigade from the 5th Division – was ordered back from France to be shipped to Norway as reinforcement.

Though the scale of British operations was small and the forces few they spanned a huge area. The British troops consisted of 49th Division (Major-General Mackesy) made up of three brigades, 146th, 147th and 148th. Of these only 146th and 148th actually took part, although 147th was earmarked for one operation which never took place. General Mackesy was also allocated 24th Guards Brigade. He himself was ordered to command the troops at Narvik – RUPERTFORCE. The attempt at Namsos was made by one of Mackesy's brigades (146th), as part of a force under Major-General Sir Adrian Carton de Wiart V.C., to be called MAURICEFORCE. And the landing at Aandalsnes – SICKLEFORCE – was to be undertaken by Mackesy's second brigade – 148th – under its own Commander (Brigadier Morgan). Mackesy, Carton de Wiart and Morgan each received instructions from the CIGS in London as "independent commanders under the

War Office". Major-General Paget arrived later to take command of
SICKLEFORCE, by which time it had been joined by 15th Brigade, at a
critical moment in its fortunes.

Thus, command of each detachment was retained by the War Office
in London, although in the case of Central Norway – MAURICEFORCE
and SICKLEFORCE – a commander, Lieutenant-General Massy, with a
small Staff, was established in London to coordinate their operations.
Massy never left London and it is unlikely that he could have contributed anything useful if he had, in fact, been able to visit Namsos and
Aandalsnes. Each force had a general officer in command, each was
extremely small, each had intractable problems, and the ultimate
decision to solve them by evacuation could only be taken at government
level.

Inter-Service collaboration was also exercised from London,
although at a later stage the Flag officer, Narvik, Admiral of the Fleet
the Earl of Cork and Orrery, was put in command of all forces in that
area. Meanwhile each Department sent orders to its own Commanders, naval, army and air. This placed a premium on excellent cooperation within Whitehall, which in these early days of the Chiefs of Staff
Committee at War was not as straightforward a matter as it later
became. No campaign more demanded the close coordination of all
Services than did that in Norway, and the common understanding of
the others' problems. It is tempting, in the light of later experience, to
suggest it would have profited from a united command – tempting, but
unconvincing. The difficulties met by each Service and the scale of
each contribution were very different. The army never had more than
four brigades ashore in the whole of Norway, whereas the navy, at one
time or another, had virtually the whole of the Home Fleet committed –
and vulnerable. Admiralty direction of naval operations (whether
wisely exercised or not) was inevitable. An overall land force commander could have done nothing to affect operations, and since the actions
of each detachment had serious political implications each, inevitably,
had to refer to London. The command arrangements for Norway
appear laborious and inept, but it is unlikely that efficient alternatives
could have been successfully improvised in time. Nor is it likely that
they would have affected the outcome.

Operations in Norway were thus divided into two brief campaigns, one
in the area of Trondheim, the other at Narvik, separated from each
other by over 400 miles. Of these the operations near Trondheim were

briefer, lasting a mere fortnight, from 19th April to 3rd May: a fortnight of much tragedy.

Trondheim is a city of considerable importance to Norway, both economically and historically. It was seized by the Germans in their original descent upon the Norwegian ports on 9th April. Within a week the original assault force was built up to some 4,000 men, and the Germans, believing as always in speed and exploitation, began pushing out in several directions, ready to take the offensive against any attempt at a counter-stroke.

The first Allied plan for the capture of Trondheim was by direct assault. A naval force would sail up the Trondheim Fjord, past Trondheim itself, and land a force of two brigades (15th Brigade and 147th Brigade – the third, uncommitted, brigade of Mackesy's 49th Division). But Operation HAMMER, as it was called, was abandoned on 19th April by direction of the Chiefs of Staff in London (although not before yet another General had been nominated to command the troops making the attempt – constituting a fourth independent commander under the War Office). It was feared, almost certainly rightly, that the enemy's air power would make it too hazardous. The Germans had made prompt use of the bases they had seized, principally Stavanger, and a feature of the campaign was the virtually complete mastery of the air to be achieved by the Luftwaffe.

Once HAMMER had been abandoned, the landings under way at Namsos and Aandalsnes assumed new importance as it was hoped to develop enough strength to advance towards Trondheim from the two directions as a pincer movement. The landing of troops had started at Namsos (146th Brigade) on 17th and at Molde and Aandalsnes (148th Brigade) on 18th April. The following day a demi-brigade – three battalions – of French Chasseurs Alpins joined MAURICEFORCE at Namsos, where, as at Aandalsnes, a large number of base troops and stores were landed. One light anti-aircraft battery was deployed with SICKLEFORCE at Aandalsnes, and one French anti-aircraft detachment at Namsos. Both places were soon heavily attacked by air and made near useless – and Aandalsnes was anyway much too small to support a force the size of SICKLEFORCE. In fact MAURICEFORCE and SICKLE-FORCE had no effect upon each other as far as ground forces were concerned, being separated by mountain, water and some 200 miles of inhospitable country.

The circumstances of embarkation of 146th Brigade and of their arrival at Namsos – MAURICEFORCE – were not such as to help puzzled men. They had no transport, although each man arrived with three kitbags. They had no artillery support, and one battalion had been

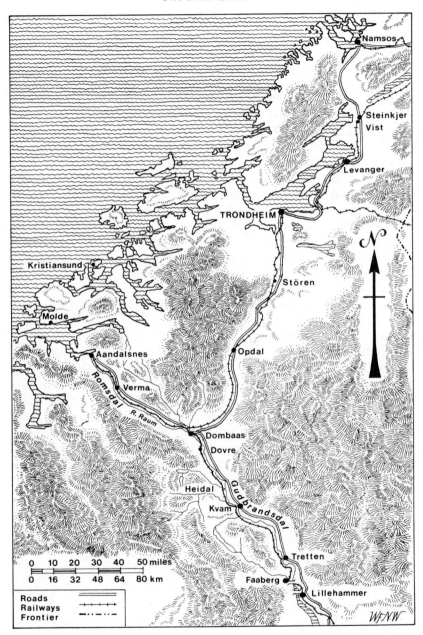

Trondheim

separated from its mortars. In unpromising condition the two leading battalions of MAURICEFORCE were set on the road towards Trondheim, to hold a front astride the narrow road by the Trondheim Fjord a few miles south of Steinkjer. On the morning of 21st April the first German attacks came in.

The Germans were advancing from Trondheim. They came on foot, assisted by motorcyclists (and light mortars mounted in sidecars) and using what carts and sledges they could find in the farms. They were physically fit, and when they came under fire they climbed and outflanked. In all their advances in Norway the Germans were based on roads, as were the British, but they managed to manoeuvre with more agility, helped by a few ski-troops. Against MAURICEFORCE they were at a slight numerical advantage. Soon 146th Brigade reported, for the first of many times, that their position was untenable, and they must withdraw.

Next day was disastrous. Two battalions were holding a number of roads converging at Vist, three miles south of Steinkjer. The main road was unmasked by the precipitate withdrawal of one battalion to a point in the woods to the east, and the second battalion began to withdraw to avoid, as it seemed, being cut off; and did so in a way which their Commanding Officer found impossible to check. The three battalions of 146th Brigade were now strung out down the road south from Namsos and very much on the defensive. MAURICEFORCE's first taste of battle was brief and inglorious. They were in no condition to attempt any further advances towards Trondheim and they were badly shaken. Fortunately the Germans had no intention of advancing further, and the situation was quiet until British and French evacuation a week later. The northern arm of the pincer movement on Trondheim came to its undistinguished end.

This was the first British encounter with the German Army in the Second World War, but a very different sort of encounter from any previously envisaged. Battle took place, however, in conditions of equal difficulty for both sides – in snow (for deep snow lay everywhere except on those roads where it had been beaten down), in extreme cold, and within days of landing in utterly strange surroundings. The British had the advantage of a more cooperative population, and some Norwegian local forces, including ski-patrols. The Germans, however, had the advantage of expecting to fight and of being organised and equipped to do so; and, above all, they enjoyed a level of air support which soon paralysed their enemies' communications and supply, and made movement as dangerous as it was exhausting. "I see little chance," signalled Carton de Wiart, one of the most daring of officers, on 20th April, "of carrying out decisive or, indeed, any operations unless enemy air activity is considerably reduced." The Germans, furthermore, were trained to go forward, to find ways round, to climb to higher ground where it could be done, to infiltrate positions, to keep up the offensive, as a matter of instinct and basic training as much as a response to order. German tactical ability, at every level and particularly the most junior, was here experienced for the first time – and the discipline which harnessed that ability and directed the whole. The experience shocked the British Army.

Such a shock was all the greater because of the three British brigades engaged in Central Norway two were Territorial. The Territorial brigades of the British Army in 1940 had had all too little chance and help to develop the fundamental qualities of the soldier. They had been starved of equipment. They had suffered from an unplanned and unprepared expansion, and the equally unprepared introduction of conscription just before the war. Their soldiers had not the experience which a long tradition of National Service gives to successive generations. They were splendid men. The vast majority of Territorials had reported for duty in 1939 with punctuality and enthusiasm. But there had been too little system and sense of urgency in their training. Their officers knew too little; the blind had too much to lead the blind. General Nye, later VCIGS, told a friend before the expedition sailed that what frightened him was the deplorable state of training of the troops we had available to send to Norway.[1] The bill was now being paid.

Few men are born heroes. Few are incorrigible cowards. Most can be either; and to help them towards the former rather than the latter state an army uses leadership, discipline and training – a mix which produces confidence and pride. The man well-led can believe there is sense in what he is ordered to do, and that his commander both cares for him and knows his own job. The disciplined man knows that the habit of obedience and united action distinguishes a self-respecting body of soldiers from a mob. The trained man knows his profession enough to do what he has to do, and do it by instinct amidst great dangers. Without these characteristics in the body to which they belong soldiers cannot behave well in battle; and when they fail the fault is not theirs but lies in the system which has placed them there unprepared.

The story of SICKLEFORCE had some similarities, but many differences, from that of MAURICEFORCE.

The Norwegian authorities had been stunned by the German

1 Fraser Papers.

onslaught. At first, however, only the capital and the western parts had been seized, and in the following days attempts were made to mobilise the considerable Norwegian militia forces for resistance. Norway is a huge country, and it was hoped that the enemy's power would take time to penetrate. The King and government escaped from Oslo. The Norwegians established a military Headquarters to coordinate armed resistance and to collaborate with Allies. The British Military Attaché, Colonel King-Salter, made his way to this Headquarters on 14th April and started to inform London of the situation (as far as it was known) of German forces and Norwegian militia. When the British began to land at Aandalsnes, King-Salter made contact with them on 19th April. Thereafter the requests made by the Norwegian authorities had a significant effect on the actions of SICKLEFORCE.

To the Norwegians Trondheim was a prize of great political importance. The Norwegian Government could be established there, if a campaign were to be launched for the reconquest of the country and the ejection of the Wehrmacht. More immediately, however, the Norwegian Commander-in-Chief, General Ruge, was concerned with the actions of the German forces established in the south, in the area of Oslo. These had been strongly reinforced. The Germans were now pushing up the country, to clear opposition and make contact by road with their isolated detachments at the western ports. No attack towards Trondheim (as envisaged in the orders to SICKLEFORCE) could be made unless the south-facing flank of such a movement was itself secure. German columns were already in the Gudbrandsdal, the valley running north towards Trondheim via a road junction at Dombaas fifty miles south-east of Aandalsnes. The Norwegians argued with urgency and passion that the first British task must be to hold the German northward advance, as Norwegian militia had been striving to do for days. This could only be done by SICKLEFORCE.

SICKLEFORCE consisted initially of 148th Brigade under Brigadier Morgan, who, en route to Norway, had received from the CIGS a new order. He had first been told to secure Dombaas, and operate offensively northwards towards Trondheim. Now he was ordered to "prevent Germans using railway to reinforce Trondheim" (this would involve a blocking position at or near Dombaas), and also to make contact with the Norwegian Headquarters, thought to be at Lillehammer, in the Gudbrandsdal, a further seventy-five miles south of Dombaas. Morgan was also told to "avoid isolating Norwegian forces operating towards Oslo", an obscure instruction. The tasks set SICKLEFORCE by the War Office, therefore, were to secure a road and rail junction at Dombaas, fifty miles from their landing place: to "operate offensively" against the Germans in Trondheim, one hundred miles north of Dombaas; and to make contact with the Norwegians in the Gudbrandsdal, seventy-five miles south of Dombaas. To carry out these orders Morgan had two Territorial battalions, with a third due to land two days later, one battery of light anti-aircraft guns, no transport and no supporting artillery. He moved troops forward to Dombaas by train immediately they landed at Aandalsnes, and secured the position there. At Dombaas, on 19th April he met King-Salter, who told him that 148th Brigade had been placed at the disposal of the Norwegians, and urged him to deploy as fast as possible south of Dombaas, where the Norwegians were hard-pressed. Morgan referred the matter of his relationship to the Norwegians back to the War Office (who told him in due course that he was not under Norwegian orders, as King-Salter had stated, but should do his best to help them), and moved all his troops yet landed – two battalions – to Dombaas. He now acceded to Norwegian pressure and set in hand the movement of his two battalions south down the Gudbrandsdal. Movement was by train.

Morgan then effectively gave up operational control, by agreeing that his two battalions could be split up into detachments, under Norwegian authority. His position was difficult. The Norwegians knew the ground and the situation, and it was SICKLEFORCE's task to help them. The consequence was unhappy. By the evening of 20th April both battalions were spread out on a wide front, by detachments of company or two company size, in reserve behind Norwegian troops in contact with German columns, and some ten miles south-west, south and south-east of Lillehammer. The impossibility of controlling, administering or supporting newly arrived troops in such circumstances may be imagined; and their commanders had given up the power to attempt it.

In these conditions, after incessant movement in deep snow and with little chance of comprehending the situation or the task, the Territorials of Morgan's two battalions were ordered to relieve the Norwegian detachments to their front on the afternoon of 21st April. A strong German attack had already developed, and later in the afternoon the Norwegian General in command ordered a withdrawal north of Lillehammer. The withdrawal of each detachment could expose its neighbours to envelopment. The synchronisation of such a movement, difficult at the best of times, demanded that transport be available when ordered. It was not; and a number of British troops, after their first contact with the enemy, were cut off during an exhausting march through the snow. In the early hours of 22nd April the remainder of both battalions straggled into a position at Faaberg, north of Lillehammer (having discarded the equipment they could not carry), which they were to defend, unsupported by the Norwegians. During the after-noon the German attack developed – heavy mortar fire and an out-flanking movement – and Faaberg was abandoned. Attacked from the air as they moved, the remnants of SICKLEFORCE went further back to Tretten, ten miles further north. There, on the following afternoon, the Germans attacked north up the main road, supported by the fire of their light artillery and by three tanks against which the defenders had no effective weapon. By the evening of 23rd April, 148th Brigade was reduced to nine officers and 300 men. Its fighting capacity was virtually non-existent. With the aid of Norwegian buses SICKLEFORCE raced to the Heidal, a steep valley forty-five miles to the north, likely to provide some sanctuary against bombing.

Few troops could have performed effectively under the conditions of SICKLEFORCE's committal to battle, and although some gallant deeds had been done the British were inevitably broken. The road to Dombaas lay open.

On 23rd April Major-General Paget was given command of SICKLE-FORCE. On 25th he arrived at Aandalsnes; at the same time a new brigade – 15th Brigade, from France (Brigadier Smyth) – had dis-embarked and hurried south. By the evening their leading battalion was in positions at Kvam, on the main road up the Gudbrandsdal, just south of the Heidal Valley where 148th Brigade had taken refuge. The German advance was here confined to the main road and the ground immediately beside it – their movement assisted by tanks, armoured cars, and readily available mortar and artillery fire, beside the incessant action of dive-bomber aircraft which had already made Aandalsnes near unusable. The Germans had seven battalions available, although so narrow a front confined their attacks to the spearhead unit of the advance.

On 25th April, at Kvam, British Regular troops (as opposed to Territorials) first fought the Germans in the Second World War – for the 15th Brigade consisted of Regular battalions. For the next four days the brigade conducted a fighting withdrawal, as ordered, to Dombaas.

15th Brigade's actions were very different from those of the preced-ing days. At each successive position the troops were well entrenched. They gave a good account of themselves whenever attacked. They were supported by the brigade anti-tank gun company; and their with-drawals, leap-frogging battalion through battalion, were orderly. The Germans manoeuvred the defenders out of each position by superior numbers and fire-power, by sometimes climbing higher in the flanking mountains to make defence untenable, and by the use of ski-patrols. But on several occasions the attackers, with superior numbers, were driven back with very heavy losses, and did not resume battle. The conduct of the 15th Brigade is the more creditable because on 27th April Paget received the inevitable orders to withdraw all of SICKLE-FORCE to Aandalsnes for evacuation, and it is not easy to maintain the morale and staying power of troops knowing that the only reward of victory will be a retreat, and that ships are awaiting them. The withdrawal was admirably performed throughout.

The contrast between the performance of 15th Brigade and that of 146th and 148th Territorial Brigades is striking. It undoubtedly owed much to the fact that in 15th Brigade were Regular battalions. The withdrawal to Dombaas did not demand great power of imagination or manoeuvre. But outfacing the enemy in a defensive position was another matter. That required discipline, sensible orders, skill with weapons and a sufficient grasp of minor tactics. It demanded *esprit de corps*. These things the Regular battalions of the army possessed. But 15th Brigade was committed to the battle in very different conditions from those of 148th Brigade. The latter not only consisted of inexperienced and inadequately trained troops, but were so ill-used and exhausted that more seasoned warriors than they would have failed to pass the test.

The evacuation of Central Norway was conducted with great skill and courage by the Royal Navy. The air situation made sea movement close inshore and on a predictable course highly dangerous; casualties to ships and embarked troops were suffered. But the great majority of those committed to this ill-starred adventure got away. The evacuation of SICKLEFORCE was complete by 2nd May. That of MAURICEFORCE was more hazardous for the navy, but simpler for the army, since the Germans made no move towards Namsos after their first successes. Carton de Wiart's troops were clear on the same day.

The operations of RUPERTFORCE in North Norway were intended to seize Narvik. They began earlier and ended later than elsewhere. In the end Narvik was taken – although it had by then been decided that the Allies should evacuate the area completely thereafter. The campaign not only lasted longer than in Central Norway, it also occupied considerably more troops.

On 11th April, General Mackesy received his orders from the CIGS, sent to him at Scapa where he, his Staff, and two battalions and Headquarters of 24th Guards Brigade were embarked. Mackesy was

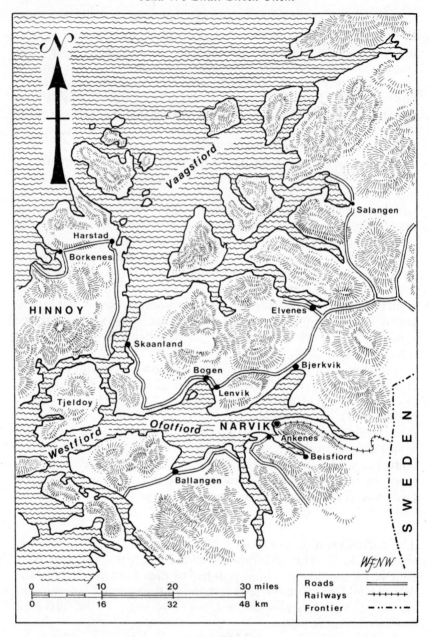

Narvik

given his object – to eject the Germans from the Narvik area and establish control of the town. He was directed to base his force at Harstad if possible (the nearest port to Narvik, and on an island some forty miles away, but twenty-four hours sailing by big ships). Mackesy was ordered to collect information (little was known of the Germans) and plan further operations. He was also told what troops to expect. RUPERTFORCE, as well as 24th Guards Brigade, was to receive two Territorial brigades within days and the rest of the 49th Division – Mackesy's division – in about a fortnight. There would also follow "British formations from the BEF". This looked a comparatively large scale and deliberate affair. Like his colleagues to the south, Mackesy was ordered not to attempt an opposed landing; but in a handwritten message from the CIGS, Ironside, he was told, "You may have a chance of taking advantage of naval action, and you should do so if you can. Boldness is required." Mackesy's orders were amplified verbally by the Brigadier who brought them from the War Office. He was told that the first task was to get ashore and make contact with the Norwegians, and that it was well understood that it might not be possible to make any plan for weeks.

While RUPERTFORCE was at sea major changes were made. The two Territorial brigades were diverted to Central Norway, where their adventures have already been described. Mackesy reached Harstad on 14th April, and in the next few days the rest of RUPERTFORCE was disembarked and deployed to various points on the mainland, all some considerable distance from Narvik itself. The force now consisted only of 24th Guards Brigade, one light anti-aircraft battery (as yet without its guns) and two field companies of Royal Engineers. The diminution of RUPERTFORCE's fighting strength was not accompanied by any reduction in stores, and large loads of every description arrived, including some for forces in other areas, and even for units earmarked for the Finnish expedition and since disbanded. The little port of Harstad overflowed with the logistic support, much of it irrelevant to real need, which the British Army tends to send behind its expeditions, and there were problems of clearance and handling under the ever present threat of air attack. Congestion and confusion were made worse in that everything, as throughout the Norwegian adventure, arrived higgledy-piggledy, and much that was urgently needed did not arrive at all. The story was no different from that at Namsos or Aandalsnes, but on a larger scale. Some shipping losses had also contributed to the general lack of essentials.

Operations in North Norway had three phases. In the first of these RUPERTFORCE was still small, but it seemed to be possible to take Narvik by a bold *coup de main*, substituting speed and surprise for strength. The first chance for this had arisen when ships of the Royal Navy had entered Narvik Fjord and destroyed a number of German warships. The guns of British warships dominated Narvik, which appeared to have been evacuated by the occupying German troops, reckoned to be about a brigade in strength. An immediate assault seemed a possibility. There were, however, no troops yet to hand – this was two days before the arrival of RUPERTFORCE – and such moments pass with disappointing rapidity. The German soldier is resilient, and an opportunity not taken at once is unlikely to recur.

When Mackesy arrived and met the Senior Naval Officer, Admiral of the Fleet the Earl of Cork and Orrery, on 15th April, the chance had certainly passed. Cork had been briefed verbally by Churchill in London. He had sailed from Rosyth the same day that Mackesy left Scapa. A fiery fighting man, he ordered *Southampton*, a warship containing part of RUPERTFORCE, to rally with him off Narvik with the idea of trying an immediate landing. The idea was soon dropped, but the spirit behind it – a very admirable spirit if tempered by understanding of what is feasible – persisted. Cork's sense of urgency was sharpened two days later, on 17th April, by messages to Mackesy and himself from London, urging immediate action to occupy Narvik. The moving spirit behind them was Churchill, now Chairman of a Military Coordinating Committee set up to deal with the direction of these operations.

Mackesy remained at all times determined not to commit the troops to a suicidal assault. The snow was lying even deeper than in Central Norway – four to five feet down to the waterline, in spite of the assurance given in London that there was no snow after mid-April. Snow blizzards took place at frequent intervals. Tactical movement on foot ranged between the laborious and the impossible. A direct assault on Narvik would have to be made in open boats, on too easily predictable and narrow beaches, certainly covered by German machine guns. The General told the War Office – and the Senior Naval Officer – that the operation was impracticable. To this Cork countered that a naval bombardment would reduce the place, and there would be no coherent opposition. There was a difficulty here: a bombardment of Narvik itself would cause, inevitably, serious Norwegian casualties and loss of Norwegian goodwill. On these and on moral grounds Cork's military colleagues described it as indefensible. Mackesy agreed, however, that if bombardment by the guns of the fleet were restricted to designated military targets, and if subsequent reconnaissance showed the enemy to be absolutely reduced by it, he would land troops to occupy the place. The operation was scheduled for 24th April. Meanwhile Cork was placed in supreme command of the expedition.

The effectiveness of the naval bombardment was a great disappointment. It was clear beyond argument that it could have had little effect on the defending Germans. Direct assault on Narvik was shelved for the moment, and the troops disembarked. All was by no means lost as a new plan took shape to attack Narvik from the west. One battalion of 24th Guards Brigade was shipped to a point only a few miles west of the town, and a village – Ankenes – was occupied on 28th April, only to be lost a few days later when the Germans drove out the British in a spirited counter-attack. German reactions were sensitive in this area, where they had little depth, and it seemed that by building up here the Allies might take the place without too much delay and by methodical approach. But on the same day that Ankenes was temporarily occupied one company of 24th Guards Brigade was detached and sent by sea to Bodö, over one hundred miles to the south, to forestall a German landing. This was a portent of things soon swiftly to come.

The Allies were evacuating Central Norway. Their standing with the Norwegians was gravely affected. The essential cooperation of the four Norwegian battalions in the Narvik area was now under strain. The Allies needed to show some sign of continuing resolution. Once again they decided to concentrate on Narvik and to send considerable reinforcements. One demi-brigade (three battalions) of Chasseurs Alpins had landed on 28th April. Now two battalions of the Foreign Legion and a Polish brigade of four battalions were shipped north. On 1st May it was agreed in London that when transports became available 5th Division should be withdrawn from the BEF in France and sent to Narvik (a move which did not occur), along with two French light divisions. Less ambitious, but more welcome because they actually arrived, one battery of close support artillery, a troop of tanks and the first of the much needed reinforcing anti-aircraft batteries were also despatched from England. RUPERTFORCE was expanding – not, of course, simply to take Narvik but to operate on a grander scale against the Germans in Norway.

There was, however, still serious dissension at Narvik itself. On 3rd May, Cork returned to the proposal to assault Narvik direct. Mackesy, supported very strongly by the acting Brigade Commander (the Brigadier had been wounded on a reconnaissance near Ankenes), said that the attempt would fail, for well-rehearsed reasons. Little had changed. The snow was melting, but the beaches were covered by the Germans, and no covering fire available would keep their heads sufficiently down. Cork was unconvinced. There was pressure on him from the naval side since ships were required elsewhere. He referred the dispute to

London. Such a way of running a campaign may seem remarkably unsatisfactory, but it cannot be held that more authority in Cork's hands at that juncture would have solved the matter by an imposed "unity of command"; the responsible commanders, whose troops would make the attempt, were flatly opposed to it, and on grounds where they and not he were experienced. The dispute was, by direction from London, deferred until the arrival of Lieutenant-General Sir Claude Auchinleck, who had been ordered to Narvik to report on the situation – and with sealed orders to supersede Mackesy and take command of all troops if he judged it necessary. Auchinleck was due to arrive on 12th May. Thus ended the first phase of operations, which had been concerned with the landing of troops and stores, the creation of a base many hours' sailing time from the objective, and with much dissension over the possibility of taking Narvik by direct assault.

The second phase began on 10th May, when one battalion of 24th Guards Brigade was sent by warship to Mo, over 200 miles south of Narvik as crow or aircraft flies, and very far indeed by sea route. On the same day an independent company at Mosjoen was attacked by the Germans, now pushing up from their lodgement areas in the south. On the same day 400 Germans landed from the sea at Hamnesberget, south of Mo and north of Mosjoen. On the same day, after a stormy debate in the House of Commons, Chamberlain's Government was succeeded by a coalition led by Churchill. Some have thought it ironic that a Parliament dissatisfied with the conduct of the war, and particularly with operations in Norway, should in consequence find itself with a Prime Minister who was the chief architect of those operations. But there was a more deep-seated unease at what seemed the indecisive flabbiness of the government, and the change came not an hour too soon. For on that day, too, the great battle of the West began in France, and thereafter Norway could play but a peripheral part in the unfolding drama.

The battalion despatched to Mo was accompanied by a troop of field guns and a troop of light anti-aircraft artillery, but was short of one of its companies previously sent one hundred and forty miles by road and ferry to Bodö in the north. Like the unfortunate leading battalions of SICKLEFORCE three weeks before, it was taken from an operation, with a secure base, designed to work towards Narvik, and became instead the leading element of a south-facing defence at a great distance from reinforcement or support. After the landings of Hamnesberget it was clear that a German advance by road would not take long to follow, and there was always the chance of further landings from the sea. RUPERT-FORCE gave orders for the remainder of 24th Guards Brigade to be shipped south to the area of Bodö. Placed under their command were five "independent companies" which had been formed from volunteers drawn from Territorial divisions in England. These companies had been deployed in the southern sector – at various points south of Bodö – to act as guerrillas and harass the enemy as he advanced, in cooperation with the local population: a difficult mission at any time, however stouthearted the attempt. It was clear that the independent companies could not stop a determined German advance, nor was that their task. They came to be used, inevitably, as reinforcing detachments during what now became a long withdrawal.

The position of 24th Guards Brigade at Mo and Bodö was especially precarious. The only effective way of reaching them from RUPERT-FORCE's base in the north was by sea, but German air supremacy made the movement of ships in the narrow waters highly dangerous. Enemy air power also made movement by road extremely hazardous, particularly as the long Norwegian winter was now ending and the sun shone throughout twenty-four hours in these latitudes, giving no respite. Nevertheless Auchinleck, who had now taken over command from Mackesy, ordered the Bodö area to be held at all costs, and Mo as long as supply by road proved feasible.

On 17th May the Germans launched their first attack against the battalion at Mo. On 18th May the acting Brigade Commander (Brigadier Gubbins) agreed that the battalion should withdraw. Thereafter, retreat took place through a number of intermediate positions on the road north, followed up by the Germans. At each position companies were ordered to withdraw if strongly attacked, and at each position the German method was, as elsewhere, to work round the flanks. And all the time, overhead, was the threat from the clear sky.

Meanwhile disaster had struck the rest of 24th Guards Brigade. The ship in which the second battalion was embarked, sailing for Bodö, was bombed and the casualties included all the senior officers. The discipline and behaviour of the battalion attracted the admiration of all: this was the Regular Army at its best. Then a warship on which men and stores of the third battalion were travelling south ran aground, and although there was no loss of life the troops had to return to Harstad for re-embarkation. The battalions of the brigade, therefore, apart from the one struggling back from Mo, only began to reach Bodö on 20th May, and some companies had still not arrived five days later. On 24th May, 24th Guards Brigade, less the force withdrawing from Mo and short of some companies, but reinforced by one of the independent companies, took up a defensive position at Pothus, ten miles south of the head of the fjord on which Bodö stands and about forty miles away.

The battalion from Mo, after a withdrawal of eighty miles in six days and a continuous series of engagements, passed through the position on the same day. The Germans attacked early on 25th May, and following a brisk battle the British force withdrew the following evening. Concentrated again in the Bodö area, 24th Guards Brigade was withdrawn to Borkenes, near Harstad, on three successive nights, starting on 29th May. On the preceding day Norwegian, French and Polish troops had at last entered Narvik. By then a brigade of eleven British batteries of anti-aircraft guns had been deployed to RUPERT-FORCE. Otherwise British troops took no direct part in the final attack.

The third and last phase of the Narvik story was the same as elsewhere. All troops were evacuated from the area on 7th and 8th June. The decision to abandon Norway had been taken a fortnight before. A great deal of equipment was left behind.

So ended the Norwegian campaign. The difficulties of terrain, snow, climate and distance were enormous. Movement, whether operational by sea or road, or tactical across country was laborious at all times, dangerous at most times, impossible at some. The confusion of strategic and logistic planning made the task of the troops doubly difficult on many occasions, and impossible on others. The Services, whose cooperation with each other was essential, had to respond to different orders from different Departments at home. The influence of Churchill was generally deplorable: his boldness and imagination on that occasion were not – as later was generally and mercifully the case – checked by a strong Chiefs of Staff Committee. The mixture of ignorance and interference displayed from London was seldom creditable. If the first campaigns of the British in long wars tend to be ineptly launched and incompetently executed, Norway was no exception.

The army was committed to battle without proper support, whether from artillery, anti-aircraft artillery or air power. Equipment was inferior to the enemy's. The huge significance of the enemy's air superiority was appreciated for the first time: its effect on the performance of the troops was considerable.

That performance was at some points brave and skilful. At too many others it was unimpressive. Casualties were not high, but morale was too quickly destroyed by reverses. The standard of discipline and training was uneven; in some cases it was poor. This was the first British contact with the German soldier, and his tactical and psychological superiority made a most disagreeable impression. He seemed a natural winner. Compared to the enemy, British training appeared, even at its best, to have produced an army over-deliberate, slow, reactive. There was a sense of shock, of lessons as yet unlearned and basic qualities so far unacquired. It was, perhaps, the beginning of the end of the beginning.

3

Flight from the Continent

On 10th May Operation SICHELSCHNITT began – the German offensive which was, within a few weeks, to eliminate France, Belgium and Holland from the war and drive the British Army from the Continent for nearly four years. The campaign was a German victory of a speed and completeness which caught even the victors unprepared. To the defeated it was a catastrophe.

British soldiers reacted to it differently according to their experience, training and character; but to all it was a shock of unprecedented magnitude. To the senior generation – to the Generals, the Colonels, the older Sergeant-Majors – it appeared that all recent history was turned upside down. Brought up in the warm afterglow of triumph in 1918 they had shared in that triumph and felt its fruits permanent – even though they may have worried over the resurgence of Germany and fretted at British unpreparedness. To find, within days of the first encounters, the great French Army nipped in two, their own troops near surrounded, pursued and frequently outfought – this was something for which no previous experience nor study had prepared them. For a brief moment, in the great German offensive of March 1918, the feeling had been the same. Then, also, a breach had been torn with little means of filling it. Haig had referred to our "backs to the wall". But German energy had run out, the front had held, the cause had prevailed. Now it all seemed for nothing. Now there was no shortage of German energy. The Panzer divisions seemed irresistible as a hurricane sweeping across the map. Beside and behind them, supported by horsed transport and artillery only, but enormous in number, marching and fighting with skill and endurance, flowed a torrent of infantry divisions, not very different in character and appearance from those remembered twenty-two years before, but with an exuberant confidence, a new-found strength; and swooping above them all an apparently all-powerful and unchallenged air force. This was the Wehrmacht.

To those fresh to battle, whether or not brought up in the undemanding life of the Regular Army before the war, the shock was equally violent. They had of course realised that in too many cases their equipment was inadequate; that some of their training had been sketchy; that there ran through the officer corps a certain lack of professional edge, to put it no less mildly. But they, like the whole army and nation, had been encouraged to form a picture of future operations based on the trench lines of the First World War. Provided, it seemed, they did their duty from defensive positions when ordered, their deficiencies of skill and material would, with time, be made good, and all would come right in the end. Nothing prepared them or their seniors for the storm which now broke. The sheer speed of events was numbing. The psychological shock was profound. It was necessary to struggle against both physical exhaustion and paralysis of the will. Campaigns are won and lost in the hearts of men.

The BEF reached its position in Belgium on the River Dyle – Plan D – without disturbance. Allied plans were based on the Germans violating Belgian and Dutch neutrality, as they did; and assumed that the German right wing advancing through these countries would carry the main German strength, just as General Count von Schlieffen, first architect of the great advance in 1914 which had taken the German Army to the Marne, had preached. "Keep the right wing strong," he is said to have murmured when dying, and failure to do so on that occasion had led to check, recoil and defeat. Now, surely, Schlieffen's lesson would have been learned. There would again, the Allies reckoned, be a "giant wheel", and this time the right would indeed be strong.

In fact SICHELSCHNITT was a completely different concept. The Germans had changed their original plan and now placed the weight of their effort not on the right, but in the centre. On their right, or northern, wing, Army Group B (General von Bock) comprised twenty-eight divisions, including three Panzer divisions. Bock's frontage of advance included Holland, and extended south to a line running from Cologne through Liège and Namur, and thence towards the Franco-Belgian border around Mons and Valenciennes. In the south Army Group C (General von Leeb) had seventeen divisions, none of them armoured, and was directed toward the Maginot Line, between the southern tip of Luxembourg and the Swiss frontier. Between these two, through Luxembourg and the southern part of Belgium, against the French frontier in the area of Givet, Sedan and Longwy, and directed on the plains of Northern France came Army Group A (General von Rundstedt) with no less than forty-four divisions, and seven out of the German total of ten Panzer divisions. Army Group A, therefore, was designed to smash the centre of the Allied front and to cut the Allied forces in two. The BEF was deployed in the area of advance of Bock's Army Group B. It was on their neighbours to the south, the French First and (above all) Ninth Armies, that the main German blow would fall.

The BEF deployed with two corps forward. On the right[1] I Corps (Lieutenant-General Barker–Dill had returned to England to be Vice-Chief of the Imperial General Staff) with 1st, 2nd and 48th Divisions: and on the left II Corps (Brooke) with 3rd and 4th Divisions. There were three divisions in the line and each corps held one division in depth (48th and 4th respectively). In addition to these five, two other divisions – 5th and 50th – were in general reserve (elements of these had been drawn towards Norway before the clock struck); and two more divisions (42nd and 44th) were deployed in depth on the River Escaut under III Corps (Adam), some fifty miles behind the front line. Four more divisions of the BEF would also be caught up in the battle: three of them divisions in little more than name – the "labour" divisions, 12th, 23rd and 46th, which had been sent out for pioneering work and to "complete their training", and which lacked most of the support which the word "division" should imply, including any artillery. Finally there was 51st Division, which had been detached in April to the Saar area to gain experience in the Maginot Line under French command, and which remained divorced from the main body of the BEF throughout.

On the left of the BEF the Belgian Army had deployed: on their right the French First Army (Blanchard). The leading British troops took up position on 11th May, and on 13th May their light reconnaissance regiments (cavalry regiments equipped with armoured cars and light tanks) had their first contact with the enemy. The first German attacks on the British position came on the evening of 14th May. During that day the reconnaissance regiments, withdrawing in conformity with the French cavalry screen on their right, recrossed the Dyle.

Next day, 15th May, there were further attacks on both corps sectors. The fact that the German main effort, their *schwerpunkt*, was in the centre of the front and entrusted to Rundstedt did not mean that Bock's troops were instructed to take their time. On the contrary, they were spurred on, not only on their right through Holland but on their left, in Belgium and opposite the BEF, where Sixth Army (General von

---

[1] When listed, troops, unless otherwise stated, will be given from right to left.

Reichenau) had been told the importance of breaking through between Louvain and Namur. All German divisions were going hard. Throughout 15th May attacks were launched on the BEF. Ground was lost, and retaken by counter-attack. At nightfall the front was intact.

By now, however, after only five days of campaign, the position on the flanks of the BEF, rather than the actions of the enemy to its front, was chiefly determining events. In the north, on 14th May, Holland capitulated, and the French Seventh Army on the extreme left of the Allied line fell back, exposing the Belgian left until the latter rested, as it soon did, on the mouth of the River Escaut. In the south the French Ninth Army had been stunned by the strength and speed of the German advance through the Ardennes. All their cavalry and light armoured covering forces were withdrawn west of the Meuse on 12th May. That night German infantry seized small bridgeheads, and on 13th the Germans managed to ferry across, bridge the river and start getting tanks to the west bank. The appearance of German armour and the incessant attack of dive-bombing aircraft had a devastating effect on the defenders. On 14th May the dent in Ninth Army's front became a breach. Although at the remove of one army's front, the southern flank of the BEF was now in the air.

On 15th May a German attack penetrated the front of the French First Army. The fire was spreading north. On that day the first British withdrawal was ordered, to conform with the French. Next morning General Billotte, Commander of the French 1st Army Group, and now exercising his authority over the Belgians, the BEF and his French Armies for almost the only time, ordered a phased withdrawal, over three successive nights, first to the River Senne (a line running through Brussels) then to the River Dendre (some ten miles behind Brussels) and finally to the Escaut (a further twenty miles to the rear). No withdrawal was envisaged behind the Escaut.

For the next ten days the Panzer divisions of Army Group A drove westwards, through the shattered French divisions, preceded as everywhere by a mass of refugees choking the roads, all the time driving a sword ever deeper into the southern flank of the BEF and of the French First Army. The threat from south and south-west was quickly to become more menacing even than the enemy to the east, destroying any possibility of a coordinated front with the mass of French Armies, and cutting off the BEF from its base in North-Western France. The events of those nightmare days are best given in the form of diary and comment. The map tells the tale more dramatically than any prose.

The Area of Sichelschnitt

Night 16th/17th May

I and II Corps withdrew to the Senne Line, through Brussels.

17th May

To the south the Germans crossed the River Sambre in the area of Maubeuge.

I and II Corps on the Senne Line.

A garrison was established for Arras, the GHQ and railhead: one battalion, and assorted troops from base units, formed detachments manning eighteen field guns and a squadron of armoured fighting vehicles from depots.

A force was formed – "Macforce" – to protect the right rear of the BEF, initially to deny to the enemy the line of the River Scarpe: the force consisted of a brigade from 42nd Division, two artillery regiments and other scratch units. It was placed under Major-General Mason Macfarlane, Gort's Director of Intelligence.

All available Engineers and Military Police on the lines of communication were grouped into *ad hoc* battalions in GHQ reserve. The three "Labour" divisions – 12th, 23rd and 46th, whose condition has already been described – were deployed to defensive positions respectively at Amiens; on the Canal du Nord, east of Arras; and at Seclin, south of Lille. They thus lay in the path of the German Army Group A.

Night 17th/18th May

I and II Corps withdrew to the line of the River Dendre. The enemy tried to get crossings over the Senne, north of Brussels.

18th May

To the south the Germans reached the area of Cambrai – St. Quentin. I and II Corps were on the Dendre Line, with four divisions – 48th, 2nd, 1st, 3rd.

4th and 5th Divisions were moved to the Escaut, to join 42nd and 44th Divisions.

The garrison of Arras was placed under Major-General Petre, GOC 12th Division and henceforth known as "Petreforce". Petre was also given command of the two brigades of 23rd Division, one deployed on the Canal du Nord at Arleux, ten miles east of Arras, and one on the canal ten miles north of Peronne. The three brigades of 12th Division were deployed at Abbeville, Amiens and Doullens.

Night 18th/19th May

I and II Corps withdrew to the Escaut Line, leaving rearguards on the Dendre until next morning.

19th May

In the south Army Group A reached Peronne on the Somme. There were now no French troops between Rundstedt's spearheads and the sea. It was clear that no move of the BEF southwards towards the Somme would be possible. The Allied Forces were cut in two. Further British withdrawal could only be in the area north of the German penetration – west, or north-west, and in contact with the Belgian Army. That evening Gort, for the first time, discussed with his commanders evacuation.

On the Escaut Line the Germans – Army Group B – followed up fast from the Dendre, and at one point got across the Escaut itself. They were driven back, and by nightfall the BEF was established on the Escaut Line, with all three corps and seven divisions in line. 5th Division was ordered to the area of Seclin in GHQ reserve. On the Escaut Line the right of the BEF was at Maulde, its left at Oudenarde.

Night 19th/20th May

50th Division was ordered to move to Vimy Ridge, north of Arras, in reserve.

Gort now had seven divisions facing east on the Escaut, and two in GHQ reserve, beside three "labour" divisions finding garrisons and bridge guards.

One brigade of 23rd Division withdrew from Arleux and joined "Petreforce".

20th May

In the south and south-west Army Group A raced west in the corridor between Arras and the Somme, and reached Amiens, Abbeville at the mouth of the Somme, Doullens, Le Boisle and Hesdin. Four Panzer divisions, with three following up, now threatened the deep flank of the BEF on the Escaut Line. Two German divisions – 7th Panzer and SS Division "Totenkopf" – surrounded "Petreforce" in Arras. Troops of French First Army were in position facing south between Arras and Maulde – the right of the British line on the Escaut.

As Army Group A advanced:

The second brigade of 23rd Division, ordered to withdraw from its positions north of Peronne the preceding night, was caught in motor transport and marching on foot by the tanks of 8th Panzer Division. The brigade was broken up, and the remnants which got away and assembled fifteen miles north of Arras numbered only some 200 men.

One brigade – 37th – of 12th Division was overrun and destroyed at Amiens and Albert by 1st Panzer Division. Another – 35th – was smashed at Abbeville by 2nd Panzer Division. The little now left of 12th and 23rd Divisions became part of "Petreforce". But during Army Group A's advance these battalions, ill prepared, under-equipped and unsupported nevertheless on occasion held up the enemy for several hours. At Doullens, as the Germans reported, "In spite of numerous tanks it was only possible to break down their resistance after about two and a half hours." At Peronne, 1st Panzer Division failed to break out from the town at all on the evening of 18th May because of the defence put up by one battalion supported by a troop of four field guns.

At Arras "Petreforce" was attacked all day by 7th Panzer and SS "Totenkopf" Divisions.

As Army Group B advanced:

On the Escaut Line the main body of the BEF repelled numerous attacks; but the enemy achieved lodgements on the west bank both in the extreme north and the south of the line.

The CIGS, Ironside, flew from England and visited Gort's Command Post. He brought a direction from the British Cabinet, of which the first paragraph ran: "The Cabinet decided that the CIGS was to direct the C-in-C BEF to move southwards upon Amiens, attacking all enemy forces encountered, and to take station on the left of the French Army."

At the time of the Cabinet deliberations the day before, the German Army had not, it is true, actually entered Amiens, although five Panzer divisions lay by then along the Canal du Nord only twenty-five miles to the east. To comply with this instruction Gort would have had to disengage his main force from the Escaut Line where it was under pressure, and arrange the south-westward movement of three corps across the front of an armoured enemy, at that moment engaged in advancing across the line of such a movement. The BEF and the nation could be grateful that Gort did not make any serious concessions to so ludicrous a direction from so

61

remote a source. He had already planned a limited southward attack by his two reserve divisions – 5th and 50th – in the area of Arras, and he proposed to do this and no more. The visit at least had the merit of showing Ironside the truth of the situation. The BEF was about to be under siege, and its only secure flank was the coast. The visit also, however, demonstrates the anomalies of Gort's position. His operational instructions, to make sense, must emanate not from the British Government but from his French superior; and he received none – or none of practical value. And that day General Maxim Weygand took over from Gamelin as Supreme Commander of the Allied force.

21st May

The Panzer and SS divisions of Army Group A were now established south and east of Arras (three divisions), at Hesdin, Le Boisle, Abbeville, and Amiens. Rundstedt reckoned that the encirclement of the Allies in the north was complete. He had dealt the decisive blows. Now he was content with the role of anvil to the hammer of Bock from the north-east. His eyes were fixed on the south, where, he assumed, major and decisive battles were still to be fought with the French Armies south of the Somme.

As a result of a series of Allied conferences held at Ypres it was decided that the Belgian Army, on the left of the BEF, would relieve one British division, and that the French First Army, on the British right, would relieve two British divisions in the defence against Army Group B; that the defence should be based on a new line – the old frontier defences north of Lille, to which the BEF would withdraw by pivoting on its right at Maulde and pulling back from the Escaut; and that a counter-attack to the south would be made by the British divisions thus relieved. For Gort had already committed his existing reserve – 5th and 50th Divisions – to a limited counter-attack at Arras, which was at that moment taking place. The later counter-attack now being proposed would be made in conjunction with a major northward effort by the French from south of the German penetration. It could not start before 26th May.

At Arras the counter-attack went in at about 2.30 in the afternoon. It was a small affair, as two brigades from the two divisions involved (comprising between them only four brigades) were committed to strengthen the Arras garrison, and one was held in reserve. Only one brigade advanced, and since it held one battalion in reserve the "Arras counter-attack" was made by two battalions. In support, however, it had the only tanks – of 1st Army Tank Brigade – in the

BEF, apart from the light tanks of the reconnaissance regiments. And although these tanks were slow and underarmed their appearance sent a wave of alarm through Army Group A. Highly exaggerated reports were, as is usual in war, made by the Germans of the strength of the attack. The 7th Panzer Division command map showed five British divisions attacking – a creditable front to have been made by two battalions and seventy-two tanks, of which only sixteen boasted an anti-tank gun. By the end of the day the operation was over, and the troops committed to it withdrawn. It was a "spoiling" attack. It disturbed and delayed the enemy. It also demonstrated what real preparedness and strength might have achieved. Small though it was, it constituted the only true manoeuvre the BEF was able to make during the campaign.

On the Escaut Line the main body of the BEF met heavy attacks all day. A number of counter-attacks eliminated most of the enemy's bridgeheads except in the far north (44th Division) where, after fierce fighting, the Germans retained a lodgement on the west bank near Oudenarde and near the junction of the BEF and the Belgian Army.

22nd May

Churchill sent Gort a telegram from Paris, where he had been conferring. The second paragraph set the tone: "The British Army and the French First Army should attack south-west towards Bapaume and Cambrai at the earliest moment – certainly tomorrow with about eight divisions – and with the Belgian cavalry on the right of the British."

These romantic visions were far from reality and Gort could only ignore them. Later he received an incomprehensible order from Weygand, of which the relevant sentence ran: "*Les forces nécessaires à ces contre-attaques existent dans ce groupement . . . savoir . . . l'armée britannique, qu'il a lieu de porter tout entière à la droite du disposatif en accentuant les mouvements déjà commencés . . .*"

This sort of juggling with distant forces, as on a chessboard, sadly bore little relationship to the awful facts of the battlefield.

On the main position of the BEF on the Escaut orders were given for the withdrawal that night to the "frontier position". In the north of the BEF line the Germans repeatedly attacked in attempts to break through towards Courtrai.

Night 22nd/23rd May

The BEF withdrew to the "frontier position" – the places whence it had hurried forward on 10th May. The right of the army rested at Maulde, the left at Halluin. On the left the Belgian Army deployed on the River Lys, at an angle to the BEF. The Belgians had declined a proposal to withdraw further, in conformity, to the Yser. To do so would have shortened the line to be held and, because of the terrain, made it more easily defensible, but it would have yielded most of Belgium to enemy occupation, and the King of the Belgians, himself in command in the field, did not believe that the state of the Belgian Army made such a further withdrawal feasible without probable disintegration.

23rd May

Gort was perfectly clear where, for the moment, the chief danger lay – to south and south-west. His previous reserve – 5th and 50th Divisions – having been committed to the operation at Arras (whose defence they still supported), he deployed only four divisions under I and II Corps on the main position on the frontier. He moved the 2nd and 48th Divisions to Lille, to the now threatened line of the La Bassée Canal, between La Bassée and St. Omer, for Gort was now facing Army Group B from the east, and the threat, which could materialise at any moment, of Army Group A's refreshed Panzer divisions swinging round at the rear of the BEF from south-west and west. Gort kept 44th Division in GHQ reserve. The BEF was vulnerable on three flanks, and desperately tired. In this situation Gort had now to consider the "decisions" of the Ypres conference two days before. In harmony with a promised and major French attack from the south he was due shortly to launch an operation from the north against the flank of the massive German penetration – the corridor filled with the Wehrmacht, running from Germany to the Channel. When Blanchard (French First Army) visited him for discussions Gort said grimly that any operation from the north would have to be very limited.

The La Bassée Canal, and its extension, the Aa Canal, was the only defensible position covering the area – the southern and western flanks – of the BEF. Along it Gort deployed two divisions – 2nd and 48th – and whatever *ad hoc* forces he had been able to collect under various expedients from base troops and logistic units, now transformed into infantry. Posted at the main crossings, sometimes supported by a single field gun firing over open sights, these detachments were in many places all that lay between the BEF and encirclement. It was not enough. East from St. Omer, on a twenty-mile front, the Germans of Army Group A, now operating northwards, seized crossings over the canal. In a valuable delaying operation Arras held out far to the south-east with the survivors of "Petreforce", and 5th and 50th Divisions – by now at the southern tip of a long salient since Army Group A had crossed the La Bassée Canal and Army Group B pressed I and II Corps on the frontier position. Now the evacuation of Arras was ordered, and during the night 23rd/24th the gallant defenders withdrew northwards along roads where confusion reigned.

Brooke, commanding II Corps, wrote in his diary that evening: "Nothing but a miracle can save the BEF."

24th May

In the west, the Germans consolidated and dangerously expanded their bridgeheads over the La Bassée Canal, but suffered severely in trying to make further crossings. In the east Army Group B launched a strong attack on the Belgian Army in the area of Courtrai, about ten miles from the British left. The Belgians withdrew. The uneasiness, present now for several days in the minds of Gort and (particularly) Brooke, commanding the lefthand II Corps, about the left flank of the BEF, grew stronger. The BEF was only under severe pressure that day in the extreme south-west, across the La Bassée Canal: but the Panzer divisions had only been halted, to be conserved and restored for future operations.

Gort now ordered III Corps (Adam) to prepare for a limited counter-attack to the south, in conformity with the decisions of the Ypres Conference. As at Arras, 5th and 50th Divisions would be used, with the attack launched two days hence, to coincide with a French attack from the south northward. Unbeknown to Gort, however, the French, this day, abandoned the idea.

25th May

On the eastern front, held by I and II Corps, a serious German attack had driven back the Belgian Army, leaving a gap on the British left. But German plans, captured that day, showed that two German Corps of Army Group B were to be launched towards the area of Ypres – driving a wedge between the Belgians and the BEF. The left of the BEF was now threatened. Were it not secured the British Army would be encircled by a German westward thrust to the sea on the BEF northern flank.

Gort had that morning once again and for the last time, considered with his Corps Commanders the possibility of a breakout to the south, across the flank of the German penetration, in addition to the southern counter-attack to be made on the morrow by two of his divisions and three from the French First Army.

He had conferred earlier in the day with Blanchard (now commanding the Army Group – Billotte had suffered an accident). They had discussed the southern counter-attack. Neither man knew that the French northwards attack from the south side of the German penetration had already been cancelled, making their own planned operation futile. The larger idea of a mass breakout to the south did not last long. Brooke discussed it with his Divisional Commanders and was thoroughly sceptical – the threat to the left was too strong. Even the "limited" southern attack was by now a most questionable operation. At six o'clock in the evening Gort, on his own authority, cancelled the preparations for the attack of 5th and 50th Divisions, and ordered them instead to move to the British left. His instinct, fortified by the recent information on German deployment in Army Group B, was that the threat in the north was now extremely serious. The left of the BEF – and its route to at least one port – must be secured. There was no further question of a major move south.

By this decision Gort saved the BEF.

26th May

Blanchard himself now recognised that only a bridgehead, covering Dunkirk, could be held by the French First Army, the BEF and the Belgian Army. He issued orders accordingly, for a progressive disengagement and withdrawal over the next three nights, to bring the armies back to the line of the La Bassée Canal (and its continuation to the sea, the Aa Canal) and the River Lys.

On this day of decision Gort received a telegram from the War Office authorising him "to operate towards the coast forthwith in conjunction with French and Belgian Armies". London now appreciated the realities of the situation.

But to "operate towards the coast" required more than simple adherence to Blanchard's orders for a phased withdrawal. For on the left of the BEF the Belgians, still deployed on the Lys (which was to constitute the east flank of the "final position" – the north end of the bridgehead covering Dunkirk), were severely attacked and reported that they could do nothing to close the gap between the Belgian and British Armies, and that they were not in a condition to withdraw. The German road to Ypres lay open.

On the southern front there were probing attacks by Army Group A north and north-eastward across the canal lines and towards Dunkirk. But the real threat now was from Bock's Army Group B to the north of the BEF, where his thrusts were driving the Belgians northwards, away from the British.

That evening the British Government ordered Operation DYNAMO to begin. This was the evacuation of the army from Dunkirk.

Dunkirk was not the only port open to the BEF when the withdrawal to the old "frontier position" began. Twenty miles west of Dunkirk is Calais, and a further twenty miles beyond Calais is Boulogne. As the German Panzer divisions cut their way to the sea at Abbeville on 20th May the importance of these ports grew paramount. Two days later 20th Guards Brigade, with two battalions and some anti-tank guns, arrived from England, disembarked at Boulogne and received orders to hold it. The town already contained units improvised from individual French soldiers, but an expected French division never arrived.

That day 2nd Panzer Division of Army Group A was directed on Boulogne, as the left flank guard of a corps of three Panzer divisions advancing parallel to the coast toward Dunkirk. 2nd Panzer Division began their attack at 5 p.m. and attacked continuously, with tanks, infantry and air support until 6.30 p.m. the following evening, when the two defending battalions were ordered to withdraw and embark from the blazing harbour. Some were safely embarked. Some were captured. Some held out for another day before finally overwhelmed. Some fell at Boulogne and never left it. By 25th May the port was in German hands.

On 22nd May, while 20th Guards Brigade was moving to Boulogne, a Territorial battalion landed from England to defend Calais. It had no supporting arms of any kind but was joined by a battalion of forty-eight tanks, half light tanks, half cruisers, which moved to an assembly area two miles west of the town. This was part of the 1st – and only – Armoured Division, now for the first time being deployed in France. Nobody at Calais knew the general situation. A patrol of light tanks set out from the town, ran into the German 6th Panzer Division, and withdrew after loss.

By then – 23rd May – reinforcements were unexpectedly arriving. 30th Brigade, with two battalions and formed only four weeks previously as the Motor Brigade of 1st Armoured Division, had been embarked in England and ordered to land somewhere in France and help with the defence of Boulogne – which had been under heavy attack since the evening before. Disembarked at Calais 30th Brigade found the underarmed Territorial battalion and the depleted tank battalion about to face a German onslaught. It was clear that, so far from moving to support the defenders of Boulogne, to defend Calais itself was going to be difficult. All available troops were deployed in defence of the perimeter. 10th Panzer Division had already reached the high ground south of the town, while 1st Panzer Division was advancing on Gravelines, between Calais and Dunkirk.

At this point – having just arranged the hasty disposition of his force – the commander of 30th Brigade, Brigadier Nicholson, was ordered by signal from the War Office to escort 350,000 rations for the BEF to Dunkirk. The perimeter was immediately weakened to provide a convoy guard. Meanwhile Calais was effectively ringed by three Panzer divisions, one between it and Dunkirk. Patrols soon established that no convoy could possibly get through.

On 24th May Calais was attacked from all three sides. The defending battalions were without much of their equipment, which had not been disembarked, and were short of ammunition. In spite of this they inflicted severe casualties on the enemy, giving ground only under great pressure. They punished every incursion of the attacker. Nicholson was ordered, in a message from the CIGS, to fight to the last; there would be no evacuation "for the sake of Allied solidarity". Since it was clear that defence could not last long this meant that all hope was gone. By 25th May the defenders had three tanks, no anti-tank guns, no artillery. They had never had the explosive to blow the bridges over the canals. Next day the Germans brought up more artillery and, under cover of air attack, drove the defenders back into the northern part of the old town. There was no surrender. There was no evacuation. Broken into small parties, the gallant commander and troops of 30th Brigade were finally overwhelmed.

By nightfall on 26th May the British decision had been made. There was no possibility, they rightly reckoned, of counter-attacks, of breaking through the German penetration, or of holding a bridgehead in Northern France beyond a very limited period of time. The remnants of the French First Army, the BEF and the Belgian Army were hemmed in with their backs to the sea, boxed in between the victorious forces of Bock and Rundstedt. But the decision to evacuate was not immediately communicated to the Belgians on the left flank. There was confusion between Allies, a certain refuge in ambiguity which has since led to much mutual recrimination. The French were not directed to seek evacuation for several days: and the following day the King of the Belgians requested a cease-fire. His troops had borne the brunt of the German attack for the last three days, and they had little motive to sacrifice themselves to ensure the safe departure of the French and the British, of whose intended evacuation they now – on 27th – heard for the first time. Belgian capitulation, however, left an immediate and appalling vacuum on the flank of the British Army. When Gort heard the news, at 11 p.m., he commanded an army that was fighting off, back to back, two German Armies, armies attacking from south-west and north-east – and under twenty miles apart; and his left flank rested on air, with a gap of over twenty-five miles between the British left and the sea.

Once again the BEF faced the combined might of both Army Group A and Army Group B.

Rundstedt, encouraged to advance again, towards Dunkirk, had an imperfect instrument: all the German Panzer divisions were now in his Army Group A and the tanks of his Fourth Army were less appropriate to the low lying Flanders fields than the infantry of which Bock – short of tanks – disposed of plenty. But Army Group A now attacked strongly and surged forward between St. Omer and Robecq, towards Armentières and Lille; and attacked persistently all day at Cassel, penetrating between there and Hazebruck. Six Panzer divisions, the SS "Totenkopf" and four motorised or infantry divisions pressed and probed against the extended and exhausted remnants of two Territorial and one Regular British divisions. St. Venant and Robecq on the left of our line were attacked without respite; but 2nd Division managed, with considerable losses, to hold apart the jaws of the assault – the German Fourth and Sixth Armies, from south and east, each directed on Kemmel-Kemmel, that wooded hill dominating the plain, monument to years of savage fighting two decades earlier. Everywhere the Germans reported that the defenders were "fighting tenaciously, and to the last man remain at their posts".

On the eastern front Army Group B's main attack was directed south of Ypres. Here the British II Corps bore the brunt, with 5th Division suffering worst on the very ground another BEF had defended a quarter of a century before. Brooke strengthened the division with battalions from his right; deployed 50th Division on the left of 5th; and, during the night of 27th May, moved 3rd Division across the enemy's front from his right to his and the BEF's left. At the same time two divisions were drawn back to the River Lys from the old frontier defences, and 1st Division was moved to Dunkirk itself, where Adam, with III Corps Headquarters, was ordered to prepare a perimeter defence, in consultation with the local French command.

All day, on 28th May, the BEF faced Bock from new positions on the Lys, while to their rear a few miles away Rundstedt continued to press or penetrate the remnants of three divisions holding the southern front. The BEF's position was still that of a finger extended into a trap. But during the night of 28th the south-facing divisions were somehow extricated and withdrawn to the River Yser, covering Dunkirk itself, while the east-facing divisions withdrew from the Lys and from the Ypres Canal. By morning the BEF was reunited, deployed covering Dunkirk on the perimeter line, and on the River Yser: while two divisions – 3rd and 50th – forward between Poperinghe and Noordschote, were holding firm, against Bock, a door behind which the exhausted divisions from the Lys and from the southern front could withdraw northward towards Dunkirk.

Some divisions of the BEF now consisted of little but shattered remnants; others still had strength and cohesion. Some had lost many men, many as prisoners. Some had left behind isolated detachments, to fight delaying actions of great value but from which few escaped. Nowhere had the Germans succeeded in breaking through, dividing the BEF, or isolating and destroying a major part of it. Now it was a question of holding the perimeter, of withdrawing from it step by step in good order, of hoping against hope that the assortment of little and great ships, being hastily assembled to sail to Dunkirk, could carry off as much as possible of the army, to fight another day. The last phase was about to begin.

Evacuation of part of the British Army had begun several days before. Gort's orders were to get away as many men from the rear installations as possible, and before Operation DYNAMO began some 26,000 had been shipped. Immediately DYNAMO was ordered, but before the fighting formations of the BEF had withdrawn, a further 58,000 were embarked. Now it was the turn of the rest. But could the perimeter be held, so that thousands of men could be taken on some craft or other behind its shield; and could the shield itself be finally lowered without disaster?

West of Dunkirk the perimeter was held by French forces, strengthened on 29th May by the remnants of French III Corps from First Army (General de la Laurencie) at less than divisional strength but splendidly led and animated. East of Dunkirk the perimeter was entrusted to the BEF, with II Corps holding the extreme east flank and I Corps the line between the Franco-Belgian frontier and the port itself.

70

The German attack was handed over to General Kuchler's Eighteenth Army. The attackers were ordered to take Dunkirk and to halt evacuation; to help them the Luftwaffe, from 27th May onwards, mounted incessant bombing and dive-bombing attacks. The BEF and their French comrades to the west had to hold their positions, and then embark, against attacks by a total of about nine divisions, under continuous air attack against a crowded bridgehead, and, in the later stages as the perimeter shrank, under heavy artillery fire as German guns were brought within range of the beaches and the harbour itself. From the evening of 30th May the BEF in the beach-head was commanded by Lieutenant-General the Hon. Sir Harold Alexander, GOC 1st Division, who had been placed in command of I Corps. II and III Corps HQs had been evacuated, and Gort himself was expressly ordered to leave by Churchill, and did so on 31st May. By then a total of 126,000 men had been shipped to England.

Swimming and wading from the beaches, they were ferried by small craft to larger ships, or taken from the mole of Dunkirk Harbour itself as ships braved the wreckage and fires to come alongside; and whether waiting on the beaches, on the mole, or in the trenches deployed to beat off German attacks on the perimeter, they endured the ceaseless attentions of the Luftwaffe. German aircraft seemed to dominate the sky. "Where are our cavalry?", British infantrymen in the squares at Waterloo had shouted at Wellington as Ney's cavalry surged round them, apparently unmolested. "Why don't they come and pitch into these French fellows?" In the same spirit the men of the BEF cursed the Royal Air Force and asked where they were. The sentiment had been natural but largely unjust in 1815: it was wholly unjust now. The Royal Air Force flew sortie after sortie from their bases in Kent, and suffered severe losses over Dunkirk, but they inflicted heavy losses too. And, above all, their sortie rate had to be strictly limited, by order. Another battle was to come.

The next days saw violent German attacks against the perimeter. On the final day of the evacuation, 3rd June, the last of 224,717 British troops reached England. From 29th May, when the French, too, received orders to evacuate, the policy was to bring away equal numbers; and of the grand total between 29th May and 3rd June half were British, half French. Due to a confusion and against the intentions of Churchill, the rearguards were French, and finally surrendered on 4th June. Operation DYNAMO was over.

The evacuation of the British Army from Dunkirk marked the end of a calamitous campaign. The return of the BEF was greeted in Britain with emotions of relief and even jubilation. Churchill was quick to remind that this was no moment of victory. It was, nevertheless, a deliverance.

A long retreat, in the knowledge that there is to be no counter-attack, is the most demanding of operations. On the whole the spirits of the BEF remained high until near the end and in some cases beyond. As generally happens the morale and order of the front line units, those who had been continuously fighting, was often better than those engaged on duties in the rear. In the confusion of much of the campaign large numbers, too, had become separated from their own units and commanders. These arrived at Dunkirk somehow, muddled, exhausted, hungry and in many cases without arms. Such can easily become a rabble and, particularly in the early stages of DYNAMO, this undoubtedly happened. There was drunkenness, looting, insubordination, violence and confusion. An army without its order and discipline is a mob, and almost every retreat recorded in military history can show deplorable scenes, now re-enacted at Dunkirk. A few officers, too, betrayed their trust, seeking their own safety by deserting their men, fearing to assert their authority, failing in their duty. These examples, too, were not unique to Dunkirk but they occurred.

Against this dark side of the coin should be set the other – officers leaving ships on which they had been embarked on learning that all their men were not present and that some wounded were not accounted for: the cheerful humour with which tired men faced the Germans on the perimeter, short of sleep, food, water, ammunition and everything else save regimental pride: battalions marching on to the Dunkirk mole in perfect order, as on parade; and a thousand small acts of heroism and unselfishness which happen, unrecorded, in any army at even the worst times and are its true glory.

On 4th June, when the last of the BEF had been evacuated from Dunkirk there were still 140,000 of the British Army in France. First, there were large numbers of troops on the lines of communication, in depots, workshops, reinforcement units. These had been thinned out, and some men had already been evacuated. *Ad hoc* battalions had been formed and organised as a division of three brigades under Brigadier Beauman, commander of the northern district of the lines of communication – "Beauman Division". The second element, 51st Division, under Major-General Fortune, although Territorial, had within it a number of Regular as well as Territorial battalions of the Highland Brigade. The division had been deployed to the Saar Front on 30th April, to gain experience of combat under French command. When

SICHELSCHNITT began the Germans mounted little more than "holding" attacks on the Maginot Line. On 13th May the division was attacked under heavy artillery fire and successfully defended the forward line – the *ligne de contact*. But as the general situation to the north worsened 51st Division was withdrawn on 23rd May, and ordered to North-Western France. By then the Wehrmacht had reached the sea, and already cut the lines of communication of the BEF.

The third element of British troops still in France, 1st Armoured Division, the first and only armoured formation available to the BEF, had only now started landing in France. It was without artillery. It was without infantry, its motorised infantry having been diverted to Calais. It had, however, 257 tanks, of which 143 were cruisers. The orders given to this division and the way it was committed to battle gave it little chance.

1st Armoured Division landed at Cherbourg. On 21st May its commander, Major-General Evans, received his first order: to seize crossings over the Somme, and to concentrate south of that river and thereafter operate north of it. The division was still in process of disembarking, but by the time it had begun to assemble, on 22nd May, the Germans already held the Somme crossings, and Army Group A was racing towards Abbeville. Rundstedt, whose eyes throughout the campaign were on his southern flank, had been prompt in securing the Somme.

On 23rd May, the day 51st Division moved west from the Maginot Line, 1st Armoured received orders from GHQ, BEF, to "safeguard the right flank of the BEF during its southern advance to cut German communications between Cambrai and Peronne" – the projected attack by Adam's III Corps astride the Canal du Nord, cancelled by Gort two days later. As an instruction to 1st Armoured Division there was nothing practicable in this. The BEF was by now separated from Evans's Division not only by the Somme, over which the Germans held south-facing bridgeheads, but by most of Army Group A. Small parties of 1st Armoured were ordered to seize crossings between Amiens and Abbeville, but inevitably these attempts proved futile.

The chain of command to this unfortunate division was confused and inefficient. At different times Evans received orders direct from the War Office in London, from GHQ BEF, from General Georges commanding the army groups engaged in the battle wheresoever, from General Altmayer, commanding the left wing of the French Seventh Army – the lefthand French Army on the general line of the Somme – from General Frere, commanding Seventh Army, as well as from

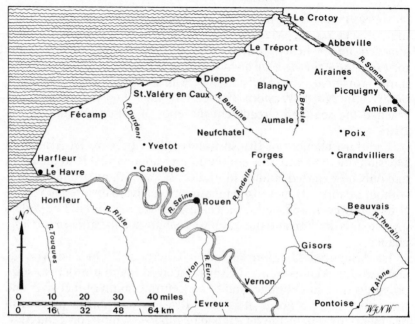

Between Somme and Seine

General Weygand, Supreme Commander, himself. None of these was based upon realistic information or understanding and none was capable of being obeyed with the smallest chance of operational success. Thus, Evans was directed by the War Office to place himself under the orders of French Seventh Army, which had been encouraged (by the War Office) to "employ both [i.e. 1st Armoured and 51st Division] offensively, and go all out". From the French Command Evans was directed to hold the Somme Line – already in German hands. Then, on 27th May, under French command, 1st Armoured Division supported two French divisions in an attack from the south towards Abbeville.

The attack was made against German infantry and anti-tank guns, well-sited and strong in numbers. Carried out by tanks alone, at least as far as 1st Armoured Division was concerned, it was made without artillery support. The result was tragic and predictable. Unsupported tanks – and these were not heavy tanks for infantry support, but light and cruiser tanks, built for speed – can exploit and manoeuvre. But if the defender is in sufficient strength, with infantry and anti-tank guns well positioned, they cannot punch a hole. Beating without avail against the German bridgeheads the division had, by the end of the day, lost sixty-five tanks.

74

Meanwhile 51st Division had been moved to the west of the French line south of the Somme and put under command of IX Corps of the French Tenth Army, facing Abbeville. They took over the same task as their comrades of 1st Armoured – to drive the Germans from some of their bridgeheads across the Somme. Two French divisions were placed under Fortune's command, and with these and 51st he was ordered to attack on 4th June. These attacks were put in with spirit, in the early hours of the morning, on the villages south of Abbeville, and many of the objectives were taken. It was to be the Highlanders' last chance of attack. Next day, 5th June, the Wehrmacht went over to the offensive. The last remnants of the BEF had been evacuated the day before. Now the three German Army groups launched what all were convinced would be the decisive phase of the campaign, the battle for Central France. It was for this that Rundstedt had tried to husband his armour, against opposition from some of his more thrusting subordinates, wishing to drive harder towards Dunkirk.

51st Division was on too wide a front to withstand the offensive now launched. On 7th June the division was holding on the River Bresle, south of the Somme, while, in dreadful re-enactment of what had taken place in the north, German divisions were already driving south and south-west past the division's right flank. IX Corps, 51st Division with it, were about to be cut off from withdrawal across the next major river line, the Seine. Meanwhile the remnants of 1st Armoured Division had been assembled to strike at the southern flank of the German movement, but were visited by Weygand himself and instead given orders to hold the line of a river, a tributary of the Seine, facing east – a role for which with their remaining tanks and no supporting arms they were entirely unsuited. In the path of the new German drive towards the Seine were thus 1st Armoured and some scattered battalions of Beauman Division. On 8th June these were all withdrawn south of the Seine.

The Germans were now nearing Rouen on the Seine. Although there might be respite for Allied troops withdrawn south of the river, there could be none for 51st Division. Only on 8th June did the commander of IX Corps order Fortune to withdraw from the Bresle to the Seine – a move of fifty miles, planned to take four days, and already pre-empted by German 5th and 7th Panzer Divisions, spearheads of the whole of the German Fourth Army, and about to enter Rouen itself. Whatever 51st Division's line of withdrawal, it could no longer be to the Seine.

Instead, withdrawal was ordered westwards to Le Havre. Fortune sent a force of two brigades (one from Beauman Division) to cover Le

Havre itself from the east, and ordered the rest of his force to withdraw through positions on the small rivers, Bethune and Durdent. The covering force for Le Havre – "Arkforce" – reached its position before the Germans. But 5th and 7th Panzer Divisions, having entered Rouen, turned north and raced towards the coast across the path of the retreating Allies. On the night of 10th June, Fortune learned that the crossings over the Durdent, planned as an intermediate position for his own withdrawal, were in German hands. 51st Division and French IX Corps were surrounded. The only possible harbour of embarkation was tiny St. Valéry-en-Caux. Thither the whole force, Highlanders, Frenchmen, transport, horses, were directed along densely packed country roads and through chaotic traffic reminiscent of Dunkirk. A perimeter was selected for defence. The navy, anticipating a withdrawal through Le Havre, was at hand.

On 11th June tanks of General Rommel's 7th Panzer Division broke through the western defences and seized high ground on the cliff tops overlooking St. Valéry and its harbour. Fortune hoped that if ships came that night he could still evacuate a large part of his force; but the ships were prevented by fog, and even had they arrived casualties would almost certainly have been appalling, with the Germans covering the harbour with direct fire. In launching a last, desperate attempt to clear the Germans from their commanding positions the Highlanders' fire had been masked by French troops carrying white flags. The French Corps Commander, General Ihler, under whose orders Fortune was serving, ordered surrender. For a while Fortune declined to comply – he refused to accept what had become inevitable until clear beyond hope that no ships would arrive while he could still defend. During the morning of 12th June, with white flags being everywhere displayed by the French and a signed order from the French Corps Commander in his hand, Fortune ordered the cease-fire. 51st Highland Division surrendered.

On the evening of 13th June Lieutenant-General Sir Alan Brooke arrived at Cherbourg. The British Government was still honourably determined to reinforce France with all that could be brought to do battle. With this object another Scottish division, 52nd (Major-General Drew), had been embarked, and its leading brigade had already arrived and been placed under French orders. It was also intended to send 1st Canadian Division. Others were planned. Brooke had been ordered to make contact with the French and to take command of what was to be a new BEF.

At Orléans, on 14th June, Brooke found Weygand, and together they visited Georges. Weygand made no secret of his views. The French

Army had ceased to offer organised resistance. There had been agreed (he said) a strategy of holding a "redoubt" in Brittany, with both flanks resting on the sea. Brooke asked what troops would hold it – at least fifteen divisions would be required. Where were they? Weygand and Georges gloomily agreed. The plan was absurd. Weygand went further. An armistice was imperative. He had – although he did not say so – already advised the French Government to seek one.

Brooke did not hesitate. If the British Army still in France was to be saved there was no time to be lost. That evening he spoke on the telephone to Dill, now CIGS, and to Churchill. With considerable difficulty he persuaded them. There must be no question of a "Brittany redoubt". There must be no delay. There must be no British troops left under French command. There must, above all, be no more reinforcement. Evacuation as soon as possible must be ordered. Three days later Marshal Pétain broadcast to the French nation in terms which made clear that resistance to the enemy would cease. By then nearly 160,000 troops south of the Somme, including most of the British except for the heroic 51st Division, had been evacuated. There was enormous loss of stores and equipment, some of it no doubt avoidable. Brooke, however, with the memory of Dunkirk still fresh, was determined that at all costs the men must be got away. It was a second deliverance.

Thus ended the campaign of 1940 in France and Flanders. It administered to the British Army an appalling but necessary shock. The army had been committed, after years of neglect, against one of the most efficient and competently led war machines that have ever taken the field. The first hammer blows fell on the French Army and were quickly decisive. In one week from the initial attack SICHELSCHNITT had achieved its object, although neither enemy nor ally could yet appreciate that awful fact. With no reserves available to form a front behind the shattered divisions of the French Ninth Army the High Command could not stem the tide. No limited counter-attack (even had mobile forces existed and been concentrated to undertake it) could be effective unless there were also counter-penetration, and unless the enemy could be steadied by some sort of defence to his front as well as attacked upon his flanks. The speed of events, the absence of reserves, and the momentum of the attack was such that nothing, after the first great breakthrough, could prevent Army Group A cutting the Allied forces in half and severing the lines of communication of the BEF. Thereafter the Allied High Command, in the persons of Gamelin and then of Weygand, either suffered paralysis of the will or gave orders based on unreal assumptions. Direction of the campaign broke down.

The interventions of the British Government and CIGS, before 26th May when evacuation was agreed, were unhelpful. Some appear ludicrous. The attempts to hold Boulogne and Calais by the sacrifice of brave men are hard to justify. Small garrisons of the kind deployed could not possibly have had significant effect on the operations of Army Group A at that juncture. London, however, was short of information – as were most men in authority. The language used to Gort about the "southern counter-attack", and the directions to withdraw the BEF southwards, were based on ignorance of the situation. And the shock of events had stunned the government at home as much as it had the army in the field.

Gort was in an impossible position. He was utterly loyal, by conviction and by character, to allies. He knew that it was deplorable for the BEF to become separated from the French withdrawing southwards: as late as 25th May he was considering the possibility of a move to the south. It is debatable whether any other course, after the first days, was feasible but the one he was forced to adopt. Gort never received orders based on the real situation with which he could comply. He was not responsible for the course of the campaign, and when it had reached a point where there was only one way of saving the BEF he took it. It has been suggested that he could have decided to withdraw the BEF to Dunkirk much earlier and in better order. The proposition is absurd. Gort was a subordinate commander – and the British Government could not possibly have sanctioned such a course until absolutely necessary. Gort's cancellation of the southern attack was just in time. Had he delayed he would have had no forces to extend to his left, and Belgian withdrawal, followed by surrender, would have left a gap impossible to fill. The BEF would have been cut off by Bock in the north and Rundstedt to the south. The best was made of a very bad job. Gort never again held a field command. He was tarred by the brush of early failure – one of a long line of unfortunate commanders who came to the head of a British Army at the beginning of a war for which successive governments had failed to prepare. Gort paid the penalty. He was not a clever man, neither quick nor persuasive in debate. He would not have been at home in the Whitehall of Churchill's premiership, and it is doubtful whether he had the breadth of vision for high command. He was stunned and dispirited by the course of events. He was, essentially, a regimental officer, and a fighting man. He was criticised, perhaps fairly, for being obsessed with details, but he was a thoughtful and educated soldier, and he could "read" the battle as well as any. That he did so in May 1940 saved the army.

The performance of the troops, as in Norway, was uneven. As in most campaigns there were instances of heroism and scenes of disgrace. The skill and enterprise of the German soldier made a deep and unwelcome impression. At their best our men felt that, in a fair field, they were a match for the enemy and would one day prove it, but others were not so sure. Nor was this entirely due to the "Panzer Arm", the "blitzkrieg", the sense of fighting modernity with anachronism. On the contrary the BEF was, on its main front, attacked by the infantry divisions, supported by horsed transport and horse-drawn artillery, of Army Group B. The divisions protecting the southern flank certainly faced the leading Panzer divisions of Army Group A, but these were halted for several crucial days. Main British contact with the German armour was by 5th and 50th Divisions and by the gallant defenders of Arras, Boulogne and Calais; and south of the Somme.

Main contact – but not all. Units of the "labour" divisions, 12th, 23rd and 46th, were posted to man strong points in the path of Army Group A. These troops, untrained except in the most rudimentary fashion, unsupported by artillery, employed hitherto purely on field works or fatigues, found themselves defending critical points on the German armoured thrust lines, often with little but their small arms. There was no reason to hope from this expedient any sort of success; but on several occasions the enemy was checked for hours and German war diaries refer to the tenacious defence put up by these outnumbered and completely outgunned detachments. Here was some unsung glory, greater than victory.

When given a chance to attack, as at Arras, German accounts pay tribute to the energy displayed by the BEF. On successive defensive positions local infantry counter-attacks often successfully restored the line. In general, however, the British defended and withdrew, and could do no other. In defence against the German infantry the British divisions held their own on most occasions, but to withdraw is a discouraging experience and the general uncertainty of where it would all end made this withdrawal not only dispiriting but alarming. The roads packed with refugees and the chaotic traffic conditions deepened the sense of despair. Dunkirk was humbling for all. The British Army had much to learn, but some of the lessons had been demonstrated in the most vivid of all schools.

When all has been said about the unpreparedness of the British Army for Continental war in 1939 and 1940 – unpreparedness which was a direct consequence of earlier rejection of such a task – the question still remains – "How much did it matter?" Given the collapse of the French Army, was there anything the British could have done to stem the tide of battle? Was not all done that could be done?

It is, of course, impossible to cast the balance sheet with certainty. Britain was now to stand in mortal need of an army for her own defence – a large, modern, mechanised army. Had such been deployed to France in 1939 what difference might it have made?

It is unlikely that the campaign would have gone as it did. It is improbable that the Germans would have accepted the risks they did. It is possible that French sentiment, always volatile, would have responded, would have taken a different course, but with what ultimate outcome cannot be known. We should certainly have been readier to face the perils of the late summer of 1940. And certainly, although we do not know their names, some who died might have lived. The collapse of Britain's ally, however decisive for the outcome on the Continent, provides little reason to argue that no stronger British effort was worth the making – or that the decline in the British Army's quality, strength, and sense of direction since 1920 was not a tragedy indeed.

Part II

Reforging the Sword

4

The Tools of the Trade

It has been said that for Britain the Second World War began in earnest at Dunkirk. At that point the British Army, in process of major expansion from a minuscule base, had been committed to battle in generally poor condition. The nature of the expansion itself, the organisation and purpose, had now urgently to be reconsidered, and the weapons of war, with even greater urgency, to be scratched together. The field army had left virtually all its equipment in France and Flanders. Over 2,000 guns had been lost. The returning soldiers had in most cases their personal weapons, but everything else, from light machine guns to heavy artillery, had to be reprovided. And the munitions factories of the country were still in the stage of build-up to the full needs of intensive war.

At last, however, the urgency was clear. Wellington, long ago, had emphasised to Englishmen a neglected truth. The Duke had written:

> Admitting the truth of the expense, I say that the country has not a choice between Army and no Army, between peace and war. They must have a large and efficient Army, one capable of meeting the enemy abroad, or they must expect to meet him at home: and then farewell to all considerations of measures of greater or lesser expense, and to the ease, the luxury and happiness of England.

Having comfortably and for years been persuaded they had a choice the British now realised that their legendary immunity was at mortal risk. Everybody expected Britain to be invaded. To defeat that invasion was the first task of the Army. Beyond the Channel, Operation SEELÖWE – the invasion – was now being planned. Thirteen divisions of the Wehrmacht, supported by two airborne divisions, were to be landed in the first echelon, followed by nine Panzer and motorised divisions. Forty-one German divisions in all were to be committed, on a frontage of assault between Folkestone and Brighton. The challenge was formidable. As the Royal Air Force fought their glorious battle above Britain and the Channel, so the British Army was sorted out, reconstituted by units, brigades, divisions; made ready to receive equipment as it became available, and now set the twin tasks of defending Britain in a battle which all assumed would shortly begin, and training for a long war of which some, at least, had had a startling and bitter taste. But Britain now stood alone, and the experience was invigorating as well as awe-inspiring.

As the returning soldiers from Dunkirk were sorted once again into employable military packages, and joined by new recruits from the training establishments, Britain resembled an armed camp, and would thus remain for many years. Men were called to the Colours in huge numbers. 275,000 men joined the army in June, July and August 1940. The training organisation was inadequate to deal with the influx, and deployment was governed more by what equipment was available than by any more scientific calculation of the army's long term needs. Since there were more infantry weapons than anything else, the infantry expanded fastest, and 120 new infantry battalions were formed in three months. Soldiers were billeted in houses, schools, inns, warehouses, outhouses and bus depots. Every existing barracks and camp was crammed to capacity, and extended by temporary constructions. As vehicles became available side roads, playgrounds, scrap yards and paddocks all over the country became parks. The roads of Britain became ever fuller with military convoys, the trains were packed by men in khaki, the countryside was covered by requisitioned firing areas, improvised ranges, and echoed to the sound of military manoeuvres. Much of the coast was designated an operational area, with civilians denied access, and obstacles laid against landing craft. Road blocks and concrete pill boxes were erected on all likely – and some highly unlikely – enemy routes inland.

The defence of the country was in the hands of Sir Alan Brooke, recently Commander of II Corps in France, now Commander-in-Chief, Home Forces. Brooke was a man of great clarity of perception. Quick-witted, he got through many men's work. He did not expect to need to say things twice. He started a ruthless weeding process among the army's commanders, and he established over his entire command a dominance which he took with him to his next appointment – in December 1941 – that of CIGS. Above all Brooke was strong. He was utterly professional, and if he assessed a military plan as unsatisfactory no power or pressure would get him to agree it. He now had to determine how best to face the Germans if they landed in Britain. Brooke was sceptical of reliance on obstacles. The enemy would only be beaten, he knew and ordered, by the concentration against him of mobile reserves, brought to the critical point of the battle and determined to hurl the invader into the sea. These mobile reserves, established as a first priority for the army, would initially move in requisitioned buses. They would be pitifully short of modern weapons. They would be almost entirely unarmoured. But they would at least have the power of concentration; and they must attack. Brooke had no intention of leaving the initiative with the invader. He needed, and immediately began to form or re-form, a sufficient number of properly constituted and mobile divisions. He assessed his minimum requirement for a field army to grapple with an invader at twenty-two divisions, eight of them armoured; and eight independent brigade groups, together with ten army tank brigades for support of the infantry. To hold the beaches of Britain there must, additionally, be twelve static "County" divisions.[1] Here was a pattern for the reconstitution of an army, first – to defend Britain but one day to take the offensive again.

The basic element in army organisation, the tool of the trade, is the division, a formation of all arms necessary for combat. It must have its own artillery, engineers, communications and logistic support. An infantry division consisted, in the Second World War, of a number of infantry brigades, generally three – each of three battalions. An armoured division consisted of one or more armoured brigades, with three or four tank regiments or battalions; an armoured brigade also included a motor battalion, a "light" battalion on a special establishment designed for intimate cooperation with the tanks, carrying the infantrymen in trucks or half-tracked vehicles with cross-country capability. The organisation of divisions, both infantry and armoured, was frequently changed in the light of experience and according to the demands of a particular theatre of war. Some were disbanded during the war while others were raised. Some changed their basic function. Some were organised purely on paper, for deception of the enemy. Not all divisions existed simultaneously – totals, therefore, can mislead. Thirteen divisions, of very varying quality, had composed the BEF. Now the "Order of Battle" had to be reconstituted and expanded.

During the Second World War the British Army formed eleven armoured divisions (of which two had their origins before war began) and fourteen independent armoured or army tank brigades – brigades, each of three tank regiments or battalions, for infantry support. There were thirty-five infantry divisions, including the old Regular and

---

[1] Nine were, in fact, formed.

original Territorial divisions; and two airborne divisions,[1] as well as the nine "County" divisions formed for beach defence. In addition there were, of course, the divisions of the Indian Army, and the five colonial divisions of the British Empire, all of them with a requirement for British officers and British arms. Completely separate constitutionally, but often grouped under the same operational command overseas, were the armies of the Commonwealth – Australia, Canada, New Zealand, Rhodesia, South Africa – independent nations which had freely entered the war, and whose troops formed the major part of the field army in several campaigns. In theatres of war the story of the British Army was inextricably interwoven with the story of Commonwealth and Empire.

The British total of divisions – the equivalent of about fifty field divisions, of which a number had been disbanded before others formed – did not rise near to the total of the First World War, when there were over sixty divisions on the Western Front alone. As the war went on, the Prime Minister was apt to grumble at the statistic, and would point to the considerable ration strengths of a particular Command and the comparatively small number of fighting formations therein. But the reasons for this apparent imbalance were many. The large number of theatres of war each demanded a huge overseas base, a line of communication, a training organisation, and thus manpower. Anti-Aircraft Command, in active contact with the enemy from the first, could be counted as the equivalent in men of some twelve divisions, manning about 2,000 guns. The complexity of weapon systems and equipment necessarily involved a much larger proportion of men than hitherto in the repair and re-supply services: as weapons became more sophisticated and more deadly they needed fewer men to fire them but more in support. Unlike the earlier war, the claims of the Royal Air Force had to be considered. Its strength rose to a million in 1943, compared with army numbers at the same time of 2,700,000 – yet people somehow persuaded themselves that only the army was a major consumer of manpower.

The army had a new man at its head in Sir John Dill, a soldier of high intelligence and utter integrity. No General in the army was more profoundly respected. He had, however, a task which he found intolerably taxing – to deal with the pressures placed upon the Chiefs of Staff by the Prime Minister. For Churchill was now goading his military advisers with the same vigour with which he inspired the nation. Only Churchill could arouse the people, make them fully awake, fully alive.

[1] All listed in Appendix I.

His oratory was like a warming flame. His pricking of his Chiefs of Staff was inevitable – often necessary – but a sore trial to busy and often exhausted men. Dill, who was highly strung, found life particularly hard.

But Brooke, not Dill, was the chief begetter of the new army. His own dynamism was felt throughout. He was quick, abrupt, impatient with failure. Commanders were replaced from top to bottom. Inadequate staffs were galvanised. Brooke also had profound reservations about the stamina of the troops, compared to what he had witnessed only twenty-five years before. He felt and said that both army and nation had grown soft. The tests of battle had not been passed with flying colours. The only way to improve was by hard, rigorous training. The army must not only expand but train, and train again. Training was impeded for a long time by lack of equipment, but minds and bodies could be trained and toughened. There could be more energy, more systematically applied. Not only the field army expanded hugely but the training organisation, too: arms schools, technical schools, tactical schools and schools for every particular facet of military art. There were schools for chemical warfare, for aircraft recognition, for camouflage, for mountain warfare, and to train instructors for divisional battle schools. There were schools to teach men how to teach. Training within units and formations was also rigorously inspected. In new divisional battle schools companies and platoons practised battle drills, used their weapons in combination and were themselves fired upon. Everywhere there ripened a determination to harden and excel. The scale of training began at last to enlarge: great exercises, involving most of the divisions in the United Kingdom, mock battles of several army corps, indispensable rehearsals for major operations. The British Army had long been unfamiliar with such practices, which alone could train higher commanders and Staffs in at least some of the realities of the battlefield. There was but one aim: the creation of a great national army, skilled, and once again worthy of the nation.

The soldier did not move from civil life to a fighting division. He joined a branch of the Service – a corps or regiment: or, as the war went on, he was first enlisted into a "General Service Corps" and there underwent tests to determine where he should best serve. The need for selection was pressing. The sudden introduction of conscription in 1939 and the simultaneous doubling of the Territorial Army with willing volunteers had led to a good deal of wastage of human talent. Round pegs were not all in round holes. The whole army was short, for instance, of what are called military "tradesmen" – specialists, particularly in the electrical and mechanical crafts; and the problem was compounded after Dunkirk, because expansion of munitions production demanded the release of trained operatives from the army – and they tended, of course, also to be military tradesmen. It was essential to make wise use of the skills and aptitudes men possessed, although a man's own wishes, if he had any, to join a particular corps or regiment were at least taken into account. Thus from the General Service Corps, or on enlistment before it was formed, a man joined one of the Arms of the Service – that is, armour, artillery, engineers, signals or infantry; or he joined one of the logistic corps – service corps, medical corps, ordnance corps, electrical and mechanical engineers or the military police.

Thereafter a man underwent individual training at a depot and then, either quickly or after some intermediate process, he joined a fighting unit, probably itself part of one of the divisions of the army. Every Arm had an Arms School, some had several.

If an armoured soldier – a tank or armoured-car crewman – a man joined the Royal Armoured Corps: this was, so to speak, his nation. But within the nation were many tribes, called regiments – the regiment, in this case, being the fighting unit. Each regiment had its own name, place in the *Army List*, capbadge, customs, likes and loathings. A man absorbed these, and the regiment was his family, a source of support in a world often alien and alarming.

A member of the Royal Armoured Corps would probably find himself in an armoured division or army tank brigade as a crewman in an armoured car or a tank. In 1940 tanks were in remarkably short supply. Those sent out with or to join the BEF had been lost. There had been produced in Britain in 1939 only 969 tanks of all types. Some were in Egypt, and the balance by now in Britain was small. Production was increasing. The output figure grew to over 8,600 (including self-propelled guns) in 1942, but even this was little enough to deal with expansion, the needs of Allies and battle wastage. From 1942 the British Army was equipped with considerable numbers of American tanks in the armoured divisions, while retaining British heavy tanks in the army tank brigades. Tank design was a particularly weak point in British armaments policy. Individual components were sometimes excellent, but the result was too often a tank inferior in some vital respect to the enemy's. In France our tanks had hardly been tested. The general impression of their users was of mechanical unreliability and insufficient armoured protection, while the anti-tank gun (mounted only in some) was the barely adequate two pounder.

In the desert, the great testing ground for tank and anti-tank warfare, our tanks' main armament, the two pounder, initially gave excellent service. Later, however, our armour suffered from German development of the long-range high velocity anti-tank gun, and skilled German tank manoeuvring behind screens of mobile guns. Against these equipments and tactics we produced tanks with too thin a skin or too feeble a weapon, or both. In the desert, the terrain and visibility meant anti-tank engagements could take place at extreme range. It was a theatre for the big gun; and our tanks were often under-gunned and too lightly armoured for the purpose to which they were put.

If a man became a Gunner he joined the Royal Regiment of Artillery. This was a different usage of the word "regiment", for although the Royal Regiment was the tribe as well as the "nation" – it comprehended all Gunners everywhere with one capbadge, and under one name in the *Army List*[1] – it was not a unit. Instead, the unit a man joined was a particular numbered regiment of the Royal Artillery. And this particular regiment might perform any one of a large number of different functions. It might be a light anti-aircraft regiment, an anti-tank regiment, or a field artillery regiment: in this case it was probably part of the artillery of a division. It might be a heavy anti-aircraft regiment or a medium or heavy artillery regiment. In these cases it would be in a special artillery formation, probably deployed under Army Command, or Anti-Aircraft Command itself. The different functions of artillery were, of course, so distinct and so unlike each other that there had to be complete retraining if a man were transferred from one sort of gunnery to another, and each became a sect within the tribe.

Members of artillery units were adept not only at serving their guns but at knowing where they and others were – to arrange that guns could fire not only in unison, but according to harmonised assumptions about topography, was a vital element of their art. Artillerymen, too, were generally skilled communicators, and their radio linkage provided invaluable duplication of the normal command net. This was logical, for modern communications had greatly increased the power of artillery by enabling orders and information to dispersed guns to be transmitted instantly, so that a commander could quickly concentrate the fire power of a whole divisional artillery and more, without moving a single gun. The range of modern guns and the instancy of modern communications gave to a commander his greatest single method of affecting a battle. But communications had to work. They were part of

[1] This, although true in peacetime, must be qualified. Some units – for instance some Yeomanry Regiments, previously horsed cavalry – were converted to artillery but did not strictly belong to the Royal Regiment.

the artillery system. And gunners were, on the whole, well-equipped. In anti-tank gunnery the enemy outpointed the British at times – not least because of his versatility in using anti-aircraft guns in an anti-tank role. But, for the rest, British guns were good; and although, in 1940, they were painfully few in number, their quality never betrayed the troops they supported.

If a man became an Engineer he joined the Royal Engineers – he became a "Sapper". No corps was more constantly in demand, so much master of so many tasks. The Sapper might join one of a hundred different types of unit engaged on specialised work in some remote theatre or line of communication. He might be employed running a port or a railway, building an airfield in the middle of a jungle, running a postal service, tunnelling beneath the Rock of Gibraltar, rafting over a river or building a camp. If he joined a field squadron or company he would need – beside being expected to turn his hand to virtually any task of construction or demolition – to become master of all the arts of combat engineering. He would become expert in the laying and lifting of mines, in the creation or removal of obstacles, in blowing a bridge or building one. He would be part of a team expected to impose the maximum hindrance on the movements of the enemy, while ensuring the utmost mobility of our own troops.

As the war continued and the tide turned, a major engineer require-ment was to enable our assault forces, and especially our armoured assault forces, to beat a path through obstacles. Special armoured engineer equipment was developed to enable tanks to cross ditches and streams, to pass through minefields by detonating the mines. Some of those equipments were handed over to the Royal Armoured Corps. Some remained in the hands of armoured engineers. Whether armoured or not, Sappers were needed in the van of any attack on a prepared position, just as they were needed to prepare any position for defence.

In June 1940 the need, as in all corps, was to train a hugely expanded engineer force. But overshadowing this were the actual and urgent demands of the operational situation. Everywhere engineers were in demand for building works to house a large army, now suddenly and unexpectedly occupying the United Kingdom as an operational theatre; and for work on anti-invasion defences and anti-aircraft posts. And some noble Royal Engineers were responsible for bomb disposal.

If a man became a communicator he would join the Royal Signals. The new situation which faced the army in June 1940 meant that a completely new framework of communications had to be hurriedly improvised. GHQ Home Forces had to be established as an operational headquarters, and the various area commands of the United Kingdom had suddenly to become operational headquarters capable of exercising command in the field as, in effect, several army headquarters with army corps and divisions subordinate to them. This involved a considerable re-organisation of such signals capacity as existed. At the same time signallers were needed for a greatly expanding number of field formations – divisions – as well as for the large demands, especially in highly skilled men, of Anti-Aircraft Command.

A signaller would become proficient in radio, radio mechanical repair, telephone and switchboard, line-laying and maintenance, telegraph operating, as well as physical communication by a despatch-rider service. Communications had to be established not only up and down a chain of command and laterally, but also to obtain air support in mobile operations; to enable ship-to-shore traffic in amphibious operations; to use to the practical maximum existing civil resources, and to safeguard security by ingenious use and control of cypher. The Second World War was the first in which radio played a dominant part in tactical control. Before it ended over half a million wireless sets of one sort or another had been issued to the British Army. The Royal Corps of Signals (including reservists and Territorials) was 34,000 strong in 1939. Six years later the total was over 154,000. Furthermore within a unit, be it armoured, artillery, infantry or whatever, communications were manned not by Royal Signals but by men of the unit itself – regimental signallers. Royal Signals, too, played the key part in communications interception – and in deception.

A man might join the infantry. In this case he became a member of one of the regiments of Foot Guards or infantry of the army. The regiment then was his tribe. He wore its capbadge and spoke its language.

A regiment of infantry, however, was not an operational unit – that was the battalion. Each regiment had many battalions. There were the old Regular battalions – two, in the case of Line infantry: the Territorial battalions, which doubled in number in 1939; and the new battalions raised, and in some cases disbanded, during the war. Sometimes battalions of the same regiment served together in the same infantry brigade; indeed some brigades were formed entirely from battalions of the same regiment. In other cases battalions of the same regiment never served in the same operational theatre throughout the war.

The regiment was traditionally the focus for *esprit de corps* and loyalty; and among Regulars, men with longer service, this was so. For the majority, however, the focus of a man's loyalty was his own battalion, and he could feel isolated and bereft if moved from it, even to another battalion of the same regiment. The virtue of the British regimental system was, ostensibly, that it fostered the strength of the tribe – the regiment – through individuality: that a different capbadge, a different history and a jealously guarded distinction all contributed something priceless to the spirit of the unit and the morale of its men. This could be so – but it imposed on the authorities an obligation to support the system by a manning and reinforcement policy which conformed to it. This was not always done. Intentions were good, but it was, of course, often difficult and uneconomic to fill the depleted ranks of a battalion with soldiers of only that regiment; and widespread failure to do so as the war went on meant that many soldiers, particularly in infantry battalions, found themselves fighting in a regiment of whose identity they were barely aware, to whose "family" they were strangers.[1] It took longer for them to become accepted and to find the strength which comes from the friendly and the familiar amid the loneliness of the battlefield; and some never did.

The infantryman had his rifle – the Lee-Enfield .303 – and his light machine gun, the Bren: the army started and finished the war with these robust equipments. He was supported by infantry mortars of various kinds, production of which grew from 2,800 in 1939 to 29,000 in 1942; and from 1942 he was equipped with the Projector Infantry Anti-Tank, the PIAT, a primitive short-range weapon of dubious efficiency. He had the anti-tank rifle, in which there was little faith (but which was still produced in large numbers until 1942); and he had, in the anti-tank platoon of his battalion (if a motor battalion) or brigade, an anti-tank gun, first the two pounder and later the six pounder, excellent equipments for their time but inadequate as German armour thickened.

The infantryman's function was to fight on his feet. Sometimes he marched to war, sometimes he was transported, but in battle he relied on his legs. Being unprotected against shell and mortar fire he depended greatly on his shovel – to get below ground was the first requirement of an infantryman on a position. He relied, or needed to rely, greatly on darkness. The infantryman was not a member of a vehicle crew, bound by the compulsory order of a vehicle's walls. He was a member of a team, but at the same time, and alarmingly, an individual, vulnerable as no other to the isolating pressures of the battle. He was the most difficult of soldiers to train to a really high

---

[1] Indeed in Italy, in March 1944, it was formally agreed to regard infantry reinforcements as available for any battalion needing them.

standard, so delicate was the combination required of discipline and initiative. But when skilled he was indispensable to victory in any conflict, and there was never enough of him.

A man might join one of the logistic services. These provided the essential support behind every formation – army, corps, division, brigade – without which the men serving guns, fighting tanks, laying minefields, maintaining communications, or patrolling against the enemy could not do their duty – because they would have no food, or ammunition, or fuel for their vehicles; supplies carried to them by the Royal Army Service Corps. Or they would be wounded and uncared for unless evacuated to the casualty clearing stations or field hospitals of the Royal Army Medical Corps; or they would not receive new equipment because it had not been distributed through the provisioning organisation – the Royal Army Ordnance Corps; or their vehicles would break down, their equipment be damaged and never mended, unless in the workshops or by the detachments of the Royal Electrical and Mechanical Engineers, a new and essential corps formed during the war to handle most of the repair functions for the army.

And supervising the conduct of troops when outside the unit, the traffic flow of formations on the march, the general discipline and good order of the machine was a large Corps of Military Police. The army was, furthermore, supported by a large and efficient corps of women in the Auxiliary Territorial Service, whose work freed men from many logistic functions and who also played a key part in serving the batteries of Anti-Aircraft Command.

These were the Arms and Services which composed the army. These were the principal corps and regiments to which Britain's manpower was directed. These corps and regiments managed the enlistment and manning policy and the primary training of an army over one and a half million men strong in June 1940: a total which would rise to nearly three million and over 300,000 women before the war was over. For five long years the army was not only an instrument of war but a great factory of warriors.

The traditional Arms of the Service no longer comprehended all the military skills. Of all the special formations raised for particular operations in the Second World War, two were to gain an outstanding place in the annals of the British Army. Commando forces were raised for raiding enemy coastlines – forerunners of a mighty structure for combined operations and landings from the sea. Airborne forces were

93

formed for the first time, to bring whole units into battle by parachute, glider and aircraft, using the enemy's open flank, the sky.

British airborne forces were born in June 1940. The Russians had demonstrated mass parachute drops some years before the war. The Germans had paid thoughtful attention, and had formed one parachute and one airlanded division in 1938. Airborne troops were used in a small way by the Germans in Norway, and in a very decisive way in the invasion of the Low Countries, when 7,000 men of "Fliegerdivision 7" landed in Holland, and 600 in Belgium, including in their tasks the capture of the vital frontier fort, Eben Emael.

In Britain airborne forces had a slow start. It was clear, with Britain emphatically on the strategic defensive, that their time was not yet. To transport them would mean the assignment or construction of aircraft by a Royal Air Force difficult to convince of their priority, and an aircraft industry pressed to meet the urgent needs of the Battle of Britain. Nevertheless 500 volunteers were trained as parachutists, and embodied in what was first christened 11th Special Air Service (SAS) Battalion.

Little more had been done, and that little under difficulties, by September 1941. Thereafter the pace quickened. 11th SAS Battalion was renamed 1st Parachute Battalion. A parachute brigade (Brigadier Gale) of three battalions began to form with volunteers invited from all infantry battalions. In November it was agreed to add a specially assigned airlanding brigade, carried in gliders, and greatly to increase the number of glider pilots under training. A new regiment – the Glider Pilot Regiment – was established in the *Army List*, soon followed by a distinctive Parachute Regiment. In November 1941, too, a divisional headquarters was agreed: the 1st Airborne Division (Major-General Browning).

This division had the twin tasks of experimentation in a new method of warfare, and training as an operational division, for fighting once landed. All Arms of the Service now needed to develop new and light equipment suitable for the airborne role. The whole division underwent a programme of hard training that became legendary. Sceptics, some of whom were in key positions, had to be convinced. Air-Marshal Harris, Commander-in-Chief Bomber Command, doubted the effectiveness of airborne troops. He did not believe that resources diverted from the strategic air offensive against Germany would justify the investment. The Chief of the Air Staff, Air-Marshal Portal, was only slightly less sceptical and certainly not wholeheartedly converted. It was fortunate for airborne forces that the Commander-in-Chief (and from December 1941, CIGS), Brooke, was an enthusiastic supporter.

Somehow a way ahead was found; aircraft were made available both to carry parachutists and to tow gliders, and a glider production programme was agreed. On 1st May 1943, 1st Airborne Division completed mobilisation, as ready for war. Now a second division – 6th Airborne Division (Major-General Gale) was ordered to be formed. Each airborne division consisted of two parachute and one airlanding brigades, with specially equipped supporting units and divisional troops.

The two airborne divisions were not the only airborne forces. In the Far East special airlanding brigades were later formed under General Wingate, for deep penetration. Their exploits belong to another chapter of this story. In North Africa and in the United Kingdom Special Air Service Regiments were created – one with its origins in the Long Range Desert Group – which were combined with certain Allied parachute units into a SAS Brigade (Brigadier McLeod). These had the task of carrying out special missions behind the enemy lines. Because one of the methods of delivering their patrols was by air, the SAS Brigade came under the general direction of British airborne forces. Its task, however, was strategic and irregular, whilst the task of the airborne divisions was tactical and conventional.

After the ejection of the army from France it became clear that return to the Continent would one day be necessary. Although some believed that Germany might be brought to defeat by strategic bombing alone they failed to carry their point, then or later. There would, ultimately, have to be an invasion. It would be an arduous business. Meanwhile experience had to be gained, the enemy needled and the offensive spirit kept alive by a policy of raiding.

In June 1940, a Director of Combined Operations was created, with Admiral of the Fleet Sir Roger Keyes appointed the following month. He commanded six independent companies (which we last met in Norway), and ten "Commandos". The Commandos were units of light battalion size, composed of volunteers from infantry battalions or, later, formed from the Royal Marines, and equipped for raiding an enemy-held coastline.

Battalions, therefore, found volunteers for airborne forces and for Commando forces. It was natural that often the most adventurous volunteered, and that the best were accepted. This policy, of forming Commandos from volunteers, was criticised by some. Parachute troops were recognised as being in a particular category, but the sentiment was widely held that all troops could and should be trained for raiding. Brooke himself never approved of the Commando policy. He thought it a dangerous drain on infantry battalion quality, and that it deprived normal divisions of the challenge of maintaining and training their own raiding forces.

Nevertheless the Commandos flourished. The raiding policy, of which they were the spearhead, led to an increasing expertise in amphibious operations – landings from the sea. Some raids, like the brilliant and successful operation against a German radar station at Bruneval in 1942, combined airborne and seaborne operations: the raiding party parachuted in, achieved their object and were taken off by sea. Combined Operations Headquarters supervised the complex training and evolution of the special equipment that the art demanded. Sailors and soldiers combined with alacrity. The combination bore triumphant fruit in Sicily, in Italy and ultimately in Normandy – the greatest operation against a defended coast in the history of war.

In the summer months of 1940 the invasion was expected daily. On one September day the church bells rang and people believed that it had come, but SEELÖWE never happened. The precondition Hitler himself had laid down – that British air power must be decisively beaten – was never met. Men began to believe, in Britain, that the ultimate challenge was not going to be thrown down after all – that England would not be trod by the foot of the invader. As this sense turned into conviction – and into certainty after the German invasion of Russia, unless Russia were to collapse – so the army became not a counter-invasion force but an invasion force itself; a source of supply for active theatres of war overseas, and an ultimate army of liberation. A change of emphasis took place. Once again there had been a deliverance.

5

Officers and Men

A great national army is not a small Regular Army writ large, but an entirely different creature. Where the Regular Army is a small, professional minority that cherishes its exclusiveness a mass army is composed of all. Soldiers of the Regular Army tend to be bewildered at an influx of men, resembling them in uniform and acquiring at least some of their tone, but innately different, being civilians at heart. Where a nation does not, in peacetime, have National Service as a normal and acknowledged practice, the process is harder for both sides, the adjustments unrehearsed.

In Britain, although the Military Training Act introducing conscription became law on 26th May 1939, only one intake had actually joined by September. The National Service Act, passed by Parliament on the first day of war, decreed universal compulsory service. Because of shortage of equipment this had led to a slow moving enrolment by age classes. Now there had to be a mighty acceleration. In June 1940 the country needed to feel and to see that every able-bodied man was engaged in its defence.

Universal service meant that all sorts were now conscripted.[1] The small Regular Army had freely discharged volunteers if their conduct or attitudes were unsatisfactory. The Territorial Army had consisted of men willing to give their spare time – a moral élite. Now, in common with the general run of men quietly if reluctantly accepting the demands of the hour, there was conscripted every resentful or maladjusted misfit, provided he passed the simple medical test imposed. These took time to sort out. They were a tiny minority, but they heightened the disturbance felt by the majority at the sudden plunge into uniform.

To most the army was a strange and unnerving experience. They had not undergone National Service in time of peace, with its healthy and routine introduction to military life. They did not know what to expect.

[1] For various reasons the Royal Navy and Royal Air Force could be more discriminating, and the army's problems were compounded thereby.

They were mostly townsmen: open country and darkness, the natural environments of the soldier, were entirely alien. They had, in many cases, never been far from home. Their knowledge of Service discipline derived largely from popular caricature, a combination of the fearful with the resentful. Transition to a soldier's life did not represent a voluntary act, but the operation of "call-up", the bleak official notification, sudden immersion in an unnerving atmosphere, subjection to a huge, impersonal machine. Furthermore, and for the first time in life, it was a machine which a man could not quit if he did not like its ways. And nobody knew how long this would go on. The future seemed indefinite. The British have sometimes been described as "unmilitary", as if this were some congenital state or virtue. The epithet is hardly supported by history. For much of its past the British Army has shown as "military" a front, and its members as professional a bearing and expertise as any of their opponents or allies. But it is certainly true that the men who composed the army of the Second World War came of a profoundly unmilitary – indeed anti-military – generation.

This chiefly derived from a rather muddled spirit of aversion from the experiences of the First World War, the same spirit which had so signally contributed to our unreadiness. A vague pacifism had been widely preached. The prevailing ethos, during most of the time in which these men had grown up, was that life in the army was nasty, brutish and probably short: that soldiers were treated as dirt, their efforts disregarded, their feelings ignored and their lives squandered by distant and indifferent commanders. Much of this was myth, but myths matter. From the day that conscription was introduced in 1939 the popular Press tended to colour its comment and address its readers with something of the same prejudice. Public vigilance was appropriate, but it sometimes merged with irresponsible bloody-mindedness. Convinced by now of the need for service, men were still warned, explicitly or implicitly, that their time and trouble might be abused. It was not the most helpful spirit in which to bring men to a new and demanding life, and it differed sharply from the simple and accepting enthusiasm with which their fathers had flocked to the Colours. That the earlier spirit had been exploited and betrayed can be argued. That it provided a better base on which to build a disciplined and resilient army can hardly be doubted.

These men, too, were children of the Depression. They had been young during dark years of high unemployment. In or just behind the conscious minds of many were attitudes towards authority of suspicion and resentment. Illusions about the Soviet Union were plentiful and favourable. It was portrayed as an egalitarian and well-managed paradise. But there were few illusions about the powers-that-be at home. It was a generation prepared to believe that unless a man were careful of his rights they would be trampled upon. An older generation had, it may be thought, at least as much reason for similar prejudice, but it had, perhaps, been offset by a certain lingering belief in the paternal aspects of authority. There was little of that now. At best, these sentiments intensified a passion for "fairness" – in any case a profound national emotion. At worst, they led to a querulous readiness to evade the necessary demands of discipline and duty.

This was one side of the picture – certainly not universal, but by no means caricature. On the other was a generation full of comradeship, loyalty to each other, and a wry, irrepressible humour which is the peculiar characteristic of the British soldier. These men were sceptical about themselves. They had pride but little vanity. They cocked a wary eye at their commanders, but they knew that to command such as them was no simple task. They were suspicious of slogans, detested bluster, resented injustice, but where their trust was won they performed great things. Their loyalty had to be earned. Once earned it was generously and affectionately given.

Such a generation and such an army had to be led rather than driven. To become truly disciplined, as an army must, discipline had to be combined with a certain charisma in those who demanded it, or in enough of them. Mechanical processes could achieve something – and something necessary – but only if combined with those touches of human communication, inspiration and example men call leadership.

This leadership was far from easy to provide at first, for its most effective expression is success, and of success there was all too little. By 1940, the army, tarred with the brush of failure, was low in the estimation of Press and public, unlike the navy and the air force, who basked in their triumphs. Soldiers were both suspicious of failure and felt degraded by it. Some might know in their hearts that they shared some of the fault – but they rightly reckoned that more of the fault lay above their level and beyond their powers. To believe in themselves they needed to believe in the capacity of their commanders, low and high. They had to believe that their lives lay, at every level, with one who was, in Napoleon's term, *heureux* – that he had within him the stuff of success. And men of this army needed to know what was happening. They needed to warm themselves in the confidence of their commander. In order to trust they needed to feel trusted. In truth there had to be a little make-believe in this. No army can function on the basis that its members require rational explanations before they obey: obedience must be absolute, immediate and enforced. But although, in practice, men had "blindly" to obey, they needed to feel they were not blind – that they knew as much as could be managed, and that it made sense. They needed to know, above all, that their destinies were in good hands.

And in this army not only respect for competence, fairness and even strictness, but liking – however roughly disguised or disclaimed – was an important factor. Montgomery, sometimes regarded as inhuman in his judgments of ability, always recognised this. "I don't agree," he would say after visiting a command whose chief was reported to him as no good, "I don't agree. And they *like* him. That's important. They're good judges."[1] Suspicious of mere charm, Montgomery knew the strength affection could bring to the military bond, how it could warm necessary respect, how it could stimulate confidence of the led in the leader. To inspire that confidence lay with the men's officers.

The huge expansion of the army and the pressing needs of the moment set in sharp relief the most difficult of military problems – the shortage of trained and efficient commissioned and non-commissioned officers.

It is probably hard to exaggerate how much the effectiveness of the German Army's expansion owed to the strength and quality of the officer and non-commissioned officer cadre. It was said that the "100,000 Mannheer", the small Reichswehr to which Germany was limited by the Treaty of Versailles, was an army of officers and NCOs. In Britain no such cadre existed. The concept of a small army able to expand in war through every man being competent to do a job several ranks higher was entirely absent. The quality of many Regular officers was not what it should have been, and the Territorial officers – often the most valiant of the nation – had too little basic experience. Now instructors as well as leaders were everywhere in demand. The Officer Corps had to be considerably expanded, diluting its quality. The parallel expansion of the NCO strength of the army was undertaken by the various Arms of the Service, and (for junior ranks) within units, rather than on a centralised basis or according to army standards and policy. Commissioned Officers, however, were a different matter.

Over 200,000 officers were commissioned in the British Army in the Second World War. This matched establishments, and replenished losses. It is, however, questionable whether the army became overweighted with officers, and those of too senior a rank. It is generally

---

[1] Recounted to the author.

true that the fewer the officers the more, perforce, vill be done by their subordinates, whose qualities in turn will increase. It was an article of faith in the British Army, for instance, that a troop or platoon of men had to be commanded by an officer. In practice, troops and platoons were, on frequent occasions, commanded by NCOs – in battle, with great success, and to the complete satisfaction of th)se they led. The proportion of officers to men overall increased as time went on: one to fifteen when the war began, one to thirteen when it ended – an increase of about thirteen per cent on a huge total. It is possible that a policy of having fewer officers from whom more responsibility was demanded would have made better use of human resources – possible but not certain. The example of some other armies (and the Indian Army) encourages the belief, but to introduce a radical departure from custom in the middle of war was probably impracticable.

From whatever cause the supply of officers began to make difficulties early in the war. From September 1939 it had been decreed that all candidates for commissions (with certain exemptions, for instance in the technical and medical services) must spend some time in the ranks, and earn the recommendation of the Commanding Officer of the unit. Armed with this, the aspiring officer was seen by an interview board. If he passed, the candidate became an Officer Cadet, and spent a period of intensive training at an Officer Cadet Training Unit – the pre-war Royal Military Academy and Royal Military College were closed for the duration of the war. The length of training differed by Arm of the Service; it was, on average, about four months.

The system seemed to work adequately at first. Naturally, a very large number of men of all ages and all occupations, anxious to serve and with the human qualities likely to fit them to be officers, came forward and were absorbed in the first eighteen months of war. Indeed, in June 1940, since casualties had been comparatively few and the expansion of the army was only just beginning, highly recommended applicants queued for as yet non-existent commissioned posts. Some were excellent. Some were unduly confident that the army could have little to teach them: they attempted, with varied success, to acquire its skills while rejecting its professional characteristics. Some were simply inadequate. By 1941, dissatisfaction was being expressed. Commanding Officers simultaneously complained about the quality of some of the officers reaching them and – under the pressure of a major expansion and training programme – avoided sending their better officers and NCOs to instruct at the Officer Cadet Training Units – the OCTUs – of which there were now thirty-five. The interview boards were also criticised. With only a permanent President (the other

101

members were field officers co-opted for the day), there was little continuity and the chances of a candidate could, it was said, be subject to individual whim or prejudice. The lack of any uniformity of standard imposed between Commands was questioned. Good men feared rejection and hung back from candidacy. The radical Press was quick to suggest that the prejudice of the interview board favoured the influence of class and background rather than an applicant's fundamental qualities. The method of selection simply by recommendation and short interview was also criticised as unscientific and haphazard.

The philosophy of the German Army, at that time enjoying a pretty well unbroken record of success, was scrutinised. The Germans were known to subject candidates not simply to interview but to several days of personality tests, whereby their behaviour, their initiative, their power of communicating with and inspiring others, their speed of perception, as well as their courage and intelligence, were all rigorously assessed. The Germans were also known to make extensive use of psychology and of trained psychologists in their selection process. Thus early in 1942 the War Office, with much the same philosophy, set up an experimental board on similar lines, with two more following by mid-summer. Careful steps were taken to monitor their product. The reports were entirely favourable. The system was widely and quickly promulgated, and, by the end of 1942, seventeen War Office Selection Boards were in operation, and the principle was extended to overseas theatres (where there were also OCTUs) in the following year. Simultaneously there was a drive to bring younger officers, with battle experience, to command and instructor posts in the OCTUs themselves. The revised system certainly gave more satisfaction. Complaints – whether from injured members of the public or dissatisfied Commanding Officers – diminished. And the general philosophy behind the new and increasingly respected selection process survived until victory and very long beyond.

This was to make the best – and to be seen fairly to make the best – of the human material available. This involved having sufficient material of high quality, and in this the army, from first to last, had problems. The Royal Air Force, in particular, was in strong and clearly justified competition for the sort of intelligent and resourceful young men the army needed. The numerical needs of the army, as has been said, may have been overstated by the army itself, with consequent acceptance of less than the highest standards. But the best were very good indeed and the system was justified and glorified by them.

The expansion of the army required a huge expansion of the Staff. The output of the Army Staff College at Camberley, and the Indian

Army Staff College at Quetta had, in peacetime, been small. The British Army never possessed a General Staff Corps on the Continental pattern (although this had originally been planned under the army reforms of the beginning of the century). There had never been explicitly produced that "brain of an army", acting according to established precepts under the direction of one chief, to which Moltke had attached such supreme importance. The British had, however, evolved an excellent teaching institution for the instruction of selected regimental officers in the duties of the Staff and the general conduct of war. In a small, peacetime army the fact that a generation of selected officers had the suffix "psc" (Passed Staff College), knew each other, and had been through the same mill, had produced something of a General Staff Corps in fact if not in name.

Once great numbers were required, the course of instruction (two years, before the war) had to be shortened, the intake increased and the catchment area of candidates broadened. The Staff College courses were at first shortened to four months, and then again increased to six. The intake on each course was enlarged from sixty to two hundred. The students were more and more drawn from Territorial and Temporary as well as Regular officers. Entry examination was abolished, and attendance was by nomination and selection. An additional Staff College was established, in March 1940, for Middle East Command at Haifa. And at Camberley the college was divided into senior and intermediate courses to cater for different ranks and Staff levels. The object could no longer be military education in any but the most shallow sense. The syllabus was tailored to produce certain officers fit to perform specific functions, not to consider the conduct of operations objectively. Staff Colleges were required to impart, not to evolve, doctrine.

At all three Staff Colleges – Camberley, Haifa and Quetta – the selection of candidates caused increasing difficulty as the war continued, and complaints were increasingly made about the quality of officer selected. The standard of Directing Staff – who had generally proved themselves in battle – remained high throughout. The standard of student deteriorated, and the Staff work of the army suffered accordingly. There was a natural and general disinclination of the best to leave the regimental family for Staff employment – and of commanders to make the best available. Many a Commander-in-Chief could have echoed the words of Wellington in 1812, faced with this recurrent problem:

I do not know that the Colonels of regiments have any right to interfere to prevent the appointment of officers to the Staff from their regiments, or to occasion by their influence the relinquishment of their offices on the Staff when they think proper . . . I admit the necessity of keeping regiments well-officered but I should wish to know who is more interested in keeping regiments well-officered than the Officer who Commands the Army?

Leadership was one thing, and essential to high morale. Equally important, intertwined with and reflecting it, was the administration, the system, the élan, bearing and self-respect of the regiment or unit a man joined and, indeed, of the depot in which he underwent his first apprenticeship. This last could be, and at best was, harsh and demanding. Provided it was fair, well-organised, and touched with occasional humour a man responded well to rigour. He had heard old soldiers' tales. Now he, too, could show he could "take it", that the army was no soft institution, but that he could show himself to be as hard as was required. By challenging his self-respect, tough initial training started to breed in a man respect for the institution he had joined. This respect was at the root of his loyalty. He needed to feel part of an organisation that worked, that was better than most others, and that could protect him as well as control him. Competent, understanding leadership, and a well-run and pride-filled unit were the conditions of a man's ready acceptance of what the army now demanded of him. This was a questioning generation, and the factors which could unsettle discipline and diminish performance needed always to be countered by positive influences and strong, effective command. The army had the stuff in it to do great things, but it was vulnerable. To the very end it would need thoughtful management. To maintain its morale would always be a challenge, brilliantly met, or, sometimes, disastrously failed.

There were other factors of great importance to morale. Montgomery observed that, "The surest way to obtain [high morale] is by success in battle."[1] The early withdrawals, in several campaigns, were particularly bad for morale – and not only among those performing them. To go forward in time, it became widely known that not only at Dunkirk but in Crete (May 1941) and Singapore (February 1942), to take but two instances, there were scenes of panic and indiscipline and all the evidences of shattered morale. This was not universal – it never is. Nor

[1] *High Command in War*, F. M. Viscount Montgomery of Alamein. War Office pamphlet.

did rumour distinguish between corps or even nationalities. Tales lose nothing in the telling, however, and while men did not feel inclined to condemn those who had failed tests to which they had not themselves been subjected, they felt a certain contamination. They also felt, instinctively, that things must have been mismanaged; and the corporate morale of the army suffered. Indeed, probably the low point of the army's morale was not in June 1940, a moment of immediate and stimulating challenge, but in summer 1942 when all, still, after two more years, seemed going downhill.

In the same way victories, when at last they came, spread their intoxication far beyond those who achieved them. The army needed to feel it was winning. It needed to feel its equipment, its command, its plans were sound. It needed to feel large enough – everyone knew, and the despatches of commanders confirmed, that exhaustion, lack of relief, shortage of numbers had contributed much to earlier breaks of morale: a small army is an army without rest or staying power. It needed these assurances. Its confidence was fragile.

Another factor of great importance to the morale of the army was the connection with family and home. A man could be away for a very long time. From theatres of war overseas home leave was not granted until September 1944. A Regular soldier might by then have served seven, eight, even nine years abroad, a conscripted man four. During this time the bombing of the United Kingdom created anxiety and, often, hardship. Families were uprooted and bereaved. The high incidence of unfaithfulness of wives and sweethearts (as evidenced through the universal censorship of mail as well as in the complaints of the soldier to his superiors) caused great suffering among soldiers afar, and great resentment against those (especially Allies) serving in the United Kingdom or exempted from the Services in civilian occupations. Not that soldiers at home were free from these pressures: they constituted the main cause of the most prevalent military offence in the United Kingdom, absence without leave. But time and distance exacerbated suspicion, and, with loneliness and anxiety, were potent factors working against high morale. They struggled, as the war went on, against the bright influence of victory.

Discipline and morale are interdependent. Strict, just discipline is likely to be a prerequisite of high morale, but cannot alone create it. Low morale produces bad discipline, but is not its only cause. Laxity and inadequate training also contribute to those failures of duty charged as disciplinary offences, especially dangerous as they must be in battle itself. Of all the offences committed in the army in the Second World War the most serious and the most prevalent was that of desertion.

Statistics give some indication of the problem. In 1942 eighty-two per cent of men serving sentences in detention barracks had been found guilty of desertion or of absence without leave.[1] The number of convictions by Courts Martial for desertion or absence rose from 15,000 in the year 1940–41 to nearly 20,000 in the year 1943–44. By far the highest annual total in overseas Commands was in 1944–45, the last year of the war, when a total of 8,400 were found guilty of desertion by Court Martial. These were desertions on active service in a theatre of war.

Much research was done, notably in Italy where the particular features of the campaign led to statistics of epidemic proportions. A prime consideration, naturally, was the question of punishment and deterrence. Throughout the First World War the death penalty had been mandatory for desertion in the face of the enemy. In fact it had been commuted to a sentence of imprisonment in all but a tiny minority of cases – only 266 men had been executed out of 31,000 convicted. The ultimate penalty remained, however, until abolished by Parliament in 1930, against, it should be said, the advice of the military authorities. The mood which had led to abolition was understandable. The horrors of war had been vividly portrayed in many brilliant books, and was increasingly brought home by film and photograph. It was widely held that the stresses of war could lead sensitive and honourable men to crack, and that to execute them for action or inaction when they were no longer masters of themselves was abominable. The mood matched the times.

In the Second World War, with a smaller army, about the same number of convictions for desertion took place. Commanders-in-Chief, commanders, regimental officers – and psychiatrists – were united in the view that the existence of the death penalty in theatres of war would sharply reduce the desertion rate, and formal recommendations were made, to no effect. It was their contention (and the experience of all with first-hand knowledge) that this was not a question of harsh treatment for the man who "cracked" – overcome by circumstances. He was recognised as needing medical treatment, restorative care. On the contrary it was pointed out, and well estab-

---

[1] If a man absent without leave did not return to his unit after a specific time a Court of Enquiry declared that there was, in effect, a prima facie case against him of desertion – that is, leaving the service with intention not to return; and his name was posted accordingly.

lished by investigation and interview, that the crime of desertion was in
the great majority of cases a cold calculation of risk and advantage. In a
letter to *The Times* after the war a correspondent wrote:

> Some months spent in daily contact with deserters in Italy taught me
> that, although there were a few very sad cases caused by nervous
> strain or domestic troubles, the offence was usually a carefully
> thought out plan, and the belief in a pardon after the war was
> widespread.

It was by no means difficult for a man to disappear before an operation,
leaving his comrades to face proportionately greater toil and danger –
and suffer proportionately greater losses; and where the choice lay
only between the risk of death or mutilation on the battlefield and the
security of a prison cell for a period all thought would be limited, it was
too easy to choose the latter. In other words, it was contended by the
fighting soldiers that the absence of the death penalty for desertion in
the face of the enemy placed an intolerable burden on men's courage
and determination, by removing any comparable fear of the consequences of failure. To those who argued against the death penalty on
grounds of its finality and ferocity they countered, bitterly, that the
bullets of the enemy had no mercy on those who did not choose to
abandon the field. The highest desertion rate did not correspond with
the lowest point in morale, generally given as 1942. The latter was
closely related to how the war was going: a consequence of failure. The
highest desertion rate overseas, on the other hand, was in 1944–45,
when victory on all fronts was already within grasp. But so, too, was the
end of the war, and men wished to be alive to see it.

The offence of desertion was proportionately highest in the infantry.
This was unsurprising. The circumstances of the infantryman's battle
demanded most from the individual, and thus gave him a latitude he
could abuse. The member of a vehicle crew was carried forward. The
infantryman had to direct his own reluctant limbs towards peril. He
could the more easily evade notice. Against the instincts of fear he had,
or should have had, loyalty to his own comrades, his tribal home, his
own battalion, his familiars. Where this was not so he was deprived of
yet another vital support.

Sometimes, it was found – or considered – an inevitable expedient
to send reinforcements to battalions, regiments, divisions not their
own. This could lead to indifference, low morale and a high desertion
rate. It could also lead to serious corporate acts of insubordination. An

example occurred at Salerno. In a private letter to the CIGS, Brooke, General Alexander wrote on 23rd September 1943:

> One of the steps I took was to wire back for 1,500 Infantry reinforcements . . . since then I have heard that as there were only 700 Infantry reinforcements at Philipville the balance was taken from details of 50th and 51st Divisions in the Tripoli area. When these men arrived at 10 Corps 191 of them refused to join the units they were detailed to go to . . . I have recommended that they are all tried by Court Martial for refusing orders. There is no doubt that these two divisions have got word of the fact that they are earmarked to go home, and of course they have both had a terrific amount of fighting – but they must be dealt with very firmly.[1]

Certainly this was right, but the occurrence was symptomatic. Many of the men concerned in this case had fine records. They had correctly understood that their parent divisions, with which they had fought the length of the North African desert, were due to return to England, to prepare for the invasion of North-West Europe. Now they found themselves as individual reinforcements destined for different divisions, strange units, unknown officers. Disappointment at the future – the sense of "fairness" which, of course, makes an army unworkable if carried beyond a certain point – was combined with resentment at being directed to an alien "family". The tribal sense of the British Army reinforced the grievance, and exploded in an act of corporate insubordination which discipline was inadequate to deter, and administration too inflexible to pre-empt.

As we have seen, it was common at this time to compare the practices of the British Army with those of the hitherto victorious enemy, in search of lessons. If we contrast the various elements in morale and discipline we find that the German soldier suffered rough, even brutal initial training: he was expected, in and out of battle, to show discipline in its most formal expressions of saluting, rigid position of attention when reporting, and so forth; he enjoyed, on the whole, a very high *esprit de corps*, a strong camaraderie; and he suffered draconian punishment, instantly meted out, for disobedience or failure. It was customary to mock the German way and extol the milder systems of the British. Nevertheless the military performance of the Wehrmacht throughout the war was seldom equalled and only on very rare occasions surpassed.

Questions of discipline, failure, crime and punishment, as well as

[1] Alanbrooke Personal Files.

organisation, training and achievement have to be dealt with in any honest appraisal of an army. They are a part of the story, as are the battles, the defeats, the triumphs. Cracks in morale can be as decisive, if they occur at the crucial moment, as the surge of skill and courage which can bring men to victory. But it would be mistaken to imagine that the blemishes formed a large part of the whole. They happened: a mass army is not composed solely of patriotic heroes. Unfeeling, foolish or weak commanders existed in the Second World War: so did bad and badly administered units, and undisciplined, unprincipled men. This did not poison or particularly discolour the great, generous and loyal body which was becoming the British Army. Men from a suspicious and "unmilitary" generation, many from an unpromising background in their formative years, many with grave anxieties and real hardships to plague them at home, became a proud, efficient, cheerful army, a force deserving better preparation than their country had expended on them in the prewar years. Worthy heirs of noble fathers, they added some glorious pages to the story of the British Army, once they found a High Command that understood their generation and their needs. They did their duty and made their sacrifice. In the Second World War 145,000 British soldiers were killed. It was only one quarter the death list of the First World War, but it was enough.

Part III

The Habit of Defeat

6

False Dawn in Africa

A great army was being reconstituted at home, but it would be some time before it engaged the enemy. Meanwhile Britain carried out a series of campaigns which, although they included glorious episodes, almost all ended with the sour taste of defeat. For every painful or exhilarating step forward there seemed to follow another back.

For two years – between the evacuation of the BEF from France and the early summer of 1942 in Africa – only four British divisions fought the Germans: 1st, 2nd and 7th Armoured Divisions and 70th Division. There were independent brigades, army and corps troops, and British units in Indian formations. But apart from these the fighting in North and East Africa, Greece, Crete and Syria was carried out by two Indian, three Australian, one New Zealand, two African and two South African Divisions.

On 10th June 1940, Italy declared war. At first the act seemed greatly to add to our dangers, menacing British possessions in Africa, or areas for which Britain was responsible such as Egypt, threatening Mediterranean shipping, and compelling most sea transport for the Middle East, India or the Far East to go round the Cape of Good Hope, adding many thousands of miles and many weeks to every passage. Nevertheless Italy's hostility had long been thought likely – a contingency that would have had to be considered at every turn. Danger was transformed to advantage and an opportunity was given and taken for what Britain and the British Army needed above all else – a victory in the field, albeit short-lived. There was to be dawn after darkness – a false dawn, to be succeeded by another night, but splendid while it lasted. Without it spirits would have been low indeed.

The new enemy focused British eyes on a new theatre of war – the Middle East – and on a different army from the remnants of the BEF. Middle East Command was an almost entirely Regular Army, largely untouched by the expansions, traumata and changes of character undergone by the army at home. It had also become an Imperial and

Commonwealth rather than a British Army, with the first winter of the war bringing reinforcements; Australian, New Zealand and South African formations, and divisions of the Indian Army, in which some British units were serving.

Middle East Command, now suddenly in the front line of war, had responsibility for the security of Egypt, Palestine, Aden, the Sudan, and the British East African possessions in Kenya, Uganda, Tanganyika and British Somaliland. The Command was also responsible for operations, should such occur, in the whole area of the world between the Mediterranean, the Caucasus and the Indian Ocean. Its strategic importance did not simply lie in territory marked red upon the map, but in the oil on which Britain depended. The collapse of the British position in the Middle East could mean that those oilfields could fall to the first intruder. The Middle East was also the western bastion of the defence of India. And it was a stepping stone for movement by air and a shortened passage for movement by sea to India and the Far East.

General Wavell had become Commander-in-Chief, Middle East, in August 1939. A silent, enigmatic man, he loved books, poetry, beauty and originality. He disliked the superficialities of social life. He also disliked the confusion, ugliness and inefficiency of war. Wavell was a scholar, who had deeply studied his profession. His humour was quiet. He inspired confidence while never seeking publicity. He gave the accurate impression of not greatly caring what men thought of him, and, perhaps in consequence, most thought a great deal. Wavell sometimes seemed to lack great energy. Churchill could never get on terms with one so inexpressive and so taciturn, and at a later stage of the war wrote with exasperation that Wavell appeared to take a very detached view of some disaster although the responsibility was his. Dill, too, once wrote to Brooke from India (whither Wavell had gone from the Middle East) that "drive" was not his outstanding characteristic. There was something in this comment. Wavell did not, as the war went on, always project dynamism. His interventions with his subordinates and his strategic judgment are open to criticism. Nevertheless he seemed to stand like a quiet colossus, uncommunicative, intelligent, imperturbable, full of inward imagination touched with a certain stoic melancholy.

By land the Italian threat to Middle East Command came from two directions. In Italian Somaliland, Eritrea and Abyssinia (the last recently added, as a first acquisition, to Mussolini's new Roman Empire), some 250,000 men, under the Duke of Aosta, menaced the tiny garrisons of Kenya, British Somaliland and the Sudan. In Libya, once French neutrality was assured and the Italians' Tunisian frontier secured, fourteen Italian divisions, under Marshal Balbo (succeeded in June by Marshal Graziani), could be concentrated against Egypt.

To confront this threat Wavell had, in the Sudan, the British-officered Sudan Defence Force and three British battalions; in Kenya two East African brigades, shortly to be joined by a South African brigade; in British Somaliland four battalions – two Indian, one East African and one Rhodesian – reinforced by a British battalion brought across from Aden; in Palestine a small garrison, reinforced before the war to deal with the troubles arising from the British Mandate, and now constituting a reserve for the defence of Egypt. Egypt itself had a miniature field army and a base – as yet of modest size – all under the command of British Troops Egypt, Lieutenant-General Sir Henry Maitland Wilson. Included, however, was that rare commodity in the British Army of 1940, an armoured division.

This mobile division, christened the 7th Armoured Division on 7th February 1940, had formed in September 1938 under Major-General Hobart, who had been sent from England. There could have been no better choice. Hobart was one of the original prophets of British tank forces, who had fought with great pugnacity and singlemindedness not only for the development of armour but also for, as he saw it, the modernisation of an outdated and amateur army. A crusty, difficult man with more genius than geniality, he was perfectly suited for the task of creating a new force, according to principles as yet untested but in which he passionately believed, it was all the better that, for a year, he remained well away from the War Office and with the mighty training area of the Western Desert on his doorstep. His vigour and imagination redeemed his prickly intolerance.

Hobart took the components assigned to the mobile division – those units and equipments which happened to be there, rather than a planned establishment – and trained them with the utmost energy. He trained them in living in the desert, by practice and experiment, in moving across the desert, maintaining their vehicles in the desert, and communicating in the desert. He oversaw the conversion of a cavalry brigade to a light armoured brigade. He laid the foundations of the support group of motorised infantry and anti-tank guns which could be deployed as a pivot of tactical manoeuvre, a fixed point in the feature-less terrain. Above all, perhaps, he developed and trained his division in an administrative system appropriate to mobile forces. All this was experimental. To maintain mobility a force needs replenishment – fuel, water, ammunition. Without this an army comes to a halt, is defeated, starves. To provide them in the huge sand sea of North Africa required system both within the unit and behind it – and transport in the right place to save time, but so drilled and deployed as to be able to move secure from the enemy. Just as the administrative planning of the High Command was crucial to success, so were the systems evolved within unit and formation. Hobart was their progenitor.

The area over which the British were to fight for nearly three years has been described as a tactician's paradise and a logistician's nightmare. The phrase is apt. The final advance of the British Army from Egypt to Tunisia covered some 1,500 miles, and the range of operations over such huge distances was governed by the laborious business of supply. Every gallon of petrol and water, every carton of ammunition, every box of rations, had to come from a sequence of supply depots in the field, established behind the moving armies. The capture and retention of workable ports through which supplies could be brought in bulk (or denied to an enemy) was crucial. But whatever the port of origin the distances meant that an army could only be maintained by a huge train of load-carrying transport. These vehicles, and the men who drove them, needed care, maintenance and rest. No grand manoeuvres sketched on a command map had chance of success unless anchored to the realities of supply, maintenance and track mileage.

To the tactician, however, the terrain was an exhilarating challenge. There were few impediments to movement. Manoeuvre was possible. Mobility came into its own. There was a railway and a track, later developed into a good coastal road, hugging the Mediterranean. To the south rose an escarpment, sheer in places, which touched the coast at various points, such as Bardia, creating narrows. Elsewhere it rose well back from the sea, overlooking a coastal plain. The few passes from the high plateau to the low road were of obvious tactical significance, leading to names such as Halfaya taking on considerable importance in the desert story. Above the eastern escarpment the going was generally good, manoeuvre unimpeded, features few. In Cyrenaica, however, between Derna and Benghazi, lay a considerable range of hills, the Jebel Akhdar. Here there was rainfall, roads and cultivation; and the coastal strip was particularly confined. South of the Cyrenaica Hills, on the high ground, the terrain was boulder strewn and difficult, a challenge to the passage of vehicles, a different proposition from the great plateau above the escarpment between Tobruk and Mersa Matruh. This whole area was now to be the scene of high and bloody drama. This was the Western Desert.

In June 1940 Lieutenant-General Richard O'Connor took command of the Western Desert Force (later XIII Corps) – the fighting formations of British Troops Egypt. It consisted of one armoured division, and the equivalent of some two infantry divisions. O'Connor was ordered to defend Egypt against Italian attack. He was perfectly content, and asked no questions.

On 4th July 1940, in Abyssinia, the small post of Kassala and several other places near the border with the Sudan were attacked by three Italian columns including armour. The Italians were opening their East African campaign.

It was not, however, towards the huge expanses of the Sudan that Aosta, the Italian commander, first moved in strength. The colony of British Somaliland, with neighbouring French Somaliland now neutral, looked an easy target. Italian forces massed on three of British Somaliland's borders, and on 3rd August Aosta invaded. Twenty-six Italian battalions, in three columns and supported by tanks, armoured cars and aircraft, advanced from the south-west towards Zeila, Hargeisa and Odweina.

The Italian force was met by the five defending battalions – (two) Indian, African, Rhodesian and British – on a line of hills only fifty miles from the sea. Here was the first defensible position, but it could not be defended indefinitely against a much larger force with no impediment whatever to movement round the flanks; and Major-General Godwin-Austen (who had arrived unexpectedly, diverted to British Somaliland from another assignment, on 11th August) had no intention of giving the enemy time. He ordered withdrawal to the port of Berbera, and evacuation, as British Somaliland was untenable unless hugely and unjustifiably reinforced. Two thousand Italian casualties had been inflicted for two hundred and sixty British and Imperial. The evacuation was naturally a matter of jubilation in Italy. For the British it was bad for morale and for prestige, but inevitable. Wavell, who disliked abandoning territory, had no alternative. Nevertheless he decided that there should be a sequel, not too long delayed. Meanwhile the Italians made no further move for the present in East Africa.

In Libya, Marshal Graziani, like Aosta in Somaliland, had also been ordered to take the offensive. The Italians were to march against Egypt.

Since Italy went to war the Libyan-Egyptian frontier had been the scene of incessant raiding by British light mobile forces and armoured cars. The Italians had constructed a tall fence along the frontier, and manned small desert forts behind the wire. The British gapped the wire and attacked the forts, taking prisoners and ambushing replenishment columns. They did not occupy the forts. They concentrated on

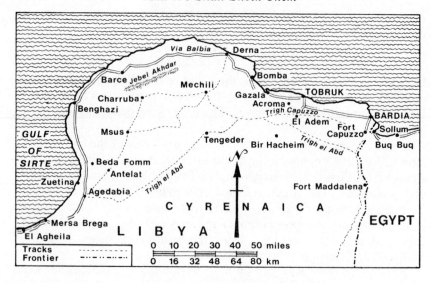

becoming masters of the open desert, on dominating the desert sea.

Graziani, after some procrastination, had received a direct order from Rome. He was to advance on Egypt and attack not later than 9th September. Finally on 13th September, five infantry divisions, short of motor transport and supported initially only by some 120 tanks, began moving towards the frontier. The Italian Army, like the British, had been starved of equipment and of the means of mobility. Their artillery was excellent and their engineers first-class. They were also adept at creating tolerable, even luxurious, living conditions in the middle of the desert, just as in the past enterprising Italian colonists had brought some sort of order and material civilisation to an inhospitable land. With not dissimilar spirit and ingenuity Italian soldiers adopted a position, fortified it, and provided living quarters, storage and refrigeration. Nevertheless they did not make the desert their own. They did not become the nomads that the desert war demanded. They had little mobility. It was an army pedestrian in mind as well as material that Graziani now pushed towards Egypt.

Preceded by an artillery bombardment, the leading corps of two divisions, accompanied by a mobile group on the southern flank, descended the escarpment by the Halfaya Pass and entered the little port of Sollum from which its British occupants, a platoon of infantry, had withdrawn. The Italians suffered severely from mines laid by Western Desert Force on this predictable approach. They also suffered from the harassing fire of the support group and artillery

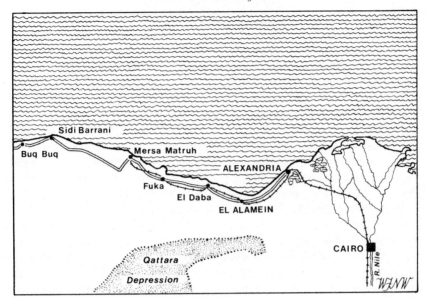

Western Desert

of 7th Armoured Division, and from attacks by the Royal Air Force. Ultimately they massed below the escarpment and continued the advance by the coastal road. It was slow moving, devoid of surprise, and laborious.

O'Connor hoped that the Italian advance would be driven on towards Mersa Matruh, a further 120 miles towards the Egyptian Delta. He could then attack the vulnerable and extended columns from the southern flank. To his disappointment the Italians stopped fifty miles from Sollum, at Sidi Barrani, where they started to construct fortifications, as well as at three points to the south on a frontage of twenty miles – at Tummar East, Tummar West and Nibeiwa. These became large fortified camps. Further divisions were deployed to Derna, Tobruk, Bardia and Buq Buq. The Italian Tenth Army, three corps and twelve divisions strong, had gone on the defensive. The advance was over. British Somaliland, and fifty miles of Egyptian littoral were in Italian hands. Two pawns had been advanced upon the board.

In August 1940 the British Government took a decision of great courage. At home, invasion was expected at any time, and the army

119

struggled towards reconstitution and re-equipment. Production was beginning to get into its stride – but only beginning. Although only 1,400 tanks were produced in the United Kingdom in 1940 (compared with nearly 5,000 the following year), three tank regiments (one each of light, cruiser and infantry tanks) were ordered to the Middle East Command. Forty-eight anti-tank guns, twenty light anti-aircraft guns and forty-eight field guns, twenty-five pounders, were sent at the same time. The convoy was despatched via the Mediterranean, and despite the hazards from a hostile Italy, it arrived safe in Egypt. Wavell now had a formidable addition to his army. His armoured formations could be made up to strength. His infantry could be supported in any attack by the slow but heavily armoured Matilda infantry tank.

Wavell now planned a blow at the Italians in the desert – a brief, brisk offensive – a raid, no more. He also meditated on a counter-offensive in East Africa. He kept his own counsel and shared his thoughts only with the few who needed to know. He planned the operation in the Western Desert for December. Thus was born COMPASS, a small-scale operation in terms of the troops engaged under British command, but one with disproportionate effect on the morale of both the Italian enemy and the British Army. COMPASS was the achievement of troops led by the Commander of the Western Desert Force, General O'Connor.

O'Connor was a small, alert, modest man. His deprecatory gentleness masked a strong will, speed of perception and great professional understanding. His manner was quick and bird-like. Those who knew him well felt an aura not only of inner assurance but of goodness. He had, too, the intelligence to see risks clearly and the courage to take them. Now he was ordered to take 30,000 men and attack an army over five times as large. As to the strategic aim, his Commander-in-Chief proposed to leave the matter open. Wavell wrote to O'Connor at the beginning of December that, "It is possible that an opportunity may offer for converting the enemy's defeat into an outstanding victory." Wavell, in other words, was prepared to see how the operation went. If the "raid" were really successful and the enemy showed symptoms of more than local disarray, it might be exploited. If there were doubt on that score, O'Connor should not overreach and get his fingers burned. Such flexible instructions placed much responsibility on the commander receiving them, perhaps wisely. Had O'Connor been a nervous, or unimaginative, or simply a very prudent man there was every chance for him to rest on what were to be his early laurels. Instead, O'Connor was to "put it to the touch to win or lose it all", and Britain reaped the benefit.

As the first British offensive of the war, Operation COMPASS was of great psychological importance. Western Desert Force had under command 7th Armoured Division with 270 tanks, and 4th Indian Division. There were also 16th (British) Infantry Brigade, and two brigades – 16th and 17th – of 6th Australian Division which took part, complete with all three of its brigades, after the opening stages. O'Connor had five regiments of artillery, in addition to the artillery of the divisions. He also had under his control, for allocation where needed, the Matilda infantry tank regiment recently arrived from England.

O'Connor took immense pains to conceal every preliminary step. The approach march on 6th December was masked as a training exercise. By 8th December, the Western Desert Force had concentrated ten miles from the Italian fortified camps, twenty miles south of Sidi Barrani. These places were to be attacked from the rear – generally at the point where reconnaissance showed that Italian replenishment columns themselves entered – while some sort of demonstration would be made on the east flank, the "front". Each assault would be carried out by infantry and Matilda tanks, preceded by a sharp, hurricane artillery bombardment. The fortified camps south of Sidi Barrani would be attacked first followed by Sidi Barrani itself, as the opening phase of COMPASS. And simultaneously, to cut off an Italian withdrawal, O'Connor directed 7th Armoured Division, his *corps de chasse*, at the coast road to the west.

At dawn on 9th December 4th Indian Division attacked the camp at Nibeiwa, achieving complete surprise. The effect of the tanks was devastating and all was over in an hour. Tummar West, the next camp in O'Connor's sequence, fell to the same division a few hours later after hard fighting, for there was now no question of surprise; and Tummar East surrendered next morning. At 6 a.m., on 10th December, 16th (British) Brigade, fighting as part of 4th Indian Division, attacked Sidi Barrani from the south. Four hours later it had fallen with 20,000 Italians taken prisoner. The first phase of COMPASS was over.

At this point, when the "raid" might have been regarded as complete, Wavell, without any previous warning, ordered the 4th Indian Division to be sent back to Egypt for transfer to East Africa, leaving O'Connor to decide how best to exploit victory. He could rest upon the field, triumphant, with a haul of prisoners and booty. This was not O'Connor's style. He chose to go forwards and strike again, operating under the continuous support of the Desert Air Force, with the complete 6th Australian Division in place of 4th Indian Division. First

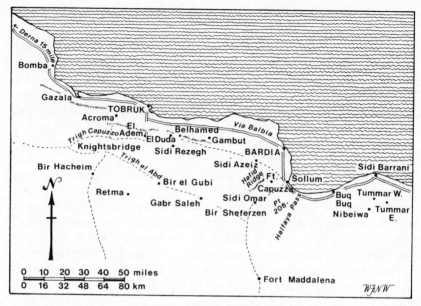

From Sidi Barrani to Tobruk

he directed 7th Armoured Division at Sollum, on the frontier, and an Italian division was "swept up" while attempting to move west from Buq Buq. Western Desert Force had not only taken 38,000 prisoners in three days, but also 73 tanks, 1,000 vehicles and 237 guns.

The second phase of COMPASS now started. The Italians had been driven from Egypt and could now be expected to fight in their fortified places: Bardia, Tobruk, Derna. O'Connor therefore directed a mobile force down the escarpment to cut the coast road west of Bardia, itself some fifteen miles north of Sollum, inside Libya. He entrusted the attack on Bardia to 6th Australian Division, plus British tanks. On 1st January, Western Desert Force was renamed XIII Corps.

The assault started at 5.30 a.m. on 3rd January and continued for two days. By the early afternoon of 5th January all was over. O'Connor was master of Bardia and another 40,000 prisoners. The fighting had been hard – storming bunkers and machine-gun nests at close quarters, duels with Italian tanks, gapping of wire under fire. The Italian artillery, throughout, was accurate and effective, the guns bravely served. Now O'Connor's eyes were on Tobruk, eighty miles farther west, as they had been from the start of operations. Tobruk was a prize worth having – and worth denying to an enemy. Through its port bulk supplies could come, and a new advanced base be constituted for the onward movement of XIII Corps. By 5th January, 7th Armoured Division had already passed El Adem, twenty miles south of Tobruk, had swung north and cut the road running westwards from Tobruk towards Gazala. By 9th January, Tobruk itself was invested.

On 21st January Tobruk was attacked by the Australians. Again, the fighting was bitter. When Tobruk finally surrendered, a further 27,000 prisoners were herded into the hastily constructed cages before eastwards evacuation – cages, in which, despite all efforts, conditions were at first appalling. No major epidemic broke out, but prisoners were among O'Connor's greatest administrative problems. He had taken captive over 100,000 men. The remaining divisions of the Italian Tenth Army were now scattered, apparently without mutual support and inviting destruction in detail, over Central and Western Cyrenaica.

O'Connor now determined to drive his mobile forces south of the Jebel Akhdar, 250 miles across some of the most difficult terrain in North Africa, to cut off the entire Italian Army before it could escape into Tripolitania. At the same time he planned to press along the coast road and overcome Italian garrisons at Derna, at Barce, at Benghazi. To start the operation there would be a twin advance, on Derna by 6th Australian Division, and on Mechili by 7th Armoured Division. Derna, on the coast, was the northern point and Mechili, at a junction of desert tracks, the southern point of a new line of widely separated Italian defensive positions. O'Connor also hoped to trap an Italian armoured force at Mechili, to catch it withdrawing northwards towards the Jebel. But the operational aim of his southern thrust was to reach the sea just south of Benghazi.

British patrols entered Mechili on 27th January, to find it empty of troops. O'Connor was disappointed in his hope of catching the Italians withdrawing; they had slipped away, the trap unsprung. Two days later, after some hard fighting, the Australians found Derna, too, evacuated. Meanwhile the British tanks and vehicles were showing the strain, for O'Connor was driving the armoured forces hard. He was impatient with their reluctance to move at night, but they and their vehicles had come far and reliable maps hardly existed. The pace of advance was now governed not only by terrain but by logistics. A field supply depot would, it was reckoned, need to be established near Mechili, to replenish the armoured forces for the final great drive across the Cyrenaican "bulge", south of the Jebel Akhdar to the coast. This was becoming a pursuit which, in traditional military language, must be "to the last breath of man and beast". But logistics now apparently compelled a pause.

The pause, however, was very brief and interrupted. On 3rd February, the Australians, advancing both along the coast and into the Jebel, found that the Italians had fled – Graziani had ordered the evacuation of Cyrenaica. Now if the remnants of Tenth Army were to be caught there could be no waiting. The logistically impossible must be achieved. Every vehicle that could move forward from Mechili must do so, carrying two days' supplies on vehicles, careless of subsequent replenishment. The difficulties of the terrain south of the Jebel were now brought painfully home. Progress was frustratingly slow. Tracks broke, tyres punctured, engine sumps cracked on boulders. To speed the pace of at least some of 7th Armoured Division the tracked vehicles of the leading brigade were separated from the wheeled, and the latter were pushed ahead to join the armoured-car regiment, the same indefatigable armoured-car regiment that had first ranged the Libyan frontier in June. It was appropriate that they should be the first to see the Gulf of Sirte and the coastal road running south from Benghazi, which they reached at midday on 5th February, ten miles south of Beda Fomm. They were followed by some infantry from the support group, and some guns. The road was blocked; a thin line as yet, but timely. Thirty minutes later the head appeared of the Italian columns escaping towards Tripolitania.

The last scene of the last act was played on 6th and 7th February. The enemy still had plenty of tanks in running order, and, as the blocking force astride the escape route was reinforced, the Italians mounted attack after attack to get through or round the last of their opponents between them and Tripoli. They met a wall of fire astride the road, and from the flank came attacks from O'Connor's tanks. One hundred Italian tanks were destroyed or captured in those hours. Behind them the Australians were advancing on Benghazi.

Soon after dawn on 7th February white flags in profusion were displayed from the huge mass of vehicles, armoured and soft-skinned, confronting the British. The Italian Tenth Army laid down its arms. A further 25,000 prisoners moved eastwards. COMPASS was over.

In two months O'Connor's force had advanced 500 miles. 30,000 strong, it had destroyed an enemy army of fourteen divisions, taken 130,000 prisoners, captured nearly 500 tanks, including light tanks, and over 800 guns. Meanwhile XIII Corps suffered under 2,000 casualties, of which 500 had been killed.

Losses in equipment arose as much from wear as from enemy action. Only one-fifth of the vehicles with which Western Desert Force had started COMPASS were still usable. There would need to be near total replacement. But units of a new armoured division – 2nd Armoured

Division – were arriving in Egypt from England. O'Connor could see little opposition in front of him. Despite the logistic situation he believed that, after the briefest of halts, he could hurry forwards everything that could move, and could drive the Italians out of Sirte and out of Tripoli itself. Only through the port of Tripoli could come German reinforcements, if, as was suspected, Hitler had decided to assist his Italian ally.

In fact the decision to do so had been taken in Berlin a month before. At the same time in London another decision had been taken; in January the British Chiefs of Staff had agreed that O'Connor's offensive should continue only as far as Benghazi. Thereafter we should stand on the defensive in Cyrenaica and all available troops should be withdrawn for a very different venture. There was to be no exploitation after Beda Fomm.

O'Connor received these orders in their final form on 12th February. On the same day General Erwin Rommel arrived in Tripoli, followed two days later by the first two units of the "Deutsches Afrika Korps".

O'Connor was brought back to take command of British Troops Egypt, and XIII Corps was dispersed to different duties. The garrison of Cyrenaica was reduced to the minimum thought essential to defend against a new move forward from Tripolitania – not anticipated for several months. O'Connor's immediate future was tragic. Sent up by Wavell to advise General Neame (now commanding in Cyrenaica) when Rommel attacked on 31st May, he would probably have taken over command, but was taken prisoner on 6th April when his car ran into a German patrol. Thus there fell into enemy hands one who, in a few short weeks, had proved himself as gifted, agile and energetic as any.

O'Connor felt strongly that he could have driven XIII Corps forwards to Tripoli, and that had he been allowed to do so it could have pre-empted the long and deadly struggles of the next two years. This may be so. To deny North Africa to the Germans was a great prize. The subsequent loss of Cyrenaica (and its airfields) was to place both Egypt and Malta in peril. All this must remain speculative. Rommel, regardless of his orders, hurried the first two German units eastwards towards Cyrenaica immediately they disembarked. A German reconnaissance battalion reached Sirte (halfway between Tripoli and Beda Fomm) by the night of 16th February; O'Connor reckoned he could have got there and hustled the Italians out four days earlier, had he gone straight forwards at full stretch after Beda Fomm. It would have been a near run thing and none can say with certainty how it might have gone. Certainly a British occupation of Tripolitania at that time would have raised questions for the French authorities in neighbouring Tunisia – and therefore for the Germans.

Despite these questions O'Connor's achievement, and that of his troops, stands in its own right. It was a brief campaign, undertaken by small forces, but in it the troops of the British Empire showed that they, too, could attack, that they, too, could achieve surprise, could move, could win. This was the Desert Army, merry, enterprising, with a comradeship all its own. They were all to see many changes, suffer many jolts to spirit and confidence, and reach ultimate triumph. COMPASS was their awakening. One day, in the hour of victory, Churchill was to say to them, "After the war, when a man is asked what he did it will be quite sufficient for him to say, 'I marched and fought with the Desert Army.' " The mirage of that final victory was glimpsed in COMPASS.

The British Army also produced in O'Connor a field commander who, although he received little public acclaim, showed himself a master of the battlefield. The whole army felt, for a while, cleansed. There was, it is true, an uneasy feeling that Italians were not Germans. The Italians had often fought with great courage, but neither in equipment nor in habit of mind had they been exponents of man-oeuvre. They had proved too easy to isolate and surround, to destroy piecemeal. War is like a game in that respect: an opponent's lack of skill can flatter the prowess of a performance.

For the British, the comradeship in arms of Australian and Indian formations produced healthy competition. All races were on their mettle. These were British Regular soldiers. Their virtues were traditional. Their shortcomings, due to a generation of neglect, have been identified. But the training of Hobart and the leadership of O'Connor had gone far to overcome for a season the influences of the static-minded, the over-deliberate and the amateur. The British again discovered for themselves the tonic power of the offensive in war. A warm glow was felt, not only in Middle East Command. It seemed the dark night of defeats might be over.

At about the same time that O'Connor was starting the final phase of COMPASS, advancing on Derna and Mechili, far away to the south two remarkable campaigns opened that ultimately became one. Within a short time they destroyed the Italian Army in East Africa as surely as it had been destroyed in Cyrenaica, but this time with more finality.

In the Sudan on 19th January Lieutenant-General Platt, commanding the 4th and 5th Indian Divisions, each containing British battalions, advanced into Eritrea. The key to Eritrea was the Asmara Plateau: the key to that plateau was Keren; and the key of the door opening the road to Keren was the town of Agordat, strongly garrisoned by a reinforced Italian colonial division, with ten medium tanks. Platt had to seize Agordat and batter his way to Keren through a precipitous gorge and against a considerable superiority in enemy numbers. The terrain was formidable: great mountain ranges, sheer escarpments, steep sided valleys covered with camel thorn, "going" almost as hostile to the infantryman as to every sort of transport – except animal transport, of which Platt had none, while the Italian were well furnished with pack companies.

On 28th January, 4th Indian Division attacked Agordat. The battle involved the climbing of a steep hill to the south, followed by the storming of the crest and the enemy trench lines below the hill. Platt was fortunate in having four Matilda tanks to support his infantry, both British and Indian. Infantry attacks in the Second World War needed where possible the intimate support of tanks, which could devastate defensive strong points by close range, deadly fire from tank and machine guns firing from behind a shield of steel; and thus cover the movement forwards of the infantryman, who alone could ferret out the enemy from every quarter of an objective, and defend it thereafter.

The fighting, both then and later, was extremely hard. The Italians and their colonial troops fought with great energy, counter-attacking with spirit when they lost a position, seeking to infiltrate men forwards to within grenade-throwing range and to storm any exposed point taken by their enemy. Nevertheless in two days Agordat was taken. Platt then pushed on towards Keren.

The road to Keren passed through the Dongalaas Gorge – wild country in which the army could not advance until the enemy had been systematically cleared from the craggy heights which dominated the pass. These heights were tenaciously held. Every successive strong point needed a new plan, a new battle. It became a "slogging match" of a kind with which the British Army was historically familiar – but not yet in this war. Platt soon appreciated that to force his way through to Keren and dominate the Asmara Plateau would need a forward base, a methodical build up, a mountain of ammunition. One great advantage had been won. The advance into Eritrea had enabled the Royal Air Force to operate from forward airfields and henceforth greatly to assist the operation. A diversion was also created. A force composed of two Indian battalions and two Free French battalions was moved by sea from Port Sudan to Karora, on the border of Eritrea. Thence this force advanced towards Keren, and kept the eyes of the defenders from concentrating solely on Platt.

Meanwhile, nearly 1,000 miles to the south, the Italians were thrust backward by another vigorous hand. In Kenya, Lieutenant-General Sir Alan Cunningham had assembled three divisions: two African, with British-officered troops from Nigeria and the Gold Coast, as well as East African brigades of the King's African Rifles; and the 1st South African Division. On 10th February, Cunningham launched a part of his force eastwards into Italian Somaliland. The port of Kismayu was taken on 14th February. The capital, Mogadishu, was occupied on 26th February, and by 5th March Cunningham had overrun some 50,000 of the enemy (they were killed, captured or simply disappeared into the bush), and was marching north into Abyssinia.

Cunningham sent part of his force north-west to join hands with a division marching north from Kenya. With the rest he advanced from Mogadishu to Jijiga, which he entered unopposed on 20th March. His troops had now covered 1,000 miles from their starting point in Kenya. Meanwhile a force from Aden had landed at Berbera. British Somaliland was reconquered. On 6th April Cunningham entered Addis Ababa.

On 15th March, in Eritrea, Platt began his main assault towards Keren, a battle of great ferocity, fought by 4th and 5th Indian Divisions. On 26th March it ended in total victory. Platt now pushed a force to the coast at Massawa, which surrendered on 8th April. Eritrea was clear of the enemy by the middle of April. Six Italian divisions had been routed. Forty thousand prisoners and three hundred guns had been taken.

In some parts of Abyssinia the Italian régime had been less unpopular than that of the Emperor, and the Allies found little sympathy with their campaign. In the west of the country, however, a tribal rebellion against the occupying power broke out in April. It was ably fomented by Brigadier Orde Wingate, assisted by two battalions from the Sudan. The 12,000 strong Italian garrison surrendered. Only in the north, at Amba Alagi, 250 miles north of Addis Ababa, was there still resistance. Here the two British expeditions joined hands. Platt had returned the 4th Indian Division to Egypt. His work was almost done, and brilliantly. He now sent the 5th Indian Division southwards towards Amba Alagi. At the same time 1st South African Division advanced from Addis Ababa. Amba Alagi was assaulted in the first week in May, and after another bitter fight the Duke of Aosta, Viceroy and Commander-in-Chief, surrendered on 16th May.

The campaign was not quite over. Seven Italian divisions, still in the

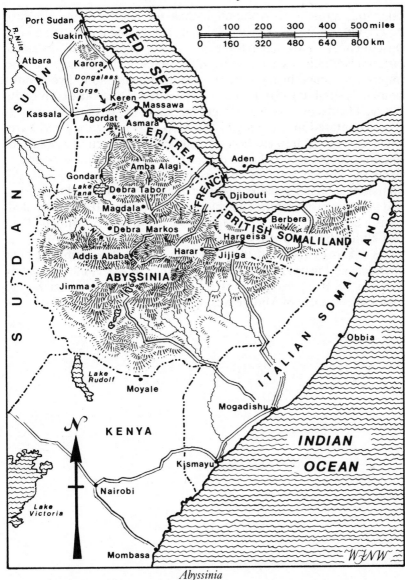

Abyssinia

region round Gondar, north-west of Addis Ababa, were defeated in a
sharp battle and surrendered to Platt in the last week in June. The
Italian East African Empire was at an end. No longer could it threaten
the vital British sea route to Egypt round the Horn of Africa.

This remarkable campaign, in which British, Indians, and Africans
from north, south, east and west all served together under British

129

command, attracted less attention than the battles of the Western Desert, but was no less sensational in its results and more lasting in its consequences. Two small forces of, in all, five Imperial divisions, starting from points separated by 1,000 miles, had invaded an Italian Empire garrisoned by a quarter of a million men, and in five months completely subdued it, and captured or destroyed the entire body of the enemy. The distances covered were immense, the terrain as testing as any encountered in the Second World War. The fighting was hard. There was no requirement here for manoeuvre and tactical mobility, of which the Italians had shown themselves indifferent masters and at which the British were by no means always to shine. Instead, the campaign had been a matter of bitter infantry fighting, and the sort of hard pounding with artillery at which both British and Italians excelled. It was a campaign, also, which tested the nerve of commanders. Platt and Cunningham had little behind them when they set off into the great spaces of Eritrea and Abyssinia. They were heavily outnumbered, both separately and in aggregate. Their achievement was a fine one, finely executed by their troops: a rare but worthy additional feather to COMPASS in the cap of Middle East Command.

7

The Wehrmacht Once Again

In the Western Desert and in East Africa the British Command – and the British, Australian, New Zealand, African and Indian divisions – had shown or were showing what they could do to the Italian Army in a fair field. The next chapters in their saga were to be against the Germans, against whom it was very necessary to win victories, if only on a small scale. Norway and France had created a certain myth of German invincibility. It had to be exploded. To manage this, however, needed not only fighting quality but favourable conditions, which were certainly not present in the campaigns of 1941. Instead the army seemed to be condemned to the habit of defeat. The false dawn of Beda Fomm was quickly to fade.

When the COMPASS offensive was halted on the Gulf of Sirte, the defence of Cyrenaica was entrusted to Lieutenant-General Sir Henry Maitland Wilson, with the 6th Australian Division and part of the newly-arrived 2nd Armoured Division. Their tanks were by no means in mint condition, but were in better shape than those of the 7th Armoured Division, whose vehicles had been almost entirely worn out by advance and battle. But within weeks all changed. The 6th Australian was relieved by the 9th Australian Division, largely untrained. Only one brigade of the 2nd Armoured Division was deployed in Cyrenaica. Wilson himself was relieved by Lieutenant-General Sir Philip Neame, and was appointed to a new and difficult task: commanding an Imperial expedition to Greece, which had been attacked by Italy on 28th October 1940, and had become Britain's ally in war against Italy thereafter. British support for Greece had taken the form of deployment of seven squadrons of the Royal Air Force to the country. Operating from Albania, which they had invaded the previous April, the Italians gained initial success, but were driven back by a series of spirited Greek counter-attacks. But these, and the winter campaign which followed, cost the Greek Army dear. Its determination to hold the Italians remained high, but, unaided, it was in no condition to resist a new attack from another quarter. The Greek Army was exhausted and at full stretch – although how exhausted was not entirely appreciated by the British Middle East Command.

Meanwhile Hitler, who had reached an agreement with Rumania whereby German forces were stationed on its soil, issued his Fuehrer Directive No. 20, on 13th December 1940. In this he stated his intention to move German divisions from Rumania into Bulgaria, and thence to the Aegean coast in Thrace, and, "should this be necessary", into the rest of Mainland Greece. Bulgaria was to be the launchpad for Operation MARITA, as it was called. It was due to start early in April 1941.

Hitler aimed to eliminate the British air bases which were seen as posing a threat to the Rumanian oil-fields. He also wished to help his Italian ally, whose progress on all fronts was manifestly disappointing. His principal if underlying motive, however, was to clear his southern flank of any possible complications before the attack on Russia (Operation BARBAROSSA), and planning directives for the two operations were issued only five days apart. Germany was not at war with Greece, and although German intentions were suspect the Greeks naturally hoped to avoid trouble from a second enemy with whom they had no direct quarrel. The Greeks were, therefore, reluctant to accept British support of a kind that might be claimed by the Germans to be incompatible with neutrality, even though such claims would have been far-fetched. Greece was fighting for her life against Italy: Britain was at war with Italy; and Germany had no common frontier with Greece. Nevertheless, Greek anxieties not to provoke Germany were understandable. The Greeks did not wish British troops – offered in a series of conversations in January and February – to arrive unless and until German troops had entered Bulgaria. But if help *was* needed, they wished it in numbers sufficient to drive out the Germans in a counter-offensive. Support, in other words, must be strong, timely, and effective, yet neither provocative nor premature. On every count this was to hope too much. It was the syndrome of Belgium once again.

An expedition to Greece could come only from Middle East Command. But Wavell, even by accepting every risk he legitimately could in the rest of his vast area of responsibility, could offer little to Greece. The British Government had made clear from before the capture of Tobruk that a Greek venture, if made, must have priority, but in February and March 1941 Wavell could – by stripping Cyrenaica to the bone – only send as a first echelon to Greece one Australian and one New Zealand division, and one armoured brigade group from the British 2nd Armoured Division. More might follow: a second Australian division and a Polish brigade were planned. It would never be more than a small force, however, and initially it would be very small indeed.

A further factor was Yugoslavia, whose geographic position was crucial to any strategic plan for the defence of Greece. If Yugoslavia were neutral and her neutrality respected by Germany, then the inner flanks of the Greek defence facing west on the Albanian front and north and east on the Salonika front could be assured. If she were friendly, the flanks could be secured by her alliance. If, however, Yugoslavia were hostile, acquiescent in German demands, or overrun by the Wehrmacht, then the defence of Greece could hardly be undertaken except upon a line well to the south, east and west of the Pindus Mountains, with both flanks resting upon the sea. As a great many diplomatic overtures failed to elicit much from the Yugoslav Government, an Anglo-Greek deployment plan was, with some difficulty, approved without any firm assumption being possible on this essential point.

If an expedition was sent, General Wilson would, it was agreed, take under his command British Imperial forces and also three Greek divisions. A defensive position would be adopted on the so-called Aliakmon Line, with its right on the Gulf of Salonika and its left on the Yugoslav border north of Veve. This line, with the barriers of Mount Olympus, the Pieria and the Vermion Mountains was of great natural strength. But it involved sacrificing Salonika and Grecian Thrace, with its three Greek divisions, which would, in all probability, be impossible to withdraw. It also depended crucially on the Yugoslav factor, since a broad valley ran from Monastir, in Yugoslavia, south across the border and past the left flank of the Aliakmon Line; while the west-facing Greek Army on the Albanian front was fifty miles away.

On 2nd March, German forces crossed the Danube, and Bulgaria joined the Axis Powers. Five days later the British acknowledged a Greek call for assistance. But nobody was under illusions. The expedition might be a failure. Its outcome must depend critically upon the performance of the Greeks – and the attitude of the Yugoslavs. Wilson's forces would be unlikely to achieve much against a full-scale assault by the German Army. If, however, things went well (and the terrain of Greece is eminently defensible), it would show the world that the British Empire did not desert its allies in need, even if the prospect of success appeared bleak. It might encourage the Turks. The policy of Yugoslavia might yet be favourably affected. In this decision all, including Wavell, fully concurred. So, to his credit, did Wilson, even after the event, when the military consequence had proved disastrous.

British troops began landing at Piraeus on 7th March, the same day the final British Government decision was made. Two days later, the Italians launched an offensive on the Albanian front. On 20th March, it was learned that, following considerable pressure from Berlin, Yugoslavia had offered to sign a pact with Germany, but on 28th March a coup d'état in Belgrade, in the name of the young King Peter, displaced his uncle the Regent, Prince Paul, and gave some hope to the British that the situation might possibly be reversed.

Meanwhile British Imperial contingents continued to arrive in Greece. The 1st Armoured Brigade, with one regiment, was sent forward towards Salonika to cover the concentration of the force – Wilson's Command, known as "W" Force – on the Aliakmon Line. Wilson deployed the 1st New Zealand Division (Major-General Freyberg) on the right of the line, where there is a narrow coastal plain between mountain and sea. In the next major gap in the mountain barrier – the Verria gap – he deployed a brigade of the 6th Australian Division (Major-General Sir Ivan Mackay). Between the two he placed a Greek regiment, in the mountains, and on the left (the north) of the Australians the balance of the Greek forces – about one and a half divisions. Behind the left of the position, at Amyntaion, Wilson established a small task force – the second tank regiment of 1st Armoured Brigade, with supporting arms from the Australian and New Zealand divisions. For a threat from the direction of Yugoslavia would mean that the left of the Aliakmon Line was in the air. The two remaining brigades of 6th Australian Division were to be held in the rear, behind the centre. The Australians and New Zealanders were combined into a corps – the Anzac Corps – under Lieutenant-General Sir Thomas Blamey. It was a thin deployment, on a front of sixty miles, and Wilson was already worrying about the security of his left flank and the threat from the Yugoslav direction before hostilities began.

Wilson was an elephantine, imperturbable man, known throughout the army in which he had served over forty years as "Jumbo". He was fifty-nine, older than most field commanders even at that time, and he was thought by some to have lost his "edge". An indefatigable correspondent, his letters show a meticulous if somewhat ponderous mind. Wilson's was not a character to leave much to chance. He was well read in military history and strategy, cautious, conservative, tolerant and essentially sound. Although unlikely to bring off daring manoeuvres, he was also unlikely to lose an army which could be saved, which in the conditions of the Greek campaign was the more important quality.

A forward dump with seven days' supplies was established at Amyntaion, where Wilson had his task force watching the left flank. Road and rail communications were exiguous, and maintenance

Greece

difficult. Throughout March Wilson's troops moved up to their concentration areas, but part of the 6th Australian Division was still to come when, on 7th April 1941, Germany declared war simultaneously on Yugoslavia and Greece. Operation MARITA had begun.

Twelfth German Army (Field Marshal List) advanced from Bulgaria with three army corps, XVIII, XXX, and XL, two of which were

135

directed southwards to the Aegean Sea, and swept aside the three Greek divisions in their path. The Germans entered Salonika on 9th April. Wilson withdrew the 1st Armoured Brigade from Thrace to the main front at Edessa, and thence, to strengthen his left, to join the task force he had established at Amyntaion.

The righthand German Corps, XL Corps, with three divisions, advanced into Southern Yugoslavia, its progress little impeded by Yugoslav resistance, and Wilson looked with renewed concern at the gap in the hills south of Monastir. So far there had been no German move across the Yugoslav-Greek frontier, but it was clearly imminent, and he did not believe that the Aliakmon Line could then be held. On 9th April, two days after the invasion began, Wilson decided that the Aliakmon position must be evacuated. The troops were digging in, to retire would be immediately discouraging, the line itself was strong. But Wilson was not prepared to be outflanked. He forecast a succession of withdrawals. His information, greatly expanded by the information on German plans and intentions being received through ULTRA, was excellent and without it – like most commanders in the Second World War – his situation would have been even more parlous. It was a remarkable fact that because of early British acquisition of the ability to read German coded messages British plans were often made with an intimate knowledge of enemy intentions which, at least in theory, should make the conduct of battle relatively simple. But warning of the enemy's disposition and intentions is only a step on the road to victory. German moves may have been more accurately predicted by this means than the generality of public or soldiers were ever permitted to suppose. But these moves had still to be opposed by sufficient skilful and determined forces. To turn information to successful account strength is needed. Wilson was already discouraged by what he saw of the Greek forces – they were ill-equipped, tired and poorly organised. His original deployment had "sandwiched" Greek units between Australians and New Zealanders, because he reckoned they were more used to mountain fighting than the troops of the British Empire. The device had its disadvantages. It made command more complicated, coordination doubly difficult. With the anxious precedent of Gort in Flanders no doubt always in mind, Wilson was determined not to leave his withdrawals until too late nor to place his force at the mercy of the movement of Allies over whom he had no control. He ordered the occupation of a position further south, based on a line from Mount Olympus through Servia to the mountains at Klisoura. The 1st Armoured Brigade was ordered to Grevena, behind the inner flank.

On 10th April, the German XL Corps, composed of one Panzer, one

136

SS and one infantry division, crossed the Yugoslav-Greek frontier south of Monastir. The divisions were to operate in conjunction with XVIII Corps, driving down from Salonika between mountain and sea with a further four divisions, including one Panzer and two mountain divisions. "W" Force was facing a strong enemy, an enemy so composed as to have cross-country mobility on tracks where the terrain permitted and on foot where it did not: an enemy likely to have his vehicles and equipment in prime condition, while the British tanks were already suffering from such track wear, spares shortage and weakness that when they broke down they were frequently abandoned; and an enemy, above all, fired with the spirit of the offensive, the strongest form of war. The enemy's aim was simple. In his Directive No. 27, issued immediately before the campaign opened, Hitler had written, "The object of this operation will be, by a quick breakthrough in the direction of Larissa, to encircle and annihilate the enemy forces there, and to prevent the establishment of a new defensive front."

Wilson had no intention of being encircled and annihilated. He was, however, finding that the coordination of withdrawal between Greek and Imperial forces was particularly difficult. On 14th April, "W" Force was on its new position. The 1st Armoured Brigade, harried by the enemy armour during the withdrawal, had given a good account of itself and destroyed a number of enemy tanks, but mechanical failure was alarmingly reducing the British tank state. On 15th April, both wings of the German advance fell on "W" Force. The most savage attacks were in the east, where the leading divisions of XVIII Corps pressed the New Zealand division hard, and Wilson reinforced it with an Australian brigade and held the Vale of Tempe running between Mount Olympus and Mount Ossa towards Larissa. Larissa was the vital junction through which all north-south traffic east of the Pindus Mountains would pass.

On 16th April, Wilson met Papagos, Greek dictator and Commander-in-Chief. The general situation was deteriorating fast. On the Albanian front the Greeks could hold no longer. Their army in Epirus, west of the Pindus Mountains, was collapsing. The Greeks had been, from the start, lamentably ill-equipped. They and their material were now equally exhausted. Papagos himself suggested that the British evacuate their troops from Greece. Wilson was not entirely surprised. He had preserved a calm front, but had by now little belief in anything but an effort to save his expedition. He was concerned to withdraw to a line which he could hold with British Imperial forces alone – for he reckoned that Greek conduct was likely to be unpredictable – and to select a line which would cover ports and beaches of embarkation if, as it surely must, it came to that. He chose a line at Thermopylae, where, north of Mount Parnassus, he thought the gateway to Attica could be held. "W" Force had withdrawn from the Mount Olympus position by the night of 18th April, but the withdrawal of the left wing was absolutely dependent on the New Zealanders holding their positions on the right.

By now the Luftwaffe had gained complete control, and movement by road could only be by night. The effect of total enemy air superiority upon an outnumbered and retreating army was, once again, shown to be devastating. The movement of supply columns was ceaselessly attacked from the air, with the usual effect upon morale. Drivers would leave vehicles immediately an aircraft was heard overhead – a most understandable reaction, hard to avert without special measures which "W" Force had not time, experience or facilities to put into effect. By 20th April, bruised but intact, "W" Force was back on the Thermopylae Line. It was perfectly clear to the Anzac Corps Commander, Blamey, that this line could not be held for long.

On 19th April, Wavell visited Greece. When he left, British evacuation had been agreed at a meeting at the Tatoi Palace by the King and Government of Greece. On 21st April, the Greek Army in Epirus capitulated. It was now a question of withdrawing through a succession of covering positions to ports or beaches selected for the rescue of "W" Force, and these included some in the Peloponnese, further from the enemy's air bases, as well as some in Attica. Movement to the Peloponnese meant crossing the Corinth Canal, holding the bridge over it, and destroying it at the last. On 26th April, in mid-evacuation, two German parachute battalions dropped to seize the bridge and to enable their pursuing forces to break into the Peloponnese. The bridge was, nevertheless, blown, and both from Attica and Sparta the soldiers slipped away. At Kalamata, the ultimate port in the Peloponnese, the pursuing German column caught up with the evacuation, and, after a fight, 7,000 were taken prisoner. Nevertheless over 50,000 were taken off by the Royal Navy. The soldiers' spirits remained remarkably high, fortified by the extraordinary and moving expressions of gratitude they received from the Greeks, right to the end. Trouble and risks were taken to save portable equipment, but all guns and vehicles were lost. By 1st May, the Greek campaign was over.

The evacuation of the Greek mainland left one Aegean disaster still to be played out.

When Italy invaded Greece, the British, as allies, assumed responsibility for the defence of Crete, not least because an Italian air base on the island could extend formidable hostile air power in the Eastern Mediterranean, and towards Egypt. Crete stands sentinel over the Aegean Sea, and Suda Bay could provide a convenient fuelling place for both the Royal Navy and the Royal Air Force. Therefore, Crete, if ever threatened, should be held.

Although the island had three airfields – Heraklion, Retimo and Maleme – only Heraklion had any of the facilities of an air base. The others were air strips only, although a small number of fighter aircraft were deployed to Maleme, to defend the harbour (Maleme is only ten miles west of Canea, the capital and port at the neck of the Akrotiri Peninsula, east of which is Suda Bay). The British 14th Brigade composed of Regular battalions, and a small number of anti-aircraft guns were stationed on the island. To deter the Italians and to reassure the Greeks this might have been adequate. It was not enough, however, if a serious threat developed, as soon it did.

When, at the beginning of 1941, German intentions in the Balkans were becoming clearer and the British began to consider assistance to Greece, the question of Crete assumed a new significance. If the Germans were to attack Greece (on which British help was predicated), and if that attack was successful (as was gloomily recognised as not improbable), then Crete would be exposed to the full fury of the Luftwaffe operating from Greek airfields. And there would probably be an attempt to invade the island, under the Luftwaffe's cover.

These deductions did not, however, lead to increased tempo in the preparation of Crete for war, a failure for which Wavell has been justly criticised. No works were undertaken which could have protected aircraft on the ground, nor were the Cretans organised, although their goodwill was heartening and their martial spirit undoubted. Six different officers in succession were placed in command in Crete, and into none of them did Wavell seem to breathe fire or purpose. Initially the threat was at two removes. It did not appear vivid until the Germans invaded Greece, nor imminent until they emerged as conquerors. The attention and resources of Middle East Command in the first months of 1941 had many claims, but if Crete was as important as was soon to be confirmed by the British Government and by Wavell himself, its importance merited earlier attention. The island was there all the time. It did not rise, like Aphrodite from the waves, at the end of April after the fall of Greece.

By then, however belatedly, the threat to Crete was fully appreciated. An attack would, it was accurately assessed, come from airborne assault, followed (it was thought) by a seaborne expedition. Wavell signalled to London that he assumed Crete would be held, to which Churchill warmly responded that "it would indeed". Wavell visited Crete on 30th April and confirmed the order. Crete would, whatever the difficulties, be defended to the last. Whether this was strategically sound can be debated. Crete played little subsequent part in the war. It is certain, however, that both Germans and British rated its importance high, and if both were in error, brave men on both sides died for it.

Most of the British and Imperial troops evacuated from Greece were taken first to Crete, in order that ships could be turned round quickly for the next load. At the beginning of May, therefore, the garrison of Crete was augmented by thousands of men, many without arms and some both demoralised and leaderless. Even three weeks later several thousand soldiers were still without weapons. But there also arrived from Greece Australian and, above all, New Zealand units, formations of exceptional fighting quality, once order had been reimposed, and once a sense of urgency (which took time) had been instilled. Indeed, the island, sunny, beautiful and hitherto unscarred by the current war induced at first a relaxed and holiday mood in which the next logical step seemed a return to Egypt, after an agreeable respite from life and war.

The New Zealanders formed the majority of the fighting troops, and the Commander of the New Zealand Division, Major-General Freyberg, was placed in command of the defence of the island. He received telegrams from Churchill and from Wavell, full of exhortation and encouragement. He received too little else, although he did not complain. Freyberg was a man built on heroic lines, like Gort a holder of the Victoria Cross won in the First World War, in which he had been nine times wounded; and, like Gort, a man simple and direct in all his dealings, one who inspired the immediate liking as well as respect of fighting men. Brought up in New Zealand, he had joined the British Army in 1914 but retired from it between the wars. He was called from retirement to command the New Zealand Expeditionary Forces in the Second World War, a man by this time brave rather than original, more rock-like than dynamic. He now received the most difficult assignment of his career, a task to break a heart less lion-like than his.

Freyberg regarded the defence of Crete as probably a forlorn hope, particularly as it was made clear to him that nothing could be done to reduce the Luftwaffe's absolute supremacy in the skies. In his stolid and loyal way he therefore got on with his job, with misgivings he never allowed to infect the spirit of his troops. The first and urgent need was to sort out his forces. In addition to large numbers of disorganised and unarmed men he had the 14th (British) Brigade, a strong brigade of Regular battalions, already in garrison, as yet unblooded in action but unshaken by the experiences of Greece. He created a composite force from the Mobile Naval Base Defence Organisation – primarily a force manning coastal or static anti-aircraft guns. Soldiers from various corps, who could be, were armed, together with some Greeks and stiffened by one battalion from the 14th Brigade. Freyberg had a much weakened Australian brigade – 19th Brigade – from the 6th Australian Division, from Greece. And he had two brigades from his own New Zealand Division, the rest of the division having been evacuated direct to Egypt. Freyberg also commanded a number of Greek regiments, some almost without arms and ammunition at first; regiments whose fighting potential tended to be underestimated, in a way not uncommon among British military men faced with customs utterly different from their own, but whose conduct was often both valiant and successful.

Freyberg's plan was imposed by the topography of Crete. The four vulnerable areas were the three airfields, Maleme, Retimo and Heraklion, and the port and capital town of Canea and anchorage of Suda Bay. To each of these was assigned a force, aimed to be as self-sufficient as possible. One road only, along the north coast, connected these points, and it would clearly be painfully easy for the Luftwaffe to prevent day communication between them. There was very little transport. A central reserve would probably never reach a threatened point. Each garrison must be able to fight off and counter-attack an invader, using only the slender resources that Freyberg could allot. The forces defending Canea from the west and those at Maleme were sufficiently near to be able, possibly, to assist each other; and these two areas were, therefore, grouped under the command of the New Zealand Brigadier Puttick, commanding the New Zealand Division, while Freyberg himself commanded all forces on the island.

At Maleme and west of Canea, under Puttick, were two New Zealand brigades, 5th (Brigadier Hargest) and 10th – the latter an improvised formation, under New Zealand command (Colonel Kippenberger), with some New Zealanders and two Greek regiments. In the same area was 4th New Zealand Brigade (Brigadier Inglis) in reserve. Defending the Suda Bay-Canea area itself was the composite force, under Major-General Weston, Royal Marines. At Retimo, and responsible also for Georgopolis, ten miles to the west, was the Australian 19th Brigade, under Brigadier Vasey. At Heraklion was the British 14th Brigade (Brigadier Chappell). As information became ever clearer that the Wehrmacht would make a mighty effort for Crete, the

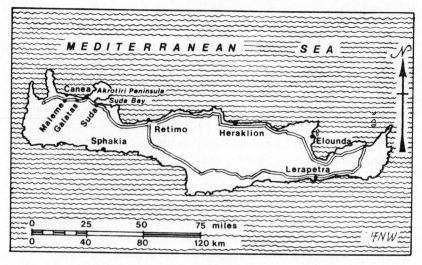

Crete

preparations of the defenders intensified. Lack of earlier work could not be made good; but the insouciance of the first days disappeared. Hard work, careful reconnaissance, and contingency planning were undertaken. Equipment arrived from Egypt – even a few light tanks and six Matildas were shipped to Crete, in woeful condition but deadly against parachutists if committed quickly: they were divided by Freyberg between the various sectors. The worst shortage was of communicating equipment. The fact that commanders could seldom convey information or orders to each other and their men increased the customary fog of war to an intolerable level, and played a tragic part in the fate now to befall the defenders of Crete.

On 25th April, Hitler issued his Directive No. 28: Crete was to be occupied, to provide a "base for air warfare against Great Britain in the Eastern Mediterranean". The operation would be the responsibility of the Luftwaffe, of which the German parachute troops were part. General Student's Fliegerkorps XI would carry out the assault from Greece.

Student's plan was straightforward. He believed that if he committed his entire parachute and gliderborne force to the attack on all three airfields on the first day he would certainly capture one of them. He could then bring in powered aircraft with reinforcements – three rifle regiments from 5th and 6th Mountain Divisions, assigned for the operation. With these and his own airborne soldiers he was confident of completing the conquest of the island, but he would be supported by a

142

seaborne expedition, including elements of the 5th Panzer Division. For the initial attack Student's command included the 7th Air Division, of three parachute regiments, each of three battalions, and a special Assault Regiment of three further battalions. Assault from the air would be preceded by intensive bombing by the aircraft of Fliegerkorps VIII – over 430 bombers and dive-bombers, with over 230 fighters. To oppose this Freyberg had no aircraft (the few undamaged Royal Air Force fighters were withdrawn before the battle, having suffered severely in a gallant but hopeless struggle against odds: if left they could only have been destroyed on the ground), and only thirty-two heavy and thirty-six light anti-aircraft guns for the whole island.

On 14th May, the Luftwaffe began its attacks on the airfields, and kept up this preliminary and attritional bombardment for six days. Freyberg was in little doubt about what was coming. Intelligence, assisted by ULTRA, was good. As a result of this, the timing and direction of the German assault was made known to the defending commander in a manner remarkable in the whole history of war.

Freyberg made what he correctly reckoned was his last tour of the defensive positions on 16th May and signalled to Wavell that he felt "reasonably confident". He felt that his men could deal with airborne assault, but was particularly concerned about Maleme. There was nothing to be done about the devastating power of the Luftwaffe, but Freyberg felt that he had arranged all he could with the resources he possessed. His men were in good trim.

On 20th May, a particularly heavy attack on all airfields and the defences around them began at dawn. To the defenders it was the most terrible experience yet. Anti-aircraft positions were suppressed by saturation bombing. The air was filled with a choking dust, reducing visibility and clouding the senses. The Luftwaffe appeared everywhere. At eight o'clock the sky above Maleme, south-west of Canea, above Retimo and over Heraklion was suddenly and astonishingly filled with the silent presence of gliders and floating parachutes. Operation MERKUR, the invasion of Crete, had started.

Student planned to drop four regiments, one each near Maleme, Canea, Retimo and Heraklion. His aim was to land the regiments where there were no defending troops, to concentrate and to seize the objective. As soon as possible, and certainly on the following day, the Mountain Division regiments would fly in to a captured airfield. Student gave himself no airborne reserve, but as one of the flights did not take off as ordered he found himself with 600 parachutists fortuitously in hand on the second day.

The assault was in many places entirely unsuccessful. Some of the drops were, as planned, on unoccupied ground but many took place among the Australian, New Zealand, British and Greek defenders. Instant and savage close quarter fighting followed, much of it with the bayonet, all over the area of assault. The German parachute troops suffered very heavy losses. They were, however, able to concentrate some – albeit gravely diminished – force at each of their points of attack; but their casualties and the vigour of the defence took much of the sting from MERKUR within hours of its launch, and was unexpected and shattering to the Germans. In one area, however, German success was early, avoidable and just enough to tilt the balance of the brief and bloody campaign. At Maleme the German Assault Regiment was in possession of the airfield by dawn on 21st May. Without communication, and without accurate knowledge of the situation in his own battalion area, the local New Zealand battalion commander believed the worst and withdrew from the airfield and the high ground commanding it during the first night. There was insufficient locally deployed strength to right the situation. On 21st May, Student's uncovenanted reserve battalion was dropped at Maleme, to restore to the assault troops some of the strength which had almost drained away the previous day. Later on that day transport aircraft began to arrive, as the paratroops forced the New Zealanders ever further from the airfield. A counter-attack to retake it – the only hope – was deferred and then too weakly put in. It was the decisive moment for Crete.

In all areas fighting was bitter, and initially, at least, on approximately level terms. The small packets of tanks were committed but their condition and their numbers were inadequate to affect the battle decisively anywhere. They broke down or were destroyed by air attack, for when some sort of rough lines formed between attackers and defenders the Luftwaffe was again able to bomb without fear of hitting their own men, and the incessant, remorseless attacks began to have their inevitable effect. Among the fighting men, however, spirit remained high, and except at Maleme the defenders held their own. They felt they were masters of the situation. But Maleme was the key. The battle turned upon it. A small seaborne follow-up expedition had been routed by the Royal Navy in the darkness, for although the waters around Crete were dominated by the Luftwaffe in daylight, the navy could intercept during the short hours of night. How long this could have continued is speculative. British ship losses off Crete were appalling. But in the first and only week of the campaign, if the Germans were to build up enough strength in Crete to win the battle they had to come by air and hold an airfield; and they did.

With Maleme in their hands the main German effort was now made in the west of the island. The New Zealand defenders of Maleme were temporarily withdrawn to reserve in the area of Canea, whence a front was formed to the west. The village of Galatas, three miles west of Canea, was unsuccessfully attacked by seven German battalions, then taken, then retaken by New Zealand counter-attack on 25th May. Fighting was as hard as anywhere in the war – close quarters, hand-to-hand, man-to-man. Everywhere and on both sides casualties were mounting. And everywhere the Luftwaffe ranged the skies supreme.

Freyberg's situation was grim. In the vital sector his troops were outnumbered and hard pressed. The enemy had a place of entry for reinforcements, while Freyberg's forces could be neither significantly reinforced nor supplied from outside Crete. It has been said that he remained for too long apprehensive over a threat from the sea which did not materialise, and thus dispersed his forces unnecessarily and held back troops from immediate committal to the battle against Student's paratroopers. In fact, through ULTRA, Freyberg was perfectly aware of German intentions. Besides, he had no right to assume that the Royal Navy could indefinitely operate north of Crete. Sooner or later the Germans could, if they chose and needed, come by sea; for the Luftwaffe dominated land and water alike. On 26th May, Freyberg told Wavell that the fall of Crete could only be a matter of time. On 27th May, Wavell informed the Chiefs of Staff in London that he had ordered evacuation.

It was a bitter blow. 14th Brigade at Heraklion were still strongly holding. They embarked from there during the night of 28th May, only to lose 200 men from a single battalion when the ship in which they were taken off was sunk. The Australians at Retimo received no orders, could not be rescued, were cut off and ultimately ordered to surrender. They had fought magnificently and were unbeaten. The New Zealanders from the western sector, after no less valiant a struggle, made their way with the majority of Freyberg's men south across the mountains at the waist of Crete to the little fishing port of Sphakia, where all but 5,000 were taken off. There was hard fighting to the last, but the Germans were as exhausted as their opponents. As in all such tragic conclusions, instances among the withdrawing troops of indiscipline and a breakdown of order were redeemed by many an act of heroism and by the steadfast obedience of the majority. The rearguard was embarked on 1st June. The Royal Navy could do no more. They had lost off Crete three cruisers and six destroyers sunk; one aircraft carrier, three battleships, six cruisers and seven destroyers had been damaged. They had lost over 1,800 men killed. In Crete nearly 12,000 men, of all Services and all four nations involved, passed into German captivity.

The total casualties of the British, Australians and New Zealanders in Crete itself was 3,479, of which over half, including 612 British soldiers, were killed. German losses were over 6,000, of which nearly 4,000 were killed or missing: the flower of their parachute troops and many of their best officers in the new Arm had fallen. Crete, like Norway in 1940, was the scene of a campaign where the actions of very small forces had large strategic consequences. Yet Crete was a defeat of very different character, although like Norway, and France and Belgium the end was evacuation and bitterness.

In the earlier disasters the German soldier had, in most cases, achieved a certain moral superiority. Not only in air support and in material but in tactical skill, fitness, discipline and leadership the enemy had proved superior, and the British Army knew it. In Crete, on the other hand, although the enemy fought with very great skill and energy, he suffered very heavy losses and was everywhere met by defenders as vigorous and ruthless. This applied to the New Zealanders, who were the majority. It applied to the Australians. It applied to the Greeks. It also applied to the British. When the British Regular battalions of 14th Brigade, or the British gunners serving the pathetically inadequate numbers of guns, met the enemy they held their own and avenged their wounds with interest. They fought savagely and with tenacity. They were well led, at regimental level at least. This was of great psychological importance. The soldier did not feel he was faced by a better man. He had less confidence, however, in those on high who had placed him in a situation with so inglorious an outcome. The British Army might be recovering some of its hardness, but it needed victories.

Could Crete have ended in a British success? The Germans were only able to attain local superiority by the seizure of Maleme Airfield. Since Maleme might not have been lost – its defenders were neither outnumbered overall, nor downhearted, nor were they unsupported – might Crete not have been held for the British cause, had the German Assault Parachute Regiment attacking Maleme been destroyed, or its power of further offensive action been neutralised by the sort of vigorous offensive and counter-attack which was occurring in other parts of the island? The Germans were certainly very tired.

Freyberg reckoned that the effect of the Luftwaffe's incessant attacks was so devastating that it would irresistibly wear down the defence; and that soldiers could not endure that punishment beyond a limited period. Furthermore, German control of the skies meant that enemy supplies and reinforcements could arrive by landing or air drop, while it virtually isolated our own forces in Crete. Nothing could reach Freyberg's men by air. Seaborne supply was becoming impracticable. The movement of ships by daylight – necessary for some hours if they were to reach the northern ports – could surely not be envisaged for long. In those circumstances it could only be a matter of time before Crete must fall.

On the other hand, although neither Freyberg nor Wavell could know it, Hitler had already fixed the date of 22nd June for the German invasion of Russia, a date later than originally hoped. To attain the quick victory in Russia which was essential would demand all Germany's resources. It is possible that, had Crete held, and some sort of exhausted stalemate been temporarily achieved in the olive groves outside Canea and Heraklion and in the hills south of Maleme, the power of the Luftwaffe might have been relaxed by claims on it elsewhere, and British resupply of the island again become possible without grievous loss at sea. Had that been so, reinforcements might have turned the scale. It would have been the turn of Student's men to be isolated from the world. As with all hindsight the issue must remain speculative. What is sure is that the immediate effect upon the troops was depressing in the extreme. The army was once again being rescued, taken off by sea after a wretched defeat. Despairing self-mockery, in the British way, covered raw flesh. The British Army were known as "the evacuees". Once again they were losers, men being accustomed now by habit not to win. To all involved it was a dreadful experience, all the worse to men who felt they had been unbeaten in the field.

An equally dreadful experience had taken place in North Africa. Before the invasion of Greece, an enemy offensive, led and inspired by a new and very different enemy commander, had begun in Cyrenaica. By the end of MERKUR, the occupation of Crete, Rommel and the Afrika Korps stood at the gates of Egypt. The fruits of O'Connor's valiant offensive had been lost. The false dawn in Africa was indeed over.

After the triumph of Beda Fomm the victorious troops had been withdrawn for other service. The Australians were prepared for the Greek adventure. The 7th Armoured Division returned to Egypt for re-equipment. No imminent danger was expected from Tripolitania. The Italians had suffered severely. Rommel was known to have arrived in Tripoli, and advance parties of German units were on their way: the Germans planned to send some limited assistance to their Italian allies, and their opponents knew it, but factors of distance, supply, movement and acclimatisation combined to convince Wavell that no serious attack could take place for several months. There might be probes – Rommel was known to be a vigorous commander. Nothing serious, like an attempt to take Benghazi, need be anticipated. The desert flank of the Middle East Command would not be unduly troubled for a while. The assumption was queried in London but it suited all to accept it, for Wavell was being urged to find as many troops as possible for Greece, and his campaign in East Africa was under way. Wavell thus reduced the forces in Cyrenaica to what he regarded as the acceptable minimum. A static Cyrenaica Command was established, under Lieutenant-General Sir Philip Neame.

Neame was yet another commander who held the Victoria Cross. With a fine fighting reputation, he had little experience of senior command – an inevitable and unimportant defect in a trade in which a man either possesses or does not the "divine spark", and needs originality and will-power more than practice. But he had little chance to find his feet.

Neame was given 9th Australian Division, two of whose brigades had just been replaced by two different and largely untrained formations. He was also given 2nd Armoured Division (Major-General Gambier-Parry).

The Australian division was short of transport. Infantry formations, in the desert war, could defend or attack strong points: defiles, ports, particular features. For manoeuvre, however, every army had to depend on troops who could simultaneously fight and move – and engage the enemy over the long ranges the desert made possible. The desert war demanded tanks, mobile anti-tank guns, with infantry used only for specific infantry tasks if and when they arose: the desert war demanded armour. Neame's armour was 2nd Armoured Division.

The division was, however, wholly inadequate to its task. It had two armoured brigades, of which one was sent to Greece, with many of the division's support echelons. The other – 3rd Armoured Brigade – was now Neame's only tank force. It had three tank regiments, two of them equipped with light tanks and captured Italian M13s, and one regiment of cruiser tanks of which twenty-three were fit to run. All vehicles were in poor condition. The division and its commander were new to the desert. More important, they had not experienced the sort of hard, merciless training to which Hobart had subjected 7th Armoured

Division. Rommel himself had never before been to Africa, and habitually brought German units into battle in the desert immediately they disembarked at Tripoli, with notable success. What was lacking, too often, in British formations was not knowledge of the desert so much as understanding of the mechanics of war itself, and experience of working together as a team of all arms. And in the case of 2nd Armoured Division the situation was gravely exacerbated by the state of the division's equipment.

Neame was ordered by Wavell to be prepared to withdraw if attacked – a contingency the latter did not expect. Troops should fight a delaying action back to Benghazi. Benghazi itself could be abandoned if that were necessary in order to preserve the force from being cut off. Hindsight is always easy, but it must be said that this permissive concept seemed to neglect both the known boldness of the enemy and the geography of Cyrenaica. Cyrenaica could be held against attack from the west by troops in position on the borders of Tripolitania, which was where O'Connor had reached. Immediately that position was surrendered, however, a defender was bound to be faced with the threat of a bold outflanking movement of the kind O'Connor had just performed, in reverse. Such a move must cut off troops fighting "a delaying action back to Benghazi". It must inevitably lead to Mechili and Derna. It could only be dealt with by a force able to manoeuvre on favourable terms on the southern, desert flank, south of the Jebel Akhdar. Without such a force – and 2nd Armoured Division was pathetically inadequate to provide it – there was no defensible position east of Mersa Brega on the Gulf of Sirte, where Neame deployed the (very weak) support group of 2nd Armoured Division, with the division's 3rd Armoured Brigade some miles in rear and inland, in support. Neame ordered Gambier-Parry that this support group (one battalion, with some guns) must block the coast road as long as possible. 3rd Armoured Brigade must not be committed without Neame's permission, but was designed to take the enemy in flank if he attempted to turn the blocking position. 9th Australian Division was deployed to the area of Benghazi, with one brigade detached to garrison Tobruk. So it was on 31st March when the British first met the Afrika Korps.

Immediately Rommel landed at Tripoli on 12th February he flew to the front to inspect for himself this terrain which the Italians told him was so hostile. He also set in hand the movement eastwards of German troops immediately they arrived. If they disembarked during the night or early morning they were on their way toward the Cyrenaican frontier the same afternoon. "Speed is the essence of war," wrote Sun Tzu, and Rommel was that principle incarnate. Rommel was given command of Italian motorised troops – he interpreted the term to give him full command over all Italian formations committed to the field army at the front. With similar firmness he interpreted his nominal subordination to the Italian Commander-in-Chief, General Gariboldi, as having little relevance to the needs of the hour. There must, he decided, be an attack on the British in Cyrenaica at the earliest possible moment.

Rommel made up his mind that such an attack must have distant objectives and ambitious aims. He himself would lead it from the front and set the pace. He had in mind the Suez Canal as a finishing line. The Italian authorities in Tripoli and Rome, like the German General Staff in Berlin, were determined that he should not overreach himself and drag them into overcommitment. They drew comfort, as did Wavell, from the logistic difficulties which would surely and sharply limit an advance. Rommel kept his counsel. He reckoned – rightly – that quick victories and attractive possibilities of exploitation would bring Hitler to his support. Success would be reinforced, boldness approved. He had in hand the first German division to arrive – 5th Light Division – and three Italian divisions, including some tanks. 5th Light Division had about 120 German tanks, and had strong anti-tank gun units, including some of the new 88 millimetre converted heavy anti-aircraft guns. He had the promise of 15th Panzer Division. But the latter had not yet arrived when, at 10 a.m. on 31st March, Rommel sent 5th Light Division into the attack at Mersa Brega.

The sweeping of the British and Australians from Cyrenaica in the first fortnight of April 1941 had a grim inevitability about it. The armoured strength of the opposing sides made the outcome probable. Against the 120 tanks of 5th Light Division, and the Italian divisions' light tanks and M13s, 2nd Armoured Division could muster twenty-five light tanks and twenty-two cruisers, numbers reduced within days to single figures, largely by mechanical defect. But the handling of the opposing forces provides a painful contrast. Rommel had the initiative and kept it. His enemy from the first danced to his tune, treading a sadly elephantine measure. And Rommel had superb energy. His command responded to the leadership of one will and one mind that knew what it wanted.

The first attack at Mersa Brega was sufficient to lever the British out of positions from which they had anyway been directed to withdraw if there were the smallest risk of envelopment. The northwards movement of the British began, towards Benghazi. On 2nd April, 5th Light

Division took Agedabia, forty miles from their starting point. On the same day Wavell visited Neame. Neame's concept was that 9th Australian Division should cover the coast road along which their own withdrawal, should withdrawal be forced, would take place; and that 2nd Armoured Division should cover the desert flank – which meant that it should retain the ability to manoeuvre against an enemy seeking to cut across south of the Jebel, and should cover Msus, where dumps supplied the division. This concept certainly provided for the most likely contingency – that the Germans would primarily seek to outflank, by advancing south of the Jebel Akhdar. It did, however, leave the coast road south of Benghazi clear for the enemy. Wavell, who still seemed persuaded that the enemy could not be aiming at any more ambitious success than to take Benghazi, countermanded Neame's order to the armoured division, and instead directed that its task must be to impose maximum delay on the enemy's advance to Benghazi. The coastal road must be covered at all times. The peculiarity of this order is not diminished by the fact that it arrived too late to be obeyed. At the same time Wavell sent for O'Connor, from Egypt, and planned to relieve Neame of his command.

On 3rd April, the tanks of 3rd Armoured Brigade, 2nd Armoured Division's only formation and the only British armoured force in Cyrenaica, had been very sharply diminished in numbers since the start of the fight. A few had been lost in action against 5th Light Division at Mersa Brega. Most had broken down. Gambier-Parry reported that his armour was being reduced by one tank for every ten miles of movement. The division was also very short of petrol, and was dispersed over a wide area of desert north of Agedabia and east of the coast road. This slender and puzzled force was subjected to the orders of its own Divisional Commander, Gambier-Parry; of the General in charge of the Cyrenaica Command, Neame; of the Commander-in-Chief, Middle East Command, Wavell – with O'Connor summoned to support. Such an arrangement would have stultified the attempts of a much fitter formation. By 3rd April, 2nd Armoured Division had little fighting capacity left as a coherent formation of all arms. If the Germans chose to drive across the chord of the Cyrenaican arc there was little to stop them.

Rommel had already determined to do so. On 3rd April, the reports he received convinced him that the British would not, and probably could not, fight for Cyrenaica. He had divided his force into four mixed columns of tanks, armoured cars, motor cyclists, anti-tank guns and motorised infantry. He set these columns, under able subordinates, on roughly parallel thrust lines. He already had part of 5th Light Division

151

marching north-east across the desert towards Tengeder, south of
Mechili, on a wider sweep than even O'Connor had performed. He
had taken Agedabia and Zuetina on the coast. He now set in hand both
the advance by the coast road, and two "hooks" – towards Antelat and
Msus, and from Benghazi to Charruba; hooks which would meet at
Mechili and be exploited towards Derna and Tobruk. His troops
entered Benghazi on 4th April, and next day his columns reached
Tengeder, Msus and Charruba.

O'Connor, meanwhile, summoned from Egypt, had persuaded
Wavell that there should be no change of command in the middle of the
battle, but that he would remain with Neame and give him what help he
could. On 6th April, Neame was away from his Headquarters when
information reached it confirming what O'Connor had believed from
the start – that the Germans and Italians were embarked on a great
outflanking movement. O'Connor, in Neame's name, gave orders for a
general withdrawal and for all that remained of 2nd Armoured Division
to concentrate at Mechili. The 3rd Armoured Brigade had, in response
to at least some of the orders which reached it, withdrawn from
Agedabia to Msus, and on 5th April had moved north towards
Charruba at the same time as a column of the Africa Korps approached
from the west. The Brigade Commander decided that he had insufficient petrol to reach Mechili, and instead led what was left of his
formation to the coast road in the hope of reaching Derna. The 9th
Australian Division and 3rd Armoured Brigade were thus sharing one
road to Derna. In Rommel's path in the desert to the south of the Jebel
was little but the Headquarters of 2nd Armoured Division (which had
received and obeyed the order to move to Mechili) and 3rd Indian
Motor Brigade, a formation which had been added to Cyrenaica
Command and which consisted of infantry riding in unarmoured
trucks without supporting arms or anti-tank weapons of any kind.
Gambier-Parry and most of his Headquarters, together with 3rd
Indian Brigade, were taken prisoner at Mechili. O'Connor and Neame
ran into a German patrol south of Derna on 7th April and were
captured. On the same day a German column reached the coast road
east of Derna. It was Beda Fomm in reverse.

By then, however, some sort of order was being imposed on the
chaotic conditions of the battlefield. The 9th Australian Division had
withdrawn east of Derna and were untrapped and astride the road
between Derna and Tobruk. They were moved into Tobruk itself,
whither a fourth Australian brigade and a regiment of tanks were
despatched from Egypt by sea. Lieutenant-General Beresford-Peirse
was placed in command of a reconstituted "Western Desert Force"

with an incomplete 6th Division, and a mobile force under Brigadier Gott. One of the division's brigades, 22nd Guards Brigade, was deployed to Bardia, and the mobile force formed small columns, each based on a company of infantry, some field guns and light tanks, to range the Libyan frontier, and to sting and harass the exhausted columns of the German-Italian advance when they appeared. Rommel noted on 10th April that the pursuit should be pressed as far as the Suez Canal, but his opponents were recovering something of their balance and his troops were very tired. He determined to attack Tobruk while simultaneously pressing eastwards. He was successful in neither object.

The first attack on Tobruk was made on 13th April. A small lodgement was made in the long perimeter, but the attack was held by a skilful and aggressive defence. Given the chance to come to grips with the enemy troops face to face, the Australians met them with the same vigour as their compatriots in Greece and Crete. A second attack was made by the Italians three days later. It met with no greater success. Rommel's men could go no further. Tobruk was invested, and again unsuccessfully attacked on 30th April. Positions were established on the frontier. 15th Panzer Division arrived in Tripoli, was deployed eastwards and took over responsibility for the frontier so that the exhausted German and Italian divisions of the great advance could refit. The Cyrenaica airfields, menacing both Egypt and Malta, were in German hands. The gallop was over. A British attempt on 15th May to counter-attack in the area of Sollum and Capuzzo, and to clear the escarpment at the top of the Halfaya Pass met with very limited success. A brisk demonstration by the Germans on 26th May in the same area nearly surrounded a British battalion, and once again secured the Halfaya Pass for the Afrika Korps. This was, on each side, the swordplay of a tired and wounded wrist. A little time had yet to elapse before either contestant could again make a lunge with his weight behind it.

Except for the important fact that he did not capture Tobruk, Rommel's first offensive in Cyrenaica was a success. His strength was inadequate to keep up the offensive beyond the Egyptian frontier and his wilder dreams were unrealised, but there was now less disposition among his superiors to question his judgment. His strategic gains were the Cyrenaica airfields, the port of Benghazi and considerable depth to the defence of Tripolitania. The moral benefits were greater. Hard though he had driven them, Rommel had given to the Italians some

And We Shall Shock Them

sense of avenging the fate of their Tenth Army two months before. They had liberated Italy's own possessions. The German troops had been given an invigorating taste of desert war. They had had matters pretty well their own way, at least until they encountered the need for a set-piece battle at Tobruk. Their belief in their commander was fortified, their spirits high.

For the British there were few consolations. The chaos and disorganisation of the retreat through Cyrenaica were African versions of the early disasters in Norway. The Germans had appeared to be everywhere and everywhere prevail. They were better equipped, better led, more boldly and intelligently handled and had been masters of the field. Rommel began to assume legendary and heroic dimensions – not only to the troops in Africa. By contrast the British Command appeared indecisive and amateur, and not to be on terms with contemporary reality. All could see that the balance of armoured strength and of anti-tank guns had given the British little chance. But this was happening at the same time too in Greece and Crete; and when soldiers are committed to battle with little chance somebody, somewhere, at some time has been responsible. It was all too habitual. It was another defeat.

154

8

The Mirage of Victory

For Middle East Command to accept with equanimity the threat of a
German-Italian Army on the frontiers of Egypt was impossible. There
must be a counter-stroke when the time was ripe, and the sooner the
better. To the authorities in London the situation was intolerable. A
dramatic success in February had been followed by a humiliating
reverse in May. The Mediterranean was near dominated by the enemy.
The appearance of the German Army in Greece, Crete and now Libya
had been enough to send the forces of the British Empire scurrying
back to base or trudging bitterly towards ports of evacuation. Or so it
appeared, and in a war dependent on the support of public opinion
appearance mattered.

Churchill had additional reasons for impatience. The government
had, at great risk to the Royal Navy, sent a convoy to Egypt through the
Mediterranean. With minimal losses the "Tiger" Convoy, as it was
called, brought reinforcements, including 220 tanks, to Alexandria on
12th May 1941. The tanks were used to refit 7th Armoured Division,
which had been virtually without equipment since Beda Fomm.
Thenceforth Wavell was ceaselessly badgered to attack. Beside 7th
Armoured Division he had, following its triumphs in East Africa, 4th
Indian Division, made up to a strength of two brigades only by the
inclusion of 22nd Guards Brigade. He had a new commander for XIII
Corps – the Desert Army – Lieutenant-General Sir Noel Beresford-
Peirse was promoted from command of 4th Indian Division. On 15th
June, Wavell committed XIII Corps with its two divisions to an
offensive: Operation BATTLEAXE. Beresford-Peirse was to attack the
enemy in the frontier region and secure the Halfaya Pass. Thereafter
he must engage and destroy the enemy's armour. XIII Corps would
then advance to relieve Tobruk and, if successful, exploit to the general
line Derna-Mechili.

It was an ambitious programme.

After his triumphant advance from Mersa Brega to the Egyptian
frontier Rommel had regrouped his forces. Three Italian divisions

were left surrounding Tobruk, garrisoned by four Australian brigades. The German 5th Light Division was withdrawn to rest and refit in the desert south of Tobruk. 15th Panzer Division had now arrived in Africa and most of it, including two battalions of the Panzer Regiment, was deployed on the frontier with the divisional commander, General Neumann-Sylkow, commanding in the frontier area. Beside his two tank battalions Neumann-Sylkow had forty-six anti-tank guns, including thirteen 88 millimetre anti-aircraft guns to be used as anti-tank artillery, the most powerful weapon yet employed in that role in the desert and capable of knocking out any British tank at a distance of over 2,000 yards. Neumann-Sylkow held forward at Halfaya Pass, and also at Point 206 above the escarpment six miles inland from the pass. Ten miles to the rear he held a small garrison in the area of Fort Capuzzo; and a large number of anti-tank guns were deployed in depth on Hafid Ridge, seven miles west of Fort Capuzzo and about ten miles behind Point 206. The eighty tanks of the Panzer battalions were kept in reserve.

Beresford-Peirse's plan was to attack on the right with the 4th Indian Division, supported by the infantry tanks of the two tank regiments of the 4th Armoured Brigade, from the 7th Armoured Division. In this first phase of the operation the 4th Indian Division would take the Halfaya Pass and Fort Capuzzo. The righthand thrust would be immediately above and below the escarpment, to assault both ends of the Halfaya Pass: the lefthand thrust of the 4th Indian Division would aim at Point 206 and Capuzzo. Also in the first phase of BATTLEAXE, the 7th Armoured Division would advance towards the Hafid Ridge and engage (it was hoped) the main enemy tank force with the division's remaining armoured brigade, 7th Armoured Brigade, equipped with faster, cruiser tanks. The support group would advance on the left flank. Headquarters, XIII Corps, would be at Sidi Barrani, sixty miles behind the front. In succeeding phases the corps would advance to Tobruk and Derna.

BATTLEAXE took two days to fail completely, despite some initial tactical succéss in the centre, where 4th Indian Division's lefthand thrust with 22nd Guards Brigade and the tanks of 4th Armoured Brigade took Capuzzo and beat off a counter-attack. At the Halfaya Pass the tanks supporting the attacking 11th Indian Brigade met for the first time a few of Neumann-Sylkow's 88s. All tanks but one were destroyed and the attack failed. On the left of XIII Corps the cruiser tanks of 7th Armoured Brigade approached the Hafid Ridge. There they ran on to the deadly fire of the German anti-tank guns. The tanks had out-distanced their supporting artillery. They were at the mercy of anti-tank guns with greater range than they – and their own tank guns could only fire armour-piercing shot, while high explosive was needed to tackle the anti-tank gun crews opposing them. By the evening of the first day of BATTLEAXE over half the armour of XIII Corps had been destroyed. By mid-morning on the second day, 16th June, Beresford-Peirse was left with only twenty-two cruiser and seventeen infantry tanks. He had started the battle with about 200 tanks of all kinds.

It was the right moment for a counter-attack. Rommel had pushed the rested and refitted 5th Light Division, with its Panzer regiment, forward from near Tobruk towards the battle before the British attacked, for his Intelligence staff and wireless interceptions were perfectly competent to warn him of what was coming. Just before dawn on 16th June he drove forwards a two-pronged counter-stroke. 15th Panzer Division attacked Capuzzo from the north. 5th Light Division began a wide turning movement round the outer flank of 7th Armoured Division. There now occurred that engagement with the enemy's tank force which BATTLEAXE had been designed to produce. It took place in most unfavourable conditions and was generally decided in the German favour. At Capuzzo, 15th Panzer Division met stout resistance and lost a number of tanks: the British were supported by twenty-five pounder guns and by noon the attacking German division withdrew for respite, its tank strength down to thirty, its casualties high. But on the inner flank Rommel saw that the 5th Light Division was having the best of it and was pressing on across the British axis of advance. He ordered the 15th Panzer Division to disengage most of its armour from the fight at Capuzzo and join 5th Light Division, thereby shifting his weight from the left to the right. As a result the whole of XIII Corps was now threatened. Messervy, Commander of 4th Indian Division, against his orders, decided that now if ever he must withdraw his forward troops from Capuzzo through Halfaya, and did so. On the British left, 7th Armoured Division fell back to the frontier. Wavell had flown up to the front, realised BATTLEAXE had failed and ordered withdrawal. The British had lost ninety-one tanks. The Germans had twelve destroyed. As masters of the battlefield they could repair their casualties and salvage much from their enemies.

The failure of BATTLEAXE has been ascribed to many causes. Beresford-Peirse's concept has been criticised as laborious and pedestrian. It has been said that British equipment was inferior; that British training was inadequate, British organisation and tactics faulty; that

British generalship was remote and inexpert. There is something in all this.

The "Tiger" convoy had brought a mix of Matilda infantry and cruiser tanks. The latter were of the new "Crusader" type, capable of considerable speed but so far regarded as mechanically unreliable. But both tanks still had only the two pounder gun. This fired an armour-piercing round, not dissimilar in size and penetrative power to the smaller German tank gun of the time. The British tanks, however, whether cruiser or infantry, fired no high explosive round and could only engage a target at short range. The German tanks were armed with a mixture of different guns – a tank gun comparable to the British, but also a gun in a close support tank, firing a high explosive shell over a longer distance. The Germans, therefore, could engage some targets with their tanks at greater range, although they were not, at this point, greatly superior in tank versus tank combat.

But tank versus tank combat was not a German concept, unavoidable though it might sometimes be. German policy, which the British at first imperfectly comprehended and certainly never copied, was to develop and deploy anti-tank guns as the principal means of engaging enemy tanks. German tanks could therefore be kept as far as possible for manoeuvre and exploitation, seeking not the hard but the soft spots in their opponent's body. The Germans believed (and General Guderian, father of the German Panzer troops, had ceaselessly taught) that they should regard the engine of the tank as a weapon like its gun. The power to move, to threaten the enemy's rear areas, communications, supply echelons, or (if found) unprotected infantry was the strength of the tank. To destroy the enemy's tanks a powerful, long-range gun was required; and to place such a weapon in a tank would be to create a monster whose engine power and overall size would inevitably have to be huge, and whose manoeuvrability would be correspondingly slug-gish. Ultimately the Germans did this – perforce. Meanwhile they concentrated on the anti-tank gun, later mounting it on a chassis.

And in the 88 millimetre gun, although it represented only about one in four of those used in BATTLEAXE, the Germans possessed a mighty weapon in open desert. Fighting against it resembled engaging with a carving knife a man armed with a long spear. The Germans, whether in attack or defence, would deploy or push out a screen of anti-tank guns, against which they hoped to let the enemy armour waste its strength. Their anti-tank guns were manoeuvred in close cooperation with their tanks, just as their gun tanks and their high explosive firing tanks were interdependent. All this required a clear-cut tactical doctrine and a high standard of training. It also led to operational concepts which were different from the British. To the Germans, Beresford-Peirse's aim for 7th Armoured Division – to bring the bulk of the German armour to battle – would have been an extraordinary objective for an all-tank force. To hope to lead an offensive operation, to have the "feel" of a battle of manoeuvre from sixty miles to the rear, would have been equally incomprehensible to Rommel.

Successful tactics did not only require sound training, instinctive ability, quick reactions and decisive leadership. They also depended upon a correct combination of weapons immediately available. Here British organisation was less successful than German. The Panzer divisions had a mix of tank and infantry regiments – normally two battalions in each, sometimes three of infantry. They were strong in anti-tank guns. They were weaker than the British in close support artillery, but since some of the tanks could fire a high explosive shell they could provide instant although limited close-range support. They practised the forming of battle groups, often under one of the regimental commanders; groups whose composition depended on the task. The one British armoured division had its tanks organised in armoured brigades of tanks only. Infantry were concentrated in a support group. Field guns were towed, with consequent limitation on their ability to support fast-moving operations – a limitation the more important because the field gun firing solid shot over open sights was often the most – or only – effective anti-tank weapon in the battle, and saved many a day. British organisation made the intimate collaboration of arms on the battlefield more difficult than it might have been. Radical improvement, however, was virtually precluded by the international character of the forces. As their commanders had a responsibility to their several governments, Australian, New Zealand and South African divisions had to fight complete as such.

On the German side, the combination of anti-tank gun and gun tank, and the tactical skill in deployment and manoeuvre was greatly superior. But Rommel had other advantages. His tanks, with different types on similar chassis, could move at the same pace, while the British Crusaders and Matildas could hardly be concentrated (as Beresford-Peirse at one stage ordered) so disparate were their speeds. And, on the whole, the British tanks were mechanically inferior. They broke down too often, and in a withdrawal were lost for ever. In BATTLEAXE, furthermore, technical inferiority was compounded by unfamiliarity. After arriving at Alexandria on 12th May the British equipment, and especially the tanks, needed preparation and testing and modification for the desert, problems little comprehended in London. Meanwhile Wavell was doing his best to protect the army from a premature adventure, against the urgent pressures of Churchill. As a result, training time with new equipment was cut to the minimum. The 7th Armoured Division had had no new equipment and no desert training since Beda Fomm, until the "Tiger" convoy arrived.

The impression remains, nevertheless, of an all round performance inferior to the enemy's not only because of lack of practice with equipment but also because of basic fallacies about the necessary combination of all arms, and how to attain that combination and handle those arms when faced with an enemy as professional as the Germans. BATTLEAXE was for the more experienced British armoured units, and above all for higher commanders, what Rommel's April campaign had been for the beginners and what Norway, France, Greece and Crete had been for others – a grim lesson in how expert one now needed to be to wage war, and how long a lead the enemy seemed to have acquired. The British Army was still inadequately trained. The lesson took a long time to learn.

After BATTLEAXE Wavell was removed from the Middle East Command and made Commander-in-Chief, India. He had overseen two notable successes, in the Western Desert in February and in East Africa in the campaign only recently consummated. He had also borne the burden of an unsuccessful April, May and June in Cyrenaica, and of Greece and Crete. He had had many other preoccupations, not least a most difficult and disagreeable business in Syria, where the British Government had been persuaded that the resident French forces would welcome an Allied expedition in the name of Free France and de Gaulle, whereas (as Wavell expected) the exact reverse was the case. He had dealt effectively with a pro-German coup d'état in Iraq, by the despatch of a small expedition to Baghdad across the Syrian Desert. Now he was to go, to exchange posts with the present Commander-in-Chief, India, General Sir Claude Auchinleck.

Auchinleck was a man of magnificent presence and dignity. Strength radiated from him. His manner expressed calm, restraint and courage. He was admired by all who served him. He came from the Indian Army, his experience was of the East, being, like Wellington, a "Sepoy General". In the British Army he was not widely known, nor did he widely know others. He was, perhaps because of this, an imperfect picker of men. He did not always choose subordinates wisely, nor judge their performance as shrewdly as was needed. His own character as a soldier was admirable, but in knowing how much to delegate and how much to intervene his touch was less sure. In treating with politicians,

160

in particular with Churchill, he felt uneasy. He was warned by Dill how to deal with the Prime Minister, and how testing the probes and admonitions he would receive; but he still found Churchill's telegrams and interference intensely bothersome, and he said so. He did not have the skills to humour such a man. In the end all confidence between them expired. The fault was not only Churchill's.

Auchinleck took over the Middle East Command in the aftermath of BATTLEAXE and when, once again and understandably, London was bringing great pressure for an offensive. There was also pressure for the British Army to see action on a larger scale. Operation BARBAROSSA, the German invasion of Russia, had begun on 22nd June, and it appeared that the Russians were doing all the fighting. This was difficult for the government at home. The vast mass of the new British Army was in the United Kingdom. Much of the old Regular Army was in India and the Far East. The only complete British divisions engaged against the Germans since Dunkirk had been 2nd and 7th Armoured Divisions, although detached brigades had fought in Greece, Crete and as part of Western Desert Force. The first of the infantry divisions from England to reach Middle East Command – 50th Division – was sent to Cyprus and then to Syria, and the bulk of the divisions for the next offensive were Australian, New Zealand, South African and Indian. Indeed the Australian Government ultimately demanded that their troops – four brigades – be relieved in Tobruk, which they had defended superbly, with an aggressive vigour and a zeal for patrolling which had held an eager enemy at arm's length. They had composed the majority of the garrison's combat troops. They had suffered over 3,000 casualties. Between August and October they were withdrawn by sea and replaced by a British division – 70th Division – and a Polish brigade. But although most of the corps troops, the medium and heavy artillery, all the tank forces and the base units were British, there were few British divisions showing on the battlemaps over which Churchill pored, and the fact irritated him. Indeed there was only to be one, apart from the garrison of Tobruk, in the forthcoming offensive.

Auchinleck successfully resisted pressure to start before the army was ready. As on all such occasions his resistance was unpopular in London, where it seemed to him that men supposed a regiment or an equipment fit for action in the desert immediately it was disembarked at Alexandria. Since Rommel achieved exactly this with German forces reaching Tripoli the supposition was not outrageous. It was, however, unrealistic. The general standard of training of British officers and troops, and the robustness of their equipment, set their readiness for immediate action well below that of the enemy. Reinforcements, including 600 tanks and 800 guns, reached Auchinleck by October but he refused to act before he judged the moment right.

The first great undertaking of the army in the Western Desert, now christened "Eighth Army", was to begin on 18th November: Operation CRUSADER.

The battles about to begin were like nothing in the collective experience of the British or any other army. BATTLEAXE had been brief, unsuccessful and so limited in its depth of advance as to be atypical. O'Connor's advance to Beda Fomm in January and February, and its mirror-image, Rommel's counter-stroke in April, had both been attended by chaos. The fog of war had lain thickly over much of the tactical battlefield. Nevertheless the general shape and object of these operations had been clear at the time and in retrospect. In each case a push in the north had been followed by a great outflanking, a cut-off movement or movements far to the south. There had been little manoeuvre of opposing mobile forces. On each occasion one side had held the initiative throughout.

In CRUSADER, on the other hand, the tactical initiative passed from one side to the other and back again with great rapidity and little comprehension by those losing it. The confusion of the battlefield was immense, as larger and more evenly matched forces than hitherto were deployed. In the area of desert between Tobruk and the Egyptian frontier – perhaps 3,000 square miles – it has been reckoned that some 30,000 vehicles of several armies were advancing, wheeling, withdrawing, counter-marching, attacking, defending, being supplied, or simply had broken down. Since action was concentrated in particular parts of the area the astonishing density of vehicles greatly contributed to the difficulty of planning coherent tactical manoeuvres, let alone carrying them out. The desert campaigns have been likened to war at sea. It is true that the comparative scarcity of features, the freedom to move in any direction, the potential range of vision and engagement, the lack of defined flanks and fronts, created something like a maritime pattern of conflict. But the analogy can mislead. It suggests battle fleets of comprehensible size manoeuvring beyond the empty horizon. In the desert the landscape was sometimes empty, but at decisive moments it more nearly resembled a caravan site struck by lightning, as far as the eye could see.

Coherent fronts and defensible features were rare except tactically and locally. This added to the confusion. It also restricted the ability of commanders at all levels to know where they, their troops or their enemy actually were. An assault could come from any direction, sometimes in accident by an enemy equally puzzled. A threatening attack from one direction might appear a headlong withdrawal when viewed from beyond, and be reported as such. Commanders and Staffs tried to deduce the enemy's intentions from his movements. It was a difficult exercise, presuming a rationality which fighting in the desert could not always attain.

These conditions emphasised the importance of certain traditional principles of war, notably the maintenance of the aim, and the concentration of force – both tenets of the British military bible. Unless a commander could hold fast to some essentially straightforward object, which would not be hourly transformed by the shifting tides of battle and which all could understand, he was likely to find his command strewn over the desert wondering which way to go. Maintenance of the aim did not mean inflexibility in attaining it – quickness of wit and readiness to switch point of effort with changing circumstances were essential. But there had to be an underlying concept which could be maintained for a phase and could exercise a gravitational pull on disordered operations. And concentration was an essential principle in a theatre where a larger force could easily be destroyed in detail by a smaller if its component parts were not so deployed as to offer mutual support. The conditions of the desert placed, too, enormous value upon equipment, upon communications and upon administrative flexibility. Because encounters whether on a large or a small scale were so often unplanned, the best tank, gun, vehicle was that which was most robust under all conditions, was best in the mêlée, could get a blow in first, and not break down. And without communications nobody could send orders or receive information. Communication had to be almost entirely by wireless – by thousands of wireless sets competing for frequencies, dependent on a huge supply train of batteries and subject to the evening blight when natural conditions always made radio communication especially hard.

Eighth Army now had a new commander. Lieutenant-General Sir Alan Cunningham, who had achieved a triumph in Abyssinia, was now appointed to command, under Auchinleck, the only army the British Empire was fielding against the Germans. Under Cunningham were two corps for the forthcoming operation: XIII Corps (Lieutenant-General Godwin-Austen) consisted of 4th Indian Division (Messervy) and the New Zealand Division (Freyberg) supported by 1st Army Tank Brigade, with a mixture of 135 Matilda and Valentine tanks. XXX

Corps (Lieutenant-General Norrie) consisted of 7th Armoured Division (Major-General Gott) with 7th and 22nd Armoured Brigades and the support group. 4th Armoured Brigade, although part of 7th Armoured Division, was initially kept separate under Corps Command. Also in XXX Corps were 1st South African Division (Major-General Brink) and 22nd Guards Brigade. 2nd South African Division (Major-General de Villiers) was in army reserve. Under Cunningham's own command for the battle was the 70th Division (Major-General Scobie), at present holding Tobruk, with a Polish brigade group (Major-General Kopanski).

Cunningham's plan was for XXX Corps to cross the frontier in the area of Fort Maddalena and advance north-west towards Tobruk. XXX Corps's object was to find and destroy the enemy's armour. North of XXX Corps, XIII Corps would cross the frontier and attack the enemy positions at Sidi Omar, Capuzzo, and – later – Sollum and Bardia, from the west. When ordered by Cunningham, 70th Division, supported by the 32rd Army Tank Brigade, would break out from Tobruk and join hands with XXX Corps. The second stage of CRUSADER would then begin – the reconquest of Cyrenaica. But XXX Corps must first attain its – and Eighth Army's – great initial object: to find and destroy the enemy's armour. A shifting object indeed.

XXX Corps' main thrust was to be made by 7th Armoured Division,

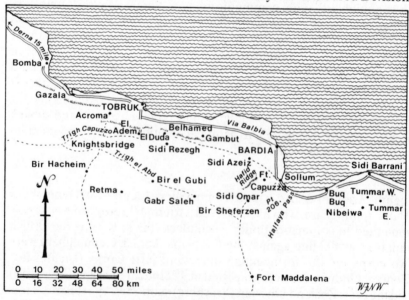

From Sidi Barrani to Tobruk

with 1st South African Division protecting the left flank, and with 4th Armoured Brigade on the right, or inner, flank, also charged with protecting the left flank of XIII Corps. XIII Corps held 4th Indian Division on the right, in order to attack Sidi Omar and Capuzzo. On the left, or inner, flank was deployed the New Zealand Division, ready to move north or west as required. In his three armoured brigades Norrie had some 475 tanks, and there were a further 130 infantry tanks with XIII Corps. 7th Armoured Brigade had cruisers, of which over half were of the old "Covenanter" pattern. 4th Armoured Brigade was equipped with the American light tank, the "Honey". 22nd Armoured Brigade, its three tank regiments fresh from England, had the latest cruiser tank, the "Crusader".

Assisted by a thorough and successful deception plan, and by extensive administrative preparations, Eighth Army moved across the frontier at dawn on 18th November. The Army Commander moved with XXX Corps Headquarters. CRUSADER had begun.

On the Axis side of the frontier wire extensive reorganisation had taken place. In August a new "Panzer Gruppe Afrika" was constituted, with Rommel its commander, comprising all German and Italian formations in the forward area – the two German Panzer divisions of the Deutsches Afrika Korps, 15th and 21st (21st Panzer Division was the former 5th Light Division renamed); and the five Italian infantry divisions of XXI Corps (General Navarrini). The DAK had been handed over by Rommel to General Cruewell. This was not all. DAK was reinforced by a new division from Germany, soon to assume the title by which it would become famous – 90th Light Division (Lieutenant-General Sümmermann). Besides Panzer Gruppe Afrika, and not formally under Rommel's command, was the "Corpo d'Armati di Manovra XX" (General Gambara). This was responsible direct to General Bastico, the Commander-in-Chief in North Africa, and Rommel's titular head. Rommel obtained operational control of the Italian divisions of this corps, however, and for effective purposes the German and Italian forces operated as one body with little hindrance from Tripoli. Gambara's corps consisted of the Ariete Armoured Division and the Trieste Motorised Division. Of about 240 tanks in the two German Panzer divisions, 70 were the Mark II light tank and 35 were the Mark IV, primarily used for close support. Ariete Division had 140 tanks. In gun tanks – for tank against tank work – it can be seen that the British had a considerable numerical advantage. For this to count the right tanks had to be at the right place at the right time. The

165

Germans, however, still retained the advantage of two anti-tank guns which they were adept at using – the 88 millimetre and the long-barrelled 50 millimetre. In all they had thirty-five 88s – including twenty-three in the frontier area – and ninety-six 50s – a formidable anti-tank strength – as well as a considerable number of large calibre Italian anti-tank guns, both on the frontier and investing Tobruk.

Rommel's eyes were on Tobruk. Under similar pressure from Berlin as Auchinleck was enduring from London, he was not, in his view, getting as much support as exhortation. The German authorities made it perfectly clear to him that the important war was now in Russia. But if he could take Tobruk and make it a port of supply, the savings in logistic support would be considerable, and an offensive eastwards in 1942 might be possible – perhaps in conjunction with a German thrust into the Caucasus, thus shaking from west and north the British position and British influence in the Middle East. Rommel deployed a considerable mass of artillery and prepared for another full assault on Tobruk in late November.

Rommel himself was at his advanced Headquarters at Gambut, north of the Trigh Capuzzo thirty miles east of Tobruk, with 15th Panzer nearby, north of the coast road, and 21st Panzer in the desert west of Sidi Azeiz, twenty miles west of Bardia. Ringing Tobruk were Navarrini's Italian divisions, and south of Tobruk at Bir Hacheim and Bir El Gubi were the Trieste and Ariete Divisions of Gambara's corps. The frontier defence positions were manned by Italians with the exception of the Halfaya Pass where there was and had been throughout a German detachment. Cruewell and the Headquarters of the DAK were in Bardia.

In his mission of "finding and destroying the enemy armour", Cunningham had directed Norrie to advance about forty miles and stop. It was reckoned that so menacing a thrust would provoke a reaction – and with luck should bring the German armour against 7th Armoured Division who could receive it and destroy it from positions they themselves selected. This did not work. Rommel refused for some time to believe that a major British offensive had started. He wished nothing to distract him from the assault on Tobruk, and when he had evidence that there was indeed an incursion he at first treated it as a minor matter, something from which the Tobruk attack could be screened. There was, therefore, no major move of German armour in response to Norrie's first advance, and on the first night Cunningham decided to push XXX Corps further forward next day: 7th Armoured Division was to advance on Bir El Gubi and Sidi Rezegh. Norrie had, from the start, taken the reasonable view that to be sure of provoking a reaction from Panzer Gruppe Afrika it was probably necessary to make a determined move towards ground vital to the defence – such as ground covering their east-west communications, the Trigh Capuzzo and the Via Balbia. This demanded a more determined and deeper thrust than had first been authorised. Now the move towards Sidi Rezegh must surely get a reaction. It also, of course, took XXX Corps further from XIII Corps, and 7th Armoured Division further from 4th Armoured Brigade, whose unchanged function was to keep within supporting distance of the left flank of XIII Corps.

The next three or four days saw some of the most extraordinary and complex movements in the history of the war. To seek to describe them in any orderly way is unintentionally to deceive, so confused were the manoeuvres themselves.

When 7th Armoured Division advanced on 19th November one brigade (22nd) drove straight at the Ariete Division in Bir El Gubi and suffered severe tank casualties. The other brigade (7th) reached the airfield at Sidi Rezegh on the Trigh Capuzzo, lying as it does on a shelf between two escarpment steps. Meanwhile 21st Panzer Division (Ravenstein) became uneasy that something was happening to the south and sent the division's Panzer regiment – 120 tanks, accompanied by four 88s – to engage. This was "Battlegroup Stephan". A wild encounter battle took place with the 4th Armoured Brigade near Gabr Saleh, where XXX Corps had concentrated the night before. British tank casualties were substantially higher than were German. All three British armoured brigades had now been engaged, facing in three different directions, at the points of a right-angled triangle whose hypotenuse (the line from Sidi Rezegh to Gabr Saleh) was about forty miles long.

Rommel still regarded all this as a minor intrusion. Determined to start his attack on Tobruk on 21st November, he decided to cut off this British raid, and told Cruewell to move 15th Panzer eastwards and to follow 21st Panzer towards Sidi Omar, thus concentrating the DAK armour between the British and Egypt. But Cruewell now began to appreciate both the strength and the direction of the British advance. He decided that the Afrika Korps must attack the British right flank as soon as possible, and on 20th November directed both his divisions against Gabr Saleh – in effect against 4th Armoured Brigade. As this movement became clear to the British, 22nd Armoured Brigade was ordered to leave Bir El Gubi and return eastwards to reinforce 4th Armoured Brigade. 21st Panzer Division ran out of fuel and a battle took place between the tanks of 15th Panzer Division and those of 4th and 22nd Armoured Brigades. The British were outnumbered at first, for 22nd Armoured Brigade only arrived towards evening, and were depleted after their encounter with the Ariete at Bir El Gubi. But although forced back by the weight and range of fire, the two brigades of XXX Corps finished the day with nearly 200 tanks; and they were concentrated. Meanwhile 7th Armoured Division's support group was ordered forward to the Sidi Rezegh Ridge, and 1st South African Division was moved up to mask the Ariete at Bir El Gubi. Cunningham now ordered that 70th Division's breakout from Tobruk should start next morning (21st November).

Rommel now at last realised what was happening. He ordered the DAK to move as early and as fast as possible back towards Sidi Rezegh.

On 21st November, therefore, 15th and 21st Panzer Divisions raced toward the Sidi Rezegh Ridge from the south-east. More slowly 4th and 22nd Brigades moved in a similar direction, towards 7th Armoured Brigade and the support group. 7th Armoured Brigade attacked northwards from Sidi Rezegh to link hands with the Tobruk sortie which started at dawn, a movement supported by the infantry of the support group who cleared the way for the tanks to advance over the escarpment north of the airfield. This was infantry fighting, bravely and ably conducted, and 7th Armoured Brigade moved forwards – only to suffer crippling casualties from emplaced anti-tank guns of 90th Light Division holding the thin line between 7th Armoured and the sortie from Tobruk. For the latter was equally bravely and grimly executed but had just been held up by the same thin line, beset on both sides and being directed by Rommel himself. And now the Sidi Rezegh Ridge was itself being attacked from the east by the DAK. They were themselves being followed by 4th and 22nd Armoured Brigades, who assumed they were following up a beaten enemy. To the remaining armour of 7th Armoured Brigade and to the support group on Sidi Rezegh Ridge, the DAK appeared very different. A British tank regiment was quickly detached to face the threat. It was as quickly and almost completely destroyed by the guns of the DAK. Only a valiant handful of the support group and a few guns now faced the concentrated Afrika Korps. By nightfall, 21st November, the east end of the Sidi Rezegh escarpment was in German hands.

But, incredibly, neither side appreciated the true position. Instead Cruewell believed he had severe problems. He withdrew north of the Trigh Capuzzo. Rommel believed that the main task of the DAK was to stop the British reaching Tobruk. The British High Command believed that all had gone well. The fog of war was thick. It was thickened by the very exaggerated estimates of enemy tank losses submitted by both sides.

Next day, 22nd November, XIII Corps in the east started its attacks on Capuzzo, Sidi Omar and Bardia. The supporting infantry tanks suffered heavy losses – mainly caused by the German 88s. In the west, Rommel directed 21st Panzer Division to attack the Sidi Rezegh Ridge from the north. Norrie ordered the South Africans to move from Bir El Gubi and reinforce Sidi Rezegh, and 22nd Guards Brigade to advance and mask Bir El Gubi. In early afternoon, 21st Panzer Division attacked with a combination of tanks, anti-tank guns and infantry, and forced the remnants of 7th Armoured Brigade and the support group to withdraw. A counter-attack by 22nd Armoured Brigade was beaten off with casualties. 7th Armoured Brigade had ceased to exist as an effective force. 4th and 22nd Armoured Brigades had about 150 tanks between them. The British were ordered to withdraw southwards through, it was hoped, the South Africans. But the southern escarpment of Sidi Rezegh was not in South African hands. A German move from the west had pre-empted them. By nightfall the whole Sidi Rezegh Ridge was in German occupation. The night was not improved for the British by 15th Panzer Division accidentally overrunning a leaguer of 4th Armoured Brigade, destroying a large number of tanks and capturing the Headquarters.

The operations of XIII Corps, meanwhile, had gone well and the New Zealand Division had been ordered to move west along the Trigh Capuzzo supported by a squadron of tanks.

On 23rd November, Gott proposed to concentrate his remaining armour somewhere south of Sidi Rezegh. Ravenstein had 21st Panzer on Sidi Rezegh Airfield and Ridge. Neumann-Sylkow, with 15th Panzer, was a few miles to the east. Rommel now ordered the Ariete Division to start moving north-east towards Sidi Rezegh, and Cruewell to take both German Panzer divisions south-west towards the Ariete – and thus he reckoned to encircle the remaining British armour. Cruewell's intention was somewhat different – to move as Rommel directed, but to join hands with the Ariete, and then to swing north and drive the united German and Italian divisions northward, crushing the British between this mass of armour and the Germans emplaced on the Sidi Rezegh Ridge.

The move of the German divisions south-west towards Bir El Gubi crashed through the supply vehicles of the 5th South African Brigade causing the utmost chaos. By 1 p.m. Cruewell had made contact with the Ariete Division and at 3 p.m. turned north with his mass of 260 tanks. He moved, with a long line of tanks, against the South African brigade and their hastily deployed line of guns, and by 4 p.m. his righthand division – 15th Panzer – was overrunning the South African

Brigade Headquarters. Meanwhile his left flank was attacked by 22nd Armoured Brigade, which advanced across the rear of the DAK advance, to join the rump of 7th Armoured Brigade and 4th Armoured Brigade. Cruewell's operation hit the South Africans hard but it did not destroy the remaining British armour. German casualties were heavy. British and German armour was now concentrated south of the Sidi Rezegh Ridge, each within a few miles of the other, each having suffered heavy casualties, but the British by far the heavier. It was the evening of 23rd November. Cunningham was deeply uneasy. His tank losses had been huge, the position was chaotic and the army surely unbalanced to meet a German counter-stroke: an invasion of Egypt. Rommel was of the same mind. He decided that the British were beaten, and that by leading the concentrated armour of the DAK towards Egypt he could entirely cut off the British expedition.

He was wrong.

On 24th November the New Zealand Division, supported by the tanks of 1st Army Tank Brigade, moved westwards towards Tobruk. It has been suggested that it was a faulty dispersal of armour to place this brigade with XIII Corps, as opposed to massing its tanks with 7th Armoured Division. The comment is surely misplaced. The Matildas and Valentines of 1st Army Tank Brigade – and those of 32nd Brigade with 70th Division in Tobruk – did magnificent service, at high cost. They enabled the infantry to do what they did. They acted as a team. Each of the two Arms enhanced the capability of the other.

On 25th November, Freyberg's men occupied Sidi Rezegh Airfield, and that night attacked westwards towards Belhamed and El Duda. Next day 70th Division took El Duda, and on 26th, after very hard fighting, the New Zealanders cleared the whole of the Sidi Rezegh Ridge. A narrow corridor now connected the Tobruk garrison with the relieving force. East of that corridor the Afrika Korps was represented by 90th Light Division, hit hard by the New Zealand assaults. Rommel's armour was nowhere to be seen. It was far to the east. At 10 a.m. on the morning of 24th, while Freyberg and his division were moving west towards Tobruk along the Trigh Capuzzo, Rommel placed himself at the head of 21st Panzer Division and led them, followed shortly by 15th Panzer Division, on what has been called the "Dash to the wire". He nearly overran the opposing Army Commander. Cunningham was visiting Norrie and, taking off in a light aircraft, evaded the drive of the Afrika Korps by seconds. Rommel's thrust line was the same, in reverse, as that of XXX Corps five days earlier – the Trigh El

Abd, by Gabr Saleh towards Bir Sheferzen on the frontier. He had 100 tanks behind him. The British armour of XXX Corps was licking its wounds to his left and rear. Rommel reckoned that he could simultaneously relieve those frontier positions that had not fallen to British assault – Bardia and Halfaya Pass were still in German hands – and could produce among the British south and east of Tobruk a headlong flight from Egypt. He would roll up the British near the frontier, from south to north.

The operation was a failure. There was confusion between Rommel and Cruewell, the former giving orders to the divisions of the latter's corps. There was administrative collapse. Rommel was disinclined to take much account of battlefield logistics: he was sometimes right to brush aside the sort of over-insurance which can stultify boldness, but on this occasion his divisions ran out of petrol, ammunition and water. His tanks ran on to the fire of British artillery in position – always a far more deadly matter than running into British tanks – and suffered heavily. The divisions of the DAK entered Bardia and replenished there. To carry out the operation at all was a considerable feat immediately after the heavy fighting of the last few days. It bore witness to the high mechanical reliability, the communications and the morale of the Afrika Korps. But it was a failure. It brought little relief to the German frontier garrisons. It did not cause a British withdrawal.

When Cunningham had reached his Headquarters at Fort Maddalena after escaping from the onrush of the Afrika Korps on 24th November, he found a resolute Commander-in-Chief awaiting him. Cunningham had asked Auchinleck to come and consult, having decided that it would be necessary to evacuate Libya. Now Auchinleck handed him a written order. The offensive would continue. The object remained unchanged. Tobruk would be relieved. Cyrenaica would be reconquered. By that firmness of decision when matters looked dark, Auchinleck saved the CRUSADER offensive; and the morale of Eighth Army, by now wavering, was given a chance of restoration. It was a decision as timely, as lonely and as courageous as that of Gort on 25th May 1940, and it marked the turning-point of the battle. Two days later Cunningham was removed from his command.

The situation at Tobruk was menacing for the Germans. On the night of 26th November Rommel was forced to realise how menacing – and that his adventure had failed. Both divisions of the DAK were ordered as fast as possible westwards, from Bardia along the Trigh Capuzzo.

The British armour had had a brief respite. 7th Armoured Brigade, whose tank casualties had been heaviest, had passed its fit tanks and crews to its sister brigades and been withdrawn from the battle. The British armour of 4th and 22nd Armoured Brigades was concentrated south of the Sidi Rezegh Ridge when, on the morning of 27th November, armoured cars reported German columns approaching from the east. This was the return of 15th and 21st Panzer Divisions from their adventures on the frontier. They drove into a British position, with the two British armoured brigades prepared to take the enemy head on and in the southern flank. But the action was broken off by the British too early, with the onset of darkness; and next day 15th Panzer Division, with forty-three tanks remaining on its battle strength, was able to move to the west of Sidi Rezegh, west of the New Zealanders defending the ridge. There now followed on 29th November a concentric attack against the New Zealanders and against the "Tip" of 70th Division at El Duda. 15th Panzer advanced from the west against El Duda, 21st from the east against Belhamed, the Ariete from the south-east. The attack was partially successful. The Germans reached Belhamed. The New Zealand Division was cut in two. The British armoured brigades were led with insufficient vigour to do much to break through a south-facing screen of anti-tank guns and the Ariete Division. On 1st December the New Zealand Division was withdrawn eastwards. Tobruk was again surrounded – with XIII Corps Headquarters now within the perimeter. Rommel sent two weak columns towards the frontier, but they suffered casualties and withdrew, at the same time as an attack against El Duda failed.

Both sides were now exhausted. The British, however, were receiving replacements and reinforcements. Behind the Afrika Korps, on the other hand, there was little. Their casualties, like those of the British, had been formidable. Some sharp, limited German attacks were mounted southwards against Bir El Gubi on 4th and 5th December, but on 6th December the Afrika Korps had only forty tanks left. On the British side 4th and 22nd Armoured Brigades had been amalgamated on 29th November, to give 7th Armoured Division a tank force of about 140 mixed Crusaders and Honeys. The British were determined as soon as possible to renew the offensive.

On 6th December, Rommel decided that he could no longer hold on at Tobruk. His tank strength, compared to what he knew of the enemy's, was inordinately low. There were few replacements and his supply position was bad. The decision was a bitter one. The German forces still on the Egyptian frontier had to be abandoned, and ultimately passed into captivity. Behind a vigorous show of strength, to inhibit too attentive a pursuit, Rommel slipped away. 90th Light

Division was sent back to Agedabia. The rest – 15th and 21st Panzer, and five Italian divisions, including the Ariete and the Trieste, formerly an independent corps but now placed unequivocally in Panzer Gruppe Afrika – were withdrawn to a defensible position on which some work had been done, at Gazala. The siege of Tobruk had been lifted. The Axis forces were withdrawn, their casualties in armour temporarily crippling. The first phase of CRUSADER was over.

The British Command has been extensively criticised for mistakes made during the first phase of CRUSADER. It has been said (notably by Liddell Hart), and echoed by Rommel himself, that the British armour was unnecessarily dispersed and that Panzer Gruppe Afrika, by observing the principle of concentration, was able to defeat it in detail. "There is no higher and simpler law of strategy," observed Clausewitz, "than that of keeping one's forces concentrated ... the greatest possible number of troops should be brought into action at the decisive point." Were the strictures just?

It is certainly true that XXX Corps' initial advance culminated in its three armoured brigades engaged with the enemy over a considerable area, and with the lead brigade – 7th Armoured – separated from 4th Armoured to the right rear by near forty miles, which might be taken as three hours' march. But the course of events does not prove this fact alone to have been disastrous or irremediable. For the general charge to be valid it is necessary to show that a concentrated Afrika Korps was able, by superiority in numbers, to overcome constituent parts of Eighth Army in a way which would not have happened had those parts been closer to each other.

There does not seem to be much in this. Excluding the sortie from Tobruk, supported by 32rd Army Tank Brigade's infantry tanks, British tank losses primarily occurred on four separate occasions: the operations of 1st Army Tank Brigade in support of XIII Corps, the engagements between 4th Armoured Brigade and 15th Panzer Division north-east of Gabr Saleh, the attack by 22nd Armoured Brigade on the Ariete Division at Bir El Gubi, and the attempts by 7th Armoured Brigade to move north of Sidi Rezegh – and then, with 22nd Brigade, to defend the ridge against the attacks of 21st Panzer Division on 22nd November.

On none of these occasions did the level of casualties derive certainly from British armour being committed piecemeal against a concentrated Afrika Korps.

In the case of XIII Corps' operations, casualties were chiefly inflicted by German anti-tank guns. The majority of their 88s, as well as a large number of the long-barrelled 50 millimetre guns, were in the frontier area.

In the case of 4th Armoured Brigade at Gabr Saleh, it is possible that had another British armoured brigade already been concentrated in the area (as 22nd Brigade was thither sent) the attack by "Battlegroup Stephan" or, later, by 15th Panzer Division, would have had a different outcome. It is not very likely: 4th Brigade's casualties (admittedly much heavier than the German) did not derive from numerical inferiority but from the superior hitting power of German anti-tank guns, and tanks handled in combination. Indeed it is an equally tenable proposition that any other brigade present would have also suffered in proportion. The exchange rate between British and German does not suggest that greater British numbers would have tipped the balance of battle. Only 15th Division was engaged on the German side, and had the Germans needed greater strength they would presumably have awaited the intervention of 21st Division as well. Furthermore had XXX Corps held back more armour (as originally intended) and met the DAK with larger and concentrated forces on 19th and 20th November there could have been no thrust in force towards Sidi Rezegh at the same time, and the entire operation would have taken a different form. Such speculations can be extended for ever. In the case of the attack by 22nd Armoured Brigade against the Ariete Division at Bir El Gubi, tank losses seem to have come largely from gallant and ineffective attempts to charge emplaced guns with tanks. The failure was not one of numbers, but of tactics.

In the fourth case, the tank losses at Sidi Rezegh, these were caused on the first day by anti-tank guns, including those 88s not deployed on the frontier. On the second day, when 21st Panzer Division attacked from the west in conjunction with an infantry attack from the north, the Afrika Korps was not concentrated. 15th Panzer Division did not reach the battlefield. British tanks remaining in 7th and 22nd Brigades outnumbered the Germans by two to one, and British losses, again, were as a result of being outfought rather than being outnumbered or excessively dispersed. Furthermore, 4th Armoured Brigade was ordered to join its sister brigades, and was only five miles away. Its operations thereafter were impeded by the fog of war, but not by distance.

On none of these occasions is the case made that British failure to observe the principle of concentration caused defeat. What of the Germans? The Afrika Korps' operations showed, as ever, great energy and flexibility. It was a more "handy" formation than the British could yet produce, more mechanically robust, needing less time to react to an order or a situation, with excellent battle drills. But its operations during CRUSADER did not illustrate that clear-cut success from concentrating superior force at the point of decision which Rommel's comments[1] and those of later historians imply. At Gabr Saleh, 15th Panzer Division attacked alone because 21st had run out of fuel. At Sidi Rezegh, 21st Panzer Division attacked alone because 15th was twenty miles to the east. On each occasion German tanks were outnumbered. Their success did not come from superior numbers or concentration, witness the following occasions: first, Cruewell's march to Bir El Gubi and his wheel north, with the Ariete Division, through the South Africans, which inflicted relatively small casualties on British armour and as a manoeuvre was expensive and indecisive; second Rommel's "Dash to the wire", which was also inconclusive – a withdrawal from rather than a march towards the point of decision.

The picture (sometimes, but not on this occasion, true) of German concentration and purpose as opposed to British dispersal and consequent destruction is inaccurate. British losses arose less from operational failure than from shortcomings in tactics, equipment and organisation: particularly from a failure to combine the fire of all arms instantly and effectively, and to organise accordingly. The British fought with considerable zest and élan. But British tactical leadership, particularly of armour, was too often marked by the same blemish for which Wellington cursed his cavalry – unduly high spirit and lack of control at the start of a venture, unduly low spirit when it did not instantly succeed: the mark of the amateur. British anti-tank weapons were inadequate in power and range; tank guns were not greatly inferior to the enemy's, but the enemy could combine them with harder hitting anti-tank guns, to which the only British effective equivalent was the use of the close support field artillery piece firing over open sights in an anti-tank role – to the detriment of its prime function. And British tanks (except the American Honeys) were mechanically less reliable.

A more valid criticism of British generalship may derive from the mission of XXX Corps, reiterated by Auchinleck when he ordered that the offensive continue: to "find and destroy the German armour". The operational concept thereafter was a sound one – to provoke a German attack against a superior British tank force. But for this to succeed it

---

[1] Liddell Hart quotes Rommel as asking a captive officer, "What difference does it make if you have two tanks to my one when you spread them out and let me smash them in detail? You presented me with three brigades in succession." The same point was made in Panzer Armee Afrika's official report to Hitler.

might have been preferable from the start to march with determination and in strength to an area which Rommel could not afford to see in British hands. The area of Sidi Rezegh suggests itself, clearly menacing both the besiegers of Tobruk and Axis east-west communications. To this Rommel would have had to react, with fury and predictability. "Those skilled at making the enemy move," observed Sun Tzu wisely, "do so by creating a situation to which he must conform. They entice him with something he is certain to take, and with lines of ostensible profit they await him in strength." The course chosen was, instead, to make a limited movement in the hope that Rommel would play his appointed part. When he did not do so, the moves to Sidi Rezegh, Bir El Gubi and around Gabr Saleh were tentative rather than decisive. The initiative was allowed to pass.

In the latter stages of this first phase of CRUSADER Auchinleck's decision to press the offensive was surely admirable. Cunningham was anxious and exhausted. He was incapable, personally, of further offensive initiative. Auchinleck was right to remove him from command on 26th November and to bring in a replacement for the Eighth Army. Auchinleck reckoned that the strength and logistic support of the Afrika Korps would not suffice for the sort of manoeuvre on which Rommel had embarked. He believed that the British, after a few days' respite, could renew the pressure. He had assets behind him. The Commander-in-Chief had always insisted on keeping reserves of tanks and equipment so that losses could be made good and energy restored. Eighth Army's logisticians had done wonders and would again. The supply columns and their tireless drivers had reached the replenishment points amid the astonishing perplexities of the battlefield, and had somehow kept Eighth Army going.

Auchinleck held on at the crucial moment in the battle, and in consequence won it. British leadership at many levels was imperfect. Morale was undoubtedly shaken by the losses suffered and the bewildering vicissitudes of the last fortnight. The army was far from an impeccable instrument. But CRUSADER was a victory – at first.

In place of Cunningham, Major-General Neil Ritchie, Deputy Chief of General Staff at Middle East Command, was appointed Commander of the Eighth Army. A large, popular, equable man, Ritchie had been an admirable Chief of Staff to Brooke, commanding II Corps in France in 1940. He had commanded a division in England after the evacuation of the BEF, before being despatched to Cairo. Brooke, now CIGS, was devoted to him, but heard of Auchinleck's appointment with alarm.[1] Where, Brooke thought, would Ritchie find the experience or the confidence? He was being made Army Commander in the desert, where he had not commanded or seen conditions except from a desk in Cairo. He was set as superior over Corps Commanders such as Norrie and Godwin-Austen who had not only experienced – with some inner bruising – the recent fighting, but were Ritchie's seniors in the army. He would clearly be Auchinleck's man, putting into effect Auchinleck's ideas rather than his own – for Auchinleck showed every sign of continuing personally to direct operations. It was a false position from the start, which only an extraordinary personality could have surmounted. Eighth Army became ever less "gripped" and coherent. Its constituent parts became more autonomous. There never had been, and there certainly was not now, a sense throughout the army of one comprehending and dominating will. The events of the next six months were to make this painfully clear.

After the relief of Tobruk, XXX Corps was withdrawn to the frontier area where a methodical campaign was mounted to reduce the enemy garrisons holding out at Bardia and Halfaya. Both surrendered in January. Meanwhile operations west of Tobruk were entrusted to XIII Corps (Godwin-Austen). The first task was to dislodge the enemy from the Gazala position, and with luck to trap him. On 15th December, XIII Corps – now consisting of the equivalent of about two divisions and one armoured brigade – attacked. The attack was a failure. A spirited counter-attack by 15th Panzer Division (the Afrika Korps was in reserve behind the Gazala line) showed that there was plenty of sting left. A wide outflanking movement by the British armour, however, although it did not affect the tactical battle, persuaded Rommel that Panzer Gruppe Afrika should be withdrawn from Cyrenaica. Attempts to cut off the withdrawal, in the manner of O'Connor at Beda Fomm, were unsuccessful. The British pursuit was weak, and the attempts of small columns were easily repulsed. Nevertheless airfields were brought into use at Gazala, Mechili and Msus, so that air support – which, throughout CRUSADER, had been the best the army had ever enjoyed – could assist the next step, the invasion of Tripolitania. Rommel had brought his whole command back to the area of Agedabia by Christmas Eve, and it seemed that all the objects of CRUSADER had been achieved – all, that is, except one. The German armour had not been finally destroyed.

On the British side a re-equipped 22nd Armoured Brigade now replaced 4th Armoured Brigade. Unfortunately the enemy had also

[1] It was first made as a temporary appointment.

profited from two convoys reaching Tripoli. The Afrika Korps was restored to a strength of about sixty tanks and 22nd Armoured Brigade had barely taken its place in the forward area when Cruewell put in two vicious attacks with the concentrated German armour on 28th and 30th December in the area of Agedabia. The Germans lost fourteen tanks and the British sixty in these engagements – a typically depressing ratio. Rommel then withdrew his front to El Agheila. He was back where he started a year ago, and the British facing him were in a comparable situation to February and March 1941.

The situation was handled in a comparable way. Once again inadequate force was deployed forward by the British in the area of Mersa Brega and Agedabia, the position covering Cyrenaica most economical in force required. Once again an armoured formation completely fresh to the desert, which had been despatched to the theatre piecemeal, constituted the tank force of XIII Corps. Where previously it had been the ill-fated 2nd Armoured Division, now it was 1st Armoured Division, whose leading brigade, 22nd, had been through CRUSADER and had been recently sent back to Tobruk after rough handling by Cruewell at the end of December. In its place was the division's other brigade, 2nd Armoured Brigade. The division itself had little recent training as such. It was placed under command of General Messervy,[1] who handed over 4th Indian Division – the other formation, beside 200th Guards Brigade, in XIII Corps – to General Tuker.

Once again, too, it was generally expected that Rommel could not possibly attack for some time, and that if he did it must be local and containable. The dramatis personae had all changed since Wavell, Neame, and Gambier-Parry had first experienced contact with the Afrika Korps in March 1941. Only the illusions remained.

Godwin-Austen deployed at the front two weak brigades, each of two battalions: 200th Guards Brigade and the support group (a brigade equivalent) of 1st Armoured Division. 2nd Armoured Brigade, with about eighty Crusader and fifty-five Honey tanks, was held to the left rear of the front. 4th Indian Division (Tuker) was responsible for the coast road and for Benghazi.

On 22nd January, Rommel's forces were renamed "Panzer Armee Afrika". Rommel had four small army corps: Cruewell's Afrika Korps, of 15th and 21st Panzer and 90th Light Division, X and XXI Italian

---

[1] General Lumsden, the Division Commander, had been wounded.

Corps with, between them, five infantry divisions, and XX Italian Corps, with the Ariete Armoured and Trieste Motorised Divisions. Rommel had decided on a limited, spoiling attack, to knock the British off-balance and delay any attempt on Tripolitania. His armoured strength had been brought up to eighty-four German and eighty-nine Italian tanks. He knew that the only British armour in Cyrenaica was one inexperienced brigade of rather smaller size. Although his supply and fuel situation was particularly bad, the opportunity could not be neglected. On 21st January, the Afrika Korps attacked once again. Rommel intended to penetrate the British front, pass the British armour and then turn and surround it. Thereafter, instead of a deep advance across the chord of the Cyrenaican arc, he planned a short thrust only, eastwards, and a strong hook to his left to take Benghazi from the east.

In the early encounters, as ever, British losses greatly exceeded German. The initial advance of the Afrika Korps went as planned. 2nd Armoured Brigade was not trapped, but met the Germans driving north towards Msus on 25th January. The brigade was completely routed, and driven headlong from the field, abandoning stores, vehicles and any early chance to salvage much reputation from its first encounter with the Afrika Korps. 4th Indian Division and 1st Armoured (which had hereafter little effective strength left) could do nothing to help each other. Godwin-Austen appreciated that there should be a general withdrawal towards Mechili.

At this Ritchie demurred – indeed he stopped this withdrawal, took 4th Indian Division under Army Command (thus leaving remarkably little to the authority of Godwin-Austen) and expressed the belief that "offensive action" could check the enemy before Benghazi and in mid-Jebel. His Corps and Divisional Commanders dissented. It did not appear to them comparable to that moment in November when Auchinleck had judged the Afrika Korps exhausted. Now Rommel might be – was – short of petrol, but his armour was largely undamaged and the Italian divisions barely committed, while the British tank force had received one of its periodic savage maulings and was in disarray. Events themselves persuaded Ritchie. The campaign dissolved into a formless and undirected retreat to Gazala, not closely pressed by Rommel, whose supply position was mercifully grave. Once again, Cyrenaica with its airfields was lost.

Godwin-Austen felt Ritchie had shown no confidence in him. Ritchie had overridden his opinion and taken one of his two divisions under direct command. Godwin-Austen asked to be relieved of his command, to which Auchinleck assented. It was an inauspicious start to a new chapter in the life of Eighth Army. It was also a profoundly depressing finale to CRUSADER, with the army back in front of Tobruk at the beginning of February. Auchinleck wrote home to the CIGS and to Ritchie in the field castigating the incapacity of the army's Armoured Corps Commanders throughout CRUSADER. He compared them harshly with Gott, a rifleman, or with the great Gunner, Brigadier Campbell, who had commanded 7th Support Group at Sidi Rezegh and received the Victoria Cross. He wrote of their faulty tactics and lack of professional instincts. The British Army had lost, in this latest withdrawal, another seventy-two tanks and forty guns. It had also lost yet more confidence in its leaders, and in the equipment, tactics and command ability which seemed to put men so often in painful and inglorious situations. The past achievements of CRUSADER – and they were real – were less apparent than the ignominy of the present hour. Once again the British had been through much for nothing. It had all gone wrong. In the end they had been beaten.

9

Burnt by the Rising Sun

In the autumn of 1941, after a long period of deteriorating relations deriving mainly from the Sino-Japanese War, the United States, joined by Britain and Holland's Government in exile in London, instituted a trade embargo against Japan. This left the Japanese, who needed to import to live let alone make war, with the stark alternatives of abandoning their protracted campaign in China, or of seizing necessary raw materials by a policy of expansion. The targets of such a campaign were likely to be American, British and Dutch bases and possessions.

Just when Rommel was giving orders for the German withdrawal from Tobruk, shortly after midnight on 7th December 1941, the Japanese Twenty-Fifth Army invaded Malaya. Simultaneously the Japanese Air Force struck forward Malayan airfields with such force and success that when the British assembled their remaining fighter and bomber force at Butterworth Airfield on 9th December only ten serviceable aircraft had survived. With 150 aircraft operating from captured airfields, Japanese air superiority thereafter dominated operations.

A few hours later, troops of the Japanese Twenty-Third Army crossed the frontier of the New Territories of Hong Kong. Thus, while a temporary sense of victory could be savoured in North Africa, in Asia a new and appalling catalogue of disasters began to unfold.

The defence of Hong Kong is a type of operation peculiarly difficult to criticise: it was sacrificial. The Chiefs of Staff and the Government recognised that the colony was indefensible against major attack, unless reinforced out of all proportion to its strategic value. The garrison consisted of six battalions – two Indian, two Canadian (recently arrived in October 1941) and two British. There were in all five batteries of artillery. The Commander-in-Chief, Far East (Air Marshal Sir Robert Brooke-Popham), had consistently pressed for reinforcement of Hong Kong, as a stimulus to confidence in British strength and will. Less convincingly, he had suggested that the colony might be held for a considerable period of time against Japanese attack. Originally it had been assumed that in war the British would send a fleet to the Far East, and that British and American maritime power would ultimately frustrate Japanese movements against British and Dutch possessions. All this had changed. The preoccupations of the British in the Atlantic and Mediterranean precluded the sending of a major fleet, although the great warships *Prince of Wales* and *Repulse* had sailed east in a last minute attempt to deter Japan. The Japanese were present in force in China. They had occupied French Indo-China, giving them a base of operations well to the south. They were well-poised, and when, on the morning of 8th December, they crossed the land frontier between the Canton province of China and the New Territories of Hong Kong they had already destroyed a large part of the United States Pacific Fleet at Pearl Harbor. Two days later *Prince of Wales* and *Repulse* were sunk by Japanese aircraft. Obviously the opening land campaigns of Imperial Japan were not going to be inhibited nor the tide quickly turned by Allied sea power. No resources could be applied to help Hong Kong, no hope could be extended. Its defence was sacrificial.

The attack on Hong Kong was to some extent unexpected. Shortly beforehand the General commanding (Major-General Maltby) did not believe that Japanese preparations were in earnest. Nevertheless plans and preparations had been made, and the garrison was ready to receive the assault when it came. The troops were divided into a mainland brigade, deployed to cover Kowloon, and an island brigade responsible for Hong Kong itself. Like Freyberg in Crete, Maltby had to divide his forces in order to be ready for an assault from the sea which never came.

The Japanese were brave, hardy, well-trained and intelligently led. Throughout the war Japanese soldiers fought to the last when cornered, and with savage yet disciplined fanaticism whether defending or attacking. At Hong Kong they also had numerical superiority – not large, but sufficient. Nor would they have had any difficulty in reinforcing had the battle been unduly protracted – it was not. By 12th December the Japanese 38th Division – nine infantry battalions – had driven the mainland brigade back, forcing it to withdraw to Hong Kong Island.

Six days later, during the night of 18th December, 38th Division landed on the north-east coast of the island. The Japanese aimed to drive the defenders from east to west, and they swiftly captured dominating ground in the centre of the island on the morning of 20th December; thereafter the garrison was cut in two. One part was forced

Hong Kong and the New Territories

towards the Stanley Peninsula in the south, the main body was driven west to an east-facing line, covering the city of Victoria on the north coast and the peak immediately above it. The colony surrendered on Christmas Day.

This bare chronicle of events comprehended fighting that was bitter, a defence that was courageous. Some of the defending battalions had received little training, as they had been specifically designated as garrison rather than field force troops. They were attacked by a skilful and numerically superior enemy with command of the air and strong artillery support. They knew that the outcome would probably be death or captivity. They suffered 4,000 casualties, including 675 killed; and inflicted upward of 3,000 on the enemy. The colony, but little honour, was lost.

The story of the British calamities in Malaya and Singapore bear disagreeable similarity to the disasters of Norway twenty months

183

before, much magnified. A vigorous and well led enemy, not particularly numerous, seemed to overcome difficulties of terrain and climate in which the British found reason for their failure.[1] In too many cases the appearance of a very few tanks was sufficient to induce panic in the defenders. The general atmosphere of ill preparation, paralysed and divided higher direction, indecision and sheer tactical incompetence seems as suffocating now as it was demoralising to the troops at the time. As in Norway, soldiers were committed to battle poorly trained (again, in some but not all cases), with inadequate equipment (they faced armour with insufficient anti-armour weapons and preparation); and without the benefit of a firm and strong-willed command overall. "When the general is morally weak," wrote Sun Tzu, "and his discipline is not strict, where his instructions and guidance are not enlightened, where there are no consistent rules to guide the officers and men and when the formations are slovenly the Army is in disorder." The words are apposite. As in Norway, preliminary coordination by the different Services had been inadequate. As in Norway, the outcome was deplorable, relieved by instances of great gallantry, self-sacrifice and skill. The blow to British prestige was far greater. It was probably irreparable.

The defence of the naval base at Singapore was the prime strategic object in the defence of Malaya, although the British also had obligations by treaty with individual Malay Rulers. It had originally been thought possible to defend Singapore by the fleet, when it arrived, and by the offensive and defensive operations of aircraft, there being in some minds very exaggerated ideas of the tactical effectiveness of air power in land campaigns divorced from the actions of land forces. Forward airfields had been constructed far north in the Malay Peninsula. These, however, needed to be defended against land attack, which could come from across the Siamese frontier or from amphibious landings. The army had thus undertaken, by implication, the defence of all Malaya, yet even on the general concept there had been little coordination between the Services before the war. Nor did matters greatly improve during 1941, despite the appointment of a Commander-in-Chief, Far East, with coordinating powers over army and air force. Coordination was all very well, but strategy had been pre-empted by the construction of forward airfields, which the army was unlikely to be sufficiently strong to defend. As to the navy, the concept of a main fleet being despatched to Singapore in case of danger

[1] It was thought that the Japanese had been specifically trained for jungle fighting. This is not so: it was as strange to them as to the British – who had been stationed there.

184

had played a prominent part in reassuring Britain's friends – and dominions – and served to reduce yet further the sense of urgency needed in the army throughout what should have been the months and years of preparation. In defending Malaya, therefore, the flanks rested on the sea – over which the navy, in the changed circumstances of 1941, was unlikely to have much control, and in fact had none; while adequate air support, if sufficient aircraft were made available, itself depended on a forward defence for which sufficient troops did not exist.

To compound all this, the British authorities in Singapore and the Malay States had so subordinated military considerations to civil and economic factors that there was no serious effort to mobilise labour nor psychologically to prepare the people of any race for war. Yet, by the autumn of 1941, the attitudes adopted by Japan and the United States made a long peace unlikely; and the explicit support by Britain for American policy made it near certain that war waged by Japan in the Far East would mean war with the British Empire.

Britain's efforts were concentrated upon home defence, upon creating a large army at home for operations against Germany and upon her (still small) military effort in the Mediterranean. Little of the British Army could be spared for defence against Japan. The only possible – and nearer – sources of assistance were Australia and India. As so often in the early parts of this story, the British Army itself was represented in the campaign by a small minority of the troops – and by the High Command. To defend Malaya and Singapore, the new General Officer Commanding (Lieutenant-General A. E. Percival) assessed his requirement as five divisions. He received from Australia 8th Division (Major-General Bennett), composed of two brigades; from India 9th Indian Division (Major-General Barstow) and 11th Indian Division (Major-General Murray-Lyon), each of two brigades (the latter included two British battalions), and two independent Indian brigades, the 12th (with one British battalion) and the 28th; and a number of Indian battalions deployed for the close defence of the airfields and Penang Island. Percival also had 1st and 2nd Malaya Brigades (five battalions, including three British). The supporting artillery and engineers for the Indian formations came from both the British and the Indian Army.

For his whole task Percival had thirty-one battalions, seven regiments of field artillery, two regiments of anti-tank artillery, five regiments of anti-aircraft artillery and eight field companies of Engineers: in all about two-thirds of what he had assessed as his need.

For the defence of North Malaya, Percival formed a corps – III

Corps (Lieutenant-General Sir Lewis Heath) – with two Indian divisions and 28th Brigade. 8th Australian Division and 12th Brigade were held in reserve. The two Malaya brigades were stationed on Singapore Island. Since Malaya had few trunk roads, any Japanese advance would be canalised. The country was so rugged as to prevent deployment anywhere on a wide front, or deep outflanking movements except slowly and laboriously undertaken. Malaya is eminently defensible – except against attack from the sea. In III Corps' area, 11th Indian Division was made responsible for frustrating any Japanese attempt to advance down the west coast of the Malay Peninsula. Both of the division's brigades were held well forward, between the Siamese frontier and the airfield of Alor Star. 9th Indian Division was given responsibility for the east – and more vulnerable – coast. One brigade of the division – 8th Brigade – was deployed to cover the port and beaches at Khota Bharu, at the mouth of the Kelantan River. The second brigade – 22nd – was placed at another vulnerable port and estuary on the east coast, Kuantan, 180 miles to the south. The corps reserve, 28th Brigade, was at Ipoh, halfway between the Malay capital, Kuala Lumpur, and the frontier. 11th Division was also responsible for the operations of a separate force – called Krohcol – based on an Indian battalion, and directed to oppose any enemy advance south across the Siamese border from Patani towards Kroh. In army reserve 8th Australian Division was deployed in Johore, and 12th Brigade at Port Dickson, on the south-west coast.

Training, however, had until recently been neglected and lacked urgency. The Indian troops were largely officered by wartime British officers, many of whom had not acquired the linguistic skill to communicate with their men. The Indian Army had been made to expand and form new divisions on an inadequate human base or cadre – with the consequent and inevitable dilution of quality. The routine of garrison rather than the aggressive character of a field force had been dominant in Malaya. The British had given little thought and practice to the problems of fighting in a country largely covered by primary and secondary jungle. There had been little realistic study of the Japanese, who were generally underrated (except by the Australians who, as often, had shrewder perceptions). The picture was comfortably formed of an undersized race unlikely to match European military sophistication, particularly in the air. The reality was disagreeably different. In almost all respects the Japanese were superior. It was a thoroughly ill-prepared British Army, which the Japanese Twenty-Fifth Army struck on 8th December.

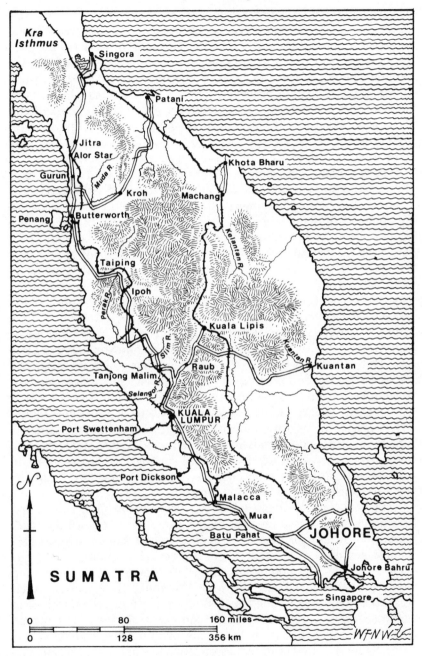

Malaya

187

Malaya Command was first warned on 29th November that hostilities were imminent. In addition to the defensive deployment it was planned to move a force forward across the Siamese frontier to the Kra Isthmus – a plan which would only be put into effect if the Japanese actually landed, or were so clearly about to do so as to justify British action (it was hoped) in Siamese eyes. Part of 11th Indian Division was held ready, but in the event this operation never took place. It is difficult to believe that it would have led to anything except another disaster somewhat further from base. Preparation for it, however, had the effect of distracting 11th Division from their prime defensive task.

Japanese plans were simple. Their 5th Division, with a strength of three infantry regiments (nine battalions), was to land at Singora, while one regiment (three battalions) landed at Patani, on the east coast of the Kra Isthmus in Siam. These four regiments, some 21,000 men, would set out immediately for the Malayan frontier, aiming to advance down the west of the peninsula by two parallel routes, towards Kuala Lumpur. At the same time one infantry regiment with supporting arms – about 5,000 men – was to land at Khota Bharu in far North-East Malaya, and advance south, towards Kuantan, after capture of the east-coast airfields.

In the east, the landing at Khota Bharu succeeded. By 11th December, 8th Indian Brigade, in face of a force of approximately the same size, had withdrawn from the northern airfields which their deployment was intended to protect; and the Brigade Commander proposed to withdraw further, to the important road junction of Kuala Lipis in the centre of Malaya. A Japanese attack at Machang, thirty miles south of Khota Bharu, was driven off with loss on 13th December. Ultimately 8th Brigade received permission to withdraw. It did so not because it had been beaten (although the Japanese landings had been successful and the airfields lost) but because the main threat was now clearly by the west-coast approaches. And in the west matters were bad.

11th Division had deployed its two brigades forward. In the first encounter, at Jitra, the Japanese attack came straight down the road, supported by a small number of tanks. Two of Murray-Lyon's battalions, deployed as a screen, were overrun. The main position was then attacked. The companies of the two inner battalions of each brigade were deployed on a wide front, over much of which, however, it was difficult to conceive the Japanese (known by now to be travelling in motor transport, supported by tanks) choosing to manoeuvre. The road itself being the boundary between the two brigades, command was instantly complicated in any attack involving troops both sides of it. The areas immediately adjoining the road were not held in strength or depth, and by concentrating as much force as the ground permitted the Japanese were able to outflank the forward companies of the two battalions concerned, one from each brigade – thus, on 12th December, there was a withdrawal, much of it chaotic. 11th Division had been fought or manoeuvred out of its defence of one simple and definable axis of enemy advance, by an enemy force weaker in infantry (for only one Japanese regiment had been so far deployed). The enemy had been supported by a small force of tanks, largely confined to the road. Yet 11th Division possessed an anti-tank regiment.

A similar story was repeated thirty miles to the south at Gurun on 15th December. 11th Division had by now been given the corps reserve – 28th Brigade. A Japanese attack down the road smashed through two Indian companies and reached a British Battalion Headquarters. One battalion withdrew due west by the only road open. The other managed to stay with the rest of its parent brigade. Murray-Lyon then withdrew his whole command south of the Muda River. The Japanese advance was now, after a week, nearing the latitude of Penang Island and had already covered 100 miles. Much of 11th Division was already clearly demoralised, with little fight left in it. 12th Brigade (the army reserve) was now allotted by Percival to III Corps, and by 18th December 11th Division, with 12th Brigade under Divisional Command, was concentrated north of Taiping. At the same time Percival authorised withdrawal if necessary behind the Perak River, a major obstacle which runs southwards to the west of Ipoh, and ordered positions to be prepared between Ipoh and Tanjong Malim, only forty miles north of Kuala Lumpur. The Japanese tide was flowing fast, and by dawn on 23rd December the whole of 11th Division were behind the Perak River.

The respite was shortlived. Heath decided not to dispute the crossing of the Perak River, and to their surprise the Japanese crossed it unmolested. On 24th December Murray-Lyon was relieved by Brigadier Paris as Commander 11th Division. The division then held a series of positions on the road north of Ipoh and inflicted considerable casualties on the Japanese. The troops were, however, becoming extremely tired and the ubiquitous Japanese Air Force, although it caused little direct loss, had its invariable effect on morale. The crux came at Slim River, where 11th Division held the main road south in considerable depth. On 6th January an infantry attack was beaten off with loss. But during the night a column of Japanese tanks with embussed infantry, broke through, straight down the road. Obstacles were ineffective. Out of a stock of one thousand four hundred anti-tank mines in the division only twenty-four had been made available and

189

only one troop of anti-tank guns (out of the divisional regiment) was deployed with the leading brigade. As a result the Japanese were able to smash completely through two brigades, leaving only scattered detachments to make their way south through the rubber plantations. Shock, surprise, and the absence of enough effective anti-tank weapons properly deployed completed the demoralisation of troops already thoroughly exhausted. 11th Indian Division had been, for a while, destroyed.

On the east coast 9th Indian Division (Barstow) was not attacked during the first phase of the Japanese advance in the west, to the Perak River. 9th Division had a brigade at Kuala Lipis, which had withdrawn from Khota Bharu, and a brigade – 22nd Brigade (Brigadier Painter) – at Kuantan on the coast. 22nd Brigade was ordered to deny the airfield to the enemy and to prevent landings from the sea. The airfield lies only a short distance south of the Kuantan River, and to prevent an enemy reaching it, as well as to deny the beaches north of Kuantan to the enemy, Painter deployed one of his battalions north of the river, covering the beaches; while a second battalion defended the line of the river on the south bank, with the third in reserve.

On 27th December the Corps Commander, General Heath, told the Divisional Commander, Barstow, that on no account should the 22nd Brigade be put at risk. To keep it unscathed was more important than to hold the airfield. This was passed on to the Brigade Commander, Painter, who said that the airfield could not be denied if all his troops were south of the river. Nevertheless on 29th Heath wrote to Barstow saying that it would be wrong to attempt to fight the enemy on the far side of the Kuantan River. The important thing was the "preservation of the entity of 22nd Brigade". Accordingly Barstow ordered Painter to withdraw his battalion from north of the river – a withdrawal which was interrupted by a Japanese attack. Some of the forward battalion got back, some did not. Painter then told Barstow that if, as he understood, his duty was on no account to risk his brigade, and since he had been ordered to withdraw a battalion from where it could, in his judgment, have defended the now indefensible airfield, he wished to withdraw his whole brigade westwards. It was clearly in jeopardy. In reply he was told it was "highly desirable" that Kuantan Airfield should continue to be denied to the enemy. Painter accordingly moved his reserve battalion eastwards to the airfield perimeter. In the same set of orders, however, he was again told of the "utmost importance" of his brigade not being jeopardised. Next day he received what appears an almost unequivocal order – to deny the airfield to the enemy for as long as possible – certainly for five days until 6th January. By now, of course, this task was impossible. The airfield was surrounded. On 2nd January 22nd Brigade was ordered to abandon Kuantan Airfield and withdraw westwards. The withdrawal was again interrupted by a fierce Japanese attack, but some two-thirds assembled in the area of Raub. The operational aim had been confused and ambiguous; the resultant orders an example of vacillating interference.

These early encounters set the pattern of the Malayan campaign. Some of the causes have been discussed. The symptoms were dispiriting. Individual battalions fought well in particular actions and were puzzled when ordered to quit. But some of the soldiers were exceedingly raw. Some had certainly never seen a tank and were ready to endow it with almost supernatural qualities. The training of some had been elementary, to the shame of the authorities who sent them to battle. The Japanese advance, like the German in France, had successfully paralysed the minds of some of the commanders opposing it. There was little grasp. Frightened men exposed to the alarming and the unfamiliar are praeternaturally quick to detect feebleness and confusion in the minds that try to control them, and in Malaya it is hard to conclude that there was not feebleness and confusion indeed. It became popular to believe that the Japanese were numerically superior, superbly equipped and had grown up in jungles. They were, it is true, experienced. They had been fighting in China. But above all they were tough, disciplined, well trained and conformed very simply to the most elementary principles of war, which their adversaries too often neglected. Defective staff work, slow reactions, poor basic training, tactical incompetence and failing morale – these were the elements in a sad and sadly familiar story for which the British authorities both in England and in India had nobody and nothing but themselves to blame. It was a delayed replay of the events of 1940 in Europe. War, and the preparing and hardening of an army for it, had not been taken sufficiently seriously. The army in India was as out of date in attitudes and equipment as the army at home. A ruthless and skilful enemy had once again been able to subject half-measures and hesitation to brutal defeat.

The withdrawal continued with its own depressing momentum. Percival's hope was to hold as far forward as possible in Malaya in order to cover the arrival of fresh troops. On 1st January the Chiefs of Staff had agreed the level of reinforcement. Two infantry divisions and one armoured brigade were to sail or be diverted to Singapore. The first of these was 17th Indian – a division which had only been due to start training in February, planned for a role in the Middle East, but which Wavell had been assured he could retain in India for the defence of Burma. The second was 18th (British) Division, sailing from England, its men already two months on board ship without a break. The armoured brigade was 7th Armoured – two regiments of Honey tanks – made available by Auchinleck in the immediate aftermath of CRUSADER. These would all take time to arrive, and some never did. Their quality and readiness for battle could not possibly be high. The urgency of the situation made it improbable that they would be committed other than piecemeal and unprepared. And so it was. The first brigade – 45th Indian Brigade – of 17th Division reached Singapore on 3rd January, its equipment three days later. It was hurried forward to Malacca, on the west coast of Malaya.

Percival's plan was now to hold Johore, the southern state of the federation. He gave III Corps the task of denying to the enemy the airfields at Kuala Lumpur and Port Swettenham as long as possible, and then to man a line in North-West Johore. This decision was overruled by Wavell, who had just been appointed to the thankless post of Allied Supreme Commander in a huge area of South-East Asia, including Malaya, Singapore, Borneo and the Dutch East Indies – the ABDA Command. He visited Malaya en route to take up his duties, and assessed the fighting potential left in the exhausted troops of the British Empire – and thus the chances of holding Singapore. He was unimpressed. On 8th January he directed – a remarkable intervention from a Supreme Commander – that III Corps should be withdrawn to rest and refit, after holding out for as long as could be north of Kuala Lumpur. Wavell also ordered that 8th Australian Division, reinforced, should prepare a defensive line in North-West Johore, and that III Corps, behind the front, should look after the east and west coasts.

Meanwhile the Japanese harried the retreating British down the Malay Peninsula, inflicting sharp losses wherever there was contact, and dealing with any opposition in entirely orthodox fashion, by outflanking movements in a series of short hooks. They crossed the Sungi Selangor on 9th January and entered Kuala Lumpur two days later. 11th Division withdrew, and 9th Division in the east conformed.

Henceforth the command organisation became increasingly unsatisfactory. Percival made General Bennett, of 8th Australian Division, Commander of WESTFORCE – which included 9th Indian Division, but did not include all of the Australians. Bennett had four brigades in his command. Heath, at III Corps, was given one of the Australian brigades as well as his own 11th Indian Division. 12th Brigade was sent to Singapore Island, to re-form. Johore, therefore, contained the remainder of 11th Indian Division, in little condition to fight; the two brigades of 9th Indian Division, from the east coast; and 8th Australian Division who had not yet been engaged. These, nominally, numbered six brigades, to which were added 45th Indian Brigade, just arrived at Malacca, and 53rd (British) Brigade, the leading brigade of 18th Division which reached Singapore on 13th January and was immediately sent forward to the front.

Percival now had three possible enemy axes of advance to cover: the east coast, where he created EASTFORCE – 22nd Australian Brigade and all troops on the east coast; the main trunk road in the centre, with Bennett's four brigades of WESTFORCE; and on the west coast the network of roads from Malacca through Muar and Batu Pahat, where 45th Brigade was deployed, sometimes under the command of Bennett (for the centre and west-coast routes directly affected each other) and sometimes directly under the command of Heath. In spite of the existence of one corps and three Divisional Commanders in Johore Percival, the Army Commander, as often as not found himself ordering the deployment of individual brigades and battalions. Whatever the cause – and there were many – coordination was often deplorable. When some troops withdrew others, whose position was vitally affected, often remained in ignorance.

In these circumstances, and helped by a network of main and estate roads, particularly in West Johore, the Japanese had little difficulty in retaining the initiative and jockeying the British out of successive positions. They had the British on the run. The principal task of British Command was seen as the coordination of withdrawal. The troops found themselves cut off, or in danger of being so, in position after position. The Japanese faced few obstacles to their advance. Demolitions were often neglected, or the orders for their firing misunderstood. And as there had been no time to rectify the tactical mistakes made earlier they were repeated.

At Muar, for instance, a vital point on the west coast, 45th Brigade was deployed on so wide a front as to make the defeat of battalions in detail as straightforward a matter as at Jitra. 45th Brigade, largely untrained, fought with considerable gallantry. It was ambushed and crumbled into pieces by the Japanese, having been deployed to tasks under conditions which made success impossible. Ultimately the brigade was surrounded, and the remaining men were ordered to break through Japanese encirclement as best they could. Thereafter 11th Indian Division, given two battalions of the equally raw 53rd Brigade, was made responsible for the west coast. Amid scenes of ever increasing chaos, order and counter-order 15th Brigade of 11th Division was evacuated by sea on 1st February. All guns, equipment and vehicles were lost. On the east coast the Australians inflicted some sharp defeats on the Japanese, by intelligent laying of ambush, and by hard fighting. In consequence the withdrawal of EASTFORCE was largely unmolested, and 22nd Australian Brigade moved back in good order to Johore Bahru, the point where the south running routes join, opposite Singapore Island. In the centre, however, coordination again failed. The Japanese drove a wedge between two brigades of WESTFORCE, and isolated 22nd Indian Brigade. Three hundred and fifty men, all that were left, took to the jungle in an attempt to get away. On 1st February they surrendered. That morning the last troops withdrew from Johore, across the causeway to Singapore.

Percival was ordered to hold Singapore Island to the last. He was exhorted to keep the Japanese engaged as long as there was breath in the body. The naval base, the protection of whose facilities had been the object of the entire campaign, was clearly no longer usable: naval personnel were withdrawn and demolitions carried out by the Admiral's order. Nevertheless Singapore was a symbol. Percival was left in no doubt about his task. In the event it was overrun in a campaign of seven days.

The island presented the usual problem for the defender of a long coastline with many landing places for an invading force. It demanded choices. The defenders could not be strong everywhere. Wavell, during his visit, had decided that the north-west coast was the most vulnerable. Percival disagreed. He feared for the north-east. In the event Wavell was proved right, but whatever the prediction the dispersion of effort which actually took place is hard to justify. The available troops – some twelve brigades, including locally raised volunteer brigades, totalling in all thirty-eight battalions – were distributed round the coast, each brigade with a wide sector. One brigade only was kept as a central reserve. There was virtually no power of concentration against an enemy who would, it could be assumed with confidence, himself deliver a concentrated attack. It is easy to comment thus, but the alternatives were painful and every course had its dangers. To create larger reserves would have meant fewer troops watching the coast and, in Percival's view, have abolished any hope of immediate counter-attack on the beaches. The upshot might have been as lamentable as what occurred. It could hardly have been more so.

Percival divided responsibility for the island between three sectors: in the north III Corps, with 11th Indian Division, and 18th Division

194

(Major-General Beckwith-Smith) just landed from England on 5th February; in the southern area the two Malayan brigades and a volunteer brigade, with certain fortress troops, under Major-General Keith Simmons; and in the western area 8th Australian Division, with a recently landed Indian brigade – 44th Brigade – under its command. Bennett thus had two Australian and one Indian brigades. Each area was supported by one regiment of field artillery per brigade, the normal allocation. 12th Brigade was held in central reserve. Little work had been done on defensive works; indeed, the north coast of the island was not even reconnoitred for defensive positions until 9th January, and a detailed plan was not produced until 28th.

The Japanese planned to attack with three divisions, concentrating on the north-west coast. There, sixteen battalions, with five in reserve, were committed to the main assault on the evening of 8th February. Such concentration was overwhelming. No sufficient weight of fire could be brought against it and the invaders got ashore on a broad front and immediately started to infiltrate inland. The attack achieved saturation by numbers. Australian battalions were withdrawn from the forward areas with considerable difficulty. By nightfall on 9th February the defence of Singapore was based on a line in the western sector – the Jurong Line – running from north to south between two small estuaries, and providing something of a funnel. The Jurong Line lay some eight miles west of the city of Singapore itself.

Thenceforth the story is as depressing as any involving the British Army so far in this war. Coordination among brigades was slight, especially in the western sector. In consequence one withdrew, another heard of it, the rumour spread (sometimes without foundation) and a domino sequence of hasty and uncoordinated retirements mocked the efforts of the soldiers which, at unit level, were often brave and successful. Many withdrawals took place not under pressure from the enemy but from what was supposed to be the necessity to conform. Flanks were suddenly found to be resting on air, and the only solution considered was to move backwards. Percival had prepared a secret contingency plan to withdraw to the perimeter of Singapore City itself. The plan was distributed as such – and in the western sector taken as an executive order and acted upon. Morale is impossible to maintain in such conditions. Furthermore a large number of individual British, Australian and Indian reinforcements had recently arrived, sent from their homelands with little training and less discipline. There was small confidence in authority or respect left for it. The streets of Singapore were full of armed, leaderless and uncontrolled men, drunken, looting and careless of anything but the possibility of forcing a way on to a ship and thus escape. All retreats are fearful, all evacuations wretched. Disgrace abounds. It was inevitable that the scale of all these things at Singapore was greater than elsewhere.

The Jurong Line was abandoned, unnecessarily, by the evening of 10th February, and an Australian plan to re-occupy it was frustrated by a Japanese attack. By the morning of 13th February all troops had been withdrawn to the twenty-eight mile perimeter of Singapore City itself. That afternoon Percival held a conference. His subordinate commanders were unanimous. No counter-stroke was possible. The administrative situation both for the army and for the city was parlous. The water supply would not last much longer.

Next morning the Japanese attack brought the fighting into the streets of the western outskirts of Singapore.

On the following day Percival held another conference. The decision was taken to capitulate. Percival surrendered Singapore on 15th February. All firing ceased at eight thirty that evening.

In seventy days three Japanese divisions had driven a British Imperial Army of comparable size down the length of the rugged and defensible Malay Peninsula; had attacked and conquered the island of Singapore, their immediate objective; and had taken 130,000 prisoners, a figure exceeding the total of Japanese troops employed. The defeat was overwhelming, the humiliation without precedent. The British Army had been engaged in some strength only in the later stages, when 18th Division arrived. But the command was British, British regiments had been involved and the shock was felt throughout army and nation. The whole business had, it was felt, been bungled. It was known that, while some scenes of indiscipline and unprincipled disorder had been played out in Singapore, some individual units had been undefeated, puzzled by capitulation, feeling only a void in the command above them. It was known that the Japanese always despised the conquered enemy who had succumbed too easily: men might be repelled by the brutality of that attitude but still feel, however uneasily, that it could be justified. "We were frankly out-generalled, outwitted and outfought," wrote General Sir Henry Pownall on 13th February, recently VCIGS, now Chief of Staff to Wavell. "It is a great disaster for British Arms, one of the worst in history, and a great blow to the honour and prestige of the Army. From the beginning to the end of this campaign we have been outmatched by better soldiers."

At the heart of the matter, however, was the unpreparedness of the British Empire for crisis, its refusal over the years to make sacrifices, to prepare against disagreeable contingencies, while at the same time supporting a policy hostile to Japan. The consequence was a system

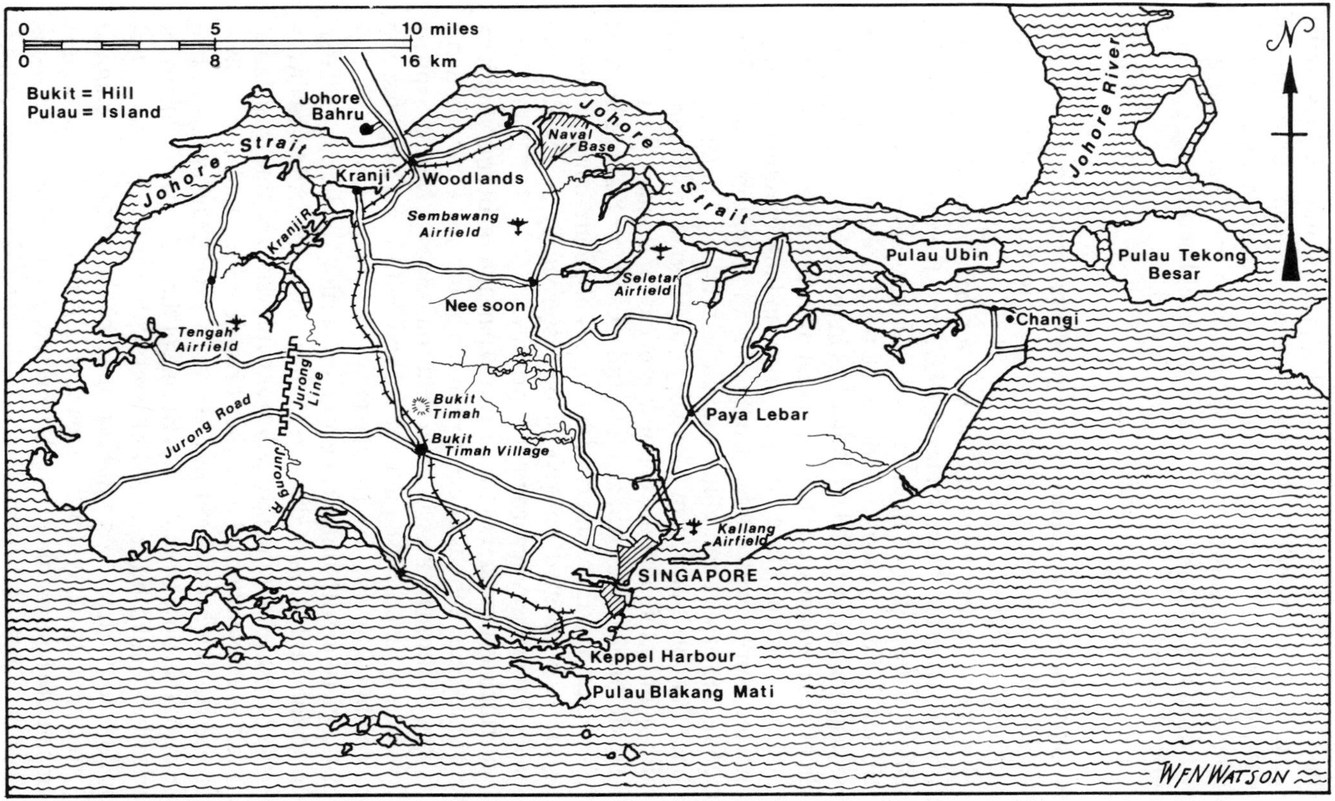

Singapore Island

Bukit = Hill
Pulau = Island

10 miles
16 km

Johore River

Pulau Tekong Besar

Pulau Ubin

•Changi

Johore Strait

Johore Naval Base

Seletar Airfield

Paya Lebar

Kallang Airfield

SINGAPORE

Keppel Harbour

Pulau Blakang Mati

Woodlands

Sembawang Airfield

Nee soon

Bukit Timah

Bukit Timah Village

Johore Bahru

Kranji

Kranji

Jurong Line

Jurong R.

Jurong Road

Tengah Airfield

Johore Strait

W.F.V.WATSON

completely unfitted to take the first shock of war. All else – the incapacity of commanders, the poor training of troops, the failure of morale, the neglect of preparations, the inadequate equipment – all stemmed from the same basic cause. The heroism of particular units and individuals, of which there was plenty, could never make good this profound defect.

The Japanese southern flank was now secure for another adventure which had started in earnest a few weeks before the fall of Singapore: the invasion of Burma.

The pre-war garrison of Burma was very small. Its administration had been separated from India in 1937, and thereafter two British battalions were stationed there, as well as four locally raised battalions of Burma Rifles, and six battalions of the Burma Frontier Force, previously the Burma Military Police. As in India the prime task of the soldiers was internal security. The threat of invasion from the east was regarded as remote. The country was wild and inaccessible. No roads connected Burma with India. A limited road system ran north from Rangoon, the capital and military headquarters – to Toungoo, Meik-tila and Mandalay; and from Mandalay the "Burma road" ran north-east through Lashio into the Chinese province of Yunnan. To the east and south no metalled road ran into Indo-China or Siam. The great valley of the Irrawaddy, screened by ranges of jungle-covered hills to west and east, seemed unlikely to be disturbed by an invader and Burma's defence was accorded little priority.

Nevertheless during 1941 a certain expansion of Burma's military forces took place, although severely limited by finance. Four additional battalions of Burma Rifles and two field companies of Burma Sappers and Miners were organised into the 1st and 2nd Burma Brigades, and then combined in the 1st Burma Division (Major-General Bruce-Scott), a division with little artillery or supporting services and, like so many in the early days, a division in little but name. Additionally, in February 1941 13th Indian Brigade was deployed in Burma from India, followed in November by a further brigade – 16th Indian. Finally – after the Japanese onslaught in December – the Chiefs of Staff had authorised the move from India to Burma of three British battalions, of two further Indian brigades – 46th and 48th – and two Indian Divisional Headquarters, 14th and 17th, of which the first was not planned to arrive until April. When the Japanese began their advance against Burma in late January, therefore, Burma was defended by two divisions (at least in name) – 1st Burma and 17th Indian (Major-General J. G.

Smyth, V.C.) – with a total of six brigades, two Burman and four Indian. Of four British battalions, two recently arrived, two were incorporated into 16th and 46th Brigades and two retained for independent tasks.

The participation of the British Army, therefore, in the first Burma campaign was minimal. But the command was British. It was a British campaign. Burma had been, to the irritation of the War Office, included in the responsibilities of the Commander-in-Chief, Far East, at Singapore. And Burma was first included, with Malaya, in the new Australian, British, Dutch, American (ABDA) Command set up when the Japanese attacked, to which Wavell was appointed. The command was short-lived and Burma was transferred on 22nd February to the responsibility of GHQ India. This was rational. Part of Burma's strategic importance was as a glacis to the defence of India, and any resources for the defence of Burma were likely to be provided, if at all, from India. Hard though communications made it to envisage, a campaign in Burma might need to be supported from a main base in India – unless Rangoon could be securely held, and nourished from the sea. Road building was set in hand to link India with Burma and remarkable feats were performed. In the meantime to defend Southern Burma, and in particular Rangoon, against attack from south and east was the first, but by no means the only, task of the Burma Command. Central Burma could also be invaded from the east, from Indo-China or from Northern Siam into the Shan States or the Karen Hills. A very long front had to be watched.

On 27th December, Lieutenant-General T. J. Hutton assumed command in Burma. 1st Burma Division with two brigades was left in Central Burma to be responsible for the routes into the country from the Mekong Valley. Hutton concentrated four brigades – 16th, 46th, 48th Indian[1] and 2nd Burma Brigades – under 17th Indian Division in the south, covering Rangoon. The line of the Salween River was to be held. This was the route the enemy were to take.

When the Japanese first struck at the British Empire, on 8th December, they planned, initially, to seize airfields in Tenasserim, the southern strip of Burma which runs down the west side of the Kra Isthmus; and this they did, occupying the airfield at Victoria Point, the southern point of Burma, from which the garrison had withdrawn. Thereafter the Japanese concentrated the Fifteenth Army (33rd and

[1] 48th Brigade was not allotted to 17th Division until 7th February. 17th Division, of course, had earlier been intended for Malaya Command.

199

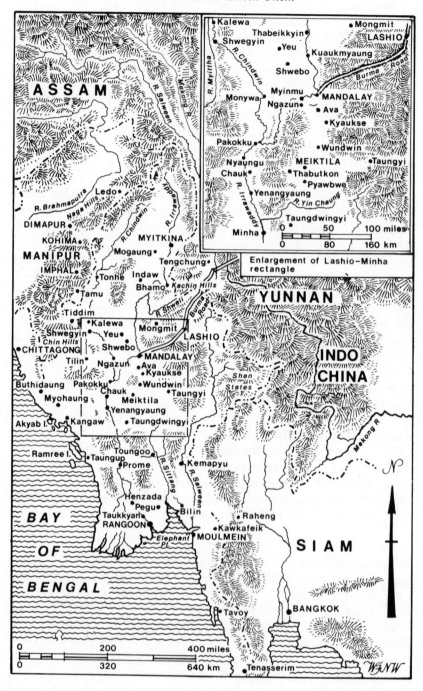

Enlargement of Lashio–Minha
rectangle

Burma

55th Divisions) at Raheng, in Siam, opposite Moulmein in Burma. Here the Japanese divisions were organised on a pack animal basis and ordered to be ready to advance into Burma when the progress of operations in Malaya made it appropriate. Their first objective was Rangoon.

On 15th January, the Japanese occupied, without opposition, the airfield at Tavoy in Tenasserim, giving them three airfields in Southern Burma from which to support operations. On 20th January the Japanese 55th Division crossed the Siamese-Burmese frontier west of Raheng and advanced towards Moulmein. They were met by 16th Indian Brigade at Kawkafeik, which was authorised to withdraw to avoid encirclement. A familiar pattern started to be repeated. The troops began to go backwards, and to feel the process unnerving and irreversible. The 17th Division, which Hutton intended should defend for as long as possible on the Salween River (whereas Moulmein itself should be given up) was levered out by the Japanese without great difficulty. In the south the Japanese 55th Division outflanked the defence by landing from the sea; in the north, by attacking in concentrated strength against a long front too weakly held, the Japanese 33rd Division established a regimental bridgehead west of the river on 11th February. Threatened by double envelopment Smyth received permission on 14th February to withdraw from the Salween to the Bilin River; meanwhile the Japanese Fifteenth Army confirmed orders – that after crossing the Salween and Sittang Rivers it was to aim for Pegu, and then swing north and south to Toungoo and Rangoon.

The Bilin position was not strong: the front some fifteen miles long, the river itself fordable. The Japanese, having crossed the Salween, marched by jungle tracks with such energy that they reached the Bilin in some places before those who were meant to defend it. With six Japanese battalions attacking the Bilin, there was little hope of maintaining a coherent line, and on 18th February Hutton authorised Smyth to withdraw behind the Sittang – the last major obstacle before Rangoon.

The withdrawal behind the Sittang River was marked by some brave individual fighting, but it was not a successful operation of war. By listening to one set of orders given uncoded by radio the Japanese knew what was afoot, and lost no time in trying to cut off the British withdrawal. One bridge crossed the Sittang River. One road ran to the bridge. The east bank was dominated by hills above the road. Two Japanese battalions set out by jungle track to cover the fifty-six miles to the Sittang and to outmarch their retreating enemies, who were moving with motor transport along a congested and inadequate road.

In these circumstances – of which the history of war provides many examples – it was and is essential to bring troops first, from whatever quarter, to provide a strong bridgehead force; to prepare crystal clear orders for the demolition of the bridge itself, with no ambiguity as to responsibility; and to make robust arrangements for liaison, so that the commander of troops responsible for the bridgehead can know as far as possible who has withdrawn through his perimeter and who is yet to come.

Little of this was done. The defence of the bridgehead was organised tardily. The Japanese attacked the Sittang Bridge itself from the north-east without success, but were able to harry the retreating British column and cut the road between one part of the column and another. The matter of blowing the bridge was confused, it being ultimately blown with 17th Divisional Headquarters on the west bank and most of the division still on the east. The bridgehead was held by gallant action of individual units, but the withdrawing column knew little of what hills were held by which side. The withdrawal was harassed by the attacks of Japanese aircraft – and of our own, through failure accurately to fix the bombline east of which all troops could be considered hostile. Staff work, in a word, was inadequate. Communications (largely a matter of equipment) were poor. There was little overall grip. The effect on inadequately trained formations was predictable. With the bridge blown, the remnants of 17th Division did their best to get across the Sittang River by swimming and rafting, after long detour through jungle. Many were drowned. The survivors were concentrated at Pegu, north of Rangoon, on 24th February: about 4,000 infantry or half the divisional establishment, and only 1,400 rifles.

Operations were taking a familiar form. The untrained brigades of 17th Division, formed during a rapid expansion of the Indian Army in 1940 and 1941, were largely unfit for battle. The division itself had had no opportunity to work as such. The training of men to handle their own weapons was largely inadequate. Artillery support consisted of only four batteries. Once again brave battalions and companies fought fine individual actions, but there was little cohesion, and morale suffered as confidence waned. Some battalions "disintegrated" under fire.

There is a further point. It is sometimes easily said that in war on land the attacker requires numerical superiority – with the implication that the defender can accommodate numerical inferiority. A rule of thumb of a three to one ratio for the attacker is sometimes glibly used. Such formulae are misleading. It is generally true that in a tactical situation, on the actual battlefield and in contact, the attacker needs superior numbers. But operationally – that is, when forces are marching and manoeuvring – no such margin is required. The attacker has every advantage. He can concentrate, where the defender is more often dispersed so as to cover all the ground for which he is responsible. The attacker can choose his point of effort. What counts is not overall superiority of numbers but superiority at the right place and time, and thus he who has the initiative has the advantage, and he who is seeking to advance and attack is waging the most successful sort of war – and the easiest. The morale of his troops, too, is sustained by the sense of progress and victory. The morale of the defender, if condemned to a series of withdrawals, can only be maintained among very well trained, well disciplined and sufficiently numerous troops. In Burma, as elsewhere, the condition in which the soldiers were committed to battle, and the circumstances of the campaign, made the outcome as unsurprising as depressing. From afar the Commander-in-Chief (Wavell), the CIGS (Brooke), the Viceroy (Marquess of Linlithgow) and the Prime Minister (Churchill) each fulminated, with good reason, at what appeared the lack of fighting spirit of the troops. They blamed the immediate command – always the easiest, often the only resource. Brooke wrote in his diary on 18th February: "Burma news now bad. Cannot make out why troops are not fighting better. If the Army cannot fight better than it is doing at present we shall deserve to lose our Empire." But the trouble lay in the past.

The gate to Rangoon was now, if not open, at least ajar. 17th Division was hurriedly reconstituted in the area of Pegu, with two brigades – 16th and 48th Indian – and redeployed to the Sittang, leaving a wide gap between it and 1st Burma Division, which moved south to the Sittang Valley to take command of 1st and 2nd Burma Brigades. 13th Indian Brigade was left at Kemapyu on the Salween, in Central Burma, where it was hoped that Chinese troops would increasingly assume responsibility.[1] The Rangoon area had only four brigades, most of them badly shaken. Rangoon was the only entry point for the British reinforcements desperately needed for the immediate battle. On the other hand if Rangoon had to be abandoned the line of withdrawal for the army would be northward towards Prome, 150 miles up the Irrawaddy, and to Toungoo on the Sittang – across an attacking enemy's front.

[1] Chiang Kai-shek had agreed that two Chinese Armies should assist in the defence of Burma. They were of uneven quality. The southernmost Chinese division was now deployed in the Sittang Valley, at Toungoo.

Hutton was thus presented with a disagreeable choice. If he left until too late the decision to quit Rangoon he would find withdrawal impossible. If he took the decision too early he would be criticised for failing to impose maximum delay upon the enemy – and the army might be unsupported by reinforcements who could only arrive through the port. 7th Armoured Brigade had been sent from the Middle East and was now due to land and fight in Burma. 63rd Indian Brigade was sailing from India. Three British battalions were on the way.

By 27th February, 7th Armoured Brigade – two tank regiments, a close support artillery battery and a battalion of infantry – had disembarked and been ordered forward to support 17th Division. Hutton now told Wavell, who had resumed the Command-in-Chief in India on the dissolution of the ABDA Command, that unless he received orders to the contrary next day he intended to evacuate Rangoon.

Wavell countermanded this. Rangoon was to be held at least sufficiently long to bring in the reinforcements now at sea – 63rd Brigade, with a regiment of field artillery, were due on 1st March. At the same time Wavell ordered Smyth, who was unwell, to be relieved by Major-General Cowan as Commander 17th Division, and requested the relief of Hutton. He believed a new personality was needed to put the necessary spirit into troops depressed by failure and retirement. On 5th March Lieutenant-General the Hon. Sir Harold Alexander assumed command in Hutton's place. Hutton had not been originally selected as a field commander, Burma being largely an administrative command until the blow fell. His own command decisions, nevertheless, were realistic; and with the means available he made a sound logistic plan for the support of the withdrawal, a plan from which his successors profited. But Hutton paid the penalty of most British Generals at the start of a British campaign. He was a commander deprived of resources, allotted untrained men in insufficient numbers, placed in a losing situation and berated for not winning, and for being too frank about the odds.

Alexander had commanded a division with distinction during the brief campaign in France and Flanders in 1940. He was a man of striking charm, even-tempered, brave, distinguished in appearance, with a good eye for the realities of the battlefield and with a blend of panache and serenity which inspired confidence. His temperament was artistic, but that of an artist in love with action. His strategic abilities were untried, his understanding of war on a grand scale untested. In Burma in 1942 the immediate need was not for strategic flair – the strategic issue was painfully clear – but for courage to take operational decisions at the right moment, and for a presence to reassure a baffled and beaten army. Wavell saw Alexander immediately before he assumed command. Like Hutton, he was to hold Rangoon as long as possible, and to withdraw north when it became necessary. In carrying out these orders Alexander was extremely lucky – and he was, on the whole, lucky: another considerable attribute in a General.

Although their patrols crossed the Sittang River on 27th February, the Japanese Fifteenth Army needed to pause before the next major step. Comparatively undemanding though their logistic arrangements might be, the Japanese had by now outmarched their supplies. They also had a dilemma; like the British it was one of timing. They knew that Central Burma was now being reinforced by Chinese troops. One school of thought in the Japanese Command wished to turn north and rout the Chinese before they became uncomfortably strong: Rangoon could be screened – the British power of offensive was reckoned negligible. This policy was rejected. Instead, General Iida, commanding Fifteenth Army, had his way and was directed to continue towards Rangoon. For Iida Rangoon was a great prize, a port through which supplies, heavy equipment and transport could come, a main base which could nourish more ambitious operations than those largely supported by animal and manpack as hitherto. By the same token the Japanese knew well what difficulties the loss of Rangoon would impose on any British Army remaining in Burma, with no line of communication to India – difficulties somewhat diminished by Hutton's forethought in moving considerable stockpiles from Rangoon into Central Burma so that as far as Mandalay the army could draw on supplies from the north. Fifteenth Army was ordered to cross the Sittang on 3rd March and advance on Rangoon.

33rd Division in the north crossed on 2nd March, and by 5th March was over the Pegu River. 55th Division in the south was directed on Pegu itself. Once again 17th Indian Division was threatened with envelopment; and little opposition lay between that envelopment and the planned northwards withdrawal route of the army from Rangoon. Some fierce fighting took place in Pegu, where 48th Brigade narrowly avoided being cut off. By the evening of 5th March – Alexander's first day of command – the Japanese felt sufficiently confident to decide to attack Rangoon by direct assault, to take it on the run. 33rd Division would march west, cross the Prome road, turn south-east and sweep down on Rangoon from the north-west – from, it was hoped, an unexpected direction.

Alexander had countermanded Hutton's orders for the evacuation of Rangoon. He had directed certain counter-offensive moves in the area east of Pegu, moves already overtaken by events. The Japanese were in considerable strength across the Sittang and Pegu Rivers and were advancing towards the Irrawaddy. On 6th March Alexander bowed to the inevitable. As Hutton had before him, he ordered the evacuation of Rangoon, already in a state of chaos. Order had broken down. Prisons and lunatic asylums were opened. Looting and arson were widespread. There was one saving element. Outstanding action by Allied air forces had frustrated Japanese attempts to dominate the air above Rangoon in the preceding weeks. But there was no other light.

Alexander's decision was only just made in time. The army was saved by coincidence. When the main body of the garrison of Rangoon began the march north on 7th March, with 17th Division and 7th Armoured Brigade providing a right flank and rearguard, the Japanese were already crossing the Prome road, the British axis of withdrawal, from east to west. This was 33rd Division's westwards march, preparatory to swinging south-east against Rangoon. The withdrawing British found what they took to be a Japanese blocking position, astride the road near Taukkyan. It was, in fact, a flank guard deployed to protect the crossing of the road by the main body of the Japanese. The British attacked without success. Their escape route appeared barred. Alexander ordered as large an attack as could be mounted – by 63rd Brigade, recently arrived in Burma – on the morning of 8th March. When it took place the Japanese had disappeared. Their work done, and fearful that the previous night's action could have betrayed their intention, the Japanese flank guard had hastily joined the main body of 33rd Division to the west, and advanced on a deserted and burning Rangoon at the same time as the British Army resumed its weary way northwards unimpeded.While 17th Division marched towards Prome, 1st Burma Division withdrew north up the Sittang Valley towards Toungoo, after fierce fighting. Having passed through the southernmost Chinese division they were moved by rail to join the main body of British troops in the Irrawaddy Valley.

Had the Japanese appreciated that Rangoon was being evacuated, and established 33rd Division where their flank guard had taken post for a different purpose, the British force would assuredly have been cut in half, and Alexander's decision seen as taken too late. It was a favourable fortune of war.

Thus Southern Burma was lost. Henceforth the war would take a different and more hazardous form, as the British struggled back, without line of communication, into the interior of the country, and as the Japanese established a main base and a major port with all that implied. Hitherto, only a small invading force had been able to be supported on the difficult route from Siam – a force which an equally limited but decently trained, organised, equipped and prepared British force could have met with success. Such a force was not deployed. Quality and organisation were defective. Forethought was largely absent. The bill for being ready to defend Burma was not a large one for the masters of India. It was not paid.

After the fall of Rangoon, Fifteenth Japanese Army was reinforced by two divisions – 18th and 56th – and ordered to advance up the two parallel valleys of the Sittang and the Irrawaddy. From the Sittang General Iida planned to march north-east to Lashio on the Burma-China road. From the Irrawaddy he intended to outflank the right of the Allied forces in that valley, and move on Shwebo. He would thus bring about a great battle of encirclement in the area of Mandalay. Taking advantage of the port of Rangoon, the Japanese could now deploy armoured and motorised columns as far as the roads reached, and their operational movements were likely to be as rapid as their tactical handling was energetic.

The British, deprived of a base, were now faced with one of the most difficult of all operations of war. They had to withdraw, carrying their base with them. An army seeks to withdraw down its line of communication. The British lacked one. Furthermore, their line of movement, were they forced to withdraw towards India, would inevitably be by jungle route and river for part of the way, along communications where no dumping programme by motor transport could be envisaged. Miracles of improvement were being performed on the bullock tracks of the Upper Chindwin, but no road worthy of the name yet connected the Burma Army with India. Alexander initially thought in terms of a withdrawal both to India and to China by the Burma road,[1] but the defence of India soon dictated priorities.

Not only the terrain but the climate now increased the troops' suffering. It was approaching the hottest season of the year. Watercourses were dry and water scarce. Men suffered, and some died, from heat exhaustion and from dysentery. And the May monsoon was approaching, bringing increased malaria and making some routes impassable. Many men survived the retreat utterly broken in health.

Alexander aimed to hold the Japanese on the general line of Prome (in the Irrawaddy Valley), and at Toungoo on the Sittang. If he lost

[1] Withdrawal to China was an idea of Wavell's: a peculiar one.

Toungoo, routes lay open through the Karen Hills into the Shan States and to the Burma road. And if he lost either Toungoo or Prome the other would, ultimately, be outflanked. He was now given a general coordinating authority over two Chinese Armies, under the command of Lieutenant-General Stilwell of the United States Army, and he requested the Chinese to be responsible for the eastern flank – for the Sittang, for Toungoo, and the Shan States. He concentrated the British – 1st Burma Division, 17th Indian Division and 7th Armoured Brigade – in the valley of the Irrawaddy, in the general area of Prome. As Commander responsible for all Burma, Alexander needed a Corps Headquarters to command the British and Imperial forces, and on 19th March Lieutenant-General W. J. Slim arrived as Commander BUR-CORPS.

The Japanese had air superiority once more, and when they resumed the attack northwards their enemies were subjected to that unremitting attention from the air which adds a particular dimension of misery to any retreat. It also denied the British commanders battlefield information, except what they could gain from ground patrolling. The Japanese may have seemed outstandingly adventurous: they were, however, not only energetic and highly trained but also well informed. They launched a series of strong attacks on Toungoo, where the Chinese divisions, fighting bravely, held out for a fortnight until 30th March. Prome was now threatened. To relieve pressure on the Chinese Slim had been ordered to carry out a limited offensive operation on 29th March. Although too far away from the Sittang area of operations for any possible effect there, the attempt was loyally made, but only unbalanced the British defence of the Prome area. The Japanese soon shrugged off this demonstration, and stormed into Prome itself, and the British, their stores and material overrun there and having lost ten tanks and suffered over three hundred casualities in the abortive offensive, again set out on the hard road of retreat. Their troops were depleted and exhausted. Low numerical strength meant little rest, and there had been no respite. Morale was weakened by the sense of going back once again into the unknown; and by incessant air attack, as well as by disease and the continuing water shortage.

Alexander wished to hold a main defensive position covering Mandalay, and south of the oil-fields of Yenangyaung, and on 8th April BURCORPS was deployed on a forty-mile front from Minha on the west bank of the Irrawaddy to Taungdwingyi, its back to the Yin Chaung River. Slim hoped to attack the flank of any enemy advance against part of his position by aggressive use of troops operating southward, from sectors less threatened. The concept needs well trained soldiers and commanders. It needs sufficient troops, or the hard core of the defence will be fatally weakened: BURCORPS brigades, on the contrary, were pitifully thin on the ground, and units at sadly low strength. When a brigade of 1st Burma Division moved forwards against the left flank of a Japanese main thrust at the centre, the result was to leave the Irrawaddy Valley itself too weak. A determined Japanese movement up the valley dislodged the troops occupying successive blocking positions. A considerable force was infiltrated, and on the evening of 16th April the Japanese seized Yenangyaung itself. The oil-fields were of considerable importance and they had, on Slim's orders, been destroyed earlier that day. On 22nd, Slim ordered a badly shaken 1st Burma Division to the area of Chauk on the Irrawaddy, and 17th Division to Meiktila, sixty miles south of Mandalay.

A withdrawal from the whole of Burma was clearly only a matter of time. An army with no base and no means of replenishment or reinforcement cannot for ever defy an enemy supported by a major port, with heavy equipment and enjoying air superiority. There was, on the map and on paper, some hope that Chinese assistance, maintained down the Burma road, could do something to redress this balance. Their uneven performance, however, their frequent disobedience of Stilwell's orders and their refusal to act except under the direct authority of a suspicious Chiang Kai-shek soon nullified this hope. Individual Chinese divisions fought, and fought as part of BURCORPS, most gallantly; but the Chinese generally mistrusted the British, recollecting that initially the British (for comprehensible reasons) had declined Chinese help on Burmese soil. When finally given it was too late.

Tactically the Japanese were as effective as ever. Large bodies of troops were infiltrated round or between defensive positions, to attack from the rear while their comrades attacked from the front. Other Japanese units were generally set deep penetration tasks, marching far behind their enemies across country, seeking to dislodge them by the fear of envelopment. But the British were learning fast: furthermore they were now supported by the two tank regiments and the guns of 7th Armoured Brigade. Small it may have been, but here was now a mobile reserve which could move and hit. On the Yin Chaung position in early April, 17th Division had a short respite from attack and some rest. The result was a refreshed and aggressive formation, very different from the one driven back to and beyond Rangoon. And from the start the personality of the Commander of BURCORPS, Slim, began to have its tonic effect on a battered army.

In the east, the Japanese outflanked one Chinese position after another, and moved towards Lashio, their objective on the Burma road, north-east of Mandalay. Thereafter they could move, unopposed, north to Bhama and Myitkina. The whole eastern border of Burma would soon be dominated by the Japanese Army.

Alexander, meanwhile, ordered the bridges across the mighty Irrawaddy to be prepared for demolition. If Meiktila was lost the army was to withdraw to the west bank. In that case Mandalay, already under threat, would be given up. And with the loss of Mandalay the Japanese would be masters of Central Burma and the valley of the Irrawaddy.

On 25th April Alexander ordered the British to withdraw across the Irrawaddy. The last act began.

The actual withdrawal was covered by some spirited and successful rearguard actions by the corps rearguard – 48th Indian Brigade. The last British troops crossed the Irrawaddy on the night of 30th April, and the great Ava Bridge at Mandalay was destroyed. Henceforth there could be no coordination between British and Chinese. Each withdrew after his own fashion, the British towards India – towards Kalewa, by the valleys of the Myittha and the Chindwin. For those moving by the road and tracks east of the Chindwin the last stage to Kalewa had to be accomplished by ferry at Shwegyin. As the possibility appeared of salvation in India and an end to campaigning, order broke down among some of the line of communication troops, and scenes familiar to any retreat were re-enacted. Gangs of undisciplined men, mindless of anything but survival, looted villages and murdered any who opposed them. The conduct of the disgraceful few, however, set in sharper relief the endurance of the stoic majority.

Now the Japanese launched a typical – and last – attempt to do that which they had so often done with success: by faster movement to cut off a retreating enemy. The Japanese 33rd Division was General Iida's left fist. He had intended it to envelop the British by striking towards Shwebo, north-west of Mandalay, and by the evening of 30th April 33rd Division reached Monywa, having moved by river and by track west of the Chindwin. There was hard fighting by 1st Burma Division, for Japanese possession of Monywa and any movement north-eastwards therefrom threatened the withdrawal of troops from Mandalay. The army completed its withdrawal – but the Japanese were free to use the Chindwin, and moving by river they made best speed towards Shwegyin, the vital ferry site for the last miles of the movement to Kalewa. Before the British withdrawal was complete the Japanese 213th Regiment of 33rd Division had occupied ground overlooking the ferry. Counter-attack could not dislodge them. Remaining tanks and vehicles had to be abandoned and destroyed. Movement to Kalewa for the survivors of the Burma Army had to be by jungle track. The army saved twenty-eight guns – about half – and eighty motor vehicles. No tanks could be brought back to India. On 12th May the monsoon started. A week later the rearguard of BURCORPS, 63rd Brigade, crossed the frontier into Assam. The first Burma campaign was over.

The soldiers of the Burma Army had retreated 1,000 miles under terrible conditions. They had no base, no reinforcement, no regular supply. They had been outnumbered – for although the Japanese attacking troops, battalion for battalion, had often met them on level terms the Japanese had an overall numerical superiority which enabled them to relieve tired troops with fresh, as well as to bring in reinforcements. The Burma Army had been indifferently trained, unlike their enemy – although they learned much under fire. For most of the time they had, above all, been subjected to the enemy's air superiority. They had moved through country of great difficulty and under climatic conditions particularly testing to the British among them. They had carried out the longest withdrawal in the history of the British Army, and had suffered 13,000 casualties, including 4,000 dead. They had, particularly on the rare occasions when they were fresh, dealt the Japanese some hard blows (Japanese fatal casualties were higher than British). But the British had lost Burma and Hong Kong and Malaya and Singapore. It was May 1942. On 26th May Rommel attacked in the Western Desert.

10

The End of the Road

The battles which began in the desert on 26th May 1942 constituted a serious and avoidable reverse for British arms. The opening situation was favourable. The British had numerical superiority in the most important equipments. In the Eighth Army Ritchie had 573 tanks in his two armoured divisions – 1st and 7th – and a further 276 in his two army tank brigades, 1st and 32nd, supporting the infantry: a total of 849. On the other side Rommel had, in all, 560 tanks of which more than half were German, concentrated in the Deutsches Afrika Korps, now commanded by General Nehring. Other arms were near even. Air forces were approximately matched, although the Germans had brought into service a particularly formidable fighter aircraft, the Messerschmidt 109F.

In quality the British had the advantage of a new tank: 167 American Grants, armed with 75 millimetre gun in a sponson – that is, with limited traverse. More powerful than any hitherto deployed against the Germans, they could also fire high explosive as well as armour-piercing shot, and thus engage the enemy anti-tank guns at greater range. On their side the Germans had a small number of new Mark IIIs with a long-barrelled 50 millimetre gun, and had taken steps to thicken their frontal armour. In anti-tank guns Ritchie received 112 new six pounder guns – an effective replacement for the inadequate two pounder, although only as yet in numbers sufficient to equip a few units, and only recently in service even with those. Rommel had forty-eight 88 millimetre guns – still the most powerful anti-tank weapon on the battlefield, and one without a British equivalent. With this important exception a rough parity existed between the two sides in the quality of armament, and the British had a three to two superiority in tank numbers.

The Axis attack was expected. Auchinleck's sources of Intelligence were good, and all in Eighth Army knew in the last week in May that battle was imminent and that Rommel would begin it. Nevertheless Ritchie's deployment was influenced by British preparations for an offensive. The government at home had been pressing Auchinleck hard. They noted his superiority in numbers, and the general strategic situation made a move imperative. Malta was menaced by Axis possession of the Cyrenaica airfields. The Mediterranean was closed. The news from Burma could not have been worse. Auchinleck had, however, resisted. He reckoned that Eighth Army needed more time – time to absorb new equipment, time to train under new organisations with which the army was experimenting. For Auchinleck had been dissatisfied with some of the showing on CRUSADER, and, like the authorities at home, deeply disappointed by its last act and the flight back to Gazala. He wanted time to correct the failings. He knew that next time the army had to win. Having put Ritchie in command, he tried to ensure the wisdom of his choice by bombarding him with a great deal of guidance and advice, whether on organisation, training or future operations. He insisted on being kept closely informed on everything. Such intimate supervision can blur responsibility, circumscribe initiative and diminish the standing of a subordinate among his own command, and this was at least one of the results. But Auchinleck was staunch in protecting Eighth Army from being impelled by government into a premature attack. He had, with some reluctance, assented to an offensive to start in June. Great stocks were built up at Tobruk and at the railhead at Belhamed, to support an advance. Now this forward logistic support was well within the range of a Rommel on first or second lunge.

Eighth Army was divided between XIII Corps (Gott) – 50th (British) Division, 1st South African Division and 2nd South African Division supported by 1st and 32nd Army Tank Brigades, with a mix of Valentine and Matilda tanks – and XXX Corps consisting of 1st and 7th Armoured Divisions. The infantry divisions each consisted of three brigades. The armoured divisions differed and the course of the story necessitates some account of their composition. In 1st Armoured Division were 2nd and 22nd Armoured Brigades and 201st (previously 200th) Guards Brigade. In 7th Armoured Division were 4th Armoured Brigade; 3rd (Indian) and 7th Motor Brigades; and 29th (Indian) Brigade. Messervy, commanding 7th Armoured Division, also had 1st Free French Brigade. The tanks of the armoured divisions were a mix of Crusaders, Honeys and the new Grants.

Ritchie also had 5th (Indian) Division in army reserve.

Eighth Army, therefore, had six divisions, of which three and two army tank brigades were British – still only a tiny proportion of the British Army being raised. Rommel had in Panzer Armee Afrika nine divisions, three of them German – 15th and 21st Panzer and 90th Light. Rommel's Italian divisions were divided between XX Corps – a mobile formation, with Trieste (motorised) and Ariete (armoured) divisions, and X and XXI Infantry Corps, each of two divisions.

For the defensive battle now imminent Ritchie gave Gott the task of manning a static west-facing position behind minefields, on a thirty-mile front from Gazala south to the Trigh-El-Abd. On this front Gott deployed 1st South African Division in the north and 50th Division in the south, each supported by an army tank brigade. 2nd South African Division was placed in Tobruk itself. Ritchie gave Norrie, with his armoured and motorised brigades, the task of dealing with Rommel's mobile thrust wherever it might come.

Norrie had to be ready for two main contingencies. A mobile thrust, obviously led by the DAK, might exploit an assault on XIII Corps' defences, probably on the general axis of the Trigh Capuzzo. Alternatively it might swing round the open, desert flank by Bir Hacheim. Either operation would take time, and the latter would involve refuelling. Either, therefore, should give Norrie sufficient hours to concentrate his armour, whether on his right, to meet a central thrust, or on his left against an enemy advance from the south. Where should such a concentration take place? There was an obvious need to cover the direct route Rommel could take towards El Adem and Tobruk, under either alternative. The base of Eighth Army must clearly be protected. For the contingency of Rommel trying to smash through the centre, XXX Corps would concentrate somewhere west of El Adem astride the Trigh Capuzzo. For the other contingency, of a southern thrust, Norrie directed Lumsden's armoured brigades to march south to join 4th Armoured Brigade of Messervy's division at battle stations south-east of Bir Hacheim. There must also, Norrie reckoned, be some pattern of pivots sufficiently far south, formations set down to man a position, even temporarily, and to provide bases for patrolling and for warning – and to help canalise an enemy advance. With all these factors in mind, 1st Free French Brigade was deployed in Bir Hacheim, in a strong defensive position. Messervy, of 7th Armoured Division, placed 3rd (Indian) Motor Brigade in the desert five miles south of Bir Hacheim, 7th Motor Brigade at Retma, twenty miles to the east, and 29th Brigade at Bir El Gubi. Lumsden, commanding 1st Armoured Division, stationed 201st Guards Brigade at the cross-tracks on the Trigh Capuzzo known as Knightsbridge, behind the left centre of 50th Division. The armoured brigades (from south to north) were deployed with 4th some twelve miles east of Bir Hacheim, 22nd near Bir El Harmat, immediately north of the Trigh El Abd and fifteen miles north-west of 4th Brigade; and 2nd astride the Trigh Capuzzo west of El Adem, eight miles north-east of 22nd. The armoured brigades, therefore, were employed on a triangle of which the longest side was about twenty miles, or ninety minutes by direct march. Any concentration would probably involve one or more brigades passing from the command of one armoured division to the other – or divided command in a single battle.

Warning time was obviously all important. To achieve a concentration of armour (which all agreed should be contrived) the distances suggested that two hours' warning time were necessary. The same consideration implied that the battle position selected for concentration must itself be such that an advancing enemy could not reach it before our own troops. Put another way, a concentration on Norrie's left, on 4th Armoured Brigade, would require information to be not only received and digested but acted upon well before the enemy was within two hours' march of the chosen battlefield. An armoured brigade or regiment would adopt by night a "leaguer" position where it could replenish, defend itself in close perimeter against patrols, and carry out maintenance and repair. It would then deploy at dawn to dispersed positions for battle, for advance or for watch. 4th Armoured Brigade's battle positions – and thus the designed concentration position of XXX Corps for any battle against a southern advance – were twelve miles from their leaguer position. And this meant that any enemy advance round the south must be reported and acted upon before it passed a line running south-west from Bir Hacheim, at the latest. Patrols were deployed in the southern desert with exactly that calculation in mind.

A German attempt on the centre presented few such problems. There would assuredly be ample time while the minefields were breached for concentration on the right. Norrie reckoned that his deployment covered the gamut of contingencies. The players relaxed and awaited their calls.

Rommel's plan was simple and audacious. He knew that he faced superior numbers of tanks although his information on British deployment was inaccurate. He decided to gamble on his proven ability to handle a united mass of armour more dexterously than his opponent. He planned to swing northwards round the south of Bir Hacheim, threatening the line of communication and the base of Eighth Army. In the ensuing mêlée he reckoned he could surround his enemy's mobile forces and pin them against their own static positions south of Gazala. For this operation Rommel ordered a demonstration by the Italian infantry divisions against XIII Corps, with sufficient armour moving in rear of it to create a deceptive impression of a main thrust (which, in fact, deceived no one). At the same time – during the night of 26th

215

May – Rommel proposed to lead the three divisions of the DAK and the two divisions of the Italian XX Corps south-east from Rotonda Segnali and then north-east round the British desert flank. This was a long march, requiring, as the British had calculated, a refuelling halt; and it took a long time. It was reported during the night by the desert patrols put out by XXX Corps, and information began to build up of large enemy columns heading south-eastwards towards Bir Hacheim in the moonlight. This was the united armoured strength of Panzer Armee Afrika, and Rommel had placed himself at its head.

The actions which took place in the next five weeks defy tidy description, but for convenience five phases can be identified. In the first of these the armoured formations of Eighth Army fought a series of disconnected contact battles against the advancing enemy, a phase which left both sides weakened, and neither side concentrated or balanced. In the second phase Rommel was able to concentrate his armour immediately east of the southern flank of XIII Corps and, while holding off attempts to crush him from the east, succeeded in smashing Gott's southernmost brigade, thus securing a supply route from the west through the minefields. In the third phase Rommel resumed the offensive, and menaced once again the rear of XIII Corps while simultaneously threatening to advance towards El Adem and Tobruk. In this fighting he successfully dispersed and inflicted crippling losses upon the armoured formations of Eighth Army, and forced Ritchie to withdraw XIII Corps to avoid encirclement. This phase ended with a general British withdrawal eastwards. The fourth phase saw the assault upon and seizure of Tobruk, undisturbed by any offensive operations by Eighth Army; and the fifth and last phase consisted of Ritchie's attempts to reorganise on the Egyptian frontier, whence CRUSADER had been launched seven months before, followed by a headlong retreat first to Mersa Matruh and then to a position only fifty miles west of Alexandria itself.

The course of the first phase ran startling and violent. Auchinleck had, personally, advised Ritchie that he thought an attack through the British centre was a likely enemy ploy – a curious view considering its obvious difficulty (Rommel appears never to have contemplated it). Although knowledge of ULTRA was confined to a tiny circle of initiates, it was generally believed that Auchinleck had secret sources of information which gave him insights denied to subordinate commanders and their staffs; and this, of course, was true. If, therefore, the

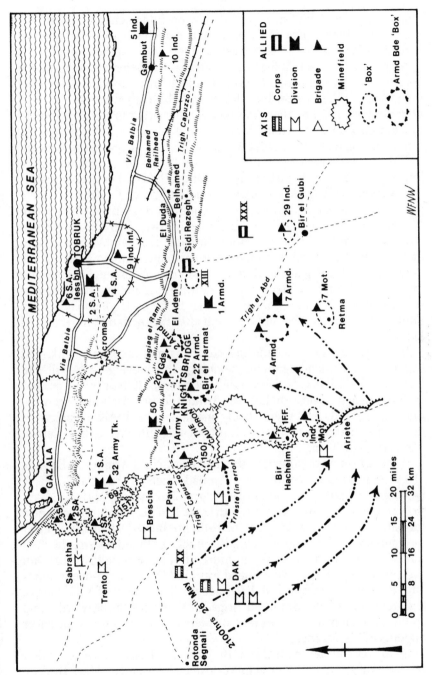

26th May 1942

ALLIED
Corps
Division
Brigade

AXIS
Corps
Division
Brigade
Minefield
'Box'
Armd Bde 'Box'

MEDITERRANEAN SEA

GAZALA
Sabratha
Trento
Brescia
Pavia
DAK
Rotonda Segnali
2100 hrs 26 May
Ariete
Bir Hacheim
Retma
Trieste (in error)
Bir el Gubi
Trigh el Abd
4 Armd.
7 Mot.
3 Ind. Mot.
1 F.F.
29 Ind.
XXX
7 Armd.
1 Armd.
XIII
Sidi Rezegh
El Duda
Belhamed
Belhamed Railhead
El Adem
Bir el Harmat
22 Armd.
201 Gds.
THE CAULDRON
KNIGHTSBRIDGE
150
1 Army TK
50
Trigh Capuzzo
Hagiag el Raml
Acroma
Via Balbia
Via Balbia
32 Army Tk.
1 S.A.
69
151
150 S.A.
XX
2 S.A.
4 S.A.
9 Ind. Inf.
6 S.A. less bn.
TOBRUK
Via Balbia
Belhamed
Trigh Capuzzo
10 Ind.
Gambut
5 Ind.

0   5   10   15   20 miles
0   8   16   24   32 km

WFW

Commander-in-Chief advanced a view on future enemy operations, even (or, perhaps, particularly) without convincing reasons, there was a natural obligation felt to give it especial weight. Whether from this or other causes there was at first a disposition not to believe that the enemy columns reported moving towards Bir Hacheim really represented the *schwerpunkt*. They might be a feint; and although the first warnings were sent out at 2 a.m. there was no executive order to any formation to move until 7 a.m., by which time air reconnaissance had reported the unmistakable truth. The delay was fatal. The distances involved meant that there could now be no hope of XXX Corps concentrating on the left as contingency planning required, and as had earlier been possible. 4th Armoured Brigade itself was too late to reach its selected battle positions. Before it had shaken out, Rommel was upon it, at the head of a concentrated mass of four divisions and over 500 tanks. He had already overrun 3rd (Indian) Motor Brigade, crushed by sheer weight of tank numbers, and manning an inadequate number of anti-tank guns. 7th Motor Brigade at Retma, in the path of Rommel's righthand division, 90th Light, which he sent towards El Adem, had only escaped the fate of 3rd Brigade by a hasty retreat to the east. Meanwhile, 15th Panzer Division crashed into regiment after regiment of 4th Armoured Brigade.

But here for the first time the Germans met the Grant tank, and experienced British regiments, shooting and moving with skill and fortitude. 15th Panzer Division did not have it all their own way, and suffered heavily. Nevertheless 4th Armoured Brigade was soon withdrawing towards El Adem, badly mauled. The DAK resumed its northward march. For the while there was, effectively, little left of Messervy's division.

Rommel's next opponent to the north was 22nd Armoured Brigade of 1st Armoured Division. Lumsden had received orders at 7 a.m. to move this brigade south, and to follow with 2nd Armoured Brigade – at the same time that 4th Armoured Brigade had been ordered to deploy for battle. But at 8.45 a.m. they had still not moved when 21st Panzer Division swept down upon them. Rommel's lefthand division had not waited to join in the final discomfiture of 4th Armoured Brigade, but had pushed on northwards. Speed was all. Only seventy-five minutes after the first armoured clash Rommel was in the heart of XXX Corps, had sent one of its armoured brigades flying north-eastwards, and could reasonably hope to prevent an enemy concentration by the sheer impetus of his advance.

In the encounter with 22nd Brigade the DAK destroyed thirty British tanks, but did not achieve a decisive victory. 22nd Brigade

218

withdrew towards Knightsbridge – no great distance to the north – and 2nd Armoured Brigade came up on 22nd Brigade's left or southern flank, facing west. Rommel's own position was suddenly uneasy. He had his two Panzer divisions west of the Knightsbridge box in the area between the Trigh Capuzzo and the Trigh El Abd which was christened "The Cauldron". He had lost 200 tanks. His force was now too dispersed to continue an immediate offensive, although, gambler that he was, he sent 21st Panzer Division on a foray northwards: it was soon recalled. 90th Light Division was far to the east, directed towards El Adem. Ariete was investing Bir Hacheim, stoutly held by the gallant French Brigade. The Trieste Division had left the column in error during the preceding night and was stuck somewhere on XIII Corps's southern minefields. To Rommel's east was a shaken but unbeaten force of British armour, now outnumbering his own by a higher margin than at the start of the day. To his west was an unbroken line of British defensive positions – "boxes", with all round defence and formidable minefields, denying to him any direct relief or replenishment. His supply columns could only reach him from the south, past Bir Hacheim (Rommel personally managed to lead in one). He needed to regather his strength, and to bring 90th Light Division back into the DAK fold. But the position of Panzer Armee Afrika was precarious. After a pause on 28th May, while breath was recovered, XXX Corps ordered 1st Armoured Division, on 29th, to attack Rommel's armour from the east. There was hard fighting, but at the end of the day the DAK was again concentrated. The second phase of the battle began.

Although Ritchie did not make it an explicit principle of the battle to get astride Rommel's south-running replenishment lines, he could have done so. Indeed Rommel had every reason to suppose that he would, and determined to open up a way from the west, and thus to create not a tenuous loop around but a wedge driven into the British position. To do this he personally led a sustained assault on Gott's southernmost brigade in XIII Corps – 150th Brigade. At the same time, the German position in the Cauldron was firmly held against the attacks of XXX Corps from the east, by a line of the usual formidable anti-tank guns. Rommel was surrounded, but he was determined to transform this encirclement into a German bridgehead and to debouch from it when the time came.

On 1st June, 150th Brigade, consisting of Territorial battalions, was crushed. At the beginning of the war Territorials had been committed to battle with totally inadequate preparation, and had failed through lack of training and time. This was behind them now and their performance was glorious. It was also tragic. 150th Brigade fought magnificently but was destroyed, while the Germans comfortably held off some singularly ill-coordinated attempts to break into the Cauldron from the east. Rommel's moves had a punch and urgency which his opponent lacked. Now the Germans had a supply route from the west. Rommel held a menacing bridgehead astride the Trigh Capuzzo, and in or behind it was the whole of Panzer Armee Afrika.

On 5th June, Ritchie launched his last attempt to destroy this bridgehead, but it was too late to affect the fate of 150th Brigade, or to threaten Rommel's lifeline. It was also a complete failure, in which 22nd Brigade lost sixty tanks and in which the gallant actions of a few units could not atone for what appears in retrospect – and appeared to many at the time – as a striking lack of dynamism and grip. Initially the infantry advanced without incident, to an objective which was, in fact, short of the enemy's position. Next, armour "passed through" – only to drive on to the anti-tank gun line of the Afrika Korps. As an accompaniment to this a tank attack from one of XIII Corps' army tank brigades was put in from the north – unsupported by other arms, uncoordinated and under separate command. As in all battles there were faults made by both sides at Gazala which are easier to discern with hindsight, but the Battle of the Cauldron was an action distinguished by the heroism shown by some at regimental level, rather than by brilliance of concept, planning or execution.

When the Battle of the Cauldron, the second phase, was over, Rommel's position was stronger than it had been since the beginning. He was concentrated, balanced and had a sure supply route. On the British side by now the failures of the armoured formations – for thus were they seen – led to increasing mistrust between arms. Once it had been our air forces which were abused by soldiers for their apparent absence when required. Now it was our armour. Eighth Army was unsettled. Too many stories circulated of armoured formations arguing against orders setting them on the move towards battle and thus (or so the tale would run) leaving less protected soldiers in the lurch. It was the old cry from Waterloo: "Where are our Cavalry?" The fault lay not with the brave soldiers of the tank units themselves so much as with commanders who had become accustomed more to discussion than obedience; and lost time and initiative thereby. It also lay with inadequate tactical doctrine, and an habitual failure to grasp the best methods of attack.

Rommel, meanwhile, had turned his attention to Bir Hacheim, where the French gave him as hard a fight as he had during the whole battle, where he suffered heavily, and whence the garrison was withdrawn on the night of 10th June. The third phase of the Battle of Gazala now began.

On 11th June XIII Corps was still intact except for 150th Brigade at the southern end of the line. The enemy concentration lay to its left rear. To the east of XIII Corps the British held strongpoints, south facing, at Knightsbridge, El Adem, and Belhamed, covering Tobruk. The three armoured brigades of 1st and 7th Armoured Division had about 200 tanks. Rommel had left 150 tanks in the DAK and 60 Italian cruiser tanks. The British were still – for the last time – numerically holding their own, but no advantage was taken of the fact, no attempts made to disrupt the enemy. Opportunities seem to have been lost that day.

Rommel now resumed the offensive. On the evening of 11th June, he moved out of the Cauldron towards El Adem, with 15th Panzer, 90th Light and the Trieste Divisions, and sent 21st Panzer northwards to create alarm to the west of Knightsbridge towards Acroma.

The ensuing confused battle was fought between the Knightsbridge box, still held by 201st Guards Brigade, and El Adem. All three British armoured brigades were put under Lumsden. 4th Brigade was driven north by the DAK, over the Hagiag El Raml escarpment. 2nd and 22nd Brigades ultimately found themselves facing south, immediately east of Knightsbridge. Tank losses were heavy. German anti-tank guns were pushed forward with their customary audacity and did great execution. By the evening of 12th June the remaining British armour was concentrated east of Knightsbridge, battered and with little thought or capacity for offensive action.

At this moment Ritchie had to decide whether the tide had finally turned against him. It was not essentially a matter of where his and Rommel's troops were: that could always be rectified in the desert, given fuel and the will to move. It was not only a matter of comparative losses: it was less definable. Ritchie appreciated that the potential of his armoured units was low. Unless they could be kept intact and used effectively XIII Corps would be cut off – a hostage to fortune. Ritchie had either to accept that he had lost – at least temporarily – and withdraw Gott's divisions while there was still a force to cover that withdrawal and time to effect it, or he had to fight it out and try to regain the initiative.

Ritchie tried to do the latter. Auchinleck was with him to strengthen his resolve. The attempt failed. Ritchie placed 1st Armoured Division under XIII Corps, and Gott attempted to concentrate the armour as an effective fighting force between Knightsbridge and Acroma. Rommel, meanwhile, directed his two German Panzer divisions inward towards

221

each other, along the escarpment north of Knightsbridge. At the end of a confused day's fighting on 13th June Gott ordered Knightsbridge to be abandoned. The British were being steadily pushed northwards. Their losses were particularly heavy, with only fifty cruiser and twenty infantry tanks surviving. Ritchie realised that his resolve of the previous day could no longer be maintained. Little now existed to prevent Rommel cutting XIII Corps off from Tobruk. Early on the morning of 14th June, Gott was ordered to move his corps east to the Egyptian frontier. Some brigades were able to comply. Some drove west out of the Gazala positions and round the south. Rommel, despite vigorous efforts, failed to cut off the withdrawal. Some resolute rearguard actions were fought, and, like Eighth Army, Panzer Armee Afrika was utterly exhausted; but they were masters of the field. Within Tobruk itself 2nd South African Division of three brigades, reinforced by the remaining troops of 32nd Army Tank Brigade and 201st Guards Brigade, prepared for the fourth phase of the Battle of Gazala.

Ritchie, in a somewhat confused exchange with Auchinleck, ultimately established that he was meant to hold Tobruk. At the start of the battle – indeed throughout this stage of the campaign – it had been an accepted principle that Tobruk should not be subjected to a second siege. Auchinleck laid down that Tobruk "should not be invested", and gave Ritchie orders for the holding of a line which would cover the place and prevent its encirclement. These orders were, by the time they were given, impossible to carry out. Eighth Army was already withdrawing to the Egyptian frontier. Tobruk, therefore, *was* invested. Its defenders were exposed to an attack for which they were physically and psychologically unprepared.

The consequence was deplorable by any standards. Tobruk had withstood a long struggle in 1941. In 1942 the Commander of 2nd South African Division, Major-General Klopper, told his subordinates on 15th June that Tobruk must be prepared for a siege of up to three months. Klopper was placed in command of all troops in the garrison. On 18th June he signalled Ritchie that all was well and that he was confident.

At 5.20 a.m. on 20th June every available German aircraft was committed to the bombardment of Tobruk. At 7 a.m. German infantry and engineers began working forwards towards the south-east perimeter. At 8.30 the tanks of the DAK began crossing the anti-tank ditch. At 1.30 high ground dominating the harbour was captured. At 5.15 21st Panzer Division began advancing toward the town itself. At

6 p.m. the Germans entered Tobruk. Klopper's Divisional Head-quarters, threatened with overrunning, had been ordered to disperse; thereafter there was no effective overall command. Some brave battalions on the perimeter, astonished to learn that the battle appeared to have been lost behind them, defended themselves to the last. Some broke out, and drove first west and then east to rejoin Eighth Army. Soon after 6 a.m. on 21st June, Klopper sent emissaries to German Headquarters to negotiate surrender. Tobruk had been held for exactly twenty-four hours. No effective actions by Eighth Army interrupted its reduction. Thirty-two thousand prisoners passed into Axis hands, of which nineteen thousand were British soldiers.

By now British armoured strength had been so reduced that any defensive plan which required a force capable of manoeuvre was thought out of the question. Ritchie planned, therefore, only to fight a delaying action on the frontier to cover the preparation of a main defensive position at Mersa Matruh, over 100 miles to the east, which was intended to be the scene of the decisive battle to save Egypt. There was, in fact, negligible resistance on the frontier, and when the enemy began to advance on 23rd June, the British began to withdraw. By 26th June, Rommel reached the Matruh position. On the previous evening Auchinleck had relieved Ritchie of his duties, and personally assumed the command. Eighth Army now had about one hundred and fifty cruiser tanks (with about fifty Grants) and nineteen infantry tanks. Panzer Armee Afrika had just over one hundred tanks, including sixty German. The British still, therefore, had a numerical superiority. But battles are won and lost in the minds of men, and this one had been lost.

Auchinleck now attempted to carry out a major reorganisation, so that divisions were to be divided between a forward and a rear element, the forward element to be a mobile group, strong in artillery, the rear largely composed of infantry. Little of this could be put into effect, however, before Rommel again caught up with Eighth Army on 26th June. Eighth Army was now organised in XIII Corps (Gott) and a new corps, X Corps (Lieutenant-General Holmes) with the New Zealand Division. Between them these two corps commanded four infantry divisions (5th and 10th Indian, 50th British and the New Zealanders) and one armoured division – 1st Armoured – with the two remaining armoured brigades, 4th and 22nd, and 7th Motor Brigade (XXX Corps had been withdrawn to plan the defensive position on the Egyptian frontier). Auchinleck wished at all costs to keep this army in being. Defence, therefore, was to be "mobile" – and withdrawal preferred to encirclement or manoeuvre. In these circumstances Rommel had little difficulty in jockeying the British out of their positions at Matruh. After a certain amount of order, counter-order and disorder, marked by some brave fighting particularly by the New Zealand Division, Eighth Army began streaming eastwards once again on 28th June in considerable disarray. Two days later Panzer Armee Afrika again caught up with their retreating foes. The Battle of Gazala was over, the fifth phase concluded. The British were back at the last position covering the Egyptian Delta. On 1st July Rommel began his first attack at El Alamein.

The battles which started at Gazala marked the last and in some ways lowest point of the long and melancholy series of defeats the British Army had suffered since May 1940. Hopes had been high. Odds had been even. At the end the army had been beaten, and knew it. The gallant actions of units and individuals could not wipe out the general discomfiture. Many causes have been adduced, and a few must be examined – or repeated.

The British were not helped by the tendency to create new organisations and experiment with new groupings, breaking up the divisional family in mid-campaign. The division is the tool of the army's trade, and the British Army suffered anyway from not being organised in peace on a permanent divisional basis. In the desert the division itself was treated often as a mobile supermarket (as indeed was sometimes necessary) from which brigades or units could be detached at will rather than a close-knit team with every cog meshed.

British equipment has been blamed. Our equipment was only inferior in the anti-tank gun – but that was an exception of huge importance. The Germans were adept at manoeuvring armour behind a screen of anti-tank guns, and of using the latter to blunt their opponents' armour, while preserving their own for exploitation, for the deep thrust. They therefore used these two arms in very close and intelligent combination – a deadly combination. Furthermore in the 88 millimetre gun the Germans possessed the most effective tank-destroying machine on the battlefield. Its comparative scarcity was balanced by its range – and the German 50 millimetre gun was a powerful auxiliary. The majority of British tank losses were caused by these guns. The British had no equivalent material or tactic.

Within the armoured formations themselves the Germans believed in manoeuvring their tanks in comparatively close order. They believed in shock, mass and control. The British had been taught to fight well dispersed – a sound system provided overall numbers and therefore depth were adequate, but a system which could expose the individual

224

troop or squadron to the threat of being too easily overwhelmed by numbers, and of thus losing a vital move in the tactical game, even while still, perhaps, inflicting disproportionate casualties. But, more significantly, the British have been criticised for failure to concentrate operationally – for allowing Rommel, once again, to overwhelm one brigade after another as he himself boasted he had been able to do.

That the British wished and failed to unite their armour in the first encounters is certain, although what would have happened had they achieved concentration must be speculative. The initial British deployment made concentration perfectly possible. It is, however, clear from map and clock that to achieve it required very timely decisions and very prompt and unhesitant action thereafter. There could never be much time. And time was what, again and again, defeated the British. Again and again they were overwhelmed by the enemy's speed of action or reaction. On the first day, despite warnings, and an order to move received at 7 a.m. – itself delayed through sluggish and apprehensive reactions – Lumsden's southernmost armoured brigade had still not started to deploy seventy-five minutes later. By then Rommel was upon it.

Why was this? Throughout the battle there runs a recurrent theme – indiscipline at the top. Orders were received, doubted, questioned, discussed. Formation commanders were sceptical of Ritchie's wisdom and independence of judgment. Was he not still, some thought, a staff officer of Auchinleck's? Were the ideas not being produced many hundred miles away in Cairo, off the map, in the face of the realities of the situation in the desert, at the front? For his part, Ritchie had Auchinleck urgently demanding to be involved in every move of the battle. And Auchinleck had to satisfy – or pacify – the government at home. Thus a fatal ambiguity and lack of authority spread downwards through the command chain. The slowness of the British, their failure to concentrate force at the crucial time and place – the secret of most victories – was not a consequence of failure to understand the principles of war. It stemmed from a failure to make the machine work. The supreme importance of unambiguous command and of instant obedience in a fast moving battle was not observed by the British. They were too genial, too conversational, too slow. At the regimental level there was, by now, crispness, confidence and competence – in many cases, if not in all. The British had travelled far since the first shocks of meeting the Wehrmacht. The British soldier knew that given a fair wind and enough ammunition he could hold his own against the German. This led to confidence – fragile but real. It was insufficiently mirrored in the higher command. There the battle was characterised by failure to impose, from the summit, a directing intelligence and will.

It was the latter the campaign required and the latter with which the British were confronted. Rommel was a fine field commander, but sometimes foolhardy. He put himself into more than one difficult position in the Battle of Gazala. Before the struggle at the Cauldron his forces were more dispersed than Ritchie's, and he was, in effect, surrounded. Yet the British counter-moves were laborious, unimaginative and unsuccessful. By the time they had failed Rommel had transformed the situation. On the British side no single will had mastered events.

Throughout the battle Rommel appears as the setter of pace and direction. British soldiers tended to exaggerate his prowess. Such awe for an enemy can be dangerous, and Auchinleck issued an order aimed at putting his foe in perspective. But the truth is that Rommel was leading his troops from the front. His opponents were, generally without success, seeking to organise theirs from the rear. A favourite British term for an operation is to "lay it on" – to deliberate, prepare, stage-manage. In some battles this is necessary and right. There is, however, little in such idiom of the instant reaction, the *coup d'œil*, the seizure of fleeting opportunity. For the latter, at which Rommel was adept, there had to be command "from the saddle": a very well-practised and disciplined machine; and confidence from top to bottom. None of this was sufficiently present on the British side. It has, for instance, been suggested by a German writer that the best British response to Rommel's concentration in the Cauldron would have been to march west to the Italian side of our own minefields and then attack from the west – an unexpected direction – rather than batter bloodily against the predictable line of anti-tank guns on the east of the German positions.[1] Whatever the merits of such a manoeuvre – and they must be entirely speculative – such an audacious movement was probably beyond British capacity or imagination.

But one further element can too easily be forgotten. At Gazala, Rommel was attacking. He could lead from the front because he knew where he was going. His natural element was the offensive, and if he was forced to stand on the defensive at any time he thought only in terms of knocking his enemy off balance by an early and vigorous counter-stroke. He could concentrate force because he could impose his own single idea, and Panzer Armee Afrika responded to it. Rommel had the initiative and was determined not to lose it. Attack is the

---

[1] Major-General F. W. von Mellenthin, *Panzer Battles, 1939–45*, Cassell, 1955.

strongest form of war, even when outnumbered, as Rommel generally was. This is not least of the factors which led to a British military performance at Gazala inferior, in many ways, to that in CRUSADER six months before. To await the enemy's attack, to place troops in a purely reactive situation, to surrender the initiative is always to face a difficult task. It can lead to defeat – even defeat by smaller forces, provided they are concentrated, well trained and led with the zest and energy which characterised the opponents of the British Army in the summer of 1942.

Part IV

The Tide Turns

11

Daybreak

The next phase in the desert war began on 1st July 1942 and introduced both sides to a placename that would, ultimately, be recorded as one of the great turning-points of the Second World War. El Alamein, a small township some sixty miles west of Alexandria, was to be fought over, on and off, for three months. Initially each side tried, in a sequence of (unsuccessful) attacks, to knock the other off balance, thereby creating a favourable situation for deeper offensive or counter-offensive. On both sides some of these actions were conducted with skill, although in Eighth Army they were not marked by improved cooperation – or confidence – between the British armour and other Arms. In many cases losses were heavy, and if Eighth Army felt dispirited so, as he recorded, did Rommel. "It can't go on like it for long," he wrote to his wife on 18th July, "otherwise the front will crack. Militarily, this is the most difficult period I've ever been through." Both sides were very tired. The long run from Gazala and the length of his communications had tested Rommel's Panzer Armee, just as the demoralisation of a headlong retreat and a beating in the field had drained the confidence and energy from Eighth Army. For a few weeks there settled over the battlefield a fragile stability bred of exhaustion.

Auchinleck was determined that when Rommel attacked again in strength – and his speed of recuperation had been consistently under-estimated – the army should not be beaten or enveloped. Although he reckoned he could hold at El Alamein (he was still performing the two functions of Commander-in-Chief, Middle East, and Commander Eighth Army), contingency plans were made for further withdrawal in extreme danger, rather than allowing the army to be crushed or surrounded. Such planning was rational, but had the danger, if it became common knowledge within the Eighth Army, of sowing doubt or weakening resolve. Eighth Army was also undergoing one of its periodic experiments in reorganisation, with divisions broken into battlegroups, brigade groups, "boxes", and batches of non-combatants being sent to the rear. It was all somewhat unsettling. The need for a new spirit and new measures was widely felt. And new measures required new men.

At the end of Book VII of his great *History of the Peninsular War*, Napier describes the peculiar sensation felt by the French Commander advancing south from Oporto in May 1809. The atmosphere had changed and so had the reactions of all he encountered. "In truth," wrote Napier, "a new actor had appeared upon the scene. The whole country was in commotion: and Soult, suddenly checked in his career, was pushed backward by a strong and eager hand." Sir Arthur Wellesley, later 1st Duke of Wellington, had just arrived to take command of the British Army of the Peninsula. A similar trans-formation of atmosphere took place in Egypt in August 1942.

Lieutenant-General B. L. Montgomery, who assumed command of Eighth Army on 13th August, had commanded 3rd Division in France and Flanders in 1940, and impressed all as a master of his profession. He had spent the next two years in England commanding first a corps, and then South-Eastern Command, covering that part of the coast where invasion was thought most likely. He had also trained his command, at whatever level, with an energy and attention to detail which had become a byword throughout the British Army.

There were two schools of thought about Montgomery. To some he was an egomaniac, insensitive, conceited, so sure he was right that he must have his way on every issue to the point of instability: as vindictive to any who opposed him as he was protective to those who gave him their adulation. Plenty of anecdotes gave colour to this view. To others he stood head and shoulders above his contemporaries as a soldier who had studied war as few other British Generals, had clear ideas and knew how to impress them memorably on his subordinates. A man who could impose his will on his command so powerfully, they thought, might yet do so on the enemy. And to balance anecdotes of unfeeling discourtesy or abruptness were less known tales of quiet kindness, friendship remembered, consideration to the young and not unhumor-ous charm. There was something in both opinions, nor do they exclude each other. But Montgomery came to Eighth Army at the right moment. A change was needed, and a firm grip. He provided both. Simultaneously Alexander was appointed Commander-in-Chief in place of Auchinleck. The latter, saddened by what he reasonably felt was lack of confidence in him, declined another command covering Persia and Iraq which he did not think workable. Later, however, he was reappointed to be Commander-in-Chief in the India he loved.

Montgomery had learned his trade in France in the First World War, where he had commanded troops as a young officer. He had also served there on Brigade, Divisional and Corps Staffs, which gave him the chance to appreciate the complex yet vital nature of preparation, organisation and planning. No one in the intervening years had studied the military art with such singleness of mind. The two years since Dunkirk had enabled him to put his ideas into effect in an army now growing in professional stature in Britain, as well as to reflect deeply on reports from the battlefronts and on the nature of the enemy. He believed in leaving nothing to chance, in "thinking through" his battles as far as could be done, and in absolute obedience to one commanding will – his own. He also believed in the offensive, and in the power of the initiative. He fought his battles according to sound and well-established principles, interpreted them into operational plans with great thoroughness, and pressed these through to victory with unrelenting authority. He sometimes harmed his own reputation for generalship by stressing how all had gone according to plan. This is seldom true in war. Montgomery was as ready with *post facto* rationalisation as most men: in fact he was prepared to change plans, to switch effort, to adjust to circumstances with as commendable agility as any, and could not have succeeded otherwise. But his emphasis – his boasting – of success in making events conform to his plan was deliberate. He realised that the army needed to feel that their commander knew exactly what he was about and what would happen, so that when he said "We will win" they could share his jauntiness, and rely upon his assurance as if it were knowledge – "I said it would go as planned. It did. It always will when I say so."

By this communication, this imparting of confidence, this assumption of personal responsibility Montgomery showed his true greatness, as well as by his iron will. This was exactly what Eighth Army required: it needed discipline and victories. Montgomery quickly impressed as a man who would tolerate nothing less than victories. He allowed no doubt, no indiscipline. He did not believe in risk or gesture, but in producing winning strength at the crucial time and place, and then driving his command ruthlessly through to a victorious end.

Montgomery was no Rupert, no Rommel. He was deliberate – and would be accused by detractors of missing opportunities, of being predictable. He did not show any particular flair in the handling of mobile forces. Whether he would have proved himself master in a battle of manoeuvre, a mêlée in open desert such as CRUSADER, whether his speed of perception and reaction "from the saddle" would have matched Rommel's, is impossible to say because he never fought

233

such a battle and had no intention of doing so. Montgomery's qualities and achievements do not rest upon particular manoeuvres, nor upon the brilliant opportunism of a Wellington, but upon the scientific organisation of battle and, above all, upon ruthless and commanding will-power. He communicated this throughout Eighth Army, and it never lost another battle.

Montgomery's first action, the evening of his arrival, was to make clear that there would be no further withdrawals. He found a tactical situation which suited his abilities perfectly. The El Alamein front was limited in width by the Qattara Depression on the inner flank, only thirty miles from the sea. Both sides established and extended southward defensive positions, with considerable depth and progressively broadened minefields. Meanwhile, Intelligence made clear that Rommel would soon attack again, and Montgomery was sure where and how such an attack would come. There would be an attempt to outflank in the south, using the limited room still available, a manoeuvre similar to that which had swung round Bir Hacheim in May.

This indeed was Rommel's plan, and because he knew that British reinforcements on a large scale were arriving while his own supply situation was failing to improve he had no time to lose. The Deutsches Afrika Korps would move east past the south of Eighth Army, south of Alam Halfa and then swing north to the coast, passing east of Ruweisat Ridge. This time the distances were less demanding than at Bir Hacheim and there would be total envelopment. Rommel would, he believed, defeat the British mobile forces, which must surely move east to react to the threat of encirclement. He would beat them as so often hitherto, by superior tactics, decision in command and speed of execution. The British manning defensive positions could be dealt with by direct assault once surrounded, or savaged as they were forced to withdraw, like the British of XIII Corps at Gazala. Then nothing would lie between Panzer Armee Afrika and the Egyptian Delta. To carry out this task Rommel had two hundred German tanks, including twenty-six new Mark IVs with an excellent long 75 millimetre gun not yet seen on the battlefield; and about two hundred and fifty Italian. His force, of four German and seven Italian divisions, included four armoured divisions. After vainly waiting for his fuel position to improve as promised, he made the decision to attack with a very narrow logistic margin, and the mobile arm of Panzer Armee Afrika moved towards the southern British minefields at 10 p.m. on 30th August.

Eighth Army had received reinforcements and tank replacements.

Montgomery assessed that he could hold the ground he considered vital with a small addition to his infantry, and 44th (British) Division, newly arrived in Egypt, was sent up from the delta at his request immediately he assumed command. Montgomery had, thereafter, five infantry divisions – one each from Britain, Australia, New Zealand, South Africa and India – and two armoured divisions, 7th and 10th, of

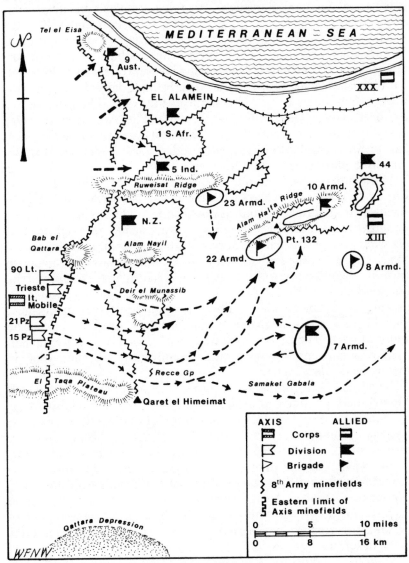

Alam Halfa

which the former had a motor brigade and light or cruiser tanks, while the latter had, either initially or as the battle developed, the mass of British armour, 8th, 22nd, and later 23rd Armoured Brigades, including all the Grants. In all, Montgomery confronted Rommel with about 700 tanks of all kinds.

Eighth Army was deployed in two corps, of which XXX Corps (Lieutenant-General Ramsden, promoted from commanding 50th Division) was in the north with three infantry divisions, and XIII Corps (Lieutenant-General Horrocks, recently arrived from England at Montgomery's request) in the south with the bulk of the armour. Horrocks held Freyberg's New Zealand Division on the main front and 44th Division facing south on the Alam Halfa Ridge, a long east-west ridge twenty miles behind the south of the front. The armour was deployed at Alam Halfa, either facing south (22nd Armoured Brigade) or south of the Alam Halfa Ridge facing west (8th Armoured Brigade): and to this concentration was later added 23rd Armoured Brigade, initially deployed in rear of XXX Corps.

Montgomery was determined on a number of points. First, he wished to husband resources for the major offensive which Eighth Army must undertake as soon as possible. He did not, therefore, wish to suffer heavy casualties in tanks or equipment. Although he had occasional hopes of a major victory, of cutting off Rommel's manoeuvre forces, he was prepared to settle for a limited success, simply to frustrate the offensive without taking risks in exploitation. Second, he intended to lead Rommel on to the emplaced British armour, in prepared and static positions. The tank would be used as an anti-tank gun. There would be no manoeuvre of the kind at which the enemy, he appreciated, had consistently shown himself superior. The terrain lent itself to his concept: Rommel would certainly turn north somewhere in the region of Alam Halfa.

Third, the British now had a formidable air-striking force, which Montgomery intended to exploit to the full (he had established his headquarters next to the Desert Air Force's). Fourth and last, but most important, Montgomery had no intention of relaxing his personal grip on the battle. By impressing his personal authority on the Eighth Army, he intended restoring their confidence that, henceforth, they would beat Rommel, as well as associating that confidence with their new commander. Since Montgomery (although sometimes seeking to disguise the fact) was human, he also had the unavowed task of personally learning from experience how to command in the conditions of the desert war.

At all these points the Battle of Alam Halfa was successful for the

British. It was, compared with previous encounters, a mercifully undramatic battle but it was a victory, limited but secure. The German-Italian advance followed its predicted pattern; very slowly, since Eighth Army's southern minefields were more formidable than expected and took longer to clear. The DAK and XX (Italian) Corps turned north earlier than anticipated, west of Alam Halfa, and British armoured positions were adjusted and reinforced to meet them: Montgomery ultimately had three armoured brigades with five hundred tanks, concentrated and facing south between the rear of the New Zealanders and the Alam Halfa Ridge. At no point did the enemy break in or break through. Neither side suffered particularly heavy tank casualties – the Germans and Italians lost about fifty, the British sixty-seven – but by the third day, 2nd September, Rommel had made little progress and called off the offensive. He was butting his head against a steel wall, and with fuel supplies running low saw no signs of that British volatility he had so often been able to exploit. He was also being pounded from the air and suffering heavily. The DAK and XX Corps withdrew the way they had come, unworried by an ineffectual – and expensive – attack by the New Zealand Division from the north against the corridor through which they passed.[1] It was Rommel's last offensive in the Western Desert.

It has been said that Montgomery inherited a plan of Auchinleck's and thereafter claimed credit for another's successful ideas. Certainly some plans had been made to meet an offensive by, *inter alia*, deploying a force on Alam Halfa Ridge and fighting the main anti-tank battle in that region. A good deal of defensive work had already been done which fitted Montgomery's intentions. The lie of the land would suggest it, anyway, to most commanders. Montgomery has also been said to have masked the part played by ULTRA Intelligence in his victory – not for the last time – in his own subsequent accounts: he is said to have sought to boost his army's confidence in him by exaggerating his own skill. Such comments miss the essential point. Alam Halfa, as fought, was Montgomery's responsibility, and he issued the orders. He did not "inherit" – he saw and decided, and it was alien to his character to do anything else. And what mattered was less the plan than the effective control of the battle. Alam Halfa was not a brilliant nor an original battle. It was, simply, the first of a long sequence of occasions on which Montgomery showed both his subordinates and his enemy who was master. For the British Army it was a moment to savour. For Rommel it was the beginning of the end in Africa.

[1] Freyberg also had one British brigade for this attack, from the recently arrived 44th Division. It suffered severely.

Montgomery now prepared for the battle he had, from the first day of his command, confidently assured Eighth Army they would win. Like Auchinleck before him, this meant holding off pressures from the government at home to start earlier than he wished. He replied to these in remarkable terms. Let Eighth Army be given until 20th October, Montgomery said, and he would guarantee victory. Few commanders in history have been prepared so to assume responsibility for the tempting of providence. Such assurance was extraordinary and compelling.

Reinforcements were arriving – but reinforcements, whether of men or matériel, had in the past been no guarantors of victory. A great mass of new equipment now reached Egypt, including 300 American Sherman tanks, with a superior turret-mounted gun to any yet in service with the British Army. And now, at long last, British divisions formed the majority of Eighth Army. On the eve of the battle, henceforth known as El Alamein, Montgomery commanded about 230,000 men, with an order of battle of eleven divisions of which seven were British: 44th and 50th, already blooded in the desert war; 51st (Highland) Division, reconstituted after the tragedy of St. Valéry over two years before, and eager for vengeance; and Eighth Army's four armoured divisions, 1st, 7th, 8th and 10th. In addition, Montgomery had four veterans – the New Zealanders, 9th Australian, 1st South African and 4th Indian Divisions.

The weeks were spent by Panzer Armee Afrika in extending and improving defences, especially minefields. Rommel had few illusions. He was temporarily a sick man, but before flying home for leave he gave minute instructions for the forthcoming battle. He knew Montgomery would attack, and was daily growing stronger. He knew that his own ability to fight, let alone manoeuvre, was at the mercy of a deplorable logistical situation, with the Mediterranean supply routes under incessant attack from the Royal Navy and Royal Air Force. His Italian divisions were largely without transport. The British had an air superiority ratio of about five to three in aircraft. In tanks the British would, by the day of battle, attain a yet higher margin – 1,030 tanks including 250 Shermans, compared to under 500 in Panzer Armee Afrika, of which only 218 were German. Rommel had 850 anti-tank guns and about 500 field guns – the British, 1460 (including 850 six pounders) and 900 pieces of medium and field artillery.

Such superiority was formidable. It need not, however, have been overwhelming. Battle could still turn on skill in execution. Rommel gave precise orders for the organisation of defensive positions. German and Italian brigades and battalions were interleaved along the front.

Each battalion was to hold a forward line lightly, a main position well to the rear. The latter, with luck, would be neglected in the first supporting bombardment of the attack, and able to produce an effective shield when the opponent's point was blunted, his lunge over-extended. Minefields were to be in great depth, so that an attacker would be entangled in positions between two and five miles from front to rear. Minefields would consist of mixed anti-personnel and anti-tank mines, so that clearance would be laborious and the progress of armour through the minebelt slow. And if British armour did, in fact, emerge, it must be dealt with instantly before superior numbers could be brought to bear: there must be immediate counter-penetration and counter-attack. For this Rommel divided his four armoured divisions into two groups, each of one German and one Italian division, with many tanks and anti-tank guns dug in within range of the rear edge of the minefield, so that any British armoured formations seeking to break out to the west would immediately encounter the sort of terrible line of anti-tank fire that had so often defeated them in the past.

The limited front, the time necessary for the British to make a breach, all implied a pounding match. Rommel knew that this, for the first time, would be a battle of matériel, with little manoeuvre; and it was a kind Panzer Armee Afrika was not equipped to win. Rommel commanded about 100,000 men, now organised in twelve divisions, four of them German. All the odds of war were against them, and their commander knew it. He handed temporary command to General Stumme, while taking leave to recover his health in Austria, and was not to return until the third day of the battle.

Montgomery fully appreciated that this was to be hard pounding. "There will be no tip and run tactics in this battle," he wrote in his first Operation Order, "It will be a killing match." Hitherto in the desert war, conditions had made armour supreme, operations "maritime" in their flow and mobility. Now armoured formations would have to be shepherded at foot pace through minefields to open country and only then – if ever – would have the chance to manoeuvre. In fact Montgomery had little intention of manoeuvring in any real sense. He sought, instead, to create a situation where the enemy's tanks would be forced to destroy themselves by attacking our own tanks and anti-tank guns. Eighth Army's infantry divisions would advance, supported by an overwhelming concentration of artillery and engineers, and would establish themselves on the far side of the main enemy defensive area and minefield. They would be followed by armoured divisions whose engineers, working immediately behind the infantry advance, were to clear lanes of anti-tank mines so that the armour could deploy in clean country beyond. Then the enemy holding ground would be destroyed in detail – Montgomery called it "crumbling" – while the British armour held the ring beyond the main defensive area and destroyed the enemy's tank forces which must (it was reckoned) advance to intervene. The object would be the annihilation of most of Panzer Armee Afrika, and particularly the armour, on its own ground. No such battle had been fought by the British Army since the First World War. This was to be a frontal attack, a battle of attrition, needing perfect preparation, moral force and persistence unto death. It could never be cheap in matériel or human life: but it could be decisive.

To put his concept into effect Montgomery organised Eighth Army in three corps. In the north XXX Corps (Lieutenant-General Sir Oliver Leese having replaced Ramsden) had, from north to south, 9th Australian Division (Lieutenant-General Sir Leslie Morshead), 51st Division, the New Zealand Division, 1st South African Division, and 4th Indian Division, as well as 9th Armoured Brigade – under command of the New Zealand Division throughout – and 23rd Armoured Brigade. In the south, XIII Corps (Lieutenant-General Horrocks) had 7th Armoured Division, 44th Division and 50th Division. X Corps, newly formed at Montgomery's request as an armoured corps under Lieutenant-General Lumsden, consisted of 1st, 8th and 10th Armoured Divisions, of which only 1st and 10th commanded armoured brigades for the battle.

Montgomery's point of main effort was in the north, in XXX Corps's area. There Leese was to attack with four divisions on a total frontage of about six miles. Behind him Lumsden's X Corps was to clear lanes for the tanks through the minefields, for the passage of 1st Armoured Division (north) and 10th Armoured Division (south): each of these two divisions formed its own mine-clearing party, including a large body of engineers. The infantry divisions were given an objective line about five miles from their starting points. The armoured divisions were to reach an objective line some two miles farther west, having debouched from the corridors and passed through the infantry.

This was a second, a revised plan. Montgomery's earlier orders had differed in one important particular. He had originally directed Lumsden's corps to press through the minefields and establish themselves astride the enemy's supply lines. Now the armoured divisions were simply to take position west of the infantry objective. Too much should not be made of this change, which was in practice (although not, perhaps, in Montgomery's mind) more one of degree than of kind. The objections voiced at the first plan by Lumsden and his commanders – and by the Infantry Divisional Commanders of XXX Corps, sceptical

240

of its realism – applied largely to the second also. Some of this arose from general distrust of the readiness of armoured units to take risks. But most arose from disbelief in the ability of armour to emerge swiftly from narrow lanes, in the face of the enemy anti-tank defence and impeded from earlier deployment by minefields. The disbelief was well founded, and justified by the event. The change of plan produced an undesirable consequence in that it virtually superimposed one corps upon another instead of clearly passing one through the other. And as the "dogfight" developed in the area of the corridors, division could only reach arrangement with division through the involvement of two Corps Headquarters and their commanders: with inevitable reference to Army Headquarters if they disagreed. As in most battles, confusion at Alamein was huge, and this device increased it.

In the south, Horrocks's XIII Corps was to attack with 7th Armoured Division clearing its own path through the minefield, in an attempt to hold the enemy's attention in the south and deter the movement north of his southern group of armoured divisions. Such a "door" would also enable Montgomery to exploit by further limited advance in the south if he chose, but he gave orders that 7th Armoured Division was not to be hazarded or allowed to be severely mauled. By these orders Montgomery gave himself (if all went well) a southern "option" which might be vital at a later stage in the battle, and something of a reserve, in that at least one armoured division was only to be committed with caution to the initial fighting.

Incessant training was now carried out, particularly in minefield clearance. An elaborate and successful deception plan was undertaken. Orders were prepared with the greatest secrecy and only imparted at first to a few. Throughout the day preceding battle the attacking troops were confined strictly to their slit trenches. Then, at 9.40 on the evening of 23rd October, 456 guns of Eighth Army opened fire. It was a bombardment unheard since the First World War. The concentration of artillery, the narrow divisional frontages of attack, the obsession with the ultimate passing through of a mobile arm, resembled the launch of the Somme Battle in July 1916.

The guns fired for fifteen devastating minutes at the known positions of enemy gun batteries. Then, after a five minute silence, they opened once more, this time on the forward positions of German and Italian infantry. It was 10 p.m. and, simultaneously, the four attacking divisions of XXX Corps rose from the ground and started forward in the moonlight, bayonets fixed, the pipers of the Highland regiments playing. This was Operation LIGHTFOOT. The Battle of Alamein.

No operation goes exactly as planned. There are few battles without crises, in which the whole concept seems in jeopardy. LIGHTFOOT was no exception.

The infantry advance started well. The artillery had done their work effectively both on the enemy's guns and upon his forward positions. But the defences of Panzer Armee Afrika were in great depth, and soon the advancing battalions came on the unsubdued defenders of the main position, surrounded by yet more minefields. Anti-personnel mines were to the British infantry at Alamein what barbed wire had been to their fathers – a lethal cause of confusion and delay. Mine-clearing, whether of anti-personnel or anti-tank mines, took longer than expected. Much of it had to be done by hand "prodding" and lifting. By dawn, on 24th October, the attacking divisions had achieved variable success and were out of line with each other. The corridors behind them, with lanes being cleared by the two armoured divisions of Lumsden's corps, were, similarly, in a state of confused and only partial achievement. Nowhere was the armour through the mined area and on to clean ground deployed for its main task. And behind the front, in and behind the corridors themselves, military police struggled to disentangle an appalling congestion of vehicles, support weapons for the infantry, minefield clearance parties of Lumsden's corps, commanders, signallers; all amid the sound and fury of battle and in thick, choking dust, smoke and sand, making darkness utterly impenetrable.

The first element of LIGHTFOOT, therefore, that went awry was time. As usual in battle everything went slower and more painfully than planned. When light came the armour was undeployed, and it took many hours' more fighting before the infantry throughout the front had reached their objectives. Throughout the day and night of the second day Montgomery ruthlessly drove Lumsden on – to force his armoured divisions through the minefields. At the end of the southern (10th Armoured Division) corridor lay the Miteirya Ridge – the infantry objective line. But when the tanks ultimately debouched and tried to reach their objective – a line two miles further to the west – they found themselves caught on forward slopes in daylight and driven back to such protection as the ridge afforded. The aim of establishing a line of armour well forward of the infantry was frustrated by Rommel's own line of tanks and anti-tank guns, dug in only 1,000 yards from the mouth of the corridors both north and south and effectively blocking British armoured deployment west of their infantry; and as the front moved west more mines were laid.

With a good deal of anger, despite the delays Montgomery decided to continue his "crumbling" operations, notwithstanding. Then and

Georges and Gort

Von Bock

Brooke and Dill

Von Rundstedt

Wavell with O'Connor

Platt

Student

Wilson

Kesselring and Rommel

Brooke and Montgomery

Percival

Iida

Alexander and Eisenhower

Bradley

Von Arnim

Patton

Clark and Alexander

Von Vietinghoff

Slim

Wingate

Kimura

Stilwell

Mutaguchi

Crerar, Dempsey, Montgomery and Simpson

Model

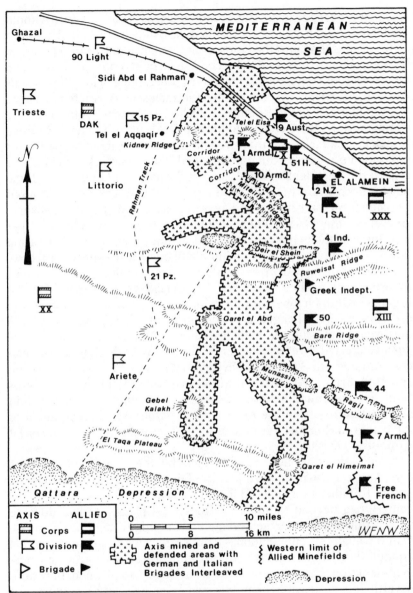

Alamein – Operation "Lightfoot"

later he blamed armoured commanders for their lack of drive at
Alamein, where at least part of the blame should have been directed
inwards, at his own failure to comprehend what tanks can and cannot

243

reasonably be made to do. But Montgomery was resilient. Even without his armour established where planned, he could, he reckoned, mount a series of attacks against the German and Italian infantry not yet overrun or engaged, and thus fulfil the second stage of his concept. To this end he carried out successful northward operations with Morshead's Australian Division. Meanwhile the German armour reacted in part as Montgomery desired. Rommel (recalled from leave and resuming command on 25th October, following the death of General Stumme from a heart attack on 24th) feared most of all a breakout by the British armour. To frustrate this he launched counter-attacks, particularly against the west flank of the Australian Division and in the area of the northern corridor mouth, "Kidney Ridge", where 1st Armoured Division's motor brigade had now repelled, with heroic brilliance, attacks by the DAK. Thus Montgomery's concept, although not working exactly as planned, was succeeding in its object of wearing down the enemy's armour while simultaneously destroying his infantry.

In the south, XIII Corps' operation had only limited success. It was, by order, not pushed *à outrance*, but played its initial part. On the evening of 26th October, however, Rommel moved his southern group of armour -- 21st Panzer Division and half the Ariete Division – northwards towards the main battlefield. At the same time Montgomery created a reserve under X Corps. By 28th October, he had concentrated 7th Armoured Division with the New Zealand Division and 10th Armoured Division, withdrawn from the main XXX Corps front. He continued his operation against the enemy infantry within and northwards from the main field of battle. And he continued to inflict loss on Rommel's armour as it faced the westward pressure of 1st Armoured Division.

A new situation had been created by the time taken to clear corridors, and the manifest difficulty of driving armour forwards in the face of Rommel's well-placed line of tanks and anti-tank guns. Montgomery had needed to adjust his ideas and plans. He had done so successfully – a greater achievement than simply steering a precise plan through to culmination – and appreciated that although his armoured divisions and his anti-tank guns were not destroying Rommel's tanks on the ground or in the scenario he had planned, they were nevertheless destroying them. His own casualties had been heavy, but he had every reason to suppose his enemy was nearer breaking point as the fighting went on, losses were reported, the RAF took their toll and the prisoners came in. Here was the moment for a last supreme effort which would destroy the cohesion of the Axis forces. Montgomery withdrew 1st Armoured Division, and now had virtually all X Corps in reserve. He planned to make this effort in the coastal area, led by Freyberg's New Zealanders on 30th October.

Rommel, however, anticipated him and moved north such reserves as he could muster. Montgomery therefore changed his plan. The culminating attack – Operation SUPERCHARGE – would go in on the old XXX Corps front of attack, north of Kidney Ridge and directed towards Tel El Aqqaqir and the Rahman track which ran from north to south behind Rommel's front. Beyond this was open desert. SUPER-CHARGE was to be led by the New Zealand Division – with two British infantry brigades under its command – and the British 9th Armoured Brigade. 1st Armoured Division would then pass through and meet the enemy's armour advancing to restore the situation. It was the concept of LIGHTFOOT, a repeat performance on a smaller scale. Again there would be a demonstration in the south by XIII Corps. And Montgomery was what he liked to call "balanced". Having constituted afresh an armoured reserve he was ready for anything. Throughout the battle Montgomery, utterly professional and steel-willed in execution, was calm, unhurried. His resolution communicated itself throughout the army. As at Alam Halfa, men felt that their commander was master of events.

On the night of 1st November, four battalions of Durham men and Highlanders under Freyberg's command went forward again for their last attack at the Battle of Alamein. It was entirely successful. By six o'clock next morning Lumsden's corps passed through and took up the running with the armour again concentrated – and again halted, as Rommel's anti-tank line for the last time stopped them on the line of the Rahman track, inflicting considerable casualties.

But Rommel had had enough. His situation had offered no hope unless Montgomery had been prepared to stop the battle. His remaining tank force stood at fifty-five. His Italian infantry had been captured, destroyed or were immobile. He was without supplies. "I haven't much hope left," he wrote on 29th October. On the evening of 2nd November he decided that, whatever the fantasies in the minds of his superiors, his duty was to save what he could of Panzer Armee Afrika. He extricated all that he could by 4th November in a brilliantly executed flight which the rather laboured efforts of Eighth Army were insufficiently urgent to prevent. The Ariete Division was annihilated. Thirty thousand men passed into Allied captivity. Eighth Army had suffered 13,500 casualties[1] but its next significant battle would be

---

[1] A figure near exactly predicted by Montgomery. He also accurately predicted the battle's duration.

fought on the borders of Tunisia, 1,500 miles to the west. The tide had finally and irrevocably turned. This was the best moment experienced by the British Army since another November day long ago in 1918.

The artillery played a crucial part in the Battle of Alamein, and fire was concentrated and properly handled. Each brigade or brigade group was normally supported by a field regiment of artillery – three batteries each of eight guns – but it was essential that the fire of all available guns could be coordinated at a higher level – that of the Divisional or even Corps Commander of Royal Artillery. By this means, artillery effort could be switched, intensified, concentrated on one section of the front, or called off as the battle required: one of the most effective as well as most immediate ways in which a commander could influence the battle. The Gunners had so far been condemned to a difficult war – often starved of ammunition, the wise handling of artillery imperfectly mastered by commanders of other arms, and dispersion rather than concentration the rule. Now they came into their own. With ample time for preparation and supply, no restrictions had to be placed on ammunition expenditure, and during the battle over one million rounds were fired by the field artillery alone.

The Sappers, too, came into their own. The clearance of mines, despite the conditions and confusions of battle, was the key task affecting the speed and success of operations. Without the successful performance of the Royal Engineers, there would have been no victory of Alamein. Engineers perforce led the armour through the corridors, and the training, skill and courage of the mine-lifting parties was beyond praise.

For the British infantry, whether in the motor brigades of armoured divisions or in the infantry divisions themselves, the battle was at last a triumph. It was expensively bought – a disproportionate share of the casualty list was borne by such divisions as 51st (Highland). But at long last the infantry had been enabled to go forward, properly supported, in conditions which suited them – and for which they were indispensable. "It all depends," Wellington observed of his chances before Waterloo, pointing at a British infantryman, "on that article." It did again, and would again.

As the remaining troops of Panzer Armee Afrika streamed westwards from Mersa Matruh on 8th November, the British Army was launched, at the other end of the Mediterranean, on another mighty enterprise.

246

The Allied landings in French North Africa – Operation TORCH – were to seal the fate of the Axis forces on the African continent. Two American forces would be landed: one at Casablanca and one inside the Mediterranean, at Oran. An Anglo-American "Eastern Task Force", once landed astride Algiers, would be built up as rapidly as possible into the British First Army, under Lieutenant-General Sir Kenneth Anderson. As the eastern wing of the Allied expedition, its orders were to advance swiftly further east, to seize Tunis and Bizerta, thereby denying them as supply ports if Hitler decided on a Tunisian front.

Two British brigades – 11th and 36th – were included in the assault force, soon to be formed as 78th Division. As well as two regimental combat teams (approximately brigade sized) from the United States 34th Division, British Commandos were also employed, these being either composite units of picked volunteers from infantry regiments or Royal Marines specially trained for assault from the sea. This was the first "Combined Operation" which was not purely a raid – the first landing intended as an invasion, and although it met little resistance it gave excellent practice for what was ahead. 11th Brigade landed, with the American combat teams, on three beaches astride Algiers. 36th Brigade, stowed ready for assault, followed three days later at Bougie, 100 miles to the east – and landed unopposed.

TORCH, too, marked the first use of a British parachute formation in action.[1] One battalion of 1st Parachute Brigade was dropped on 12th November and captured Bone Airfield a further 150 miles to the east. Further parachute operations took place in the next phase, to assist the eastward advance of the main force towards Tunis, and although more experience was needed by the dropping aircraft, and some units were too widely dispersed, these enterprises gave vital practice and played a significant part in the battle. It might, indeed, have been possible to achieve greater and more decisive results by using airborne forces more ambitiously from the beginning. For the campaign in Tunisia did not achieve the swift seizure of Tunis and Bizerta for which the High Command hoped, despite the successful initial landings at 1 a.m. on 8th November.

At first all went well. Many French Commanders and troops (there was a considerable French Army in Algeria) were uncertain of where their duty lay, and resisted the Allies, very properly, until ordered otherwise. But on 10th November, Admiral Darlan, who, fortuitously,

[1] Parachutists had already been used for raiding, notably at the very successful operation on the French coast at Bruneval in February 1942.

was in Algiers, agreed to order a cease-fire and thereafter there was cooperation, although the situation remained delicate.

After gaining their foothold, the troops of the Eastern Task Force had a huge problem in carrying out their main mission – an advance of some 400 miles over difficult terrain, with small forces and, as yet, no base. But they did not delay. By 17th November the leading British and American troops of what was now formally First Army were 400 miles from Algiers and within fifty miles of Tunis, having so far only met resistance from a few of the French at the first instance.

Now, however, all changed. German policy towards the new situation was decided very quickly and as quickly executed. Hitler decreed on 9th November (the Italians concurred and cooperated) that troops must be sent to Tunisia and hold a bridgehead based on Tunis and Bizerta. The French Government at Vichy placed its airfields at the disposal of the Axis. The first German aircraft and aircrew started arriving in Tunis the same afternoon, followed the next day by some Luftwaffe troops, and the day after by the appointment of a land commander. By 14th November a tank company, a reconnaissance company, some engineers and three infantry companies had disembarked – reinforcements earmarked for Rommel's Afrika Korps and now re-routed. In the next fortnight the Germans brought in seven battalions and about fifty tanks, the Italians a division. It was a race against time and the Germans won it.

On 16th November General Nehring arrived to take command. He had been wounded at Alam Halfa leading the Afrika Korps, and was used to the emphasis on speed of his old commander. Nehring, like Rommel, believed that the best defence is offensive, and that to save an hour can be worth a battalion. He immediately threw out mixed battlegroups, consisting of what troops he had – a few tanks, motorcyclists, some anti-tank guns – on the routes running westwards from Tunis. The Axis position was to be based on two bridgeheads hastily formed at Tunis and Bizerta, thirty miles apart, and meanwhile everything must be done to hold the line, impose delay and cover reinforcement. Nehring ordered his troops to make for Tabarka and drive the British back to Bone. German and Italian troops were to make up for being outnumbered at first by energy and skill, and by the fact that they should be operating nearer to their bases and their airfields. First contact was made at Djebel Abiod on 17th November.

Between then and the end of the month a series of brisk encounter battles took place in the general area of Tebourba, with the British mounting a deliberate attack on 24th November and the Germans counter-attacking on 27th with some fifteen tanks, but losing eight of

Daybreak

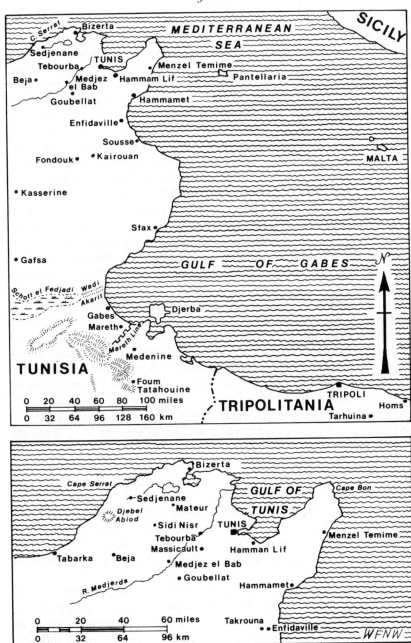

Tunisia

them. More serious was a German counter-attack on 1st December, with forty tanks and two motorcycle companies. This comparatively small force attacked 11th Brigade and an American force of two tank and two armoured infantry battalions. The attack was enterprising and largely successful, with German troops working round the flanks of the position; and the British withdrew to the Tebourba Gap, a defile to the south-west. Some of the fighting around Tebourba was particularly fierce, but First Army showed, as on countless occasions in North Africa, that the years of training in England had been put to good effect, and that the British soldier could and did once again hold his own. The German infantry, adept at infiltration, would work their way into the heart of a position or round its flanks. They would seize and mount machine guns on points of tactical significance. They would give an impression of greater strength than they possessed, yet were quick to reinforce success with infantry reserves. German tanks, closely supporting their infantry, often still appeared to dominate the field. German artillery and mortar fire was accurate, deadly and quick in reaction to circumstance, and whatever the balance of forces overall the Germans were determined to retain the initiative by concentrating and seeking a superiority of strength where they judged it mattered. Again and again the battles resolved into a series of small-scale and gallant British rushes with bayonet and grenade against German posts established where they could make British defence untenable. These were battles of junior leaders, of Company and Platoon Commanders, of Sergeants and Corporals: and these showed a professionalism and vigour which exorcised the recollection of Dunkirk. Eighth Army had so far reaped the laurels and borne the heat of the sun. Now it was the turn of the rest.

The British forces had been built up to one infantry division (78th), and 6th Armoured Division consisting of one armoured and one infantry brigade. On 6th December these were taken over by V Corps (Lieutenant-General C. W. Allfrey). It was clear that there would be no quick breakthrough to Tunis. Anderson ordered Allfrey to pass temporarily to the defensive. On 8th December General von Arnim arrived in Tunis to take over command of all Axis troops in what was to be named Fifth Panzer Army.

On 22nd December V Corps began the last Allied attempt to break through and reach Tunis in 1942. It was necessary to take high ground in the mountains and south-west of Tebourba in order to cover an advance by 6th Armoured Division. After a successful attack followed by an equally successful German counter-attack, the attempt to mount a major advance was first postponed and then abandoned. Torrential

250

rain was falling. Movement and visibility alike were difficult, and would remain so for many weeks. Both sides settled down to a long haul, to the disappointed exasperation of the authorities in Washington and London. Some minor attacks mounted by each side in January and early February made no significant difference to the situation. An Allied line, thinly held, now stretched from Gafsa northwards to the sea at Cape Serrat, a distance of some 200 miles.

This was not only the first major combined operation and the first deployment of British parachute troops, it was the first Anglo-American campaign. The Allied forces in Tunisia were at first untidily disposed. The forces from the western landings at Casablanca and Oran gradually joined the front. The intentions and capabilities of the French forces took time to clarify. By early February, three corps sectors, from north to south, V (British) Corps, XIX (French) Corps and II (US) Corps, were formed. These were not homogenous and although the intention, ultimately achieved, was that national contingents should fight under national command, at first British troops fought in all three sectors. New British formations had arrived to join 6th Armoured and 78th Divisions. 46th Division had joined V Corps. 1st Guards Brigade and 25th Army Tank Brigade were in army reserve. In addition there came into being an "Army Group Royal Artillery" (AGRA), in effect a brigade of heavy and medium artillery for massed artillery support beyond that provided by artillery regiments organic to divisions. Much of the Command system was, not unnaturally, chaotic. First Army Headquarters was not equipped to run so wide and international a front for what now appeared a major campaign; and the logistic problems of different national armies, with unfamiliar habits and staff systems, were bound to create difficulties.

Anderson, who was referred to by Alexander as a "good plain cook" – an unkind phrase which soon spread through the army – soon found himself commanding an Allied force; and his qualities did not include the necessary finesse. The Supreme Allied Commander, General Eisenhower, a man of very particular tact, found that Anderson "permitted himself to express, at times, disappointments or disapprovals in a way that seems to offend subordinates or others around him," as he delicately put it in a letter to Brooke; and Admiral Sir Andrew Cunningham, the Naval Commander-in-Chief, thought relations so strained that he made a personal signal to the First Sea Lord about it. But Anderson was not without problems. If the British had learnt the hard way how tough the Wehrmacht was as an opponent, it was now the turn of the American Army to re-enact that experience. Brave but unprepared for war, victims of a huge expansion on an inadequate professional base, they suffered as had the British some very severe shocks. Tunisia was their blooding, their Norway; but fortunately not their "Dunkirk".

Alexander arrived in North Africa on 19th February, newly appointed Deputy Commander to Eisenhower – and, simultaneously, Army Group Commander, of 18th Army Group, responsible to Eisenhower for all Allied land operations in Tunisia. A few days earlier, however, an old opponent of his also appeared upon the Tunisian scene.

Eighth Army's pursuit of Rommel's forces after the victory of Alamein has been criticised as sluggish. The delays in getting under way were, however, unsurprising given the crowded and confused conditions of 5th November. Montgomery hoped to trap his enemy with a short hook to the coast, but failed. Rommel's forces had a main road down which to withdraw and it would have needed great energy and more than a little luck to move across desert with enough speed to forestall.

As Rommel's next tenable defensive position would clearly be at El Agheila, west of the Cyrenaica bulge, an attempt was made to cut him off – to re-enact the drama of February 1941 when O'Connor had reached Beda Fomm before the fleeing Italians. On this occasion the end was different. The Germans were too skilled to be caught by so predictable a move. Flank guards held off the pursuit and Rommel reached the El Agheila position. With Cyrenaica clear of Axis troops, Tobruk and Benghazi could be brought into play as ports to supply Eighth Army over the huge distances it was now advancing. Montgomery was determined that this advance, at least, should not be followed by withdrawals; and logistics imposed constraints, as supply depots and airfields were opened ever further to the westward behind the moving front.

Rommel matched his determination not to be trapped in Cyrenaica by equal determination not to be caught at El Agheila in a battle he could not win. His own recommendation, ultimately effected, was to withdraw from Tripolitania, to move back across the Tunisian border. He still had four armoured divisions – two German and two Italian – but with very few tanks. His next position was at Buerat, on the Gulf of Sirte, but on 18th January he withdrew still further to Homs and Tarhuna, immediately east of Tripoli, and on 19th he ordered the destruction and evacuation of the port of Tripoli itself. Four days later Eighth Army entered Tripoli. The Panzer Armee Afrika withdrew to Mareth in Tunisia and prepared to meet an attack from Eighth Army, which Rommel considered unlikely for several weeks.

When Rommel's forces finally left Libya and crossed the Tunisian border on 13th February, he was now united with the forces of General von Arnim, based on Tunis. He had fifty tanks left in the Deutsches Afrika Korps – 21st Panzer Division had been detached, without its tanks, to re-form as part of Arnim's Command, and the latter had a tank force of about one hundred and forty in 21st and 10th Panzer Divisions (including one company of the new and enormous "Tiger" tanks, complete with 88 millimetre gun in turret). Montgomery was advancing towards Rommel's front. Anderson's right wing, the II United States Corps, lay to the German right rear.

On 14th February Rommel and Arnim launched simultaneous attacks on II US Corps. Rommel entered Gafsa unopposed on 15th. Anderson feared the envelopment of his whole right wing and withdrew. On 19th, Rommel took Arnim's Panzer divisions, 10th and 21st, under his own command. Thus once again, but for the last time, he had the concentrated armour of the German and Italian Armies in Africa. He was directed to attack north,[1] to cut off the Allied forces facing Tunis. On 19th, he captured the Kasserine Pass, and routed the American forces in the area.

This was, however, Rommel's last victory. Despite Allied confusion, tanks, guns and a reserve brigade were brought to the area; and behind a new front a counter-attack was prepared. Rommel, often in the past so sanguine, was convinced that his own offensive must be stopped. His fuel and ammunition supplies were low; he knew that he had little time before Eighth Army closed up to the Mareth Front. On 20th February the Axis forces were ordered back to their original start line. Considerable casualties had been inflicted on the Americans. Montgomery wrote sardonically to Brooke on 23rd February: "There seems to be a real good party going on up in Central Tunisia. We get odd people passing to and fro from that front and it appears that the Bosche [sic] does just whatever he likes with the Americans. They do not know how to fight the battle: the Bosche has got a great many of their tanks and a great deal of their equipment." Generosity about colleagues or allies was not Montgomery's outstanding quality, but his remarks would have been echoed in many quarters of First Army. Like the British, the Americans had to pay an early penalty for unreadiness; and like the British in 1940 they had gone to war with a complacent assurance of superiority which was rudely shattered by an enemy of greater

---

[1] Nominally both Rommel and Arnim were under Field Marshal Kesselring in Italy.

professional skill. On 23rd February, Rommel was placed in command of all German and Italian forces in Tunisia: "Army Group Africa". Six days earlier the British First and Eighth Armies were placed under Alexander's Army Group Command.

For the British Army the Tunisian campaign of March and April 1943 included some of the hardest fighting of the war. The first battles took place in the last days of February on First Army's front, with three determined Axis thrusts – Operation OCHSENKOPF – west from Tunis towards Sedjenane, Beja and Medjez-el-Bab. These attacks fell on the British 46th and 78th Divisions. The country was mountainous, the front long, and the actions on particular axes unconnected. The most formidable thrust, and the hardest fighting, was towards Beja, where a German battlegroup, including seventy-four tanks, fourteen of them the giant Tiger tank, attacked one British battalion of 46th Division after another, echeloned back astride the road from Sidi Nsir. But after three days of battle the German force had only five tanks left, and the approaches to Beja remained in British hands. OCHSENKOPF was called off as a serious attempt to drive First Army westwards, although sporadic fighting continued throughout March.

A larger, and even more unsuccessful attempt was made by Rommel at Medenine, south of the Mareth Line which was ordered to be held "to the last man" as the eastern bastion of Tunisia. Here, on 6th March, three Panzer divisions attacked the head of Eighth Army. Montgomery had, however, just had time to bring up the infantry and anti-tank guns that he needed, and to prepare for battle. He found time to write a characteristic letter to Brooke in his own hand that day:

> He is trying to attack me in daylight with tanks, followed by lorried infantry. I have 500 6pdr atk guns dug in on the ground: I have 400 tanks; and I have good infantry, holding strong pivots, and a great weight of artillery. It is an absolute gift, and the man must be mad.

> It is all over now [he wrote two days later] it was a model little defensive battle . . . It lasted only one day.

The Germans lost fifty-two tanks at Medenine. It was Rommel's last African battle and a defeat. On 9th March he handed the Tunisian Command over to Arnim and left Africa for ever.

Montgomery wrote frequently to Brooke, and on 4th April described the battle which took Eighth Army finally through Mareth – the gateway of Tunisia. At Mareth, Eighth Army had approximately the same strength of infantry battalions as their enemy, and about 1,000 anti-tank guns to 700. Only in tanks – 743 to 142 – was the British superiority enormous. It was, like Alamein, a position of limited extent (twenty-two miles) with one flank resting on the sea and the other on mountain. "Mareth," wrote Montgomery, "was in many ways quite a classic battle . . . Mareth had scope for subtlety and resource, and for outwitting the opponent." He suggested that after the war Medenine and Mareth "may well form the subject of study at Staff Colleges".

Not all the lessons so learned would be those assumed by Montgomery at the time. At Mareth, Montgomery delivered a frontal attack with XXX Corps (Leese) while making a subsidiary move round the German right flank with the New Zealand Division, 8th Armoured Brigade and a force of Free French under General Leclerc.[1] The frontal attack – 50th Division – after initial success on the night of 20th March, was driven back with losses by a counter-attack from 15th Panzer Division. In the belief that all possible German reserves had been committed to this stroke, Montgomery changed his plan and reinforced Freyberg's force with 1st Armoured Division – shifting his weight from his right to his left. Freyberg – and Horrocks, commanding X Corps, who was sent to coordinate – mounted a successful attack from the south-west towards El Hamma, smashing the opposition, assisted by massive air support. The Germans withdrew. The battle was successful in its object, which was to enable Eighth Army to debouch into Tunisia. It was not successful in trapping the enemy. Nor was it as masterly in higher execution as Montgomery implied. First, in some preliminary attacks four days before the main assault, one brigade (201st Guards Brigade) was launched across an unsuspected minefield and against the only sector held by German troops. Two battalions suffered five hundred and twenty casualties in one night. Second, Montgomery was mistaken in supposing that all German reserves were committed against the frontal assault, itself a failure. The Germans were anticipating and tracking his left hook, and had time and troops to deploy to meet it. Third, the movement of 1st Armoured Division took a long time because of inadequate staff work and traffic chaos – the direct responsibility, in this case, of Eighth Army Headquarters. Fourth, Montgomery had made Freyberg a "Corps" Commander for the battle: and then sent Horrocks, with indeterminate powers, to take command on the "left hook". Freyberg, very understandably, resented this – as the commander of a national contingent he anyway needed to

[1] Freyberg was in command and the force was designated "New Zealand Corps" for the battle.

be governed by consent – and the two Corps Commanders had then to reach agreement on every step. The injection of Horrocks into the situation may have been necessary but with too many Generals on the left hook, time, inevitably, was lost, because of the ambiguity of command. Lastly, Montgomery claimed that in the battle we "knocked him out". But in fact Arnim ordered the abandonment of the Mareth position some days earlier – not because of Montgomery's "left hook" but because he feared a move eastwards by First Army, and in particular by II (United States) Corps which could cut off his southern forces from Tunis.

The battle demonstrated Montgomery's excellent flexibility of mind. It also once again showed his strength and will power – Freyberg had to be pushed hard, for he needed to husband New Zealand manpower and he was disinclined to take risks. Its aftermath demonstrated, too, Montgomery's proneness to exaggerated claims for the nature of his successes, untouched by error or miscalculation. Most of all it demonstrated the excellence of British troops who, from the preliminary operations on 17th March through to 1st Armoured Division's rapid move (when movement became possible) and dashing assault on 26th March, showed a skill and energy which gave its true lustre to the day.

Arnim's next stand was at Wadi Akarit, a formidable natural barrier north of Mareth, a steep "jebel" with east flank resting on the sea. Eighth Army, in pursuit after the success of Mareth, made contact on 29th March. There was discussion as to whether to try to storm the position immediately, but Montgomery decided on deliberate tactics, to bring up the army, prepare the battle and achieve balance to exploit its aftermath. It is difficult to fault such caution. Risks might have paid – but they might have exposed the new-found confidence of Eighth Army to unnecessary setback. Montgomery has been criticised for unadventurous tactics in the pursuit on many occasions, but he never lost a major battle. He would not take risks unless they were necessary, and on this occasion he judged that they were not.

Montgomery's plan was to break in to the position with his infantry in pitch darkness and not, as heretofore, to wait for a moon. The infantry assault was to be made by XXX Corps (Leese) and be followed by the passing through of X Corps (Horrocks) for exploitation and pursuit. The battle started on the night of 5th April. The first phase went well. It was notable for the achievements of 4th Indian Division, on the left wing, whose hardy battalions climbed the precipitous Fatnessa Massif and made a silent attack[1] with deadly success in darkness, their

---

[1] That is, one not preceded by an artillery bombardment.

commander determined to possess dominating ground by daybreak. It was also notable for the hard infantry fighting throughout the area of attack, an attack made by 50th and 51st Divisions and 201st Guards Brigade, beside 4th Indian. "It was," wrote Montgomery, "the heaviest and most savage fighting we have had since I have commanded the Eighth Army." The debouchment of the armour of X Corps, however, was a disappointment. After an inexplicably slow start a line of German 88s stopped the pursuit in its tracks, and the defenders slipped away.

Equally disappointing was a move by the newly constituted IX Corps of First Army, from the west towards Fondouk, and intended to intercept the Axis forces withdrawing before Montgomery. This might have converted into a benefit the delay in Eighth Army's pursuit. It was not to be. Arnim was now determined to bring all his forces northwards into a shorter, defensible line covering Tunis. He had suffered severely at Wadi Akarit. He was in no condition for open warfare. IX Corps (Lieutenant-General J. T. Crocker) advanced with 6th Armoured Division (reinforced to a strength of one armoured and two infantry brigades) and 34th (United States) Infantry Division on the night of 7th April. In the operation it was planned to occupy high ground dominating the eastward road through Fondouk, to exploit with armour towards Kairouan and cut the road to Enfidaville. A German battle-group of two battalions with some anti-tank guns firmly held the door closed against IX Corps until their comrades of Army Group Africa were north of Kairouan. When the troops of First Army finally debouched east of Fondouk and took up the pursuit on 10th April, joining hands with the men of Eighth Army at last, the enemy was once again slipping away to fight another day.

For the final battles of Tunisia more British divisions were deployed than had been assembled on one battlefield since 1940. In First Army were 6th Armoured Division, 1st, 4th, 46th and 78th Divisions, formed in V and IX Corps. In Eighth Army, apart from the Indian and New Zealand Divisions, were 1st and 7th Armoured Divisions, 50th, 51st and 56th Infantry Divisions: a total of three armoured and seven infantry British divisions under Alexander's command.[1] The two armies, First and Eighth, sometimes regarded each other with more curiosity than enthusiasm. Montgomery had given to Eighth Army a deliberately inculcated sense of superiority: they were the battle-

---

[1] Divisions were, of course, switched between the two armies as the campaign proceeded.

winning veterans who had transformed history; they and their commander were invincible. Montgomery was also openly contemptuous of the handling of First Army. In his view, freely expressed, their battles had lacked "grip", had neglected the principle of concentration, and the balance necessary to keep up the momentum of an attack. Montgomery was also critical of Alexander's power of command. In a letter of 10th April, immediately after the Battle of Wadi Akarit, he wrote to Alexander asking that one or other army should be designated to make the final push, the *schwerpunkt* – and should be reinforced accordingly. He complained of lack of decisive purpose in the conduct of the last stages of the campaign.

These criticisms were not without foundation, but for their part First Army were by no means certain that they had everything to learn from Montgomery's men. The desert had been one thing: fighting in the Tunisian hills was quite another, and in the months since November a great deal of experience had been gained in hard unremitting infantry work which exceeded in its own sphere the experience of the divisions of Eighth Army. At Tebourba, Medjez-El-Bab and Sedjenane, there had been savage fighting, much of it successful. More was to come before 18th Army Group finally broke out of the mountains into the plain of Tunis for the last act. Both armies had their character and their glory.

Alexander's orders were that the main effort should be made by First Army. Anderson's army was to capture Tunis. Eighth Army was to "exert pressure" and keep the enemy from reinforcing his right from his left; and from withdrawing into the Cape Bon Peninsula. The offensive was to start on 22nd April. On the Axis side, Army Group Africa was by now effectively cut off from all sea supply by the operations of the Royal Navy and was critically short of fuel. Shortage of ammunition, however, did not prevent very heavy rates of defensive fire in some of the closing battles.

On the right wing of 18th Army Group, Eighth Army made one more attempt to break north towards Tunis. By hard fighting 4th Indian Division and the New Zealand Division had gained Takrouna on 19th April, and Montgomery was unwisely determined to make one final attack on the night of 28th. But he had already sent his most experienced divisions to First Army. The attack was made by 56th Division, newcomers to Eighth Army, in their first battle. A German counterattack restored the situation, and Montgomery appreciated that for Eighth Army the campaign was over. Its achievements from Alamein to Enfidaville, its succession of victories, its triumphant march from one end of North Africa to the other were by then renowned and will remain immortal.

In First Army the final attack was christened Operation VULCAN. In these last stages of the campaign British operations appeared to the Germans methodical, but dispersed and disjointed. A gallant attack would be made, but instead of being exploited by fresh troops would be exposed to bombardment and counter-attack. So it was with an attack by IX Corps from west to east south of Goubellat, with 1st and 6th Armoured and 46th Divisions: hard fighting but no breakthrough. So it was on 27th April when V Corps attacked astride the Medjarda River with 78th Division on the left and 1st Division on the right of the valley.

In this latter case, however, the operation drew so strong a German response that it paved the way for VULCAN, a parallel advance by IX Corps whose thrust line lay a few miles further east. VULCAN would be the final blow, made in enough strength at last to achieve decisive results. General Crocker had suffered an accident, and General Horrocks took command of IX Corps for VULCAN. Two infantry divisions – 4th and 4th Indian – were to attack and seize high ground. Two armoured divisions – 6th and 7th – were to pass through. On the preceding day, to distract the enemy's attention from the point of effort, V Corps were to capture the Djebel Bou Aoukaz above the Medjerda Valley to the west. VULCAN was to start in the early hours of 6th May.

The attack was preceded by an overwhelming air attack and a mighty artillery bombardment, with over 16,000 shells falling in two hours on the front of one assaulting British division alone. The infantry advanced remorselessly to their objectives. By mid-morning, 6th May, the armoured divisions were moving forward on Massicault and advancing towards Tunis to find only scattered and spasmodic resistance. Army Group Africa had no resources left. Its command structure was broken. At four o'clock in the afternoon on 7th May the leading troops of the British Army entered Tunis. Scattered pockets of resistance held out, to surrender individually to British troops as Anderson's men surged round Tunis to Hammam Lif and across the neck of the Cape Bon Peninsula. Arnim himself surrendered on 12th May. Including 4th Indian and New Zealand Divisions there were 38,000 British casualties – killed, wounded and missing – in the Tunisian campaign, including over 6,000 dead. Over 100,000 German soldiers passed into Allied captivity – a greater number than taken at Stalingrad a few months before – and nearly 90,000 Italian. Together with other nationalities the total Allied take was 238,000 prisoners. In the six months since the break-out at Alamein the British Army had ridden a turning tide of war. Norway, Dunkirk, Gazala and Singapore could be put aside as nightmares. Ahead, in the new dawn, lay the coasts of Europe.

12

Return to Europe

Now, and with suddenness, the fortunes of war changed for the British Army. Until August 1942 it seemed that in every news bulletin a brave face was being put upon calamity. Successes were shortlived, ensuing setback apparently inevitable. After Alamein, ultimate victory began to seem a certainty, merely a matter of time. The war lost a little of its awful drama, its outcome seemingly assured however bloody or hesitant the steps upon the way. No soldier now doubted – except, perhaps, some of those in a position to understand the immensity of the problems – that the British Army, with its Allies, would return to Europe, and win. This change of mood proved irreversible. It was symbolised by a great victory parade held in Tunis after Arnim's surrender. The whole strategic situation, too – at sea, in the skies over Germany, and on the economic front as well as in the east – was moving inexorably in favour of the Allies. Nevertheless strategic hopes had until recently been too often offset by present disasters. Now matters were suddenly different, and for none more than the British Army.

The army was at last receiving equipment in plenty. With the arsenals of both Britain and North America maintaining a mighty flow of guns, tanks, vehicles, ammunition, the lean times were over, while for the enemy the years would become ever leaner. Now, there was confidence in leadership, often lacking before. In the case of Eighth Army Montgomery had produced dominant authority, high and evident military competence and thus pervasive trust; and Montgomery was to command all British troops upon the next step in the great adventure and, ultimately, the great army of liberation of the West itself. In Burma, General Slim assumed command of Fourteenth Army in October 1943, a superb leader whose name became a byword for operational wisdom, unflamboyant pugnacity and a brilliant style in command – a mix of rough paternalism and self-deprecating humour. Others, senior or junior to them, were distinguished; but Montgomery and Slim dominated the field armies in most of the period of victories now to come.

Not only equipment and leadership, but training and experience now distinguished the army. The few divisions, which fought with Eighth Army in the hard times, had been joined by those of First Army, put through the arduous training cycle in England which had begun after Dunkirk, and gathered pace in 1941 and 1942 as divisions were liberated from the once imminent threat of invasion. So protracted a period of learning was not without human difficulty – a period extended for the great majority of troops in Britain until the summer of 1944. Although few men hankered for battle, most were uneasy at waiting overlong in the wings while comrades fought: beyond a certain point no training could be a substitute for action. The British Army was now, however, fielding trained divisions. Some were dashing, some were sluggish; most were now one, now the other. But none resembled the un-coordinated and creaking machines of early days.

The army could not, however, have performed its task without another immense benefit, as decisive now as its absence had been in the earlier tragedies. Henceforth British soldiers seldom fought without the Royal Air Force masters of the air above. If air inferiority in the dreadful campaigns of the first years excused a good deal of the army's performance, so did air superiority now greatly ease the march to triumph in the later campaigns. The debt was acknowledged, and should never be forgotten. A last element must be accepted in the British Army's career of ultimate success. The enemy was being worn down on the Russian front. It was there he had deployed the great mass of his forces, over 140 divisions;[1] there he suffered his heaviest casualties; there he was most deeply involved.

Following victory in Tunisia the army faced a major task: the invasion of a defended European coast. The point selected was Sicily.

Operation HUSKY would be the greatest amphibious operation ever undertaken. Although the landings in North Africa had provided practice, they had been largely unopposed. Sicily, however, was garrisoned by four divisions of the Italian Sixth Army under General Guzzoni, together with a number of coastal divisions and mobile groups. It had been reinforced by 32,000 German troops of the Hermann Goering Panzer and 15th Panzer Grenadier Divisions with a total between them of 160 tanks. Sicily was mountainous and defensible. Operation HUSKY was unlikely to be easy.

HUSKY, like any amphibious undertaking, was a complex operation.

---

[1] Albeit, as elsewhere, in greatly diluted divisional strength.

The Allies had to consider the strength and character of the opposition, and what the invading troops must seek to achieve once ashore, hence their composition. The minimum size and nature of the assault force set a minimum requirement for landing craft and ships, both for assault and follow-up – always a factor highly inhibiting on strategy in the Second World War. Air superiority would be crucial. Beaches had to be covered by Allied air power and the enemy's air effort, inevitably nearer to the beaches at first assault, had to be neutralised by air attack and by the capture of airfields. This factor could be, and in Sicily was, in some conflict with the principle of concentration. The soldiers – and, very particularly, Montgomery – wanted to land on a comparatively narrow front, to be well collected for the battle ashore. Air superiority, however, required the capture of airfields, and this factor led to more dispersed effort than was ideal for the land battle. After great argument and a good deal of acrimony all landings – British and American – were concentrated in the south-east of the island.

The invasion force was landed over twenty-six beaches, on one hundred and five miles of coast. This sufficiency of suitable beaches was the single vital factor inseparable from success. And these beaches dictated the sort of craft which could be used, whether troops would need transhipment before landing, whether vehicles and men could disembark dryshod down ramps, or need to wade. This, in turn, dictated the type of troops and equipment which could be set down at each beach, and imposed its own pattern or inhibitions on subsequent operations ashore.

The ultimate plan had, therefore, to reconcile the needs of the land battle, the irreducible demands of air power on which all might depend, the topography of the Sicilian coast, the protection of the invasion fleet and, above all, the actual availability of landing craft, troops and material. With whatever difficulty, compromise and doubt, a plan took shape. D Day for HUSKY was to be 10th July 1943. First landings were to take place at 2.45 a.m.: "H hour".

Sicily was to be invaded by 15th Army Group (Alexander) comprising on the left General Patton's Seventh US Army, and on the right Montgomery's Eighth Army. The latter consisted of XIII Corps (Lieutenant-General M. C. Dempsey) and XXX Corps (Lieutenant-General Sir Oliver Leese). In the two corps of Eighth Army were four infantry divisions (5th, 50th, 51st and 1st Canadian), one independent infantry and two armoured brigades, and one (Canadian) army tank brigade. Two more infantry divisions, 46th and 78th, were to follow up. 1st Airborne Division was to provide one airlanded brigade (gliderborne) for operations immediately north of the beach-head, to assist the break-out. Most of these divisions and brigades were veterans of the North African fighting.

These forces composed the land element of the Eastern Task Force, under Admiral Sir Bertram Ramsay. At sea he commanded 182 ships and 126 landing craft – the former including numerous warships, great and small, for escort, as well as tank and infantry landing ships: the latter containing a great mass of smaller landing craft of various types and sizes. Three immense convoys sailed from the United Kingdom, from Egypt and from Tunisia to make rendezvous south of Malta. In the weeks before D Day the defenders' airfields, communications and installations were subjected to incessant air bombardment.

Soon after H hour the four assault divisions of Eighth Army began to land between Cassabile and Castellazo. The attempt to land 1st Airborne's gliderborne force met disaster, largely through lack of experience in handling the gliders, and many men were drowned, or were landed too dispersed to be effective. It was the only major tragedy. In most places the opposition was much less than expected. By the evening of 10th July the Allied assault waves were safely ashore. The British Army stood again upon the soil of Europe. The Battle of Sicily could begin.

In the first few days after landing, Seventh and Eighth Armies moved north, north-west and west and established themselves on the general line Agnone – Vizzini – Canicatti – Palma de Montechiaro. Their aim was to win deployment room, ports, airfields and roads. The weather was intensely hot. The troops, unlike most of their experience in North Africa, were marching rather than moving in transport, for only "light scales" of vehicles had accompanied them and roads were anyway limited. A number of small German counter-attacks were defeated. Enemy reactions were greatly impeded by Allied domination of the air. HUSKY promised to be successful, and on the evening of 12th July Montgomery reported "battle situation very good". He proposed to move north on Catania, with XIII Corps on his right, and on Enna and Leonforte with XXX Corps on his left, asking that Patton's Americans should expand westwards a basically defensive front, while Eighth Army dominated the central road system, preventing enemy east-west movement, and then cut the island in two by an advance north-west to the coast. On 13th July, Alexander replied, apparently agreeing with these proposals, at least in so far as the first phase was concerned. Patton, however, strongly objected to the defensive role assigned to him in Montgomery's – and Alexander's – plan. He believed (probably

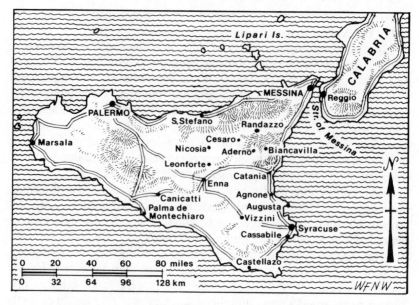

Sicily

rightly) that Seventh Army itself could advance swiftly west and north, probably to Palermo, and that he was being reined in unnecessarily. He complained to Eisenhower. Alexander had always envisaged Patton ultimately advancing to the north and to Palermo, and signalled as much to Brooke on 14th July. It was the delay which irked Patton. For his part, Montgomery believed that the road and supply system could not support more than one offensive effort. In such circumstances the higher commander responsible for decision needs the vision to see what is militarily most sound and the will to impose it. But he needs, too, the tact and diplomatic art to make decision acceptable.

Alexander had tact. He tended, however, to equivocate and to make unwelcome decisions palatable by words or glosses which blurred their sense. In this instance Patton received orders according to Montgomery's original proposals, but followed five days later by a further instruction which directed him to advance north and "split the island in two" having first formed a west-facing shield on Montgomery's left. Thus, by 18th July, both Montgomery and Patton were being encouraged to move northwards. Montgomery was to capture Catania and undertake a general advance to drive the enemy into the north-eastern corner of the island, the Messina Peninsula. Patton was to "split the island in two".

It is unclear what the enemy was presumed to be doing meanwhile.

His actual response ensured that Montgomery's original idea – to advance to the north coast – foundered. While the Allies were consolidating, the Germans were reinforcing – but simultaneously deciding that the Italians had no stomach for the fight. On the same day – 13th July – that Alexander first issued directions regulating the movements of his two armies, Hitler gave orders for a defensive line to be prepared, covering the north-east corner of the island and the Straits of Messina, the escape route. General Hube, with the Headquarters of XIV Panzer Corps, was immediately ordered to Sicily and arrived on 15th July. Also despatched were two regiments of 1st Parachute Division and 29th Panzer Grenadier Division. Hube was told to take over direction of all operations, as tactfully as possible. The Germans had already decided that Sicily must be evacuated, although in deference to Italian susceptibilities matters could only go at a certain pace. Hube planned a coast to coast defensive line in the north-east from south of Catania to San Stefano, with successive withdrawal positions to the north thereafter. While troops were brought back from Central and Western Sicily it was necessary to hold very firmly in the east, and pivot the remaining forces back from south and west towards San Stefano. Eighth Army's advance, therefore, was not to be a bold movement cutting Sicily in half as its commander hoped, but the battering at a doorpost on which the whole enemy operation hinged; while, for Patton, Seventh Army's movement northwards in the centre of the island, delayed as it had been by Alexander, was too late to trap significant forces in the west – a concept which anyway never had much relevance in view of German plans.

The Allied campaign now became a matter of pushing – expensively, often gallantly, but without hope or, indeed, much design of cutting off or destroying any major part of the enemy's forces. Montgomery wrote to Brooke on 27th July that "we have got the whole of the island and pinned the enemy in the north-east corner" – an ebullient reading of the situation, given that from the third day of campaign the enemy had intended to go there, and that he had already decided (albeit secretly) that to evacuate Sicily was inevitable. HUSKY achieved its object – Sicily was occupied. It was not, however, a decisive victory, for the enemy also acted as he intended, and withdrew his forces intact.

To have seized opportunities, however, and cut off the enemy from Italy needed a more decisive commander than Alexander. To prevent German concentration in the north-east corner would have required great energy by commanders and skill by troops determined on a northerly breakthrough in Central Sicily, thereby cutting off the eastward withdrawal of the Germans in the west. Patton, America's most resolute and headstrong Army Commander, might have done it. He had immense drive, but was held back so that Montgomery could make the main northward effort further east. Montgomery was surely right to seek to go north as fast as possible, but the timeliness of the German decision to withdraw meant that he was inevitably battering at the strongest part of the front. He believed, in retrospect, that the Germans could have been cut off from retreating across the Straits of Messina. None can tell. Had that been the object of operations – a logical object – Alexander must surely have given different directions. Montgomery at the time wrote to Brooke of having "won the battle of the Catania Plain", with little indication of any sense of missed opportunities by Eighth Army.

As it was, the advance of Eighth Army in the Catania Plain and in Central Sicily was hard, painful and expensive. The thrust lines of advance were evident to all, the terrain constricting, the land perfectly adapted for action by the efficient rearguards deployed by the Germans. Tactical mobility required pack animal transport, but Army Headquarters misread the situation, signalling on 17th July, "No pack transport required by Eighth Army in Sicily". The advance on the various axes was sometimes bold and imaginative – Montgomery particularly commended the Canadian Division, in action for the first time. In other places progress was sluggish and hesitant. Fighting was often bitter – harder, their Commander said, than any Eighth Army had yet experienced. The fact that the Germans were withdrawing did not mean an easy advance. This was close-quarter infantry work with little scope for manoeuvre, on ground where every village was a fortress, every rockstrewn, terraced hill a natural defensive position, and greater numbers not always or easily decisive.

The advance was marked by one more airborne operation – by 1st Parachute Brigade on 13th July – to capture an important bridge on the northward thrust line towards Catania. The operation was boldly performed and the bridge was won, but in too many cases men were dropped wide and casualties were heavy. Airborne forces and the aircraft on which they depended were suffering the inevitable cost of buying experience in battle. The troops themselves impressed all who saw them. "Tough, fit, efficient and of high morale," wrote Alexander to Brooke, "those units dropped on to their objectives fulfilled their tasks 100% – the remainder were never given a chance."

On 22nd July, Patton's Army entered Palermo, having driven north on Montgomery's left. Seventh Army then turned east, ordered by Alexander to advance along the northern coast road and the parallel route through Nicosia and Cesaro. By 23rd July, the Axis forces had withdrawn from eastern and Central Sicily to Hube's line covering the north-east peninsula. The line was of great natural strength, some fifty miles in length, and held by three German divisions – from right to left, 29th Panzer Grenadier, 15th Panzer Grenadier and Hermann Goering Panzer Divisions – each having under command part of an Italian division, Assietta, Aosta and Napoli respectively.

Against this the Allies could bring, in aggregate, some eleven divisions and formidable air power, and although their thrust lines were canalised by the terrain, it could only be a matter of time before Hube was pressed back to the next and then the next of a series of well-planned defensive positions covering Messina. Each successive position was, because of the shape of the peninsula, shorter than its predecessor and less expensive in troops to hold; and in these circumstances it was optimistic of Alexander to signal to the CIGS on 25th July that his plan was "a main thrust towards Randazzo to split Germans in two, then to strike north and south to encircle the two hostile pockets". The enemy was too skilled to allow such manoeuvres. He would contract slowly, when it became inevitable, and maintain a coherent front.

On the right of the Allied front, now static, Montgomery found resistance particularly hard opposite XIII Corps at Catania. He therefore planned to attack in strength at the centre of the Allied line – this was Alexander's "main thrust towards Randazzo" – with XXX Corps towards Aderno from the west and south-west. Leese put in a methodical attack on successive nights between 29th July and 2nd August, with 78th (newly arrived in Sicily and quickly to distinguish itself), 51st and 1st Canadian Divisions. This was a major "break-in" battle, and it was successful. It could not, however, lead to a "breakthrough". On 2nd August, Hube was retiring to his next line, and on 5th August the Germans decided that there should henceforth be continuous, unhurried withdrawal followed by evacuation. The contingency had been anticipated by Hitler from the first days. Mussolini's fall from power on 25th July made the Italians' situation even more difficult, morale low, commanders mistrusted by their allies; and the Germans were now taking all the decisions. Hube was in sole command. The first day of evacuation of the main body was to be 11th August.

78th Division entered Aderno unopposed on 6th August and 51st Division Biancavilla on the same day. On the day before, XIII Corps had occupied Catania. Eighth Army pressed north by the east coast highway, the Americans took up the running along the north coast and in the centre. The campaign became a slow and cautious follow-up with a predestined end, and never seriously threatened the enemy's escape. The Axis troops' evacuation was thoroughly prepared and skilfully executed. Five ferry routes were established (the sea passage averages five miles). A considerable force of anti-aircraft guns was assembled covering the straits. Assembly areas were laid out well clear of the embarkation points, which were made prohibited zones until men were called forward. Hube ordered that any panic or indiscipline was to be instantly punished by death, and none is recorded. Priority was given to men rather than equipment, but 7,000 tons as well as 27,000 men were brought across to Calabria between 11th and 16th August. By the time Patton entered Messina the birds had flown.

In view of Allied superiority in numbers and in the air, the operations of Eighth Army after the main "break-in" battle by XXX Corps at Aderna hardly appear impetuous. Yet why should they have been? Once any chance had been lost of cutting off enemy withdrawal to a line across the Messina Peninsula, there was small hope of forestalling evacuation, and every reason to minimise casualties. Montgomery's mind was already preoccupied with the next move, the invasion of the mainland. Two small amphibious operations were launched during the final phase, one of them British on Sicily's east coast, to trap the withdrawing Axis troops, but each was too late to forestall their comrades advancing overland. Furthermore, numbers overall give little picture of the tactical balance at the point of contact. Because only a few thrust lines could be used, and movement off roads or out of valleys was always laborious and sometimes impossible, action was more often than not confined to the spearhead unit of the advance. Demolitions and mines were everywhere. In such circumstances progress can only be rapid against troops whose quality is inferior, who are demoralised. The Germans were neither. Action against their main body or their rearguards, the difficulty of the terrain, the steady drip of casualties (9,000 were suffered), all gave to Eighth Army a sobering foretaste of what campaigning in Italy was likely to hold in store.

The beaches south of Salerno are perfectly formed for a landing operation, wide, clear of natural obstacles, twenty miles in length and, in 1943, just within fighter aircraft range of Sicily. Here, in the early hours of 9th September, General Mark Clark's Fifth American Army landed, with on the right VI (US) Corps and on the left X (British) Corps. Operation AVALANCHE had begun. X Corps' object was to land and seize Naples, fifty difficult miles to the west. The general area of the Allied attempt was accurately predicted by the enemy, since it was appreciated that no attempt would be made outside fighter cover.

The Salerno landings were not the first on the Italian mainland. On 3rd September, Montgomery's Eighth Army landed with XIII Corps (5th Division and 1st Canadian Division) at Reggio, opposite Messina, preceded by a mighty artillery bombardment and at first meeting no opposition. Thereafter Eighth Army's progress up the "toe" of Italy was agonisingly slow. The Germans had decided not seriously to dispute Calabria, but they deployed a number of battlegroups to impose delay, and everywhere bridges were blown, and roads were cratered. There were attempts to speed the advance by landings from the sea – at Pizzo and at Bagnara – but although these operations were successful and German counter-strokes beaten off, nothing materially quickened the pace of the main movement, nor, perhaps, could. Eighth Army was envisaged as bringing such strength from the south that opposition to Fifth Army at Salerno would crumble under double pressure. Nothing of the sort happened. On 9th September, the day of the Salerno landings, Montgomery told Alexander (who, as 15th Army Group Commander, was responsible for both operations) that his divisions were very strung out and must have two days' rest. Eighth Army extended from Reggio in two long snakes (for the advance was by both west and east coast), winding their way forward without much fighting but with great frustration. By 10th September they had reached the narrow neck of land between Nicastro and Catanzaro. Nevertheless Alexander responded to Montgomery that unremitting pressure was necessary. Not, however, until 14th September was any serious advance resumed northwards. The advance of Eighth Army posed a threat to the Germans but it did not directly affect the tactical battle at Salerno, which had already been decided by the time Montgomery moved forwards in strength. He did not play Blucher to Clark's Wellington, although Salerno was also a "near-run thing". At the same time, and as an added distraction to the Germans, 1st Airborne Division was embarked in warships and landed on 9th September at Taranto on the "sole" of Italy's "foot". After a brisk fight at Castellanata the airborne troops entered Bari and Brindisi on the Adriatic coast on 11th, and V Corps was established at Taranto.

A few hours before the AVALANCHE landings, after protracted secret negotiations, the Italians announced that they were now at peace with the Allies. The Germans had been expecting this. Within minutes of the Italian broadcast German troops started moving south in strength and German divisions in Italy, according to a pre-arranged plan, began to disarm or otherwise neutralise the Italian Army. German troops had time to take over the immediate defence of key points. Henceforth the British Army's opponents in Italy would be German. In the north

"Army Group B", to which Rommel had been appointed, had eight divisions, including one Panzer and one SS. In and south of Rome, Tenth Army (General von Vietinghoff) had a further six divisions, five of them Panzer or Panzer Grenadier – and including Hube's divisions from Sicily. In Tenth Army a Panzer corps with three divisions was deployed in the general area of Naples, with 15th Panzer Grenadier Division north of the city, the Hermann Goering Division around it and 16th Panzer Division, with over one hundred tanks, near the Gulf of Salerno itself. Hube had just handed over command to Lieutenant-General Balck.

The Salerno landings and the fierce battle which followed were the clearest example yet in the Second World War of the difficulties, as well as the opportunities, of amphibious operations in modern times. Covering air power enables the strategic mobility of maritime power to be exercised, landing troops on an enemy coast with impunity. But the build-up of enemy ground forces against the beach-head is likely to be more rapid than anything attainable by the landing force, especially when, as at Salerno, sea passage and time on turn-round are long. While the initial landings may be successful, and win sufficient room for the landing of immediately required stores and support, the crisis inevitably comes when the enemy discerns the point of effort and concentrates – provided he has the troops sufficiently near and mobile – against it. So great are the tonnages, so bulky the equipment required by modern armies, that their build-up over beaches – or even through ports – is inevitably laborious and vulnerable. Until it is complete there is acute danger. So it was at Salerno.

Fifth Army's left assault corps, the British element of the expedition, was X Corps (Lieutenant-General McCreery had taken over command from Lieutenant-General Horrocks, wounded in an air raid). X Corps had three divisions: 7th Armoured Division, 46th Division, and 56th Division. None of these divisions had fought in Sicily. All had fought in North Africa. The convoys carrying the assault divisions – 46th and 56th – sailed from Tripoli and Bizerta. X Corps was to land with 56th Division on the right and 46th on the left, with a regiment of Sherman tanks supporting. Simultaneously, a Commando force and an American Ranger brigade were to be landed west of Salerno itself, to win ground and ease further advance. The third division of the corps – 7th Armoured – could not start to land until 14th September, and it was clear that the first week, at least, would be difficult and dangerous if German reactions were as swift as all had reason to fear.

The initial landings went well. There were few mines or obstacles. The German plan was to man a limited number of strong points with

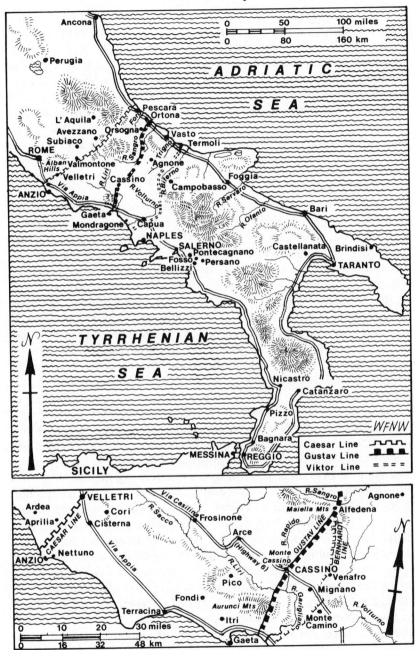

Southern Italy

small forces and to counter-attack with armoured groups held a few miles inland, concentrating, in classic fashion, only when the point of main effort became clear. At the end of the first day 46th and 56th Divisions were ashore and had established a shallow beach-head reaching inland as far as Battipaglia. By that time, however, Balck was assembling his forces, certain that Salerno was the critical area. 15th Division from north of Naples, Hermann Goering Division from Naples, 29th Division (transferred from another corps in the south) were set moving towards Salerno. Against the two British and two American divisions landed there were now concentrating, therefore, two Panzer Grenadier and two Panzer divisions, "marching to the sound of the guns".

The next three days saw a savage dogfight at many points on the rim of the beach-head, as British and American troops sought to establish themselves on defensible ground and the Germans brought up battle-group after battlegroup to dislodge them. The German reaction was sufficient to drive away any immediate thoughts of a British advance on Naples. It was going to be a hard business to hang on ashore at all, and on the evening of 12th September Alexander told Brooke, "I expect heavy German counter-attack to be imminent." The crying need, as over and over again, was for more infantry. Once the initiative passed, as after the first landings it quickly did, nothing could fill the need of infantry to hold the line against the vicious probes of German battle-groups. Now, at any moment, Alexander and Clark feared that a concentrated German thrust could reach the sea and cut Fifth Army in two. The situation was uneasy and panic in some quarters not far away.

The German attack came on 13th September, delivered resolutely and with an élan partly deriving from the mistaken belief that the Allies had already decided to evacuate Salerno. The main thrust was made with four battlegroups, each of approximately regimental size, on a nine-mile front between Belizzi and Persano, directed at the junction of VI (US) and X (British) Corps. In the British sector it fell on the righthand brigades of 56th Division, with the usual accompaniments of battle against the Germans in the Italian summer – infiltration, re-morseless shelling, local counter-attacks, confusion, heat, exhaustion and uncertainty. On 14th September a German two-divisional thrust on the American front was held, and that night, in the British sector, the Hermann Goering Panzer Division launched an attack from the north on high ground dominating 46th Division's area, an attack which was ultimately driven off after fierce fighting. Throughout that and the next nights, and throughout 15th September, the Allied air forces struck German communications with ferocity and success, and naval gunfire of great accuracy raked the attacking Germans. The last enemy attacks were made on 16th September towards Fosso and Bellizzi, and towards Pontecagnana. They achieved nothing. By next morning Vietinghoff recommended that the attempt to drive the Allies into the sea at Salerno be given up.

It has been suggested that the Allies would have done better, strategically, had they landed on beaches well to the north, for example north of Rome; and that the limitation imposed by the need for air cover was unnecessary in view of the low strength of the Luftwaffe in Italy, and the loss of surprise which so predictable a limitation produced.[1] It is, however difficult to imagine how the British Command, having suffered appallingly in the early days of war from lack of air power, could possibly have entertained such a policy; in addition the further north the landing the slower the build up. It is surely unreasonable to criticise the Allied plan.

Nevertheless the German forces in South Italy had not been cut off. They could unite and form a defensive front, but they could not reverse the tide of Allied invasion. There would be an Italian campaign.

The object of Allied operations in Italy – a matter of frequent mis-understanding and acrimony between the Allies themselves – was to pin to the defence of Italy German divisions which otherwise might be used to reinforce North-West Europe, and make more difficult the major task of invasion of France. There has long been debate as to whether, in discharging this task, the Allies may not have made a proportionately greater investment than the enemy, in numbers of divisions and troops, with the presumption that the effort was in that case self-defeating. The balance cannot be so simply cast. The varying number of German divisions in Italy – on average about twenty, roughly equivalent to the Allied total albeit at weaker strength – could have been of great value on the Western Front, whereas Allied divisions from Italy would have made a much less significant differ-ence. At the critical stage of the opening battles in Normandy the Allies needed not more troops overall but more troops in the beach-head, where the build-up was limited by logistics. Reinforcements for both sides, had the Italian front not existed, would have been of less value to the invader than to the side seeking to repel invasion. The Italian campaign proved a sound investment for the Allies and played its part to the end.

[1] See, for instance, Liddell Hart, *The Second World War*, Cassell, 1970.

Initially the Germans believed that the Allied advance in Italy would be limited, and would not seek to go much beyond Rome. Nevertheless, and to some surprise of their enemies, they decided to make a strong stand in the south. A winter line, the "Gustav Line", was to be prepared, running from Gaeta in the west, through Cassino, up the valley of the Rapido River, crossing the Maiella Mountains and following the line of the Sangro Valley to the Adriatic. At its nearest point this line was still some seventy-five miles from Rome.

South of this the Germans planned a number of intermediate positions. From south to north there were the "Viktor Line", following the Volturno through Capua and running down the Biferno to Termoli on the Adriatic; the "Barbara Line" through Mondragone, Venafro, Sessano and Vasto; and the "Bernhardt Line", following the Garigliano River in the west, then by Monte Camino to Venafro, Alfedena, and conforming thence to the Gustav Line eastwards. The German command was reorganised. Field Marshal Kesselring was allotted all German forces in Italy, in a new-formed "Army Group C", including Fourteenth Army in North Italy (General von Mackensen) and in the south, Vietinghoff's Tenth Army. Rommel left Italy for ever.

For the next three months the British Army and their American Allies struggled painfully forwards to the Gustav Line. Alexander aimed to take Rome by making the running with Eighth Army on the Adriatic coast, reaching Pescara and advancing from east to west behind the Germans facing Fifth Army. Eighth Army now comprised V Corps (Allfrey) and XIII Corps (Dempsey), with, between them, five divisions, three of them British: 1st Airborne, after landing at Taranto; 5th from Reggio; and 78th newly arrived from Sicily. There were also 1st Canadian and 8th Indian Divisions, and 4th Armoured Brigade. On the western side of the mountain spine of Italy, the British effort was represented by X Corps (McCreery), still in the American Fifth Army, and now complete with its original three divisions, including 7th Armoured.[1]

Manoeuvres of the kind hoped for by Alexander were exceptionally difficult to carry out in so harsh and defensible a terrain as the Italian, where a mile of advance was generally bought with much time and often with much blood. The advances in both east and west became frontal pushes, the only interaction possible being to reinforce one for a main effort at the expense of the other. For every intermediate German position a major battle had generally to be fought. 4th Armoured Brigade, in the east, entered Foggia on 27th September; and, three

---

[1] 7th Armoured Division was withdrawn to England in November.

days later, 23rd Armoured Brigade, in the west, drove into Naples. But the movement northwards towards the Gustav Line, the battering through of each German line in succession, was as arduous a business as the British Army had yet encountered.

For the fighting in Italy, which continued until final victory in a slow-moving, bitter campaign of twenty months, was perhaps closer than any other undertaken by the British Army in the Second World War to the murderous struggles on the Western Front a quarter century before. Tactically, of course, matters were very different. Instead of the low-lying water-logged Flanders fields, successive ranges of inhospitable mountains presented a sequence of sheer faces, steep gullies and false crests. Great cities had to be taken, hill-top fortress villages stormed, marshes and broad rivers crossed. But similar were the demands on the human body and spirit, similar the need for endurance, the emphasis on skill in minor tactics rather than manoeuvre, the primacy of the infantryman. The infantry night patrol – that great test of individual skill, courage and leadership – was, in Italy, the paramount tactic in the struggle for information and initiative in a way which was only true in other campaigns for brief and untypical periods. If the fighting itself had undertones of the First World War, the terrain and climate were more reminiscent of the campaign a century earlier in the Peninsula – the heat of summer as oppressive to the struggling infantryman, the cold of the mountains from autumn onwards as bitter, the torrential rain as cruel. Every circumstance made life in the slit trenches or among rocks as disagreeable as can be conceived; and everywhere a fierce and skilful enemy held out, his flanks secure, his forces not greatly outnumbered. The deployment of artillery was gravely restricted by the terrain, guns often overlooked by the enemy in the only positions available to them, mud fatally unresistant to their firing and recoil. Mortars, of which there could never be enough, required the carriage of heavy ammunition across precipitous ground by men already laden. Administration was laborious, supply to forward positions as often as not by mule or man portage, evacuation of the wounded by stretcher over long distances and difficult gradients.

These were challenges not necessarily greater than, but different from, those recently faced in the desert, or in the swift dramatic campaign in North-West Europe yet to come. The army was not organised for so harsh and primitive a struggle. Supported by a mass of road transport, adapted to war in the huge spaces of Africa or ready for a campaign supported by a sophisticated road system, the British Army was now to fight in mountains, over country where much of its support represented little but encumbrance. Now a soldier's personal weapons, clothing and equipment became of crucial importance; and the British Army, as so often, neglected to provide adequate waterproof clothing for its troops. The greatest pressure was upon the man not the machine. Conditions demanded hardihood, discipline and stamina of a new – or, rather, a more ancient – kind. The advance of Fifth and Eighth Armies in the autumn of 1943 and for most of 1944 was a grim business. In the fighting for the Bernhardt Line in November a battalion was ordered to seize and occupy part of a mountain – dominated by a further peak, part of the same feature but not part of the objective, the whole enterprise needing more troops than were allotted to the task.

> The Germans soon discovered the gap . . . which existed between the two halves of the Battalion, and crept round with battle patrols in darkness or under cover of mist to attack isolated platoons from every direction, and interrupt the porterage of supplies . . . The headquarters of No. 3 Company and a complete platoon of No. 2 Company were overrun . . . The two forward companies were virtually cut off for three days . . . The seriously wounded were obliged to remain on the hill top, where twelve of them died of exposure, while the walking wounded had the choice of staying in these abominable conditions or running the gauntlet of German patrols. Most trying of all was the weather. There was a bitter, tearing wind from the east, which at times grew to such violence that movement was possibly only on all-fours . . . To this were added hail and rain storms almost without pause, and the few trees which might have given the men some protection were torn to ribbons by shell and bullets. On the third day, as though every resource of man and nature was combining to complete their utter distress, there was a small earthquake.[1]

Such was much of the fighting towards the Gustav Line. Such was the Italian campaign. It is unsurprising that some of the weaker spirits failed in Italy, and that as the campaign went on the desertion rate rose. The possibility of concealment among a bemused civil population, the recurrent hardships of battle, produced a blend of temptation and fear which some had not the principle or character to withstand. This was a small minority. The great mass of men marched, climbed, dug, shivered, sweltered, laughed, swore and did their duty.

In mid-October, X Corps on the left of Fifth Army crossed the

---

[1] Nigel Nicolson and Patrick Forbes, *The Grenadier Guards 1939–1945*, Gale and Polden, 1949.

Volturno River, and in Eighth Army 1st Canadian Division entered Campobasso. Termoli fell to amphibious assault. Kesselring's first withdrawal line, "Viktor", had been carried. The Barbara Line was forced in both east and west sectors by the beginning of November – by X Corps at Mondragone, by XIII and V Corps crossing the Trigno. The German withdrawal was being skilfully conducted by General Herr's LXXVI Panzer Corps on the Adriatic coast and by XIV Panzer Corps (whose command was now handed over by Hube to General von Senger und Etterlin) facing Fifth Army. The next obstacle was the Bernhardt Line, much of which coincided with the Gustav Line – the planned "final position". An attack on Monte Camino, a huge feature dominating the Mignano Gap, and forming part of the Bernhardt Line, had been attempted in insufficient force and called off after hard and costly fighting. On both sides and on both fronts infantry were being consumed faster than replacements could possibly arrive. There were never enough for the demands of terrain and battle.

On the Adriatic front Eighth Army had been reinforced, and now consisted of eight divisions, three of them British, since 1st Division joined 5th, and 78th (it was later transferred to X Corps in the west.) 5th Canadian Division had joined 1st. The redoubtable 4th Indian had joined 8th, and Freyberg's New Zealand Division had arrived. To attack the Bernhardt Line Montgomery had first to force the Sangro River. He planned to feint by an advance in the mountains, inland, while his main thrust was directed along the coast towards Pescara. From Pescara, Alexander had always hoped to turn Eighth Army westwards in order to "loosen up" opposition to Fifth Army.

By 22nd November, 78th Division had some troops across the Sangro, a river swollen by torrential rain and for much of the time impossible to bridge. Then, during the last week in the month, Eighth Army managed to cross, and to drive the enemy from the eastern end of the Bernhardt Line. By 8th December the army had crossed the Foro River; but to win Ortona on the coast required savage street fighting by the Canadians, and Orsogna, twelve miles inland, stubbornly held out against three full scale divisional attacks by the New Zealanders. In vile weather, against the five (sometimes reinforced to six) divisions of LXXVI Panzer Corps the divisions of Eighth Army pushed valiantly forwards until the end of December, when Alexander appreciated that nothing more could be achieved in Eastern Italy before the spring. The Germans were still standing before Pescara. Eighth Army had been held by the enemy and defeated by the elements. On 30th December Montgomery handed over command to Leese, and returned to England to take command of the armies being assembled for cross-channel invasion. His sixteen months in command of Eighth Army had witnessed the turn of the tide for the British Army in the Second World War, and his own contribution had been unique.

In the west, Fifth Army had been granted a breathing space by Alexander after the first attempt to force the Bernhardt Line at Monte Camino in early November. Clark's next orders were for a phased operation which, if successful, would take his army not only up to but through the Gustav Line.[1] X Corps, as part of this operation, was again to attack Monte Camino, and thereafter to cross the Garigliano and break into the Liri Valley, seven miles south of Cassino, while on its right, II (United States) Corps was to advance to the west, bypassing Cassino and enveloping its defences from the south. Facing Fifth Army or fed into the battle as it now developed were six German divisions in XIV Panzer Corps.

The two British divisions of X Corps, 46th and 56th, stormed Monte Camino during the first week in December, supported by eight hundred guns. The Germans were withdrawing everywhere step by step but at the end of the year they still clung to positions ahead of the Gustav Line, east of the Garigliano; and held strong reserves in depth to deal with the amphibious landings which they feared were likely to feature in Allied plans. Only the first phase of Clark's operation had been achieved.

Alexander's plan now differed from his original concept – of "loosening" opposition to Fifth Army by more ambitious operations on the Eighth Army front. Instead he determined to attack in strength with Fifth Army and to reinforce it for the purpose. As far as the British Army was concerned, 1st and 5th Divisions were moved from Eighth to Fifth Army, the former to join VI American Corps, the latter to McCreery's X Corps; and Eighth Army was reinforced by new formations – I Canadian Corps Headquarters (Lieutenant-General Crerar) and a Polish corps (General Anders). The only British division left in Eighth Army was 78th. The New Zealand Division was brought into army group reserve, so that Alexander had six divisions in Eighth Army on the Adriatic coast and twelve in Fifth Army in the west. He now proposed that Clark should thrust towards Cassino and simultaneously break through the Gustav Line and attack up the valley of the Liri and Sacco Rivers towards Frosinone. These operations would coincide with a landing from the sea at Anzio, south of Rome, by VI (US) Corps (Lieutenant-General Lucas), including 1st (British) Division. All this

---

[1] Not, of course, known or assessed as such by the Allies but to the Germans the "line of no retreat".

was, in effect, to seek to achieve what Clark had hoped from mid-November on – to batter a way into the Liri Valley and advance towards Rome; the attempt supported by an amphibious landing. Clark's Army had now, however, been strongly reinforced, and sufficient landing craft were available for the Anzio Operation – SHINGLE. Eighth Army would simply hold.

First, however, Fifth Army had to dislodge the enemy from his remaining positions forward of the Gustav Line, east of the Garigliano and the Rapido Rivers. Heavy fighting, with high casualties on both sides, achieved this by mid-January 1944. On 10th January Clark issued orders for the great offensive which was to break through, isolate Cassino, trap the enemy facing Fifth Army, and lead to the march on Rome. The attack was to start on 17th January. On 22nd January, Lucas's two divisions were to land at Anzio, sixty miles behind the enemy front.

Operation SHINGLE, the landing at Anzio, and the concurrent operations known as the first Battle of Cassino started favourably. No struggles are more difficult to separate into national chronicles. Under Clark's Fifth Army were British, French and American corps, and within these corps divisions of different nationality fought side by side. The British, however, were primarily concerned in the crossing of the lower Garigliano and with the battles at Anzio.

Clark's plan was to cross the Garigliano with X (British) Corps on the left, and the Rapido with II (US) on the right. 46th (British) Division was to protect the left flank of II Corps by crossing some miles south of it. In X Corps' area the planned bridgehead was won at the bend in Garigliano and as far west as the sea, and was held against vicious counter-attack four days later. McCreery attacked with 5th Division on the left and 56th Division on the right – an eight mile front. Kesselring described the fighting in the bridgehead as the greatest crisis the Germans had faced in the Italian campaign. But X Corps had breached the Gustav Line, although the breach was precariously sealed and the bridgehead across the Garigliano narrow and expensively won.

In II Corps' area, however, things went awry. The river flowed fast, and assault boats were carried away. South of II Corps the assault brigade of 46th Division was unable to get a lodgement on the west bank. The attempt, and the crossing by II Corps, were called off, as the small detachments which had managed to get across were counter-attacked by everything the Germans could bring to the battle. Kesselring hurried towards the Cassino sector all available reserves – two

Panzer Grenadier divisions from the neighbourhood of Rome.

In the British bridgehead across the Garigliano 46th Division was now transferred to X Corps. Casualties had been heavy and both sides were near the limits of their strength. The sentence has often and accurately been used, but insufficiently describes the reality. In a regiment of tanks, a battalion of infantry, the casualties always fell heaviest on the men in the tank crews, the men in the infantry sections and platoons. These comprised only a proportion – as little as half – of the unit's establishment, the balance of which was absorbed by men performing vital but slightly less hazardous duty as specialists of various kinds; transport drivers, signallers, headquarters personnel. In the Battles of the Garigliano bridgehead, to take but this small example from the Italian campaign, casualties in the assault battalions averaged about one hundred and seventy men, perhaps one-third of the battalion's strength. But probably three-quarters of these were borne by men in the rifle platoons, amounting to between forty and fifty per cent of their effective strength.

Clark now shifted his point of effort to north of Cassino, where General Juin's French Colonial Corps of Algerian and Tunisian brigades stormed the German positions in the mountains seven miles north of the town in an operation of remarkable boldness and endurance, and II (US) Corps were brought north and fought their way through the German defences in the hills immediately north west of Cassino itself. The Allies were now on commanding ground. They had broken into the Gustav Line in three places; but they had not taken Cassino and they were still some way from debouching into the Liri Valley and moving towards Rome.

The landings at Anzio in the small hours of 22nd January 1944 achieved complete surprise. They demonstrated, however, not for the first time, that although a great logistic and organisational effort is necessary to place a force ashore in an amphibious operation, it is equally necessary that the High Command have unequivocal views on what that force is to achieve once landed and ensure that it has sufficient strength for the task. At Anzio this was not so. The operation produced certain limited strategic benefits, but at high cost and not to the extent envisaged.

VI (US) Corps landed astride the little port of Anzio – 3rd (US) Division on the right and 1st (British) Division on the left – and advanced inland with no opposition to a prescribed line, giving a beach-head of some seven miles in depth, and a corps front of about

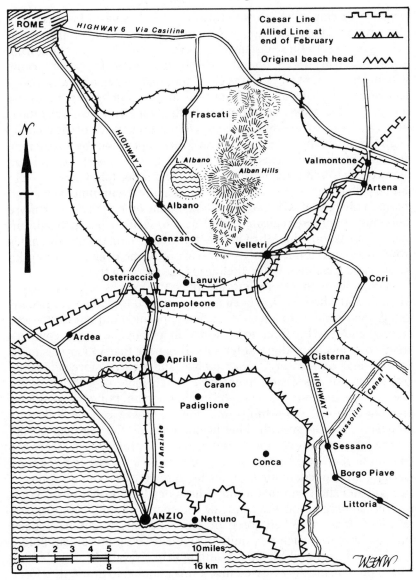

Legend:
Caesar Line
Allied Line at end of February
Original beach head

Anzio

twenty-six miles. The operation was intended as part of a successful offensive breaking through at Cassino, whereas that offensive was already failing. In these circumstances the troops in or operating from Anzio beach-head were bound to be isolated until a reversal of fortune sixty miles further south. It was clear, too, that German concentration against the beach-head would only be disturbed if there were rapid and successful operations on the main Fifth Army front, whereas these were now likely to be slow and painful. On the other side of the coin the High Command hoped to assist Fifth Army's operations by threatening the rear of the Germans in the Gustav Line. This, by definition, required aggressive action from Anzio. Alexander told Clark on 12th January that the object was "to cut enemy communications and threaten the rear of XIV Corps". Clark, on the other hand – with more ambiguity, but more realism – told Lucas to secure a beach-head, and then advance "on" the Alban Hills – the high ground twenty-five miles from Anzio and immediately south-east of Rome over which ran the Appian and Casilinan Ways, lifelines of the German front.

Matters were, therefore, left very much to Lucas as to how far to go, whether and when. He has been much criticised for failing to seize his initial opportunities to advance – when opposition did not exist – and thereby allowing his force to be sealed in a bridgehead and counter-attacked at leisure with great ferocity. It may be that VI Corps should have advanced some way deeper initially, and secured more defensible ground whose possession might have posed more of a threat to the enemy – the judgment is tactical. But on the main point, of whether a great operational opportunity was missed, there can be little just criticism. To occupy a blocking position astride the German north-south communications, and simultaneously to protect corps rearward communications to Anzio would have needed a far larger force than Lucas commanded or than could be supplied. Alexander wrote to Brooke after the event that it would have needed six divisions: "What we were aiming at was to get astride the enemy's L of C." Kesselring reckoned that an Allied force of four divisions might have been landed – and that such was quite inadequate to do more than hold a beach-head. Admiral Sir John Cunningham (Naval Commander-in-Chief) pessimistically assessed that it was impossible to supply a force of four divisions, let alone more.[1] In all these circumstances it appears that Lucas had been placed by his superiors, whatever their after-thoughts, in what would now be described as a "no-win situation". It is

---

[1] VI Corps was reinforced to a strength of four divisions within a week and ultimately to seven.

difficult to believe that, had he undertaken a major advance, he would not have suffered a major disaster. But short of a major advance – Alexander's concept – it is equally difficult to justify SHINGLE at all. Alexander and Clark both visited the beach-head from time to time, and periodically complained of Lucas's lack of enterprise. He may not have been an inspiring or lucid commander, but it is far from clear what he could have done, or indeed what Alexander and Clark wanted him to do, given the forces they allotted him; equally it is unclear why, if they were dissatisfied, they did not give unequivocal orders.

In the event, the advances of the first day were unopposed, and the British troops saw in the distance commanding ground which appeared theirs for the taking. The German response was swift. Kesselring and his superiors assessed that this was the invasion of Western Europe, rather than a subsidiary operation of Fifth Army. Reinforcements, according to an existing contingency plan, were hurried towards Italy from France and Germany. Within Italy Kesselring placed the Commander of Fourteenth Army, General von Mackensen, in command of the whole area north and south of Rome, and moved towards the battle every unit or group within range. By excellent Staff work these were assembled, sorted into coherent commands and concentrating against the Allied beach-head in a remarkably short time. The Allies were quickly contained. The framework of two German divisions was in the area by the evening of the first day, and by 28th January some four divisions, each of a different size and shape, were confronting Lucas's Corps, with more to come: a total of thirty-three battalions, a tank regiment and over two hundred and forty pieces of artillery. This was a formidable array, and to command it tactically Kesselring moved from the east the experienced LXXVI Panzer Corps Headquarters (General Herr) which on 4th February became responsible for the sector, with five divisions, including 2nd Panzer Division.

Meanwhile Lucas spent the early days digging a defensive position and authorised a number of limited attacks which, although skilful and successful, could never seriously threaten the enemy now concentrating against him. In response to pressure by Alexander and Clark to make a limited advance to Cisterna and Campoleone – ostensibly to strengthen his defensive position, although also to extend it – Lucas ordered an attack on 30th January. On the left 1st Division advanced to the railway at Campoleone, passing one brigade through another, with 1st (US) Armoured Division moving forwards on the left flank. The movement created a salient. It also had the merit of upsetting German preparations for the major counter-attack which was thought inevitable.

283

With Mackensen now reinforced and ordered to push the Allies into the sea, there began a series of battles as bitter as any in the Italian campaign. The Allied beach-head, too, was reinforced. Two American divisions – 45th Infantry and 1st Armoured – had already arrived and been in action, and, on 12th February, 56th (British) Division was withdrawn from X Corps on the Garigliano and shipped to Anzio where it took over responsibility for part of the line, while 1st Division was brought into corps reserve. Already, however, Mackensen had begun his move.

On 3rd February the forward positions of 1st Division in the salient were attacked, and although the assault was beaten off the forward brigade was withdrawn. On the evening of 7th February, Aprilia, held by the righthand battalion of 1st Division's lefthand brigade, was attacked by ten battalions, while another German infantry division thrust towards Carroceto from the west. The attack on Aprilia was again repelled, but next day was resumed by twelve battalions. Two days later, on the night of 10th February, yet another heavy attack was launched from the west towards Carroceto Station. In all these battles German infantry greatly outnumbered the defenders, pressed their attacks as hard as ever, and were driven back. 1st Division lost many men but little ground.

The main attack was delivered by LXXVI Panzer Corps on 16th February, driving south down the Via Anziate with five divisions, including two Panzer Grenadier and one Panzer, and with a battalion each of the formidable Tiger and the new Panther[1] tanks. The main thrust hit 45th (US) Division, but was entirely and brilliantly defeated after several days of fierce fighting. West of the Via Anziate the German attack struck 56th (British) Division, with equal lack of success. On 19th February the German Panzer troops penetrated the front to a depth of a mile – but were then stopped by the determination of the defence and the accuracy of the artillery fire. Mackensen's attack had failed. A final German attempt on 29th February met with no success. The German Fourteenth Army was exhausted. The Anzio beach-head was no longer threatened. Some reliefs of formations took place, and the Anzio Front remained static, dangerous and disagreeable, as positional warfare took over until May. The attempt to destroy the Allies had cost the Germans dear, and in terms of attrition the Allied operation had played its part.

That part was not, however, the intended "loosening" of the front

[1] Like the Tiger the Panther was very heavily armoured, with a long 75 millimetre gun.

opposite Fifth Army. At Cassino a separate, murderous battle was going on.

Cassino, overshadowed by its monastery-crowned mountain, was the key to the Liri Valley and thus to Rome. Clark's original attack in January had not dislodged the German defenders, and nor did a series of desperate encounters between the Americans and Germans in the first two weeks of February. Clark now made a fresh attempt. A New Zealand Corps had been formed under Freyberg's command, consisting of his own New Zealand Division and 4th Indian Division (Major-General Tuker). Freyberg was now ordered to take Cassino. He planned that 4th Indian Division should storm Monastery Hill – Monte Cassino, with its Benedictine abbey – and the New Zealand Division would attack Cassino itself from the south-east; the Indians, by now masters of the mountain, would then descend to take the place from the west. The operation closely resembled a movement by two American divisions over the same ground, already beaten off. The attack was to take place on 15th February. It was to be preceded by a heavy bomber attack on the abbey itself.

The attack, a night attack, failed completely. The attacking brigades of 4th Indian Division were cut to pieces by the deadly close-quarter fire of the defenders on Monastery Hill. The New Zealanders gained a lodgement for a few hours in Cassino town and were then driven out by German tanks. The bombing of the abbey was exploited by the Germans as excellent propaganda and remains controversial. The guidelines in such matters – the abbey was a place of international religious importance – were that if military necessity (defined as implying the saving of soldiers' lives) dictated, that factor must be paramount; but if not, such places should be treated as sacrosanct. In the case of the abbey at Cassino, agreement had been reached with the Vatican by both sides that it would not be used for military purposes; an agreement the Germans scrupulously observed. Tuker, commanding 4th Indian Division, did not believe such an understanding would be honoured by Germans, and demanded the bombing before his division attacked. Freyberg formally requested it. Clark had misgivings (there had been no evidence of German use of the abbey in all the fighting around Monastery Hill hitherto conducted) and referred to Alexander. Alexander consented, if Freyberg believed the abbey's destruction was "a military necessity". He did, and it wasn't. There were no Germans in the abbey. A considerable number of civilian refugees were killed. The military effect of the bombing on the German defenders of

Monastery Hill was negligible and thereafter they could occupy the abbey ruins without scruple. Freyberg was surely right to request the bombing if he believed it necessary, as he did; whether the belief was reasonable is another and complex question. In its effect the act was deplorable. But nobody should underestimate the influence of the monastery on the morale of our own troops, none of whom could believe that its brooding presence was of no military significance, that it did not hide enemy observers at the least. And the beliefs of soldiers, even if mistaken, are military realities if the soldiers are to be required to attack and to die.

On 15th March yet another attempt was made by the New Zealand Corps, still consisting of the New Zealand and 4th Indian Divisions, to break the German defence of Cassino to its north. Preceding it, four hundred and fifty-five aircraft poured bombs into the small area of Cassino town for three and a half hours. For five days the New Zealanders, reinforced by a brigade from 78th Division (brought across from Eighth Army) and the Indian brigades of 4th Division, fought at close quarters with the German 1st Parachute Division among the craters and rubble of Cassino. At the end there was stalemate. In a remarkable fighting achievement, although exhausted, the Germans held on. "I do not think any other troops could have stood up to it, perhaps, except these para boys," Alexander wrote to Brooke during the battle. Cassino, regarded by Alexander as vital to Clark's advance up the Liri Valley, still held. In the rubble of the town, less than a hundred yards from each other, the opposing sides settled for two more months.

The British Army's principal part at Cassino was not in the bitter fighting for the town itself, but in the ultimate break through. For this battle Alexander regrouped his forces. He wished Leese's Eighth Army to be responsible for breaking out at Cassino towards Rome, while Clark's Fifth Army should take command of forces in the Anzio beach-head, which were to undertake a separate, convergent advance and (it was hoped) trap the retreating XIV Panzer Corps. The Adriatic sector was to be taken over by an independent V Corps under direct Army Group command.[1] Both Fifth and Eighth Armies, therefore, were to operate west of the Italian mountain spine and, at long last, break the terrible deadlock in the mountains and advance on Rome.

On 11th May at 11 p.m. 2,000 Allied guns opened fire together and Operation DIADEM, Alexander's great attack towards Rome, began.

[1] Alexander's command was now designated "Allied Armies Italy".

Seldom can one battle have been conducted by so many different national allies in ostensible concert. In sum, Alexander had twenty-five divisions under his command: seven United States; five British; four French; three Indian; two Canadian; two Polish; one South African and one New Zealand.

His armies and army corps were similarly heterogeneous. From right to left Alexander had on the Adriatic coast, V (British) Corps, with two Indian divisions, under Army Group Command; on the Rapido and Garigliano Rivers, north and south of Cassino and opposite the entrance to the Liri Valley, the British Eighth Army (Leese) with X Corps, XIII Corps, I (Canadian) Corps and II (Polish) Corps, and 6th (South African) Armoured Division in Eighth Army reserve; on Eighth Army's left, the American Fifth Army (Clark) with the French Expeditionary Corps of four divisions under General Juin and II (United States) Corps of two divisions, and with a further American division in army reserve. Also in Fifth Army was VI (United States) Corps in the Anzio beach-head, a corps of six divisions including 1st and 5th British Divisions and now commanded by Lieutenant-General Truscott. The British Army was primarily represented in this patchwork quilt by three British divisions (4th, 78th and 6th Armoured) in XIII Corps in Eighth Army; and by the two divisions at Anzio in an American corps and an American Army. DIADEM was indeed a "battle of the nations".

Alexander's plan was to hold fast on the Adriatic coast while attacking west of the mountains with Eighth Army taking Cassino, crossing the Rapido River and breaking through the Gustav Line into the Liri Valley, astride "Highway 6", the Via Casilina from Cassino to Rome; simultaneously Fifth Army would attack on the left, in the sector where the Aurunci Mountains separate the Liri Valley from the sea and where a shallow bridgehead had been held through the winter. The Eighth Army attack was to be the point of main effort. At a moment judged by Alexander the troops in the Anzio beach-head would "break out" and, directed by Clark's advancing Fifth Army, might cut off the German main forces withdrawing towards Rome. The Germans were known to have a defensive line – the "Caesar" Line – in the Alban Hills covering Rome itself, and if DIADEM went well they would be prevented from reaching its sanctuary or, indeed, from withdrawing north of the capital. It was not sufficient in Alexander's view to achieve a further running battle northwards up the length of Italy.

Eighth Army now had few of its desert veterans. Of the British, only 78th Division had fought in North Africa. In X Corps Freyberg's indomitable New Zealanders had come all the way from Alamein, as had 4th Indian Division in V Corps, but as far as the British Army was concerned this was a new Eighth Army. Leese had, however, as hard a battle to plan as had his predecessor eighteen months before; the odds no more favourable, the enemy solely German.

As at Alamein the enemy had had plenty of time to prepare defences, and had put that time to good account. Cassino itself had resisted several attacks and was a wasps' nest of German defensive positions, mines and obstacles, among the ruins of the town and the dominating rocks above. Along the Garigliano and Rapido Rivers – the former so named south of the confluence of Rapido and Liri – every possible crossing-place was mined and covered by well-sited posts, while defensive positions were chosen in considerable depth and given individual strength. The possibility of outflanking moves, it is true, existed, unlike at Alamein. There were narrow defiles through the mountains north of the Liri which could be used, and which a defender had to watch; and it was also natural that the Germans should exaggerate the Allies's residual capability for amphibious action on their deep flank, an exaggeration which Alexander took pains to nourish. On the main front, however, the Liri Valley clearly beckoned any army seeking to advance towards Rome.

Leese's plan was to attack Monte Cassino with the Polish Corps (Anders). The Rapido would simultaneously be crossed by XIII Corps (Kirkman) with two divisions – on the right 4th (British) Division, on the left 8th (Indian) Division, while 6th Armoured Division and 78th Division would reinforce and expand the bridgehead and break the Gustav Line immediately south of Cassino. I (Canadian) Corps would then take up the hunt and exploit up the Liri Valley towards Valmontone. X Corps (with only the New Zealand Division) was to protect the north flank.

Facing Eighth and Fifth Army on the main position General von Vietinghoff's Tenth Army had a total of six divisions, while General von Mackensen's Fourteenth Army, with a further five divisions, covered Rome and confronted the Anzio beach-head. In general reserve Field Marshal Kesselring disposed of three divisions, one of them Panzer. The Germans were, therefore, outnumbered significantly overall and even more at the chosen point of attack. They had had, however, time to prepare: and they were not composed of different national contingents with, in some Allied cases, particular national responsibilities and sensitivities.

The first phase of the attack by XIII Corps was as confused and bloody as the first night of Alamein. The river crossing was greatly impeded by mist and by the strength of the current. Getting assault boats across was, in most cases, impossible. Small parties that did achieve the far bank were cut off and destroyed. Bridging was consequently often impracticable. Men approaching the bank or the bridging places were cut down by German machine guns firing on fixed lines or by German field guns and mortars firing pre-arranged tasks. By morning on 12th May, however, a shallow bridgehead had been won, and two bridges constructed. Bridging under heavy fire, on banks and sites which it had been impossible to reconnoitre, working in darkness lit by shell-fire, simultaneously bringing forward the equipment next required and evacuating the wounded – and all behind a thin screen of infantry to whose support the bridge was vital and without whose courage and endurance the bridging site could not be held: this was the crossing of the Rapido and the opening phase of DIADEM. Once across the river the Engineers' task had hardly begun, the enemy's position being so thickly mined and fortified.

By 18th May hard fighting had finally cracked the Gustav Line. In the south Juin's Frenchmen worked through the mountains and cut the lateral road from Itri to Pico on 17th May. In the north, on the same day, Anders's Poles, after a brutal repulse to their first attack, resumed their offensive from the north against Monte Cassino and the ruined monastery. In the Liri Valley itself XIII Corps advanced slowly, methodically but inexorably north-westward to gain Highway 6 and, in conjunction with the Poles, to try to seal the westward escape routes from Cassino. And on the German side Kesselring realised on 16th May that neither Cassino nor the Gustav Line could be held, and authorised withdrawal to a fall-back position across the Liri Valley some ten miles west of Cassino. This was the "Hitler" Line.

On 18th May a brigade of 4th Division entered Cassino. Most of the defenders had succeeded in slipping away, making their escape between the valiant and exhausted Poles moving down from Monte Cassino towards the Liri Valley and XIII Corps fighting their way up from the Rapido to Highway 6. It would be churlish to deny the defenders of Cassino their meed of admiration. They fought magnificently for months, against odds and under as heavy a bombardment as was witnessed in the Second World War. Cassino was pinched out from north and south: it was never taken. Its heroic garrison deserved their reprieve.

So far DIADEM was achieving its objects. With the Gustav Line breached, it was essential now to disrupt the German withdrawal by an operation either cutting it off by flanking moves or smashing it frontally and thereby turning it into a rout. Both were attempted and neither succeeded.

The Allied advance in the Liri Valley was infantry and tank work in close but comparatively level terrain, preceded and accompanied by massive artillery support and assisted by powerful air bombardments when conditions allowed. The French and Polish operations which made this advance possible by their "loosening" effect on the German flanks, the shoulders of the Liri, were largely mountain operations, conducted with brilliance by troops especially trained and skilled in mountain warfare, where the legs of man and mule were the instruments of mobility. By contrast the British Army had come to rely on – or, at least, to contain – a very large train of mechanical transport. In North Africa with its huge distances this had been the lifeline of the army. In Italy, in the tactical battle where advances were measured in a few miles and roads were few and constricted, so great a mass of transport tended to impede rather than promote mobility, and to pose a movement problem which British Staffs were not always sufficiently ruthless or skilled to resolve. In victory as in defeat British systems and organisations inclined to be ponderous, and opportunities were thereby lost.

On the left flank Clark's Fifth Army made faster progress than Eighth Army in the Liri Valley. Fondi was taken by American troops on 20th May, Terracina on 22nd. Also on 22nd May the French entered Pico. In the Liri Valley, however, Eighth Army were held up by the Hitler Line, strongly held, well-prepared, supported by a formidable system of anti-tank guns. Leese attacked frontally with I (Canadian) Corps on 23rd May – a methodical attack supported, once again, by a mighty concentration of artillery; under this onslaught Vietinghoff's Tenth Army fell back, planning to hold a sequence of temporary positions culminating in the Caesar Line, south of Rome.

On these successive lines, at Arce on the upper Liri, at Frosinone on the River Sacco, the Germans battled, inflicted casualties and imposed delay. Some of the fighting was as hard as any in DIADEM; meanwhile on 23rd May Truscott's VI Corps was loosed from Anzio, advancing north-eastwards. By now seven divisions strong, VI Corps might at last give Alexander the battle of encirclement he needed – a left pincer to match the slow-moving right pincer of Eighth Army. Truscott's divisions were opposed by the five divisions of Mackensen's Fourteenth Army.

VI Corps' attack was brilliantly planned and executed. The Americans achieved complete tactical surprise and by 25th May were through the German containing forces and had taken Cisterna and Cori, under ten miles from the Liri Valley itself and far behind Vietinghoff's troops confronting Eighth Army. At this stage, however,

Clark altered the main thrust line of VI Corps and directed it not north-east to Valmontone but north-west towards Rome – against rather than across the front of the Caesar Line. The Caesar Line was too strong to be taken without prepared assault, and Fifth Army was checked until 30th May. Clark's motive was unabashedly nationalistic: he was determined that the American Fifth Army should be the conquerors of Rome.

A determined thrust to Valmontone, as Alexander wished and Truscott intended, would not absolutely have cut off all Vietinghoff's withdrawal routes, for other roads lay to the east and were being used, through Subiaco and through Avezzano. It would, however, have made the escape of the German Tenth Army more hazardous. The encirclement could only have been complete if Eighth Army had already driven the Germans west of Frosinone, which occurred a week later. As it was the Germans reinforced Valmontone and held the Liri Valley door open until the troops withdrawing before Eighth Army had made good their retirement to the Caesar Line. They had no overwhelming difficulty. The roads were inadequate to the formations of Eighth Army seeking to use them, and in many places the armoured divisions, husbanded for this "pursuit" phase of DIADEM, were perforce advancing on a one tank front through wooded defiles, with inevitable delay inflicted by German rearguards and equally inevitable traffic congestion in rear. There is no more frustrating form of war than this, where preponderant strength behind is incapable of producing any but minute effect in front. As Eighth Army lumbered forwards they faced the depressing prospect of yet another major assault by both armies in parallel, this time on the Caesar Line.

It was not to be. Between Lanuvio and Velletri Fifth Army found a gap in the German defences, and on 30th May an American division moved forwards into the Alban Hills and made the breach. On 1st June Fifth Army ordered a general offensive. By 2nd June the Americans took Valmontone from the south. The previous day they had taken Velletri. The Caesar Line could no longer prevent Fifth Army's advance, and Kesselring ordered withdrawal north of Rome. Clark's victorious army entered the Eternal City on 4th June, two days before the eyes of the world turned to the beaches of Normandy.

Few Germans were trapped by DIADEM, which, like Alamein, broke an enemy front but failed to destroy an enemy army. Attacked ceaselessly from the air, Tenth and Fourteenth Armies moved north as best they could. Their casualties had been heavy both in men and equipment. They had failed to attain Kesselring's object of holding a strong defensive position across Central Italy. They were, however,

still capable of fighting another day. Whether a triumph of encirclement, a modern Cannae, could have been achieved had Alexander
been able to direct his armies more firmly will long be argued. There
was never much chance of cutting off Fourteenth Army. Certainly
Clark deliberately went against his superior's wishes in switching the
VI Corps main thrust line towards Rome rather than Valmontone; but
there might have been hard fighting to reach Valmontone, and, as has
been said, other withdrawal routes existed for Tenth Army. Alexander
put as good a face on it as circumstances allowed, in his despatches,
referring to his intention on 25th May to, "Pursue the classical
manoeuvre of parallel pursuit" with two armies. This accords ill with
any idea of cutting off Tenth Army, and perhaps Alexander recognised
the impossibility of such a consummation. He showed no concern to
Clark after learning of the latter's apparent disregard for his intentions,
simply observing, "I am for any line which the Army Commander
believes will offer a chance to continue his present success."[1] It is as if
Alexander was content to preside over events which had their own
momentum, rather than seek to attain a clear object selected by himself
and familiar to all. No greater difference could be imagined than with
Montgomery's philosophy of command – clear cut, strong-willed, decisive, sometimes abrasive. But Alexander had to deal with many and
varied susceptibilities, and he did so to the general contentment of his
subordinates. And he broke the German front in Italy. Nevertheless
Clark's action – in which he ordered his troops to prevent British
advance by force if necessary – was generally regarded as outrageous,
and had Alexander taken the matter to the Combined Chiefs of Staff he
would have had the whole British Army behind him.

The "classical manoeuvre of parallel pursuit" now followed the
Germans, checked but never held for long by their rearguards, through
the ensuing twelve weeks. Moving forward through historic cities and
country, whose beauty served only to emphasise the brutality of war,
the British Army fought its way to the enemy's next main position in
Italy, covering the approaches to the Po Valley – the "Gothic" Line.
Beyond that valley lay the Alpine passes, and the roads running to the
heartland of the Reich.

[1] Sidney T. Mathews, *Command Decisions*, Harcourt Brace, New York, 1959.

13

Fourteenth Army

In any battle the size, composition and tactical handling of the effective force at the critical point may determine the outcome; but in any campaign the ability to produce this force depends not only upon the overall strength of the army but upon the line of communication and supply. In North Africa this factor turned on port capacity and on a great train of mechanical transport carrying huge tonnages over immense distances. In Italy it was, rather, a question of engineering, road construction and demolition clearance, port development. But in no theatre of war were the limitations imposed by logistics so stark as in Burma. Over most of the country, an army could only creep forwards either by building a line of supply behind it or by capturing a base from the sea and then developing a new line of communication inland. Although construction work was largely possible only in the dry weather, from November to May, the roads built had to be usable during the six months of the monsoon. There was, in Burma, an inevitable and protracted time gap between planning and performance. Climate and conditions imposed it.

During 1942, after the grim withdrawal to Assam in early summer, the army in India was reinforced, the army from Burma restored. Wavell, Commander-in-Chief, India, had now to consider the next step. He reckoned on three separate operations – somehow, some time. First, there should be an advance in upper Burma, starting from the army's positions in Manipur, fed by an extension forwards of the road to Imphal. This advance should be directed across the Chindwin and ultimately to Mandalay, coordinated with the actions of the Chinese operating south-westwards in Yunnan. Second, there should be an advance in Arakan, on the Burmese coast. This should have as its object the seizure of Akyab Island, an important Japanese air base, and would require an amphibious as well as an overland operation. Third, the consummation of all, there should be an amphibious assault on Rangoon itself, a campaign to cut off Japanese forces operating northward into Burma. This last would need considerable maritime and air strength and a mighty fleet of landing craft.

Wavell had to plan for the next dry season, starting in November 1942. He could draw on some ten infantry and three armoured divisions.[1] Of the infantry divisions seven were Indian and two – 2nd and 70th – were British: two of the Indian divisions were converted to a special pack animal and jeep establishment. Three Indian armoured divisions were also formed, or in process of forming, and brought up to British establishment. An additional three independent Indian armoured brigades and an Indian parachute brigade were created. But the order of battle of Eastern Army (Lieutenant-General N. M. S. Irwin), which was responsible for operations in Burma, was of less importance than its communications and its supporting resources.

For any advance in upper Burma the capacity of the road to Imphal had to be increased and extended beyond it.[2] The upper Burma operations were intended as a joint enterprise with the Chinese, but after protracted negotiation it became clear that no Chinese campaign would be launched before the dry season starting a year hence, in November 1943. British operations east towards the Irrawaddy, there-fore, the first element in Wavell's concept, were confined to patrolling forwards to the Chindwin, where a brigade was planned to be estab-lished at Sittang by February 1943, and to road building on an enormous scale. As for the third and crowning element in British strategy, a seaborne assault on Rangoon required resources which, it was made clear to Wavell, could not possibly be made available in the 1942–43 campaigning season. Thus, for 1942, there could be little more than an advance in Arakan – although land communications to a force operating there would be no easier than in upper Burma – and an attempt on Akyab. The sea, however, could be used – and the rivers flowed north and south between parallel ranges of hills.

In Burma very few troops could be maintained at the point of effort against the enemy and, inevitably, those few attracted the directions of every tier of command or government. 14th Indian Division (Major-General Lloyd) was established at Chittagong, to guard against any Japanese northward move in Arakan. In September 1942, Wavell instructed Irwin to order Lloyd to push his division southwards as well as communications permitted and to establish a brigade by 1st Decem-ber at Maungdaw and Buthidaung, as a launch pad for a further effort overland towards Akyab, fifty miles to the south, combined with an amphibious assault on the island. The leading patrols of 14th Division

---

[1] "Some" because, as elsewhere, formations were removed, brought in from other theatres or reconstituted in ways not always possible to foresee.

[2] Even two years later, in 1944, it was assessed that this road could not support more than three divisions.

reached Buthidaung on 23rd October. There, on the same day that far away in Egypt Eighth Army were starting the Battle of Alamein, the British Army again met the Japanese.

The Japanese, too, were concerned with Arakan. They wished to keep at arm's length any British attempt to move towards Akyab, where they had in garrison an infantry regiment. They had wind of what was impending and moved upstream by river with sufficient speed to pre-empt any move by 14th Division to occupy Buthidaung. More strength was, therefore, brought forward on the British side. The next move came in December. By then the Japanese had withdrawn from their forward positions at Buthidaung and Maungdaw. By then, too, Wavell had decided that no amphibious effort against Akyab could succeed without considerable air support. Instead he directed that the overland operation should continue. It was decided to direct 14th Division astride the Mayu River to the coast by its mouth;[1] and thence to make a short, sharp run with small, troop-carrying craft, and storm Akyab Island.

This failed. One brigade west of the Mayu River unsuccessfully attacked Donbaik with first a battalion, then two battalions; and finally there was an assault by a fresh brigade. East of the river another brigade failed against the Japanese defenders of Buthidaung. This was hardly surprising: logistical problems, with a supply route from Chittagong which demanded a combination of ship, wheeled transport (over a usable stretch of road and track), mule and sampang, reduced the capacity of the troops, who were for long periods on half rations and whose sickness rate was in many cases severe. Training was not high and morale suffered accordingly. The Japanese were in no great strength but they had had time to prepare positions, they were well entrenched with mutually supporting machine-gun posts and they were in no doubt about their duty: there was no way back, Akyab had to be held, time had to be won for reinforcement. 14th Division's task was not easy, but the run of events demonstrated that the tide had certainly not yet turned in Burma. The battle was called off, on 5th February 1943, with nothing achieved. A final attempt to bring the offensive to life was made in March, with equal lack of success.

Throughout this Arakan campaign the impression of interference in tactical decision by Generals many hundreds of miles to the rear is overwhelming. Wavell directed the resumption of the offensive from Delhi. He directed Irwin in Calcutta – the Army Commander – to

---

[1] 14th Division included British battalions, and was reinforced to a strength of five brigades. Nine brigades took some part in the campaign, under this one Divisional Headquarters.

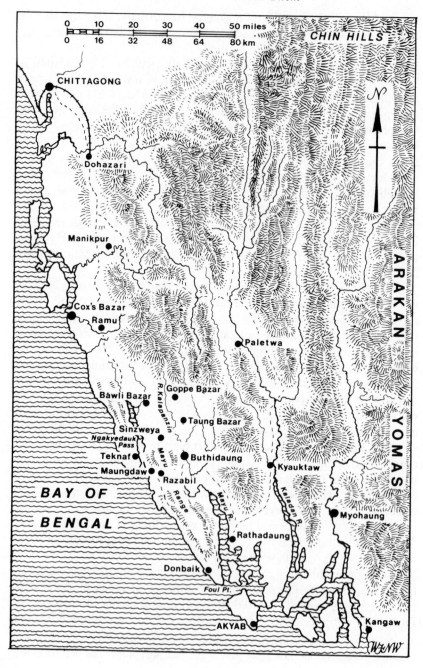

0   10   20   30   40   50 miles
0   16   32   48   64   80 km

CHIN HILLS

N

CHITTAGONG

Dohazari

Manikpur

ARAKAN YOMAS

Cox's Bazar
Ramu

Paletwa

Goppe Bazar
Bawli Bazar
R. Kalapanzin
Taung Bazar
Sinzweya
Mayu
Ngakyedauk Pass
Teknaf
Buthidaung
Maungdaw
Kyauktaw
Razabil
Myohaung
Mayu Range
Kaladan R.
Mayu R.
BAY OF

BENGAL
Rathadaung

Donbaik

Foul Pt.

Kangaw
AKYAB

W&NW

Arakan

order Lloyd, 14th Division, to use a particular British brigade. No Corps Commander was placed in command although Slim was available (and ultimately used) with XV Corps. When Lloyd made a plan Irwin overruled it. Meanwhile tired troops were being fed a diet of failure and casualty and their morale was suffering accordingly. These were Indian brigades (some with British battalions) and one all-Regular British brigade. They were placed in a situation, well known in other theatres earlier, where they could not win, despite the odds, because they were handled ineptly and their enemy had no difficulty in holding or gaining the initiative.

The Japanese now assembled at Akyab 55th Division, veterans of the first Burma campaign, and in April launched a counter-offensive. East of the Mayu River they drove the British northwards by a series of manoeuvres familiar from the past. They held off renewed and costly attempts by 14th Division to take Donbaik once again. They brought forces across the river and concentrated against brigade after brigade of Lloyd's division, cutting off troops from their northward withdrawal routes. Both Wavell and Irwin ruled that the battalions of 14th Division should "hold fast" until the monsoon broke, should counter-attack where necessary, and should occupy, before the monsoon, positions well to the south, consolidating at least a few of the gains made during the December advance. Events and the Japanese moved too quickly. The troops were exhausted, the enemy agile, confident, and aggressive. Position after position was isolated or overrun.

On 14th April Slim took command of all troops in Arakan. It was too late for anything to be done except withdraw to a defensible position south of Chittagong and covering India and, after an early attempt to hold Maungdaw and Buthidaung, Slim withdrew his forces in May – 26th Division had relieved 14th Division Headquarters – to the positions whence they started six months before. His calm and resolute character had been greatly missed in the earlier battles. During these the Japanese had demonstrated superior fighting qualities, superior leadership and superior generalship. They were better organised and better trained. The British Army, a year after the disasters of the first Burma campaign, was in that condition so familiar in other places and times – beaten, puzzled and resentful. They needed to find their confidence again, and to have it restored in the High Command. The Indian Army, and particularly the infantry on which almost all things depended in jungle fighting, was demonstrating once again its impoverished quality because of hasty expansion on an inadequate professional base. The episode belongs to that period when defeats were habitual: a period now over elsewhere, but still to run its term in the war against Japan.

The British had to accept that there was nothing to show for this first tentative and unlucky counter-stroke against the conquerors of Burma. Wavell gave orders to adopt the defensive and to concentrate on the next campaigning season, starting in November 1943, when it was hoped that a British offensive with three divisions, in conjunction with the Chinese, could begin in upper Burma. It was also planned that there should be a renewed drive in Arakan in December 1943; and that, in January 1944, a major amphibious expedition might at last be launched. Meanwhile, however, the Burma front was to be enriched by one of the most adventurous essays made by the British Army in the Second World War.

The personality and achievements of Brigadier Orde Wingate, promoted Major-General in September 1943, remain controversial. Wingate, who had made a name in the organisation of irregular warfare in East Africa, believed that in the wild and inaccessible country of Burma it would be possible to disrupt Japanese communications and exert decisive influence on the campaign by operating in strength deep behind the enemy's front. Troops would be supplied by air, completely independent of a land line of communication – a familiar enough concept. Wingate's innovation was to propose that they should be prepared to operate for a long time independent of any junction with troops moving overland. He envisaged his "deep penetration", later "long-range penetration" groups as strategically, but not tactically integrated with the operations of conventional forces. This required, he believed, specially and exhaustively trained men, inured to long periods of deprivation and hardship. It also, certainly, required a huge air effort, both to attain the necessary air superiority and to deploy and support the forces themselves. It required excellent communications. And it required inspired and inspiring leadership.

The air support which made Wingate's operations initially possible was largely American, there being a strong motive for United States assistance. Wingate's columns were intended to disrupt communication to the Japanese forces facing the Chinese in Yunnan, and China was the United States's principal client. But for such profoundly impressive American support, Wingate's notion would have remained no more than an exotic dream.

The troops were specially assigned and specially trained. Regular and Territorial battalions of the British Army, suitably "weeded" units,

298

together with Gurkha battalions and three Nigerian battalions, were converted to this role, with volunteers from other regiments and corps. Each battalion was divided into columns – each column based on a rifle company with additional platoons of combat engineers, of heavy weapons teams and for reconnaissance. Each column was accompanied by seventy pack mules. And each man, of whatever rank, was loaded with seventy pounds of equipment, ammunition or rations. These were the Chindits. Overseeing their organisation, their training, their morale and their operations was the extraordinary personality whose name was to derive its glory from theirs.

Wingate was a fanatic, a man whose energy and faith were as daemonic as his temperament was difficult. He was a quarrelsome man, suspicious of superiors and subordinates alike. He had a formidable and aggressive persecution complex. Insubordinate and disobedient, he was devious and disloyal in getting his own way or in obtaining for his troops what he thought they needed. He impressed as one with total self-confidence, sure of his task, destiny and abilities; but as one without pity or remorse. To many his methods appeared individualist and unbalanced to the point of paranoia. He was incapable of delegation; and he was so sensitive and emotionally brittle as to be unhinged by setback.

With all this Wingate had unique qualities. His energy was the expression of passionate conviction, and he could communicate his passion and make others share it. He was gloriously impatient: intolerance of mediocrity was his natural habit of mind. He was bold and original – a visionary. He had an excellent brain and thought matters out with a mind uncluttered by respect for the findings of others. He cared nothing for other men's opinions. He lacked many of the most important qualities of high command – balance, stability, patient stamina, the ability to delegate to a staff; but he was a superb, memorable leader of men. He was one of those who, with a thousand faults, nevertheless enrich an entire generation by their quality: one of Sir Walter Raleigh's "black swans" who, he said, "behold death without dread and the grave without fear", set apart from the generality of men. The Indian Army establishment needed something of the kind if it were to face the Japanese challenge to better purpose. And while Wingate was anathema to some, his claims unsubstantiated, his methods outrageous and his manners vile, to others the pity was there was only one of him. Some, quite simply, thought him mad.

The Chindits described above were to be the heirs of the first, trail-blazing Chindit expedition, when experience was gained, organisation and methods evolved and modified. Wingate commanded a

Special Force Brigade – which was moved forwards to Imphal in January. The brigade – 77th Brigade – consisted of one Gurkha and one British battalion, with a battalion of Burma rifles, a Commando company and a mule transport company. It was divided into seven columns, organised in two groups; in total some 3,000 men, of whom about eight hundred were British. Although supply was to be by air, 77th Brigade deployed by land march. Their object in this first expedition was to alarm and deceive the Japanese, to interrupt Japanese preparations for an offensive and for westward infiltration, to test the feelings of the Burmese people and – perhaps above all – to gain experience in the techniques of long-range penetration and to demonstrate the validity of the theory. There was no strategic object. Except in Arakan the British Army was on the defensive. No operations by conventional forces were planned in concert, and any successes could not have other than temporary effect. On 13th and 14th February 1943 Wingate's two groups of columns crossed the Chindwin.

The first Chindit expedition achieved little of its military object. The Japanese remained strictly on the defensive. The operation was, however, successful in teaching all who took part in it and many who did not a great deal about undertaking so extraordinary and novel a manoeuvre. The seven columns of 77th Brigade marched between 1,000 and 1,500 miles through enemy-occupied territory before they finally returned to India four months later. They inflicted some minor damage upon Japanese communications, notably the railway; but they alerted the Japanese to the fact that they could no longer count themselves safe and that to defend a jungle front was, ultimately, an impossible task.

The tactical details of the actions of 77th Brigade are confused and of little importance, since there was no coherent military objective. The movements of Wingate's columns were more often dictated by the possibility of a supply drop or the need to evade the Japanese than by the attaining of some operational aim. All columns crossed the Irrawaddy and were fortunate not to be cut off to the east. Japanese reaction was vigorous once they realised what was happening. The most important achievement lay in the lessons. The Chindits learned to depend on a jungle drop of supplies – and how to prevent those supply drops betraying them. They struggled with the problem of communications. They came to terms with the fact that most columns move in jungle on a frontage of one man. Most of all they learned how to survive in conditions of extraordinary rigour. They paid a high price. Eight hundred did not return. The authorities were sufficiently impressed to agree that Wingate's Special Force should be greatly

300

expanded. When next the Chindits were employed they had been built up to a strength of six brigades, embodied in 3rd Indian Division under Wingate's command. In each brigade were four battalions – eight columns – a field company of Royal Engineers and a medical detachment; and the force was supported by a specially assigned air component.

The monsoon period of 1943, and a large part of the dry season following it, was taken up in planning rather than action. To reconcile the views and interests of the Allies was difficult; and in a global war the resources assigned to one theatre could only come from another, so that events in the European campaign made incessant impact on the war against Japan. The British and Americans had agreed an overall strategic policy of "Germany first". In demands for such precious items as amphibious craft the claims of the Mediterranean – or the ultimate cross-channel invasion – would always take precedence over operations in the Bay of Bengal. But in their strategic perceptions of the war in the Far East the two Western Allies differed sharply, and the difference added yet another dimension of uncertainty.

The Americans saw Burma as a route – by air from India and potentially overland by the Burma road – whereby supplies could reach China. They supported any campaign in upper Burma if it would help China, but regarded with less interest or enthusiasm amphibious enterprises to take Rangoon, Akyab or any other objective. As the dominant partners in the war against Japan, the Americans' own effort in the Pacific was immense – and would be decisive. Their influence on operations in Burma was, however, crucial, for all operations in upper Burma were conceived as convergent with the advance westwards of Chinese divisions from Yunnan, and southwards of American-commanded Chinese troops from Ledo. Air supply lay at the heart of most operations, and the American transport force governed air supply. American strategic philosophy was also affected by a very general incomprehension and suspicion of British Imperial aspirations and responsibilities whether in India or elsewhere; a suspicion which a major campaign of civil disobedience waged in India in August did little to dispel.[1]

The Chinese were determined to extract the maximum in terms of supplies, and not to commit themselves to any offensive which would

---

[1] Nor did it assist the preparation of operations against Japan. Over fifty battalions of the British and Indian Armies were needed to cope with it.

weaken Chiang Kai-shek's ultimate internal position. Chiang Kai-shek was prepared for Chinese troops to take part in concentric operations against the Japanese in Burma, but he was unimpressed if the logistic support of these led to diminution in the tonnages carried by air to China. He was also certain, for whatever reason, that operations in upper Burma would need to be accompanied by a major amphibious effort in the Bay of Bengal, to distract the Japanese and menace their communications.

The British appreciated that support for China was vital, if only to ensure the continuing cooperation of the United States. They were, however, more conscious of the administrative difficulties of campaigning in upper Burma and of the limits of the line of communication from and through Assam. The British, not unnaturally, also regarded the cleansing of the whole of Burma from the Japanese as an object valid in itself; and for this they believed that major amphibious operations were likely to be necessary – operations likely to be practicable later rather than earlier because of lack of resources.

Within the British camp views differed on ways and means, and here the voice of Wingate was loud and persuasive. As the limitations of land lines of supply to and beyond the Chindwin became clearer, Wingate's solution – dependence on air supply – offered powerful attractions. He was brought to London and thence to Quebec, in August 1943, where a meeting of Prime Minister and President and of the Combined Chiefs of Staff took place. Wingate proposed the expansion of the Chindits to a force of eight groups – 26,500 men – securing certain base areas deep in enemy territory before the start of the next monsoon, holding them throughout the monsoon ready for offensive action later, and then coordinating their operations with a main effort starting in October 1944.

Auchinleck took over from Wavell as Commander-in-Chief in India in June 1943. He accepted the concept of deep penetration. He regarded Wingate's claims, however, as exaggerated. In Auchinleck's view the Chindits would be an excellent adjunct to operations but could never become a main force (as Wingate increasingly believed), since their strength and support would never make them a match for Japanese forces in sustained conventional battle. In this Auchinleck was certainly right. He was, consequently, opposed to Special Force receiving such priority as would cripple the preparation of the rest of the army. The strategic and tactical debate, influenced by so many views and factors outside the theatre, swung to and fro.

At the Quebec Conference a new figure was introduced to the Far Eastern scene. It was agreed by the Allies that an Allied Command –

South-East Asia Command – should be established and that an Allied Supreme Commander should take responsibility for all operations by land, sea and air, against the Japanese in the Indian Ocean, the Bay of Bengal and contiguous lands. The Commander-in-Chief in India was thereafter to be responsible for the organisation of the huge and expanding India base, for the defence of India and for the preparation and support of the army, but not for operations in Burma. Vice-Admiral Lord Louis Mountbatten was appointed to the new Command and arrived in India in October 1943.

Mountbatten had responsibility for the coordination of Anglo-American operations in Burma with those of the Chinese Army – fifteen divisions – which it was hoped would ultimately move west into Burma from Yunnan. This was at the extreme north-east of the huge Japanese defensive perimeter which their Burmese adventure had created. In "Northern Combat Area Command", on the north of this perimeter, Chinese troops were under the direct command of the American Lieutenant-General Joseph Stilwell at Ledo. Stilwell was also Mountbatten's Deputy, Commander of all American forces in the theatre and Chief of Staff to Chiang Kai-shek. On the west of the Japanese perimeter the British controlled Assam, and the Naga and Chin Hills, with their tenuous supply line from India and their forward base at Imphal.

Mountbatten's Land Force Commander, General Sir George Giffard, had previously commanded Eastern Army under Auchinleck.[1] As Commander-in-Chief 11th Army Group under Mountbatten, Giffard was assigned IV Corps (Lieutenant-General G. A. P. Scoones) on the Imphal or central front and XV Corps (Lieutenant-General A. F. P. Christison) responsible for Arakan. To command these two corps a new Army Headquarters for Burma was created on 14th October, with a new Commander. Fourteenth Army: Lieutenant-General W. J. Slim.

The influence of Slim on the campaign in Burma and his ascendancy over Fourteenth Army invite, inevitably, comparison with Montgomery's achievement with Eighth Army a year before. There are similarities. Like Montgomery, Slim took over when the record was depressing – with shafts of light and heroism, but depressing overall. Like Montgomery, he impressed his personality on all: Fourteenth Army was Slim's army. Like Montgomery, he turned defeat to triumph and generated total confidence. His military performance is not easily compared, so unlike were the odds and the enemy. His methods were

---

[1] He had taken over from Irwin in May. His command did not extend beyond British Imperial forces.

entirely different so far as manner went – quiet, gruff, modest, ever ready not to identify with success but to assume responsibility for failure. When asked by a lady, late in life, to what he attributed some notable French defeat, the great Marshal Turenne is said to have replied, "Madam, to my own personal and unmitigated fault; and any man who, like I, has been forty years a soldier and cannot say the same is either a liar or a fool." Slim was a Turenne: but also, like Montgomery, he had an absolute professionalism and an iron will.

Slim was an officer of the Indian Army – another "Sepoy General". The Burma campaign was largely fought by the Indian Army and by commanders from the Indian Army, although British brigades, regiments and battalions took part, incorporated more often than not into Indian divisions. Slim had commanded BURCORPS, and knew the bitter taste of defeat. He also knew the country, he knew the men, with their strengths and weaknesses, he knew his commanders and he knew, by now, a good deal about the enemy. He appreciated that in such a land as Burma troops in position could always and easily be surrounded: the essential was to train them to turn events to their advantage, to make defensive positions strong points, sufficiently remote from the enemy's main concentrations, defensible in all directions, stocked to withstand siege and strong enough to act as bases for offensive forays when the enemy's weakness or communications invited them. It was the twentieth-century equivalent of the medieval keep, essential for the enemy to reduce before he could move freely far beyond. Slim understood Wingate's enthusiasm for deep penetration. A highly intelligent and original man, he warmed to the unorthodox if it made sense, and he liked leaders. Like Auchinleck he retained his scepticism over Wingate's wilder claims. The Chindits might brilliantly influence battles. They could not win wars. For Fourteenth Army as a whole Slim became not only master but mascot – jaw jutting, taciturn, bush hat as recognisable as Montgomery's beret, quizzical gaze, earthy common sense. The British of Fourteenth Army were far from home. The name "Forgotten Army" drifted in and stuck: there was more than a little truth in it. Human problems abounded. Morale needed nursing – and, above all, needed that greatest of restoratives, success.

Mountbatten's plans for the first months of 1944 were limited by circumstance. There could be no amphibious operations – many had been mooted but in the end resources were denied. In upper Burma Stilwell's Chinese would advance south from Ledo, directed on Myitkina. In Fourteenth Army area a limited advance by IV Corps was to "contain" the enemy west of the Chindwin, where he had shown signs of vigorous patrolling and had made attempts to seize useful ground in the winter months. The actions of the Chindits would support and exploit operations by both Stilwell and Slim. Three of Wingate's brigades were to be employed in the first instance: 16th Brigade was to cross the Chindwin and march to the area of the Meza Valley, while 77th and 111th Brigades were to be deployed by air. The whole Chindit force – which might be reinforced on orders of Fourteenth Army from the further three Special Force Brigades – was designed to concentrate offensively against Japanese communications in the area of Indaw, to disrupt the rear of the Japanese forces facing Stilwell's men advancing from Ledo, and to create as much trouble as possible for the Japanese in Northern Burma. The Chindits were to cross the Chindwin in the last half of February 1944. IV Corps's actions were to start in March.

XV Corps would undertake a subsidiary operation in Arakan, where there had also been some hard fighting in December. This would start in mid-January and be directed on those familiar objectives: Maungdaw and Buthidaung.

These were modest undertakings, but all that resources and the lines of communication were assumed to permit. The Japanese were, it was reckoned, ready to punish rashness, but were standing on the defensive.

In Arakan, Christison advanced with two Indian divisions astride the Mayu Range.[1] In the west 5th Division (Major-General Briggs) was directed on Maungdaw and then Razabil. In the east 7th Division (Major-General Messervy) was to secure the road crossing the mountains west of Htindaw, and then turn east and attack Buthidaung. Christison reckoned there might be opportunities for exploitation further south thereafter. Further to the east a third division of XV Corps, 81st (West Indian) Division, was to advance in parallel down the Kaladan Valley.

The Japanese withdrew before Briggs reached Maungdaw; there was hard fighting on Messervy's front, and in the first days of February Christison reinforced him with artillery and an armoured regiment, ready to attack Buthidaung on 6th February. Japanese strength was unexpected.

On the Imphal front, too, IV Corps received, during late January, evidence of considerably greater Japanese numbers than Scoones had anticipated. Such a Japanese concentration – for Scoones now identified three Japanese divisions opposite his corps – could be

---

[1] Each brigade had one British battalion – three, therefore, in each division. The artillery units, and the engineer units in 5th Division, were British.

interpreted in only one way. The Japanese were themselves about to pass to the offensive.

Ten months earlier, in March 1943, Lieutenant-General Mutaguchi had taken over command of the Japanese Fifteenth Army, which with three divisions was responsible for the defence of Central and Northern Burma. Mutaguchi arrived at the moment when the Chindits had first penetrated deep into Burma. He was impressed by their performance. It demonstrated that no defensive line or string of positions could secure such a country against penetration; and that forces deployed in defence and remote from each other might always be individually defeated. This led him to the congenial view that the best form of defence was likely to be attack. Strategically, the Japanese had aimed to stand on the defensive in Burma. But the British, they reckoned, were bound to launch an offensive or series of offensives from India, in conjunction with the Chinese; and the best method of carrying out the strategic defensive was likely to be by an operational offensive, to disrupt and pre-empt a British attack and to win ground which would make its recurrence more laborious. Lieutenant-General Mutaguchi, therefore, sought permission for an offensive in the following spring 1944, to take Imphal and Kohima, where any British offensive in upper Burma must be based. A further advance, he thought, might follow.

Mutaguchi's superior, Lieutenant-General Kaweba, commanding "Burma Area Army", agreed. He believed, however, that an offensive should be limited to the seizure of Imphal and Kohima. The necessary reinforcement would come via an improved line of communication from Siam into Burma, along that railway on which so many thousand prisoners of war worked and died. Thus the railway was opened in October 1943. Two reinforcing divisions and an independent brigade brought the total of Japanese divisions in Burma to seven, together with one division from the "Indian National Army" formed from dissident prisoners of war. Fifteenth Army, with four divisions, was to undertake the Imphal offensive: Codename U-GO, starting date 15th March 1944. Meanwhile a new army – Twenty-Eighth Army (Lieutenant-General Sakurai) – was formed to take control of the Arakan front, with three divisions, and ordered to carry out a subsidiary offensive northwards in Arakan: D Day 4th February: Codename HA-GO. When Christison started his offensive in Arakan on 19th January he could not know that orders had gone out from the Japanese Burma Area Army Headquarters on the same day for a mirror image of his and Scoones' operations: HA-GO and U-GO. Both sides simultaneously planned to execute offensives on the same ground and within weeks of each other.

To attack Buthidaung Messervy's two leading brigades of 7th Division were deployed astride the Kalapanzin River, with one brigade in divisional reserve five miles to the north, near Sinzweya. The brigade east of the river was directed to seize high ground overlooking Dabrugyaung and the valley south of Buthidaung, and did so on the early morning of 4th February. Two hours later the divisional reconnaissance regiment sent a disturbing report.[1] Nine hundred Japanese were approaching Taung Bazar far to Messervy's north. This, which came like a thunderclap, was HA-GO.

Five battalions of the Japanese 55th Division, named Sakurai Column, had marched in close column, in the morning mist, past or through the left wing of Messervy's lefthand brigade, directed to take Taung Bazar, and then to send a battalion across the Mayu Range to cut the road south from Bawli Bazar – the line of communication of Briggs's 5th Division. Another battalion was to seize and hold a blocking position on the Ngakyedauk Pass, a road running across the range and connecting the two wings of XV Corps. The main body of Sakurai Column would then attack the British between the Mayu Range and the Kalapanzin River, in conjunction with a northward attack of two battalions hitherto deployed defensively west of Buthidaung. On 6th February the Sakurai Column attacked the Headquarters and reserve brigade of Messervy's 7th Division from the north. Divisional Headquarters was smashed and scattered. The division's righthand forward brigade was simultaneously attacked from the south. The Japanese had cut the Ngakyedauk Pass road.

Now Slim took a hand. Correctly reading the battle, he told Christison that the Japanese could not for long maintain their penetrating columns. He assessed they were in approximate regimental strength. Their numbers, if not their boldness, were inadequate to the adventure. XV Corps must hold where it was while reinforcements were assembled to take the initiative and destroy the intruders. Then the British offensive could and would be resumed. The forward troops would be supplied by air. On no account should they play the Japanese game and allow themselves to be jockeyed out of position because bypassed or surrounded.

This, at last, was effective command. The confidence of the Army Commander, as ever, communicated itself. Brigade positions were formed, covering supporting artillery within the perimeters, able to fire in all directions. Administrative units were deployed in defensive roles.

---

[1] A horsed Indian cavalry regiment, capable of superior mobility to tracked and wheeled vehicles on that and much other terrain.

Meanwhile, 26th Division was moved south and ordered by Christison to rout the Japanese in the Kalapanzin Valley.

The Japanese attacked ceaselessly to break into and destroy 7th Division. A concentrated attack on Sinzweya, in 7th Division's some-time "rear area", was beaten off after savage fighting on 14th February. This was close-quarter combat: sword, bayonet, grenade and bullet at point-blank range. On 16th, the leading troops of 26th Division, advancing southwards, made contact with the defenders of Sinzweya. For the Japanese there was now little hope. Their commanders were too able not to recognise that they had failed. Their troops were deep in enemy territory, short of every supply and suffering severe casualties. Their enemies had been unmoved by penetration and encirclement. They had no dynamism left, and the British had brought up fresh troops. They carried out a few disconnected attacks with fanatical courage, and organised, where they could and where they were not permitted to withdraw, isolated strong points. On 22nd February Christison ordered the resumption of the offensive and on 23rd the Ngakyedauk Pass was retaken, and land communications throughout XV Corps area re-established. Slim was determined that Arakan should be a convincing victory, and XV Corps had been reinforced not only by 26th but also by 36th Indian Division (Major-General Festing).[1] HA-GO was over. On 9th March Messervy took Buthidaung and on 12th March Briggs's 5th Division took Razabil.

Only one Japanese division had been employed on HA-GO. It had attacked a numerically superior force but on many earlier occasions its bold handling, tactical skill and energy would have sufficed. Instead, Fourteenth Army had met a spoiling attack head on, contained the unexpected, and shown itself capable of dealing with Japanese tactics by a combination of all-round defence, air supply, sound generalship and calm nerves. All concerned realised that it was the opening of a new chapter.

At the same time that Christison was beginning his advance and then unexpectedly meeting HA-GO, Scoones, on the Imphal front, was also preparing to receive a Japanese attack. All indications now showed that the first task of any British offensive would be, as in Arakan, the defeat of a prior Japanese offensive. IV Corps had 17th Division (Major-General Cowan) deployed in the south of the corps area at Tiddim; 20th Division (Major-General Gracey) on the Chindwin in the area of Tamu and Sittang; and 23rd Division (Major-General Roberts) north

---

[1] These divisions, too, had British battalions in each brigade: 36th Division had British artillery and was next reconstituted as a British division.

and east of Imphal, with one brigade responsible for the garrison of Kohima and the defence of Ukhrul. As in XV Corps these divisions included British battalions in every brigade (except the Gurkha brigades) and a mixture of British and Indian artillery regiments.

The forward base was at Dimapur. The road from Dimapur to Imphal, the lifeline of the army, ran through Kohima. For IV Corps the heart of the defence must be Imphal, with its airfields and stockpiles. Imphal was the necessary launch pad for any offensive eastwards – or westwards. In case of major attack, therefore, Scoones proposed to contract the corps upon Imphal. 17th Division would withdraw northwards, across the Manipur River to the area of Bishenpur, where it was hoped one brigade could hold the line and the rest pass to reserve. 20th Division would withdraw north-west through Tamu to Palel, by the only all-weather road forward of Imphal. If surrounded, defended localities would hold out, as in Arakan, supplied by air, until a major counter-attack could be mounted against the exhausted Japanese. It was also hoped that the enemy might feel increasing concern for his own rear areas, for the Chindit 16th Brigade was already marching deep into the enemy's north-east flank. The fly-in of Wingate's 77th and 111th Brigades, to create a fortress base one hundred miles beyond the Chindwin, began on 5th March. Within five days 9,000 men, 1,350 animals and two hundred and fifty tons of stores had been landed, and the Japanese began assembling an improvised force of ten battalions to counter the airborne threat. But on 10th March, too, a strong Japanese attack suddenly fell on 17th Division's line of communication at Tongzang. U-GO had started.

Japanese Fifteenth Army planned to advance on a broad front. In the south, 33rd Division (Lieutenant-General Yanagida) was to move forward in three columns. On his left, two columns would aim to envelop the British troops opposing them (Cowan's 17th Division) with one column attacking Tongzang and another column, on the extreme left of the division, marching due west, crossing the Manipur River, and swinging north up the west bank, outflanking Tiddim. On Yanagida's right a third column, under Major-General Yamamoto and supported by tanks and artillery, would advance up the Tamu-Imphal road. One week later, in the centre of Fifteenth Army Front, 15th Division (Lieutenant-General Yamauchi) was to advance by Ukhrul to cut the Kohima-Imphal road and then swing down to Imphal from the north. In the extreme north, 31st Division (Lieutenant-General Sato) was to drive on Kohima and cut the road north and south of it. All movement except that of the column moving on the Tamu-Imphal road, would be by jungle track, supported by man and animal pack.

And We Shall Shock Them

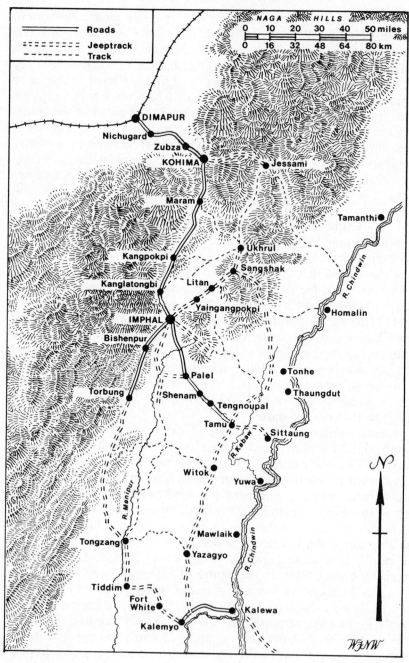

Imphal and Kohima

The attack at Tongzang, therefore, was the overture to an army operation on a front of 170 miles. On 13th March, Cowan received permission to withdraw, as planned, towards Imphal, and reached Tongzang on 15th. He was almost too late – one of the closest-run things of the campaign. By then the Japanese had blocked the road north and seized a vital bridge across the Manipur River. Counter-attacks were mounted to clear the way. IV Corps' exiguous reserves were committed. 17th Division continued slowly north. On the same day the Japanese 15th Division began crossing the Chindwin on a wide front. Gracey's 20th Division began to withdraw as ordered.

The commitment of IV Corps reserve and the obvious scale of the Japanese attack convinced Slim that reinforcement, which he had already authorised, should be accelerated. 50th Indian Parachute Brigade, with two battalions, joined him. 5th Division had been relieved in Arakan by 25th Division and was on the way to IV Corps, partly by air, as Mountbatten had succeeded in persuading the Americans to release some aircraft from the airlift to China.[1] Slim planned to follow this as soon as possible by bringing up 7th Division, similarly relieved in Arakan by 26th Division. 2nd (British) Division, from India, was assigned to Fourteenth Army. Slim reckoned that a crucial moment was now looming at Kohima and Imphal.

The first stage of the battle was the withdrawal to Imphal and the opening of Japanese attacks there and at Kohima. One feature of this strikes with particular force – the aggressive conduct of the British withdrawal unlike on earlier occasions. In any battle of movement there is some confusion, some heroism, some failure; and this was true at Imphal. But in earlier contests lack of grip, loss of confidence and cohesion had too often marked the British and Indian Armies facing a Japanese advance. It was now very different. The battalions of 17th Division, as they withdrew, carried out a series of vicious counter-attacks when opportunity offered or the local situation demanded. When required they stood fast, choosing their moment judiciously, defying Japanese assault, moving at a speed dictated by their own commanders rather than by the enemy's manoeuvres or the forces of panic. No operation is more potentially demoralising than a retirement,

---

[1] Both Giffard (by Mountbatten and his Chief of Staff, Lieutenant-General Sir Henry Pownall) and Slim (by Pownall) were criticised for losing time before appreciating the need for this acceleration of reinforcement. It was alleged that a week was lost. In this author's view no more than a day might have been lost. Typically, Slim himself said afterwards that he had been over-optimistic about Imphal.

311

and the British Army had its fill of them in the Second World War. This one was under control. So unpromising did the advance from the south appear to the Japanese that Yanagida, commanding 33rd Division, suggested the whole offensive be abandoned; and was promptly removed from his command.

The situation soon, however, became dangerous for IV Corps, operating at the end of a long and tenuous line of communication against an enemy skilled in jungle movement, even though the British armour, artillery and air support were far superior in quality and quantity. In the east, 20th Division frustrated every attempt by Yamamoto to break through on the Tamu-Palel road, and launched a number of counter-attacks – valiant but unsuccessful – at the Japanese established on "Nippon Hill", a dominant feature south of Tengnoupal. In the north-east, 50th (Indian) Parachute Brigade had a hard fight between 19th and 26th March against the southern column of 31st and the northern column of 15th Japanese Divisions. North of Imphal 5th Division was rushed in between 19th and 29th of March, and a brigade detached to strengthen the Kohima garrison; but on 29th the road from Kohima to Imphal was cut. Imphal was now isolated, menaced by Japanese trying to advance towards it on four main axes. By 4th April IV Corps was back within a ninety-mile arc covering the Imphal Plain, with a brigade of 17th Division from the south brought north to hold the Imphal-Kohima road and the rest of the division in reserve. Clockwise around the perimeter and thirty miles from the city was 5th Division, north-east of Imphal: 20th Division astride the Tamu road south-east of Palel; and 23rd Division covering the southern approaches. On the Imphal Plain were a month's stocks; thereafter the invested troops would be dependent on a massive airlift unless relieved – over 500 tons per day. Not only Imphal was isolated. Kohima, sixty miles to the north and on the main line of communication from the base at Dimapur, was the objective of Sato's 31st Division. Unlike Imphal it was not a significant *place d'armes*. It was, however, of tactical importance to any force needing the Dimapur-Imphal route, for Kohima included commanding ground and a pass vital to troops using the road. It was held by a small garrison. Now there was no way open from it to Imphal and the road from Dimapur was also cut.

Throughout the battle Slim kept a firm hold of the command structure so that men were given resources commensurate with their tasks and were not expected to exercise responsibility without the means to discharge it. When the Kohima-Imphal road was cut Slim appreciated that the Kohima battle, if there was to be one, could not be fought by IV Corps. Scoones had enough to do with his four divisions holding Imphal. Kohima was made the responsibility of the local line of communication area commander. Meanwhile Slim had brought forwards XXXIII Corps Headquarters (Lieutenant-General M. G. N. Stopford), assigned to Fourteenth Army from India. On 2nd April he gave Stopford responsibility for the whole area of the line of communication forwards to include Kohima – and for defeating any enemy attempt to advance further, to attack or isolate the base at Dimapur or even to threaten the railway and communications running north and north-east to the valley of the Brahmaputra and ultimately Ledo, Stilwell's base of operations. Although, in fact, the aims of U-GO (to the annoyance of Mutaguchi) were limited by higher authority to the capture of Imphal and Kohima, none could assume this. The Japanese thrust-line ran towards the vitals of Fourteenth Army and the entire Allied position.

Kohima was first attacked on 4th April, the day the defenders of Imphal were complete within their perimeter. Stopford had initially appreciated that it should be held if possible, but that his first priority must be to secure Dimapur and the communications running through the Assam Valley. He had, as yet, few troops – the garrison of Kohima, a brigade from 5th Division, 2nd (British) Division on its way forwards to Assam from India, 7th (Indian) Division when it could reach him from Arakan. On 5th April he sent the brigade from 5th Division (161st Brigade) forwards again to Kohima whence they had been hastily withdrawn a few days earlier when it appeared that the base of Dimapur was defenceless. For two weeks Kohima was ceaselessly attacked, the defenders driven back to within a small perimeter, two battalions on the ridge outside battling without respite against Sato's assaults with three Japanese battalions. Day and night for ten days Japanese attacks came in. The road from Dimapur to Kohima was blocked at Zubza. Water was appallingly short. Sectors of the garrison were surrounded and cut off. By 18th April the defenders were facing total exhaustion. On that day, however, the leading troops of 2nd Division, accompanied by tanks, fought their way through from Dimapur. Kohima was no longer isolated from the world.

At Imphal Scoones had resisted all attempts by the Japanese to advance further and was now planning to counter-attack. Indeed Slim on 10th April, when the attacks on Kohima were at their worst, was already thinking offensively and directing the preparation of outflanking operations eastwards from both Kohima and Imphal. On 21st April Scoones began pushing forward on the axis running north-east. IV Corps was still having a hard fight against Japanese columns north and south of the place, but Scoones had juggled his troops with skill, relieved exhausted brigades and re-created a corp reserve from 23rd Division. The first moment of acute danger had passed. The Japanese were, at least for a while, on the defensive.

In the second stage of the battle both sides struggled for the initiative in a month of the bitterest fighting of the Burmese campaign. In the north 2nd Division (Major-General Grover) and the Japanese 31st Division (Sato) fought for every spur, hill and feature overlooking the pass and Kohima itself. On 12th May, 33rd Brigade from 7th Division – Messervy was on his way forward to join XXXIII Corps – finally cleared the Japanese from the Kohima Ridge. The Kohima Pass could be used. The road south, however, was still closed and remained so for a further month while Sato desperately fought to rescue what he could of his division, and clung on still to block the Imphal road.

At Imphal, Scoones on 13th May attempted an operation by 17th Division (Cowan) to cut off the enemy south of their main body facing Bishempur while Lieutenant-General Tanaka, now commanding the reinforced 33rd Division, attempted a similar manoeuvre to cut off his opponents from Imphal. Neither succeeded. Scoones, however, was determined to keep his southern flank sufficiently strong to defeat the enemy and reduce the threat in that area. Only thus could he with an easy mind attack north towards Kohima. The fighting south of Bishenpur was so savage that two Japanese battalions of 33rd Division lost eight hundred and twenty men out of a strength of eight hundred and eighty. It was clear that the Japanese effort could not be sustained for long at this sort of intensity; and at Kohima their 31st Division, hungry, exhausted and weakened by appalling casualties had been fought to the limits of their endurance. Men were throwing away their arms and fleeing, all order gone, eastwards. Meanwhile Scoones pushed 5th Division (Briggs) steadily north-east towards Ukhrul, where Japanese communications could be threatened; and made what progress he could along the Kohima road.

The Japanese now made a last attempt on Imphal. Yamamoto's task force advancing from Tamu was strengthened with everything – and it was not much – that could be switched to the area for a final thrust towards Palel by the Shenam Pass. On the British side 23rd Division had switched roles with 20th Division and now held off every attack by Yamamoto while 17th Division held Tanaka's final desperate thrusts up the Tiddim road from the south.

By 1st June, the Japanese had finally retreated from Kohima. 31st Japanese Division were beaten after a battle in which there is no cause to withhold admiration for the courage and stamina of both sides. Stopford began pushing 2nd Division southwards. On 22nd June, 2nd

Division and 5th Division joined hands on the Imphal road. Every Japanese attempt from south and south-east had been defeated. The line of communication was re-established. The two forward corps of Fourteenth Army were united. Fresh troops were being brought forwards. Although Mutaguchi did not finally give up his attempts to reach Imphal from the south until 4th July, Slim was confident that he had won. It was now a question of how soon the enemy could be pursued across the Chindwin and the reconquest of Burma begin. The monsoon had started. Every gun and tank in Mutaguchi's army was destroyed or abandoned west of the Chindwin. One Japanese soldier in every two was a casualty. U-GO had failed, and at very high cost. The Imperial Japanese Army in Burma would never be the same again.

While the great Battles of Imphal and Kohima were finally destroying Japanese hopes of delaying or frustrating that Allied strategic offensive which they knew must come, two other campaigns were additionally occupying the attention of Fourteenth Army. In Arakan both sides had been jockeying for positions to hold during the monsoon. The British concentrated on taking ground which could open the main east-west road across the Mayu Range between Maungdaw and Buthidaung – although, ironically, the Japanese had decided to give it up as inessential for their own purpose. The Japanese were determined, before the monsoon, to attack Buthidaung – with similar irony, since the British had decided to evacuate it. XV Corps now consisted of 25th, 26th and 36th Divisions in Arakan. Christison's only reverse was in the Kaladan Valley, where a local Japanese offensive manoeuvred the defenders out of their positions and now faced them well in the rear of the main body of XV Corps, which was across the mountains to the west and thirty miles to the south. Slim was unperturbed, being confident that the Japanese lacked sufficient strength in the area for any serious offensive. As the monsoon broke on 15th June and all movement became impossible XV Corps was ordered to stand on the defensive indefinitely, including the next dry season. Fourteenth Army's strength was to be concentrated on the central front for a decisive campaign.

Slim's other concern had been the Chindits.

At the heart of the philosophy of such irregular operations as the Chindits mounted is the idea that those orthodox forces attacked – in this case the Japanese Burma Area Army – will be distracted and be forced to deploy troops in number far in excess of the attacker. This is true, in general, of genuinely guerrilla operations, especially those carried out by partisan bands supported by the population. Such was

315

not true, however, of the Chindits. The effort made to support them was enormous, in aircraft, logistic resources and training. They were deployed and supplied by the most sophisticated means imaginable. This was no band of guerrilleros nourished by the country and fading into the landscape if directly challenged, but a modern force with all that implied in terms of tonnages of stores required and relative immobility when deprived of transport. For the Chindits, humping huge individual loads, could never cover great distances nor move with speed. Furthermore their divorce from a land line of communication and their dependence upon man and animal pack and air supply inevitably meant that they could be at a disadvantage if they undertook conventional offensive operations rather than raids, now here, now there, from secure bases. In the latter they excelled: but to secure the bases also involved conventional battle and a great deal of ammunition. The Chindit concept was irregular and imaginative – and attracted leaders of irregular and imaginative mind. But the tactical reality was often orthodox and demanded orthodox method and principle.

Slim's object, agreed by his superiors, was that the Chindits should assist Stilwell's drive southwards with his American-led Chinese forces to Myitkina. To achieve this, 16th Brigade was at the beginning of February set marching through the jungle towards Indaw, and was ordered to establish a base for air supply en route – known as "Aberdeen". Wingate assured Brigadier Fergusson, commanding 16th Brigade, that he could count on 14th Brigade (Wingate's fourth brigade, now released by Slim to Special Force) to help him in an attack on Indaw, likely to be hard for tired men.[1]

In fact Wingate had no intention of reinforcing Fergusson, intending instead to send 14th Brigade south, after flying in, to harry the communications (as he thought) of the Japanese Fifteenth Army confronting Slim. In consequence, 16th Brigade's attack at Indaw on 25th March was unsuccessful. The incident shows the peculiar methods of command and processes of thought of this most peculiar man. Tragedy was now to deprive the army both of his genius and the problems his character created. Wingate was killed in a flying accident on 24th March, as 14th Brigade were flying in to "Aberdeen". His achievement was to inspire devotion in a new force, to persuade sufficient people to share his vision, and by his energy to make the

---

[1] Disappointed at the number of aircraft made available to fly 14th Brigade in to "Aberdeen", Wingate sent a signal to the Prime Minister, routing it through Mountbatten's Headquarters, complaining of the support he was receiving and incorrectly affirming that his views had Slim's support. "It looks," observed the CIGS, Brooke, "as if the strain of operations had sent Wingate off his head."

vision live. His hold on military realities does not appear to have strengthened as the span of his command grew wider. His perception of strategy, judged by his own proposals, was tinged with fantasy. He had few of the qualities the British Army normally esteems, except courage. But there can be little doubt that for most of the band of brave men who composed the force he created a light went out when he died.

Meanwhile the rest of Special Force established a base, named "Broadway", behind the Gangaw range of mountains, and thence cut the railway from Mandalay to Myitkina, blew bridges and operated from a blocking position near the railway, named "White City". 77th Brigade, flown in on 5th March, controlled thirty miles of the railway and the valley, cutting the lifeline of the Japanese in the north. Four Chindit brigades were deployed by air – for 3rd West African Brigade was, like 14th Brigade, flown in to "Aberdeen" while 111th Brigade had been deployed to both "Broadway" and Chowringee and was later based at "Aberdeen".

The heart of this first stage of the Chindit enterprise was their block at "White City", which attracted incessant Japanese attacks, incessantly beaten off. Fighting was at close quarters and merciless. "White City" was wired, mined and entrenched. It was soon surrounded by unburied Japanese corpses. 3rd West African Brigade was flown in to take over the garrison. Conditions within the perimeter were cramped and insanitary. Life was dangerous and disagreeable. But the operations from "White City" exactly met the object of Special Force – to help strangle the Japanese facing Stilwell's advance.

Other Chindit activity during this first stage, which lasted until mid-April, is harder to evaluate. There was much marching and counter-marching. A good many fuel dumps and installations were found and destroyed. Clearly the Japanese were concerned at so vast a force – and such matters are always exaggerated – at large in their communications area. The troops diverted to deal with it in no way compared, however, with the effort put forward by and to support the Chindits themselves; and any effect on the supplies of U-GO must have been marginal, for Fifteenth Army was operating on an exiguous supply chain and little of it ran through the area in which Special Force was operating. But Chindit operations were jungle warfare at its most grim. These were days before the helicopter made its appearance. Moving through jungle against Japanese who were masters of concealment and often tied themselves to trees to shoot downwards, the soldiers of the Chindit columns could expect no pity if found wounded and, because of the terrain, were sometimes impossible to carry by stretcher, so that a commander's merciful bullet was the only way to help a fallen comrade.

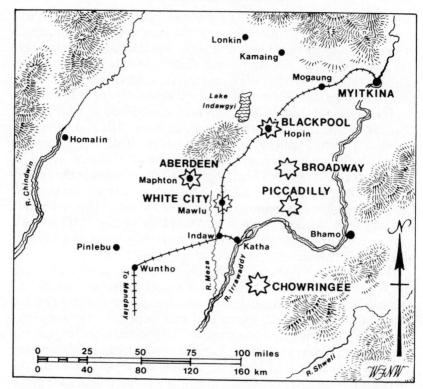

Area of Chindit Operations

New orders were given on 28th April. In May the four Chindit brigades (16th Brigade, which had come farthest and had the hardest time was to be flown out and rested) were to move north, to support more directly Stilwell's advance on Myitkina by operating offensively against the Japanese rear. This involved abandoning "White City" and opening a new base. 111th Brigade set up the new position, named "Blackpool", still near the railway but now only about twenty miles from the Japanese garrison at Mogaung, itself an objective for Stilwell's operations only second to Myitkina, thirty miles further east. Redeployment northwards, the brigades moving in the hills astride the valley, was ordered to be complete by 23rd May, and the railway was to be kept out of action against any Japanese attempts to clear the valley until 1st June.

It was clear that the enemy would react vigorously, and he did. After earlier attempts on 14th May, "Blackpool" was fiercely attacked by the Japanese on 24th May, and next day had to be abandoned. Thenceforth

318

all brigades marched in appalling monsoon conditions. A base of operations was set up at Indawgyi Lake and the brigades of Special Force pushed painfully northwards. They had their reward at last. Stilwell's offensive was moving slowly but surely southwards, and Special Force – now placed under his command – was directed to attack Mogaung. In a brilliant attack against a well-emplaced Japanese garrison 77th Brigade took the town on 24th June. After their fourteen weeks' continuous operations the brigade strength had been reduced by casualties and sickness to about five hundred and fifty men, and was decreasing daily. The attack was made without artillery support, by a force designed for different sorts of task. It succeeded, nevertheless, with one hundred and fifty casualties, a witness to the pre-eminence of human quality in war. At the same time the Chinese laid siege to Myitkina which ultimately fell in August. Meanwhile the Chinese Armies in Yunnan had crossed the Salween on 10th May and by June were investing Tengchung.

The last Chindit brigades were flown out to India in August. Special Force was disbanded. Whether this was the best course of action is open to debate. Slim observed trenchantly that "Private armies – and for that matter private air forces – are expensive, wasteful and unnecessary." But the Chindits had their own peculiar glory, resting not on well-balanced calculation of the use of resources, but upon the resilience and courage of men.

Thus, in the same summer of 1944 that the British Army drove the enemy from their bases south of Rome, and landed at last in North-West Europe, they drove the Japanese, too, from their advanced positions in Burma and finally turned the tide. The Battles of Kohima and Imphal, the operations of the Chindits, Stilwell's advance from Ledo and the long-delayed operations of the Chinese from Yunnan were all part of one great concept, converging upon Northern Burma from west, north and east. Like all Allied concepts, it was difficult and often exasperating to try to reach agreement on execution. In the end it happened. Fourteenth Army was now poised for the final reconquest of Burma. The campaign, as elsewhere, would have been impossible without the dominance of the air achieved by the Allied air forces. They were able to supply beleaguered or deep penetration forces, and they finally made movement itself a chastening experience for the enemy.

The part played by the British Army was enormous. The British Army provided the High Command and organisation, British battalions in every Indian division, British artillery, engineer and logistic units, British commanders of the formations, regiments and companies of the Indian Army. It is no derogation of the achievements of the brave Indian soldier to recall it. Two pictures stand out. First, the weary, depleted, unshakeable defenders of Imphal and Kohima. Second, the Chindits – sure of themselves, idiosyncratic, "difficult", gallant and enduring; ravaged by malaria; so undernourished at the end that on average each man lost between two and three stone in weight; undefeated.

Behind the whole enterprise was the towering figure of Slim. He never wavered in his vision – that the strategic purpose of the Battle of Imphal was the offensive one of destroying Fifteenth Army on ground where the British rather than the Japanese must ultimately hold the strongest cards. He had been confident of holding and relieving Imphal, Kohima and retaining the important ground in Arakan. Except, perhaps, for a few days in March when IV Corps' reserves were first and fully committed, throughout the battle his forces were balanced – ready for the unexpected, given tasks just within their powers, confident in their commander. He had known that the moment would come for the operational offensive, that Japanese strength was expending itself. His will was as strong as his demeanour was imperturbable.

To this must be added a last picture. The Japanese were on almost every occasion outnumbered – sometimes by a large margin. Their supply situation was often vile and sometimes insupportable. They were frequently near starvation, surrounded, wounded and without rational hope. They never surrendered. They met death stolidly. When they broke, as at Kohima, they were at the limits of human endurance. They continued to kill until they were killed. They despised weakness in themselves or others as intolerable. Callous, brave and skilful, they were enemies it was indeed honourable to vanquish.

14

France and Flanders Once Again

The eleven months of fighting in North-West Europe which began on 6th June 1944 saw the culmination of the British Army's efforts and the final act in the drama of the German War. For a significant part of the British Army it was also the first act. The majority had never fought before. Some had not fought since June 1940. Four divisions – 1st Airborne, 7th Armoured, 50th and 51st Divisions – were transferred from the Mediterranean. Otherwise the British Army's contribution to the great adventure – thirteen divisions – were being blooded for the first time.

The fighting in this consummative and decisive campaign was neither harder nor more challenging than in Italy or North Africa or Burma. Operations, however, were on a larger scale, and the attention of the world was focused upon them. For these operations troops had been withheld or removed from Alexander's command. For these operations Mountbatten had been denied landing craft and resources to invade the coast of Burma. Here at last, were operations in the principal theatre of war, directly menacing the Reich itself, and against the largest element of the German forces not engaged on the main front in Russia: operations employing, as the months passed and the build-up progressed, over ninety Allied divisions. The Supreme Commander was General Eisenhower.

The Western Allies invaded Normandy with a force of forty divisions: twenty-three of which were in General Omar Bradley's 12th (US) Army Group[1] and seventeen (three Canadian, one Polish and thirteen British) in General Sir Bernard Montgomery's 21st Army Group. Of the latter, six were armoured and eleven were infantry divisions, including one airborne division. Three months later Allied totals were massively increased when, on 15th September, the Allied Command was reinforced by General Devers's 6th Army Group which had landed in the south of France and marched north to join Eisenhower; an army group which came to consist of twenty-five divisions, six of them armoured, twelve French and the rest American.

[1] Until 1st August Bradley commanded First (US) Army – the assaulting American Army.

321

In the later stages of the campaign Bradley's 12th Army Group was also greatly increased in size, and came to number twelve armoured and thirty-five infantry or airborne divisions. Ultimately, therefore, 6th and 12th Army Groups numbered seventy-two divisions: at the same time 21st Army Group was built up to a force of twenty-one divisions – five Canadian, one Polish and fifteen British.

The division has been described as the army's tool of the trade. In 21st Army Group, however, the count of divisions at any particular moment gives an inadequate impression of its strength. Montgomery retained under Army Group Command a considerable reserve which is not reflected in the divisional total. This reserve was largely composed of eight independent armoured or tank brigades (about 1,400 tanks), of "Army Groups Royal Artillery" – in effect six brigades of heavy, medium and field artillery, totalling some seven hundred guns; and six Engineer Groups. In broad terms the effect of this (except in infantry) was to add the equivalent in fire power of a further half dozen divisions to the British order of battle. The exception, however, is important. Throughout the Allied Armies well-trained infantry were in short supply; and infantry took the brunt of the casualties.

It has often been remarked that the British Army's order of battle in this, the critical campaign of the war, was surprisingly small compared with that of the enemy. In fact, a significant number of British divisions were deployed in the Mediterranean and Far East theatres; and Anti-Aircraft Command still included a large number of soldiers. British divisions were substantially larger than German, the latter often being "run down", through lack of reinforcements, to shadow strength. Comparisons are, therefore, difficult to make, but the discrepancy is, nevertheless, huge. Germany had, at this time, some three hundred divisions in the field. How did they do it?

British industry, although women played a large and vital part, still employed considerable numbers of men, whereas in Germany fighting men had been replaced by immigrant or imported slave labour. The Third Reich, in its desperation, had resorted to conscripting even the old and the very young in a way which was mercifully unnecessary in Britain. Additionally, large numbers of divisions were formed from *Volksdeutsch*, supporters of the German cause, of ethnic German origin but in other lands. The Germans also fought from one main base, on interior lines of communication which, although long, did not make the same logistical demands on manpower as did the maintenance of overseas theatres as far removed from each other as Burma, Italy and Northern France. Perhaps above all, in Britain, the Royal Air Force made huge manpower demands – correspondingly larger than those of the Luftwaffe (which, anyway, included a large number of Parachute and Luftwaffe divisions under army operational control). Yet, when all this and more has been said, the German achievement was astonishing, and their powers of organisation and improvisation never better displayed.

The German Army in the West can only be described as it existed for the Battle of Normandy. Thereafter, for some weeks, the Wehrmacht was in such disarray that orders of battle could only deceive. In Normandy, however, the Allies had to confront some sixty German (including ten Panzer) divisions. These differed sharply in size, the SS divisions (five Panzer and one Panzer Grenadier) being numerically stronger as well as of particularly high quality. A German Panzer division had about one hundred and sixty tanks, against about two hundred and forty in a British or American armoured division. A German division of any kind had about fifty field or medium guns, against about ninety, but was very strong in mortars and *Nebelwerfer* (a multi-barrelled projector of a high explosive warhead). The Wehrmacht was strong in anti-tank guns of various kinds including the Jagd-Panthers and Jagd-Tigers – 88 and 128 millimetre self-propelled anti-tank guns, more formidable than any other anti-tank weapon on the battlefield and generally kept in army reserve battalions. When these totals are set against the Allies we get, in Normandy, an Allied superiority of about three to one in tanks (but not in anti-tank guns); a superiority of about three to two in medium and field artillery (but an inferiority in mortars); and a rough equivalence in infantry battalions. In transport and logistic services the Allies were fully motorised, while the German infantry divisions depended on horse-drawn transport, including artillery limbers; a factor which made little difference in battle but mattered greatly in pursuit. But in the air Allied superiority was complete, totally altering the significance of the above figures.

As to organisation, 21st Army Group comprised the Second (British) Army (Lieutenant-General Sir Miles Dempsey) and First (Canadian) Army (Lieutenant-General H. D. G. Crerar). Between them Montgomery deployed I, VIII, XII and XXX British Corps; II Canadian Corps later; and I Airborne Corps for a special operation. 12th (US) Army Group consisted of First and Third Armies, including seven corps. The German divisions on the Normandy front were deployed in thirteen corps and in four armies – First, Seventh, Fifteenth and Fifth Panzer Armies, fighting under Army Group B (Field Marshal Erwin Rommel) and under the overall command of Field Marshal Gerd von Rundstedt.

Like the British and Americans the Germans had spent some time preparing for the invasion. Their preparations had received added impetus from the appointment of Rommel to advise on coastal defences at all points, a function he continued to exercise even when given command of Army Group B, responsible for a particular area and stretch of coast, north of a line from the mouth of the Loire to the Lake of Geneva. Rommel believed that Allied command of the air meant that no armoured reserves, held concentrated to strike at the invading enemy's main effort in classic manner, could be used with success. Instead, he believed with passion that the German mobile formations should be held forwards, near the coast, so that there could be at least some counter-attack against the Allies' first attempt to land: a counter-attack during the fleeting hours of vulnerability. In this he was at odds with his Commander-in-Chief, Rundstedt. The latter concluded that with so long a front it was essential to retain in depth and concentrated a mobile force, in sufficient strength to affect the battle after the enemy's main thrust was disclosed. The question turned on whether such a force could, in fact, ever move; whether, therefore, it could affect the course of battle. The dispute ended in compromise. Rommel managed to get control of three of the Panzer divisions. The rest were held in OKW reserve,[1] which meant, in effect, that they were controlled by Hitler. Rundstedt, aged seventy and still Germany's most intelligent soldier, was thus deprived of much of the means whereby as a commander he could influence events, while still made responsible for their disastrous course.

On the coasts, however, Rommel's dynamism had considerable effect. New beach defences were erected in huge numbers to try to prevent landing craft coming inshore. Minefields covered every beach exit, and strongly manned blockhouses had machine guns and mortars to sweep every shore, with guns sited where possible to take the beaches in enfilade, themselves protected by banks and reinforced walls against fire from the seaward side. As to where the Allied attempt would be made, the Germans were uncertain. They thought likely an Allied feint to draw off forces, followed by a main effort elsewhere; and when the hour came they were hesitant to commit themselves prematurely to the certainty that they were facing the decisive battle in Normandy. Their hesitation was fed by a thorough and sensible Allied deception plan, aimed to draw German eyes towards the Pas de Calais. But the crucial factor in clouding German perceptions was less Allied deception than the efforts of the Allied air forces, which had so reduced

---

[1] *Oberkommando der Wehrmacht*, the High Command of the German Armed Forces.

the Luftwaffe that German commanders were virtually deprived of reconnaissance. In spite of all this, the Wehrmacht energetically accepted responsibility for every yard of coastline. They had no illusions about the pattern invasion would take, were determined to turn every invasion beach into a graveyard for invading forces, and would have the support of ten Panzer divisions, provided the latter could arrive. In the sector marked out by the British for assault the Wehrmacht had thirteen battalions of infantry – eight on the coast and five immediately in rear – supported by about two hundred and sixty guns of various kinds including over thirty self-propelled 88 millimetre anti-tank guns, and a great mass of both mortars and machine guns. This was part of the German LXXXIV Corps in General Dollmann's Seventh Army.

As in all amphibious operations the Allied design depended on beaches, tides, moon, climate, sailing times and aircraft range, as well as on the available numbers of troops, landing craft and escorts. In sequence, the following was planned:

An enormous air-attack programme, drawing on seventy-five per cent of the strategic air effort of the Allied bomber forces as well as the tactical air forces under Eisenhower's command. It was intended that this programme, which went on several months and consisted of attacks on airfields, installations, radar stations and communications, should destroy the power of the Luftwaffe to make any serious attempt to interfere with the invasion. It was also intended to paralyse enemy ability to move reserves and reinforcements towards the battle, by attacking the ways and means of movement, particularly railway junctions and railheads. In its final phase the air programme was planned to pulverise the coastal defences themselves – to overlay the naval and artillery bombardment programme up until the moment of assault and to stun the defenders. This programme, flown day and night at high cost to aircrew and aircraft, proved decisive in the success of the enterprise. It brought overwhelming air superiority over the battlefield and behind it and dislocation of German movement in Northern France. The air programme was also knitted to the deception programme, so that the pattern of bombardment targets disclosed as little as possible of the ultimate invasion plan.

A naval bombardment programme on a greater scale than yet seen in the war.

Supporting artillery fire from large numbers of guns, mounted on specially designed landing craft, firing a programme to precede the assault, and thereafter to be beached to join the troops ashore.

An assault on fifty miles of front in two sectors. On the right, or western flank, a landing on two beaches by First (US) Army, using two divisions. On the left, or eastern flank, a landing on three beaches by Second (British) Army, using three divisions: 50th Division, under XXX Corps on the righthand beach, 3rd Canadian and 3rd British Divisions under I Corps on the centre and lefthand beaches respectively. Thus there would be five Allied divisions in the first wave of landings, built up to eleven by the end of D Day. The beaching of the assault divisions was to be preceded by the dropping of three airborne divisions – two American and 6th (British) Airborne Division – on ground where they could prevent German counter-attack forces "marching to the sound of the guns".

In the following weeks, reinforcement of the army groups by the divisions waiting in England to be crammed into the beach-head, ready to burst out and win the Battle of France and Flanders once again. At the same time, a major and novel logistic effort was planned to supplement the port of Cherbourg. Seventy-four blockships were to be steamed across and sunk, followed by a line of two hundred and thirteen ferroconcrete caissons, complete with prefabricated roadway, which were to be towed over and sunk in position between the blockships to create an artificial harbour with piers: MULBERRY.

Thus the planned sequence of the immense undertaking, the prelude to the final battle of the West. All assaulting troops were under Montgomery's command. He never showed his greatness to better effect than in the months before this vast enterprise, when he spoke to all his huge command, formation by formation, and assured them that the invasion would succeed. He knew the hazards better than any man but he assumed total responsibility and communicated, as he always had done, the confidence induced by his authority, his personality and his will.

On 5th June Rundstedt wrote in his weekly comment on the situation, "as yet there is no immediate prospect of invasion". Very early that morning, after an agonising postponement caused by weather, Eisenhower made his decision. Although still uncertain, the weather forecast for the morrow was sufficiently encouraging. Loaded ships were already at sea. Midget submarines were lying submerged off the Normandy coast ready to surface and indicate with lights the invasion beaches to the assault landing craft. For all this to be recalled would involve long delay – waiting until another distant conjunction of favourable tide, moon, climate and light. Eisenhower gave the order. The following day would, at last, be D Day.

Operation OVERLORD. 6th June 1944.

During the night of 5th/6th June, 6th Airborne Division dropped out of the darkness as advance guard of the mighty assault. Dropped by parachute or coming in noiselessly by glider the three brigades of the division took all their principal objectives. It was a superb performance. They seized the only bridges over the Orne River and Canal, north of Caen, and thus from the start possessed a vital east-west funnel in the tactical battle to come. They located and destroyed the four road and railway bridges which could carry German reinforcements from the east against the beach-head. They destroyed a key gun battery at Merville, which commanded one of the beaches. They achieved all this very rapidly. They lost some of their men by mishap – no operation could have been more hazardous than this descent from the dark sky on widely separated targets in an area thick with enemy troops alert for invasion. That some craft and soldiers landed too dispersed or were destroyed en route was inevitable. But a great proportion of those launched from England arrived as planned, and were immediately effective as a fighting force. Casualties were in some cases heavy: in taking the Merville battery nearly half the force was lost. In spite of this inevitable price paid by brave men, the airborne assault was both successful and glorious, a foretaste of a remarkable day in the history of the British Army. At about seven o'clock on the morning of 6th June the great naval bombardment by fifty warships, which had followed and overlaid the bomber attack, was itself augmented by wave after wave of rocket-firing Typhoon aircraft directed against strong points covering the beaches and known targets immediately inland. Shortly afterwards the first of over 4,000 landing craft moved towards the shore and discharged their loads. Escorted by over 1,200 ships of the Royal Navy, the British Army had returned to France.

The assault troops were infantry, closely supported by tanks either prepared for "swimming", with flotation pads, or beached by tank-landing craft. Equally well to the fore and often leading the attack were assault engineers, armed with a large range of specialised armoured equipment for destroying obstacles and clearing minefields.[1] And landing immediately behind were batteries of artillery, already having fired a programme from the floating platforms of specially adapted assault craft offshore. This was the plan, and much of it worked. As in all battles some things went awry. On some beaches infantry found themselves unsupported by armour and vulnerable to enfilade from blockhouses and strong points, still unsilenced in spite of the terrible fire to which they had been subjected. And everywhere the German mortars played on the beaches.

The British Second Army landed on a twenty-four mile front. On the right, XXX Corps (Lieutenant-General Bucknall) was directed on Bayeux, eight miles inland. On the left, I Corps (Lieutenant-General Crocker) was directed on Caen. To break clear of the beaches themselves, however, to enlarge the beach-head and build up for advance inland, meant not only a fierce battle against the defenders of the coast but the laborious breaching, under fire, of the lines of dunes, of flooded marshland, of seawalls, and – everywhere – of minefields which lay behind the shore itself. Immediately behind the battle congestion began to mount on the beaches. But – greatest blessing of all – operations were unimpeded by the Luftwaffe. By ten thirty on that morning, fifteen battalions, seven Commandos, seven tank regiments, two assault engineer regiments and nine field artillery regiments of Second Army were ashore. By the evening of D Day, in the British sector, 50th Division was pressing the enemy within two miles of Bayeux, XXX Corps' objective; 3rd (Canadian) Division had fought its way seven miles inland and across the Seulles River; 3rd (British) Division was four miles inland, about three miles north of Caen; and 6th Airborne Division, with which 3rd Division had linked hands, was holdings its ground east of and astride the Orne. The only attempt against Second Army by the German Panzer reserves had been a move north through Caen by 21st Panzer Division – with a strength of one hundred and twenty-seven Mark IV tanks and twenty-four 88 milli- metre guns – with still some veterans of the Western Desert in its ranks. This move, harried ruthlessly by the Royal Air Force, was beaten off by the armour and anti-tank guns of 3rd Division. Rommel had been right in supposing that movement of German armour would be delayed and impeded by Allied air power, but wrong in assuming it could not take place at all.

---

[1] These were developed in one special formation – 79th Armoured Division, devised for the purpose – under the command of the original and inventive Major-General Hobart, first commander of the armoured division in Egypt.

Not only the assault divisions of Second Army, but elements of 7th Armoured and 51st Divisions were also ashore. The great build-up was beginning: the race to expand the beach-head, make it secure against the blows bound to fall upon it and prepare for the offensive. The evening of 6th June saw the British Army once again established in France, on a frontage of twenty-five miles and an average depth of five. Nine hundred tanks and armoured vehicles and two hundred and forty field guns were assembled. It was a good beginning.

It was purchased with about 3,000 casualties out of 75,000 in the three assault divisions and their supports, and a further 1,200 out of 8,000 in the airborne operation.

21st Panzer Division had done its best on D Day. On 7th June, 12th SS Panzer Division attacked in the Canadian sector, and on 8th June Panzer Lehr Division arrived to counter-attack XXX Corps near Tilly-sur-Seulles. Five days later 2nd Panzer Division joined the fight, blocking the way south towards Villers-Bocage. The delay in the arrival, even by hours or a day, of these divisions – badly mauled by air attack – meant that they faced ever greater strength. In the event their attacks were unsuccessful; the various elements of the Allied invasion forces joined hands, and by 9th June a continuous front had been formed.

A slow and painful expansion of the beach-head followed. Difficult though movement was for the Germans, they managed to bring enough troops to the front to stop any rapid or ambitious Allied attempts forwards, and their tactical skill was still formidable. The Norman countryside (except around Caen) largely consists of close *bocage* country of small fields and orchards, high hedges and sunken lanes. The mobility of armoured formations was everywhere checked and their prime weapon, the tank gun, could often only engage at a range limited by the next bank. Such country consumed troops in both attack and defence, offering few alternatives but to push from hedge to hedge, fighting for each an infantry battle, supported by the close range fire of tanks, themselves laboriously lumbering along the same trail. It was country in which the intimate cooperation of tanks and infantry, preferably organised together and trained together, was the key to victory; a key which, in spite of all the vicissitudes of the years, the enemy had acquired more convincingly than some of the British. In such country the huge Allied superiority in mechanised vehicles was often nullified, while German near-equivalence in infantry made its mark. German armour had been unable to intervene in force at the time

329

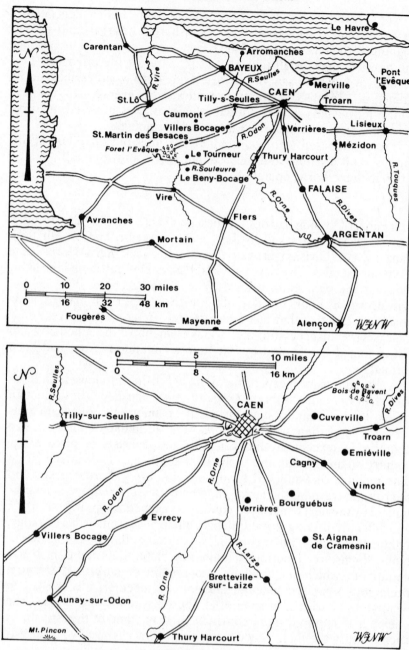

Normandy and the Caen Area

of air and seaborne landings when the assaulting troops were most vulnerable. It could now only support local counter-attacks or act defensively in protracted blocking operations, but in this it was highly effective, the Panther and Tiger tanks doing particularly deadly work. German mortars and *Nebelwerfer* were as menacing as ever. Expansion of the Normandy beach-head consisted of a huge patchwork of tactical engagements at very close quarters rather than a grand manoeuvre. But throughout June the beach-head expanded nonetheless, and within it the Allied total of divisions remorselessly increased.

Montgomery was perfectly content with the progress of operations. He had not, it is true, taken Caen, I Corps' original objective, which the Germans were defending with tenacity. But Montgomery reckoned success not in ground gained but in terms of what was happening to the enemy's body and in his mind; and this was satisfying. The German Army was being worn down and deprived of opportunity or hope. Montgomery's concept was clear and consistent for the next phase of operations. "My general policy," he declared in a personal signal to Brooke on 10th June, "is to pull the enemy on to 2nd Army so as to make it easier for 1st (US) Army to expand and extend quicker." On 18th June he wrote to his army commanders, "The enemy mobile reserves are becoming exhausted." On 25th June the Americans captured Cherbourg, and matters could now go forward with a major port supplying the Allied forces. In the eastern sector Montgomery attacked southwards, west of Caen, to the Odon Valley. Caen itself was still holding out, and Montgomery's design was to envelop the place from the west and south. His pressure in the east of the beach-head was intended to secure it against any attack from that direction: but was also principally inspired by his intention to break out from the western sector, with American forces swinging south and eastwards through Mortain to Alençon and Le Mans, and detaching a corps to drive into Brittany. Thus a concentration of German Panzer divisions and local counter-attacks against Second Army in the eastern sector, which his operations around Caen produced, was highly satisfactory to Montgomery, provided that Dempsey's front held.

This policy required unremitting activity on the Second Army Front, the country in the American sector being particularly difficult for an attacker. "In order to help the western sector I am going to set things alight on my eastern flank, beginning tomorrow," Montgomery wrote to Brooke on 7th July. But he added, "We cannot be 100% happy on the eastern flank until we have got Caen." A major Second Army attack was mounted on 8th July, with I Corps, consisting of 3rd and 59th (British) and 3rd (Canadian) Divisions, and next day Montgomery was able to signal, "leading troops . . . pushing on tonight towards centre of city." West of Caen he ordered Second Army to continue its pressure southwards to attract and pin the German reserves, by pushing towards the general line Thury Harcourt – Mont Pincon – Le Beny-Bocage. Around and east of Caen he was determined at all times to remain secure: for this was the pivot of the Allied position. On the German side the daily increasing strength of the Allies and the unremitting pressure around Caen was causing despair. Rundstedt and Rommel vainly represented to Hitler that the front could not be held, and that the best hope was to withdraw, to regard ground as less important than troops, and to try to recover some power of manoeuvre, at least with the remaining armoured forces. Rundstedt was immediately replaced by Field Marshal von Kluge, while General Geyr von Schweppenburg, commanding "Panzer Group West" (most of the troops opposing Second Army), who was equally critical of German policy, was super-seded by General Eberbach. Hitler confirmed his orders: no retreat at any point.

By now the thirteen British divisions of 21st Army Group were concentrated in the beach-head. Second Army was at full strength. Montgomery decided that, as he put it in a letter to Brooke of 14th July, "The time has come to have a real 'show down' on the eastern flank, and to loose a Corps of three armoured divisions in to the open country about the Caen-Falaise road." Such a major operation could not fail to attract such German mobile reserves as were not already opposite the eastern sector of the beach-head, and was thus consistent with Mont-gomery's strategy. He thought, however, that more dramatic opportu-nities might conceivably present themselves.

General Eberbach, now commanding Panzer Group West, faced Second Army with eleven divisions, disposed in four corps – I and II SS Panzer and XLVII Panzer Corps, and LXXXVI Corps. His armoured formations had been greatly reduced by the fighting of the last six weeks and their strength was in no way near that of the British. Nevertheless, the Germans were still strong in anti-tank guns and their positions facing north, east of Caen, were sited in considerable depth. It was here, in the funnel between Caen and the Bois de Bavent, three miles to the east of the Caen suburbs, that Montgomery ordered Dempsey to commit his "Corps of three armoured divisions". This was VIII Corps (O'Connor[1]), whose attack was to be a thrust between two

[1] O'Connor had escaped from prisoner of war camp and been re-employed (see page 152).

flanking corps – I Corps on its left, with 3rd Division taking protective positions on the eastern flank, and II (Canadian) Corps on its right, with two divisions, extending the lodgement in Caen itself.

VIII Corps, consisting of the Guards, 7th and 11th Armoured Divisions, was to be driven south into the area of Vimont, St. Aignan de Cramesnil, Verrières, astride the Caen – Falaise road. Such force, poised for further advance, would surely bring upon itself all available German armour, and produce that "writing down" of German strength which Montgomery had enjoined Dempsey to achieve. This was Operation GOODWOOD.

During the night of 17th July the three armoured divisions of VIII Corps moved eastwards behind the front towards the Orne bridges, and during the early hours of the morning the leading echelons began filing across the bridges, moved by taped routes through the mine-fields, and formed up ready for the southern attack. Meanwhile in the pale morning light the greatest aircraft concentration of its kind yet known, over 1,000 heavy and medium bombers supporting the tactical offensive, was directed on the target areas east of Caen over which the army was to advance. As the aircraft returned home, the guns of warships took up the cannonade, succeeded by further waves of bombers which continued their work well ahead of the advancing troops for two hours after the forward movement began.

At 7.45, supported by a barrage of two hundred guns, 11th Armoured Division began moving south. Opposing them were infantry of 16th German Air Force Division; but within reach were 1st SS and 21st Panzer Divisions with a combined strength, by then, of no more than one hundred tanks – including, however, a number of Tigers. The defences, to a depth of eight miles, were based on the numerous villages and farmsteads between Troarn in the east and the outskirts of Caen, and between Cuverville, in the north, and the Bourguebus Ridge. Within this area every cluster of buildings, every edge of wood and coppice, every hedgerow on reverse slope held anti-tank guns with infantry and machine-gun positions deployed to protect them. The country was open, but the front was narrow, little more than three miles, widening to no more than six.

The effect of the air bombardment was considerable. The defenders of the forward German defences were destroyed or dazed and the initial advance went well, with the tanks of 11th Armoured Division swinging down to and across the railway which ran south-east from Caen, bypassing strong points for later attention. By mid-morning, however, they were held up, with considerable casualties, north of Bourguebus. The Guards Armoured Division, following them, with the intention of swinging left and reaching Vimont, instead found itself enmeshed among the unsuppressed anti-tank guns and defenders of Cagny and Emiéville. Meanwhile 7th Armoured Division, in rear, directed to come in on the left of 11th, was so held up by the appalling congestion that it could not reach the battle in any strength.

Two factors were frustrating the accomplishment of GOODWOOD. First, the tactics adopted were those of a steamroller: following a mighty weight of air attack the armoured divisions were to surge forwards. In fact the air attack, although it stunned the defenders of the front line and numerous strongpoints, did not sufficiently eliminate the German anti-tank defence; on the contrary it was soon bravely and skilfully re-created. In consequence the tanks of VIII Corps found themselves rolling forwards into a network of anti-tank guns sited in great depth, and supported by a sufficiency of Tiger tanks which had survived the bombardment. The latter, in open country, were still the deadly superior of every other tank on the battlefield; and GOODWOOD was fought over open country.

The second factor militating against the success of GOODWOOD was the sheer congestion which arose at and east of the Orne bridges and immediately behind the battle line. To cram three armoured divisions – flanked by infantry divisions, with their own support echelons, under separate Corps Command – into the restricted area east of Caen was to ensure chaos, unless the advance went swiftly. It did not. The German line was unbroken. Six miles of ground were won, and by evening Cagny was taken, but there was no question of "a Corps of three armoured divisions . . . in the open country about the Caen-Falaise road". This great mass of armour was still hemmed into a small area immediately south and east of Caen and the German defenders, shaken but steadfast, had not been so "written down", in Montgomery's phrase to Dempsey, as to be incapable of action, although German tank losses were undoubtedly high: 12th SS and 116th Panzer Divisions from the east, and elements of 2nd Panzer Division from the centre of the Allied front had arrived upon the scene of action and had suffered. Renewed attempts by VIII Corps in the following days extended the ground gained only by small distances. A Canadian attack by 2nd Canadian Division south from Caen on 20th July was itself heavily counter-attacked by German Panzer troops. Next day Dempsey accepted that no more would be won in the area of Caen. GOODWOOD was over.

Two hundred and seventy British tanks were lost by VIII Corps – not a serious loss strategically, since replacements were plentiful, but indicative of the attrition rate suffered by the armoured divisions. A good deal of acrimony and criticism arose over GOODWOOD; the losses seemed to have been balanced by remarkably little in the way of new ground won. The Germans appeared intact, even aggressive. Montgomery issued a statement on the first afternoon of battle:

> Operations this morning a complete success ... 11 Armoured Division reached Tilly ... 7th Armoured Division moving on La Hogue ... Guards Armoured Division passed Cagny and now in Vimont, 3rd Division moving on Troarn. Have ordered the armoured car regiments of each division, supported by armoured recce regiments to reconnoitre towards and *secure the crossings over Dives* [author's italics], between Mezidon and Falaise ... situation very promising.[1]

This seemed optimistic and was received with jubilation. But it was pure fantasy and set the scene for subsequent disappointment. 11th Armoured Division was nowhere near Tilly, as it was held up north of Bourguébus. Guards Armoured Division did not take Cagny until 7 p.m. and never reached Vimont. 3rd Division was facing German troops still firmly ensconced in Troarn. And 7th Armoured Division was having difficulty in arriving at all. The River Dives lay many miles behind a firm German front, as did Mezidon and Falaise. It is hard to believe that, when he made this statement based on incorrect information (as often happens), Montgomery was not nourishing visions of a more sensational success than that he (falsely) imagined he had already won. The "crossings over the Dives" – which could not possibly have been held by reconnaissance forces unaided against serious opposition – were relevant only to a swift advance and a grander design.

In his *Memoirs* Montgomery wrote, "It was ... a fundamental object of my strategy ... to establish a force strong in armour to the south-east of Caen in the area about Bourguébus ... There was never *at any time*[2] any intention of making the breakout from the bridgehead on the eastern flank." This uncompromising assertion must, however, be set beside a paragraph in his letter to Brooke of 14th July – "The possibilities are immense: with 700 tanks loosed to the south-east of Caen and armoured cars operating far ahead, anything may happen" – and his expressed intention, as well as the pencilled arrows on the map which accompanied the letter, to direct Second Army not on Bourguébus but on Falaise, sixteen miles further south. Montgomery aimed, as he put

---

[1] "I was too exultant," Montgomery wrote afterwards. Montgomery of Alamein, *Memoirs*, Collins, 1958.

[2] Montgomery's italics.

it, "to destroy all possible enemy troops in the general area Caen – Mezidon – Falaise – Evrecy". Such a victory would have so stretched the German defence that a breakout would have been almost inevitable, and Montgomery would have presumably been ready to exploit it with Second Army if such could be done without imprudence.

The point illustrates a paradox already noted about Montgomery. He declared and reiterated *post facto* that what occurred was, in the main, what he had always intended: a very limited advance. He emphatically disclaimed any more ambitious imaginings. It is true that Montgomery had no intention of letting Second Army overreach itself. In his instructions to Dempsey he directed that the armoured divisions should "dominate the area Bourguébus – Vimont – Bretteville" while only armoured cars pushed south towards Falaise. He was determined at no time to expose the eastern sector of the beach-head to a major German counter-stroke. He told Dempsey to "write down" the German armour; and Bradley's Americans were to attack in the west a few days later. Nevertheless Montgomery, if his own words meant anything, must have at least envisaged more exciting possibilities – to be sternly eschewed unless genuinely arising, but possibilities nonetheless. To take full advantage of a situation if matters went unexpectedly well – rather than be hogtied by a previously formed concept – was surely good generalship, to be declared rather than disavowed. But Montgomery was obsessed with the necessity of showing that events had conformed exactly to his will and his predictions. He retained the obsession even with hindsight and did himself an injustice thereby. He was a better general than autobiographer.

As to the tactical objects actually set to Dempsey – to "dominate the area Bourguébus – Vimont – Bretteville" and to "write down" the German armour the objective area was certainly neither dominated nor reached: the German armour suffered, but to no decisive extent. Montgomery's declared strategic aim, however, was to attract or hold German Panzer divisions in the east. In this GOODWOOD was to some extent successful. Two reinforcing Panzer divisions were certainly drawn towards Caen. Some more deployment room east of the Orne and around Caen was won, making it easier for Montgomery to keep up subsequent pressure of a limited but expensive kind towards Falaise, consistent with his concept; and a further (9th) SS Panzer Division moved east on 24th July.

Tactically, the operation – the largest attack carried out by Second Army in the Battles of Normandy – was ill conceived. The attacking armoured divisions were crowded into too narrow a front to avoid the congestion which was itself one of the largest impediments to success;

and the unbroken anti-tank defence which they encountered needed different treatment. In spite of the stupendous air attack which accompanied it the steamroller could not roll. GOODWOOD surely needed more infantry, supported by fewer tanks, with plentiful close support artillery (the movement forwards of field guns, like everything else, was impeded by the congestion) and with armoured divisions held in reserve. As some critics would say of the first stages of the Battle of Alamein, a "corps de chasse" was used as a battering ram, and with equally inconclusive results. Nevertheless Montgomery, always resilient, at once resolved to turn this half-success to better effect elsewhere on 21st Army Group front. GOODWOOD had drawn most of the German armour facing the British to the east of the Orne, and opposite the centre there appeared to be little. Montgomery now ordered Dempsey to shift his weight from his left to his right foot: to move the whole of VIII Corps from the area of Caen to the area of Caumont; and to put in as strong an attack as he could muster on 30th July, southwards, in the centre of the Allied front. Away to the west the Americans started their major southward operation on 25th July.

The British Army was now having to fight in country for which its organisation – particularly strong in armour, highly mechanised – was ill adapted. The Normandy *bocage* has already been described. The movement of armoured vehicles over the steep banks, into and out of the sunken lanes, through narrow rides in the woods, was as painful as it was vulnerable. Crew members could be concussed by the movement of their vehicles, even when a German anti-tank gun was not concealed in the next hedge to assist the process. Winding streams in wooded valleys resembled Devon – beautiful and enfolding. Roads were few and narrow, and the congestion upon them damnable. Everywhere good infantry were needed, with tanks supporting them from hedgerow to hedgerow; and mortars, for high-angle close-range support. Armoured divisions now tended to form battlegroups of evenly balanced tank and infantry units rather than concentrate tanks in larger formations as more open country had suggested. The going was likely to be slow. The Germans had made the most of the defensive possibilities of the terrain. Their positions were well sited, their artillery and *Nebelwerfer* shoots competently conducted, their minefields extensive.

Second Army's attack south from Caumont had first to win a lodgement on the high wooded feature known as Mont Pincon, running from the banks of the Orne at Thury Harcourt to St. Martin des Besaces and the Forêt l'Eveque. On the left, XXX Corps (Lieutenant-General Bucknall[1]) was to attack with two divisions – 43rd and 50th Division – towards the western end of Mont Pincon. On the right O'Connor's VIII Corps was to attack some high ground immediately west of XXX Corps' objective with 15th Division. The infantry divisions had independent armoured or army tank brigades giving intimate support. 11th Armoured Division was to take St. Martin des Besaces, immediately south of Caumont, on the extreme right of the army. Guards and 7th Armoured Divisions were in reserve. Once again a mighty bomber assault would precede the attack.

This six-division operation – Operation BLUECOAT – continued until 6th August. During that week, mostly in intense heat, the army pushed southwards over the streams and ridges and through the woods and orchards of central Normandy. Their progress, slow but relentless, was straining the whole German fabric of defence a great deal more than appeared to the struggling infantryman or tank-crew member, his vision extending no further than the next hedgerow, apparently participating in a bloody but small-scale action. In fact Kluge was near despair. He was taking a very personal control of the battle. He moved 21st Panzer Division from east to west on the first day, to counterattack in the area won by 15th Division and to hold the high ground south of St. Martin des Besaces. On the British right 11th Armoured Division outflanked the enemy in the Forêt l'Eveque and reached the Souleuvre River: while on 11th Division's left O'Connor brought up the Guards Armoured Division and directed it on Le Tourneur.

On 1st August 11th Armoured Division fought their way into Le Beny-Bocage. The Caumont sector of the front was now clearly critical for the Germans and Kluge moved II Panzer Corps, with 9th and 10th SS Panzer Divisions, once again from east to west, from the Caen back to the Caumont sector. Using his considerable superiority and his control of the air, Montgomery was thus making Kluge dance entirely to his tune. It could not last long. The German front was near cracking. Individual German troops and units were fighting well, but the incessant air attacks and the freshness of their enemies combined to produce despair. The two newly arrived SS Panzer divisions mounted some spirited attacks in the area of Vire and at Aunay-sur-Odon, forcing back 7th Armoured Division which had been deployed on the left of XXX Corps. Meanwhile fresh British formations were brought up and a new phase of operations, a push on a broad front, began. 3rd Division was deployed on the extreme right, east of Vire: and XII Corps

---

[1] Lieutenant-General Horrocks took over XXX Corps on 4th August.

(Lieutenant-General N. M. Ritchie) came up on the left between XXX Corps and Canadian First Army (Lieutenant-General Crerar), now responsible for the Caen sector. The Germans were still fighting for every yard on a Second Army front which extended on a line from Caen to Vire. Eberbach, commanding Panzer Group West, at this point told Kluge that the best step would be to withdraw to the Seine: to give up Normandy.

Montgomery now again advanced his left. On 8th August, II Canadian Corps, with 51st Division and 1st Polish Armoured Division, launched a major attack down the Caen-Falaise road, and during the following week 21st Army Group, from north and north-west drove down towards Falaise, which fell to the Canadians on 15th August. By then the American Army was not far away to the south. The very spot in the Allied front where Second Army fought against a desperate German defence had become a hinge. The American breakout south, west and east was under way. The American Third Army (General Patton) burst from Avranches and drove on Mortain, south of Vire, where a hastily assembled German counter-attack did little to impede them. Patton drove eastwards to Le Mans, south of Angers, and sent VIII (US) Corps westwards into Brittany. On 10th August American troops, driving east towards the Seine, swung north through Alençon towards Argentan, only fifteen miles south of Falaise. The German Seventh Army, which had been holding the central part of the front, together with Panzer Group West (now renamed Fifth Panzer Army), now found themselves in a great salient. At the tip and on the north flank of that salient was 21st Army Group. As First Canadian and Second British Armies advanced, the salient became a pocket – the "Falaise Pocket". To the south the German front was now ripped open. To avoid encirclement there could be no other course except flight to the east. Pounded from the air, suffering appalling casualties in men, horses and machines, with units and detachments surrounded and surrendering, cohesion gone, the great German retreat was under way. Kluge handed over command to Field Marshal Model. German losses in the Normandy fighting totalled more than 140,000 men.

This was indeed, for the British Army, a moment to savour. The fighting in Normandy had been hard. It had ended in total victory. The task now was pursuit, and pursuit amid the congenial and sometimes distracting atmosphere of welcome and liberation.

The Battle of Normandy may be regarded as over by 15th August, the fall of Falaise. It cost 21st Army Group 83,000 casualties – 16,000 of them killed – in a little less than three months of the campaign. The army group was now directed towards the Rhine, moving north of the Ardennes. During the next five weeks Second Army crossed the Seine on 25th August, reached Amiens on 31st, entered Brussels on 3rd September, and by mid-September reached the Meuse-Escaut Canal, running east from Antwerp. Isolated German detachments fought tenaciously, and encounter battles were often vigorous and costly. But there was nothing like a coherent German front; nor did there appear significant danger from a German counter-stroke. Great numbers of prisoners came in. Although every advance had to be undertaken with circumspection, every village and bend in the road approached as if containing a resolute German rearguard (as it sometimes did), it was widely felt that if the pressure was kept up the Wehrmacht could not possibly recover. Nothing, it seemed, could prevent the armies thundering into the heart of Germany. Where serious opposition was met bloody little battles were fought, and the main body would find a way to bypass and race on once more. There were some appropriate and historic incidents. On Second Army's left First Canadian Army operated to clear the coast and take the ports. Fighting under the Canadians was I (British) Corps: and in I Corps 51st (Highland) Division entered, at the beginning of September, St. Valéry-en-Caux, place of poignant association, scene of surrender in 1940.

Logistics were now a controlling factor. In every theatre of war administrative constraints had, in differing ways, set the shape of the campaign. Although North-West Europe had a sophisticated road and rail network (the latter needed restoration to supply the armies), and the Allies possessed a mighty train of wheeled transport, only a certain number of vehicles can pass down one road in twenty-four hours, and at times and places road capacity was the limiting factor. Where distances lengthened, however, as the Allies began their great advance, the Allied transport lift was inadequate for the tonnages to be carried and the mileage to be covered. Another limitation was port capacity – and port location. Much of the supply of 21st Army Group was still, and would be for some time, coming into France across beaches. A vast maintenance area was laid out around Bayeux, stretching almost to Caen, with dumps of every sort of commodity, Ordnance depots, field hospitals and reinforcement camps.

Cherbourg was the only significant port of ingress. The Channel ports from Le Havre to Ostend (which the Germans had garrisoned) were reduced in the months following the breakout from Normandy, but the approaches to the great Scheldt port of Antwerp were not taken for some time and were of most significance. It took time, too, for ports to be brought into working condition after capture. Until all this was balanced, Eisenhower's army groups were advancing on a front from Alsace to the Channel coast – supported by a very narrow funnel of supply. And, with so constricted a line of communication, the wider the front the feebler the thrust at each point. The resources devoted to logistics were immense. Forty-four per cent of the men of 21st Army Group were in the logistic service units.

Montgomery believed in concentration of force as a principle of war. He also knew that the logistic situation meant only a limited number of divisions could be supported at any distance from the Allied bases. Thus he believed strongly that Allied strategy demanded a single punch on a comparatively narrow frontage between the Ardennes and the Channel coast, under one command. He believed that if the Allies advanced on too broad a front there would be insufficient impetus at any one point. He also demanded an increase in the transport allocated to 21st Army Group's needs.

The argument turned on fuel supply and continued until virtually the end of the campaign, since the petrol requirements of the advancing armies (and air forces) were naturally huge. Ammunition consumption was minimal at this stage.[1] Food took only a minute proportion of the replenishment tonnages. It was fuel for vehicles which set the pace of logistic argument.

A compromise was reached, and the matter remained uneasy. Nevertheless Eisenhower (who assumed, from Montgomery, direct control of the operations of the army groups from 1st September) agreed that the main effort in the immediate future should be made in the north, on the front of 21st Army Group. On 3rd September Montgomery issued a directive that the objective of 21st Army Group would be the Ruhr and the communications from it into Germany. To achieve this, the main weight of Second Army was to be directed on the Rhine, between Wesel and Arnhem, with the object of crossing the river and bypassing the Ruhr to the north, while threatening the Western Ruhr frontally between Dusseldorf and Duisburg. The next major operation, therefore, was to be an attempt to cross the Rhine itself, by the use of all available airborne forces from England, combined with a main effort by Second Army. This was Operation MARKET GARDEN, due on 17th September.

---

[1] Ammunition had been used at a great rate in Normandy, and would be again – faster than the quantities could be manufactured. But this was not a problem in the pursuit, and only reappeared as one when the front was again stabilised in the autumn – and prepared attacks supported by great artillery concentrations again were thought necessary.

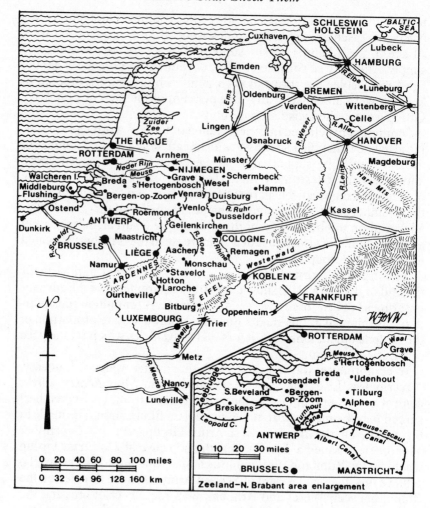

North-West Europe

These were days of tasting the heady fruits of victory for the British Army. So certain – indeed so imminent – did triumph appear that it was fatally easy to underestimate the enemy. This tendency did not much affect the forward troops where, on the Albert Canal and at other places on the road to Holland, German task forces fought as fiercely as ever, albeit surrounded. But the general mood was one of exaltation – and of a certain relaxation which did not assist the urgency which the strategic situation demanded. MARKET GARDEN was, therefore, the culmination of an advance which took the army from Normandy to the banks of the Rhine; but it also, after the event, begat a change of tempo. After it, the pursuit phase of the campaign was over. The war was certain to continue into and through the winter. "We must now prepare for a hard dogfight battle or killing match," Montgomery wrote in his orders of 27th September. And in a letter to the VCIGS, General Nye, of 15th October he confessed, "I have in fact chucked the idea of going on towards the Ruhr." The party was over.

This, however, lay in the future. As planned, MARKET GARDEN was to be the start of another major advance, this time into Germany itself. "Our real objective," Montgomery wrote, in his directive for the operation, signed on 14th September, "is the Ruhr." Having crossed the Rhine at Arnhem, Second Army was to be prepared to move eastwards to Münster, Osnabruck and Hamm, and thence thrust southwards cutting off the Eastern Ruhr. The immediate task was to advance from the Escaut Canal to Grave, Nijmegen and Arnhem, crossing the Meuse, the Waal and the Nederrijn.[1] Along the route would be dropped I (British) Airborne Corps (Lieutenant-General F. A. M. Browning) of three divisions – two American, at Nijmegen and south of it, and 1st (British) Airborne Division (Major-General Urquhart) to seize the northernmost point, the bridge at Arnhem. The spearhead of Second Army's advance, driving forwards to make contact with the airborne divisions, was Horrocks' XXX Corps, while VIII and XII Corps were to attack to widen the north-reaching corridor, on the east and west respectively. Facing Second Army, as far as was known, were a hotchpotch of German units and formations composing First Parachute Army, commanded by the redoubtable General Student, of Cretan fame. The distance from the start to Arnhem was sixty-five miles.

On the morning of 17th September an enormous cavalcade of aircraft and gliders set out towards Holland from their bases in England. They passed over the waiting troops of Second Army and moved towards the target areas. Soon afterwards the leading echelons of the airborne divisions began to drop, and the tanks of the Guards Armoured Division began to move forwards from the Escaut Canal.

From the start the operation faltered. Everything depended on time. XXX Corps had to move through country where every bridge on roads large or small could, if blown, produce a time-consuming impediment to the advance. The airborne divisions had been dropped or landed

---

[1] The Rhine separates into these two arms ten miles east of Nijmegen, the northern "Nederrijn" running through Arnhem, the southern "Waal" through Nijmegen. To cross the Rhine it was, therefore, necessary to cross both.

with orders to seize the most important of these, but they could not possibly take them all. Roads were few and vital. It was futile to suppose that great strength was being achieved at the spearhead of advance by the deployment of a mass of divisions on a narrow thrust if the fighting troops could not reach the front, or could not be supplied if they did. The ground off the roads was in many places intersected by streams and dykes, and much of it was so low lying as to make difficult or impossible the movement of heavy, tracked vehicles. Most significant would be the situation found by XXX Corps at the bridges over the major obstacles – the Wilhelmina Canal at Zon, the Willems Canal at Veghel, the Meuse at Grave, the Waal at Nijmegen and the Nederrijn at Arnhem.

The bridge at Zon – and at Best, a few miles to the west – had been blown. The crossings at Veghel and at Grave had been secured by 101st and 82nd (US) Airborne Divisions respectively, but the great bridge across the Waal at Nijmegen was in German hands, as was the town. And XXX Corps was impeded not only by obstacles but by a vigorous enemy. The leading tank battalions lost heavily from German bazooka teams covering the road shortly after the advance began. A Panzer brigade – 107th with about forty tanks – arrived unexpectedly from the east and attacked towards Zon across the line of advance. Nijmegen was held strongly. XXX Corps was running behind schedule, and only reached Nijmegen on the afternoon of 19th September – forty-eight hours after the launch of the operation. The distance advanced was over fifty miles. In most phases of the campaign it would have been a source of satisfaction. But it was not good enough for MARKET GARDEN. For 1st Airborne Division was in a position of grave danger, and as the leading division of XXX Corps entered Nijmegen from the south and attempted without success to break through to the river, a message was received from Urquhart's Headquarters that the situation at Arnhem was critical.

1st Airborne Division had dropped some miles west of the town itself (which lies on the north bank of the Nederrijn). The leading brigade advanced on three parallel routes towards the town. Only one battalion got through to the north end of the bridge, which was seized by the evening of D Day – 17th September. No help reached this valiant battalion. The southern end of the bridge was in German hands. No airborne troops were dropped or landed south of the Nederrijn until 21st September. The rest of the leading parachute brigade were held up in the woods or western suburbs at Osterbeek by a German resistance of surprising strength and ferocity; and succeeding waves of airborne troops, whose fly-in was delayed by an appalling turn in the

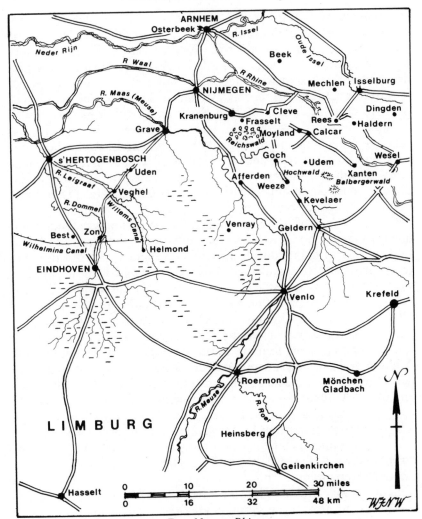

From Meuse to Rhine

weather, were able to do little but strengthen the perimeter of what was soon not an open door for the advance into Germany of Second Army but an isolated place under desperate siege.

For among the first prisoners taken by 1st Airborne Division were soldiers from 9th and 10th SS Panzer Divisions – divisions the British Army had last met in Normandy and which, much depleted in numbers and equipment but always formidable, were now being rested and refitted immediately north of Arnhem. Furthermore Field Marshal Model himself had his headquarters in Arnhem. He was there, sitting

345

at luncheon, when MARKET GARDEN started, and immediately brought his considerable energies to the organisation of the local defence and the putting together of troops from whatever quarter. The SS divisions had a few tanks and more arrived. 1st Airborne Division was thus dropped not only some distance from its objective but into a hornets' nest. When XXX Corps reached Nijmegen, therefore, and made quick plans to clear the place on 20th September, and cross the Waal if possible, time was already running out at Arnhem. Most of all it was running out at the north end of the Arnhem Bridge, where one parachute battalion had, since the evening of 17th, been resisting alone every assault the Germans could bring against it. The rest of the division could do nothing to assist and were hemmed in at Osterbeek, desperately fighting off German attacks from all directions.

On the evening of 20th September, Nijmegen, stoutly defended, was finally cleared. The town lies on the south bank of the Waal. 82nd (US) Division, in an operation of outstanding gallantry, crossed the river under fire in British assault boats,[1] gained a foothold on the north bank, west of the town, and started to move towards the north end of the Nijmegen Bridge. At 7 p.m. a column of tanks of Guards Armoured Division, the leading division of XXX Corps, rushed the bridge itself. Second Army was now across the Waal, and next day, 21st September, saw the first attempts to move north, to cover the mere ten miles to Arnhem and the beleaguered 1st Airborne Division. But soon after dawn the brave remnants of the parachute battalion holding the north end of the Arnhem Bridge were overwhelmed. The prize of MARKET GARDEN – the crossing of the Rhine – now looked beyond the winning. The sole problem was how best to support 1st Airborne Division.

The last impediment to MARKET GARDEN was the nature of the terrain between the two great rivers – terrain entirely unsuited to armoured operations; and XXX Corps was strong, above all, in armour. In this country, known as the "island", it was all too easy to hold one main artery against armoured forces. Deployment of tanks off the raised roads running along the tops of the dykes was impossible. Movement along them exposed advancing vehicles to the enemy's simple target practice. Horrocks pushed elements of 43rd Division, his largest infantry force, up to the south bank of the Nederrijn west of Arnhem, and about 250 infantrymen were taken to the other side by assault boat on 22nd and 23rd September, but it was clear that to build up enough strength to change the operational situation was impossible without a bridge intact.

---

[1] Canvas boats entirely unfamiliar to the Americans.

On 25th September, Horrocks ordered Urquhart to bring as many survivors as he could rally, by boat and ferry, to the south bank. Some 2,500 were brought out, but 3,800 fell into German hands. Nevertheless 1st Airborne Division had inflicted over 3,000 casualties on their enemies.

Many questions were and will continue to be asked about MARKET GARDEN. From the tactical viewpoint, could not different dropping zones have meant the capture of more objectives – and quicker? Why was there not greater emphasis on the Nijmegen Bridge as an objective for the airborne forces? Was it ever possible to reach Arnhem from Nijmegen quickly unless troops had also been dropped south as well as north of the Arnhem Bridge at the beginning? Polish paratroops were dropped on the south bank, but not until 21st September. Could more dynamism have led to a faster advance by XXX Corps? Traffic congestion is not a perfect excuse for delays in the advance of marching infantry and in the later stages of the war infantry often came to rely so much on overwhelming artillery support that men expected to be able to move forwards and occupy ground rather than fight for it. Skill in skirmishing by infantry, skill in tactical movement, lessened rather than increased as a natural consequence; and sometimes the ensuing sluggishness did not reduce casualties – it increased them by placing operational success at risk. Could not better close air support, which was negligible, have turned the scale at Arnhem? There are broader questions. Were large scale operations east of the Rhine, in fact, logistically feasible before Antwerp was clear – for these were the object? Perhaps as good a question as any is why advance by Nijmegen and Arnhem – by two bridges – at all? Montgomery's earlier intention had been to strike with Second Army towards the Rhine more directly on the path to Germany, somewhere between Arnhem and Wesel, and his staff were uncertain as to why Nijmegen and Arnhem (albeit nearer) were in the event preferred. It was a very personal decision.[1]

MARKET GARDEN had high aims. It was an operation where the actions of a few divisions might have had great strategic consequences. Montgomery saw it as the crossing of the Rhine. He planned to send Second Army thereafter deep into Westphalia and to do so soon. None of this could now happen. He was commendably quick to make the best of a bad job and sent a signal to the CIGS on 26th September – "The fact that we shall not (repeat not) now have a crossing over Nederrijn

---

[1] I am indebted to the late Major-General Belchem of 21st Army Group Operations Staff for discussion and information on this point. The arguments against Wesel were, largely, that the fly-in would have been more vulnerable to the German air defences of the Ruhr area. Some thought this superable.

will not (repeat not) affect operations eastward against Ruhr." This was hardly convincing. He struck a more sombre and authentic note in a letter of 2nd October: "It is my opinion that if we are to see this thing through properly we shall want everything we have got."

Strategically, therefore, MARKET GARDEN was a failure. In August and September 1944 the German Army was in a state of disarray after the Normandy fighting. Garrison detachments, reinforcement units, training units, convalescents, the very old and the very young were in process of being rounded up and formed into divisions and armies with high-sounding names but scant reality as yet. For a little while – a few weeks of August and September – the Western Front was open, and a determined effort on one part of it might have finished the war, with incalculable strategic and political consequences, and with a saving of the huge number of casualties suffered later. If MARKET GARDEN ever had a chance it was the last chance to seize this great strategic opportunity. It failed, and the war went on. Nevertheless, the fight of 1st Airborne Division was one of the noblest fought by the British Army in the Second World War, and its glory will last as long as the British Army's story is remembered.

In less than four months the British Army had landed in France, had destroyed a German Army, had advanced from Normandy to the banks of the Rhine and was now poised for invasion of the Reich itself. In the Low Countries now, as in Italy and in Burma, the curtain could rise on the finale.

Part V

Triumph at Last

15

The End in Italy

The closing battles of the Italian campaign took place against a sombre
background for those who had to conduct and endure them. After
DIADEM Alexander's two armies were in full cry north of Rome.
Although they had suffered severely, they knew that their opponents
were routed, and that if pursuit were unremitting there might be a
chance of inflicting that final and crushing defeat which had so far
eluded them. Victory is a heady wine, of which the army in Italy had
tasted insufficient until now. They had emerged into the sunlight.
They felt indomitable. The German rearguards manned intermediate
positions with their usual skill, but in the Allied Armies all felt that
pauses were temporary, that the enemy was conducting a running fight
and could be hustled to defeat.

At this point Alexander was dealt as hard a blow as any he received in
his career, when Operation DRAGOON, the invasion of the southern
French coast, was finally ordered. DRAGOON had been suspended
menacingly over the Italian front for months, a matter of considerable
acrimony between British and Americans, Brooke and Marshall,
Churchill and Roosevelt. It had little positive or immediate effect upon
the campaign in North-West Europe, save permitting French divisions
to arrive in Southern France as liberators – no insignificant factor. Its
effects upon the Italian front, however, were entirely bad. DRAGOON
required troops; as a result Alexander lost four French divisions (his
only mountain troops, of high quality, whose absence would soon be
sorely felt), and three American divisions from Fifth Army. Meanwhile
Kesselring's Army Group C was reinforced. Kesselring lost three
veteran divisions which, after DRAGOON, the Germans felt free to
withdraw: but he received five – albeit raw – replacements and the
equivalent of three further divisions in manpower drawn from Germany, Northern Europe and from the Russian front. When Alexander
first launched his "parallel pursuit" from the Tiber, his armies could
muster twenty-seven divisions, his opponents fourteen. By the time the
Allies reached the Gothic Line they numbered twenty-one divisions,
including four armoured, while Kesselring could command some

twenty-six divisions, six of them Panzer or Panzer Grenadier, nineteen of them in the Gothic Line. Although too much should not be made of this statistic – the word "division" covered a great diversity of strengths – the balance now was certainly less favourable to the Allies, and in the exhausting battles to come numbers, which enable troops to be rested and come as fresh echelons to the later stages of an attack, mattered a great deal. The odds were not in favour of decisive victory.

Many commanders would have settled for an unadventurous policy, the exercise of pressure without undue risk or loss. It is greatly to the honour of Alexander and the soldiers of Fifth and Eighth Armies that they took a different road. Interpreting rigorously their mandate to fight the enemy with such energy that he could not easily withdraw troops and should, if possible, be forced to bring in more, they conducted, instead, a campaign of great vigour and tragically high casualties, and swiftly came within an ace of that crowning achievement finally won the following spring. They did this with odds more even than in any other theatre of war; and in terrain and climatic conditions which tried the army to its limits. In the end they conquered.

The Gothic Line, two hundred miles long, ran from Pisa to Rimini. For all but the easternmost fifty miles it lay in the Northern Apennines, natural defensive country with roads through the passes easily blocked, defiles fortified, bunkers excavated, gun positions protected, demolitions prepared. In the east, on the Adriatic flank, the terrain was no more inviting to an army seeking to advance. Here the Apennine spur ran north-eastwards to the sea in a sequence of defensible parallels, between which ran broad rivers – a total of thirteen had ultimately to be crossed – with high embankments and surrounding low-lying country which rain turned easily to marsh.

In the west the Gothic Line was held by the German Fourteenth Army (General Lemelsen) with six divisions (the veteran XIV Panzer Corps and I Parachute Corps) and two divisions in army reserve. In the east the line was occupied by Tenth Army (General von Vietinghoff) with ten divisions deployed under LI Mountain Corps on the inland and LXVI Panzer Corps on the coastal flank, and a further two divisions in army reserve. German divisions were of uneven quality and strength. Some were new to the theatre, some had suffered severely, and in addition the actions of Italian partisans caused a formidable casualty bill – about 26,000 between June and August 1944. Nevertheless the Gothic Line was strong, and strongly held. Behind it, clear of the mountain barrier, ran the main Bologna-Rimini road, Highway 9, the Emilian Way, giving the Germans a lateral communication of great value.

Faced with the familiar combination of difficult terrain and an enemy with both flanks resting on the sea, Alexander could only hope to achieve decisive results by concentrating force at a chosen point, while being prepared to shift his weight to another point if the battle demanded, and to do so with greater agility than his opponent. No great manoeuvres were possible – indeed they seldom were in Italy. He determined to make his main effort in the Adriatic sector by moving back Eighth Army from West and Central Italy to the east coast. The move was accompanied by a sophisticated deception plan to mask the selected area of attack. In the week between 15th and 22nd August 60,000 tanks, vehicles and guns were moved from one flank to the other over the exiguous roads. Alexander planned that Fifth Army should also attack, in the centre, through the mountains – a move that should follow the attraction by Eighth Army of German strength towards the Adriatic.

The operation started on 25th August. Eighth Army now consisted of four corps – a total of eleven divisions. II Polish Corps (General Anders) of two divisions attacked to gain high ground north-west of Pesaro at the extreme east end of the Gothic Line. Thereafter Eighth Army moved forwards with three corps in line: on the right, directed on Rimini, I Canadian Corps (General Foulkes) with two divisions; next inland the British V Corps (Lieutenant-General Keightley), by far the strongest in Eighth Army, consisting of 1st Armoured, 4th, 46th, 56th and 4th Indian Divisions. V Corps was ordered to attack west of Rimini, to break through to Highway 9, the Rimini-Bologna road, and thereafter advance towards Bologna: this movement would menace the entire rear of Army Group C and must, it was reckoned, attract every available German division upon V Corps. On the left of Eighth Army the British X Corps, consisting only of 10th Indian Division, was directed to hold the rest of the army front across to the boundary with Fifth Army on the Pratomagna mountain range east of Florence. 2nd New Zealand Division was in army reserve.

By 2nd September, the early movements had gone well, with the Germans dislodged from their positions in the Gothic Line and driven back to the Conca River. Kesselring had only just appreciated the weight and direction of the Allied attack when the forward troops of his Tenth Army, in inadequate strength, met the main Eighth Army thrust.

The prepared positions on the Gothic Line once breached, the Allies hoped for a decisive breakthrough on the right wing. They were, however, frustrated by the terrain and by the speed of the German

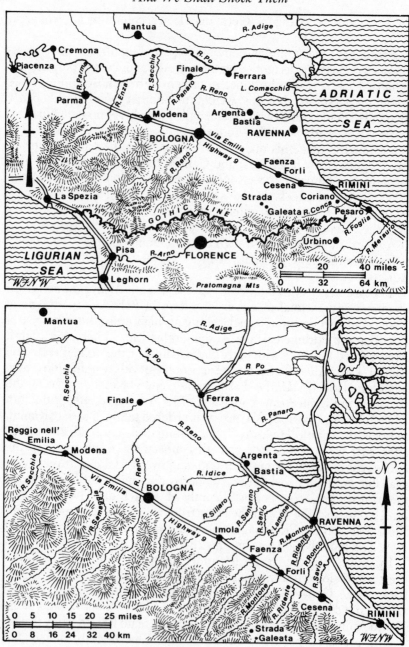

Northern Italy and the Adriatic Front

response, for the enemy was by now alert to the acute danger to the whole of Army Group C. The way forwards for Eighth Army lay across a series of ridges and rivers. At Coriano, ten miles south-east of Rimini, the last ridge before open country, V Corps was halted and failed to "take it on the bounce". Instead German reinforcements, tanks and anti-tank guns were hurried to the sector and by 5th September Vietinghoff had six divisions, including one Panzer and one Panzer Grenadier, facing Eighth Army and defending the Coriano Ridge. To break through now would demand more strength, more preparation, a mass of artillery and time. Every day that passed brought nearer the possibility of a break in the summer weather and the sort of rains which had so often before – notably on the Sangro – reduced fighting on the Adriatic Front to near-Flanders conditions.

Eighth Army now prepared a deliberate attack. They were through the Gothic Line, but they were still blocked and frustrated. The attack began on 12th September. Artillery bombardment was coordinated with bombing by the air forces and with fire from naval vessels in the Adriatic. Eventually V Corps drove the enemy from the Coriano Ridge, but casualties were high. Tank losses were so formidable that after the battle 1st Armoured Division could no longer be employed as such. Rimini was finally taken on 20th September and, inland, V Corps pressed slowly forwards from river to river, infantry and engineers once again in the lead and in universal demand.

Meanwhile Alexander, realising that there would be no early break-through by Eighth Army, and appreciating that the Germans had responded swiftly to its threat, ordered an attack through the mountains by Fifth Army under General Clark. Fifth Army, which had suffered the loss of the DRAGOON divisions, now consisted of two American Corps, II and IV, and of XIII British Corps (Lieutenant-General Kirkman), the latter containing 1st, 6th Armoured and 8th Indian Divisions. Clark was already moving forwards, for opposite him the Germans were withdrawing to maintain a coherent front with their forces under pressure in the eastern sector. On 13th September he attacked the main Gothic Line position. The Allied Armies in Italy were now fully committed right across the front. Having surrendered divisions to DRAGOON Alexander had no fresh troops with which to maintain ultimate pressure, to keep up momentum when both sides were exhausted.

Fifth Army battered its way painfully forwards through the mountains towards the promised land of the Po Valley and the supreme target of the Bologna-Rimini road, which, once reached, would cut German lateral communications between Tenth and Fourteenth Armies and force a general retreat upon the enemy. Advancing on the most easterly of parallel routes winding through the mountains, the British XIII Corps was directed towards Faenza and Forli. A combined attack by 1st Division and an American division on 17th September finally forced the Gothic Line. Many defensible positions, however, still survived along the Apennine roads, and although Clark switched his main effort from one thrust line to another, and the Allied Air Forces pounded the Germans remorselessly when weather allowed, the advance was slow and expensive. Clark concentrated strength for a renewed offensive on 2nd October, a renewed attempt to get through the mountain barrier. Such a task was comparable to the appalling march forwards south of Cassino, but with larger, steeper mountains and worse numerical odds. Men struggled painfully up and along precipitous ridges, spending their days and nights in flooded slit trenches or slithering through mud under incessant shell and mortar fire. Not a rocky hill top, not a bend in the mountain road but was disputed and then counter-attacked by an undefeated enemy. By now the weather had broken. Fifth Army attack was directed on Imola and Bologna. In the east, the enemy had been driven back towards the Savio River. Eighth Army was ordered to attack north-east towards Cesena.[1]

Throughout September rain fell incessantly and the ground became ever more impassable, a sea of mud. Movement, confined to roads, was laborious. On 19th October, Eighth Army took Cesena, inching their way north-west up Highway 9 towards Bologna, reaching Galeata and Strada. Torrential rain swept away the Savio Bridges behind them. From the south, but still held in the mountains, Fifth Army took Monte Belmonte, nine miles from the centre of Bologna, on 23rd. Casualties were high, conditions appalling, progress minimal. By the end of October, the Germans held the line of the Ronco River facing south-east and still retained a line of formidable mountain strongholds in the Apennines, facing south. As so often in Italy, weather and exhaustion imposed a halt on even the most courageous operations. The British infantry alone lost 7,000 men in the Battles of the Gothic Line. Losses were proportionately higher than in any other phase of the Italian campaign.

It is not easy to demand sacrifices, including men's lives, when the object of a campaign has become demonstrably subordinate to the claims of other theatres, and where attrition rather than victory appears the only aim. Hitherto, Alexander had been able to hold before his

---

[1] Command of Eighth Army was assumed by Lieutenant-General McCreery on 1st October. Leese went to South-East Asia to command all Allied Land Forces in that Command.

troops the vision of a great adventure into and across the North Italian Plain. He himself had visions of an even more ambitious advance – a march by Ljubljana to Vienna – a concept with which for sound political reasons Churchill had considerable sympathy, although Brooke regarded the notion as entirely impracticable, short of a general German collapse, and one which the Americans were most unlikely to entertain. Without some such stimulus, however, the Allied Armies in Italy had a hard and depressing winter ahead of them, it being clear that no further major offensive could be contemplated for several months; and even then it appeared to the soldiers doubtful whether the authorities cared if the armies in Italy advanced or not. Were not the huge army groups now advancing towards the Rhine, or the Soviet masses forcing their way through Poland, clearly going to finish the Third Reich before the Allied forces south of the Alps could play further part? The imminence of victory, the coming hard-to-imagine outbreak of peace, with the apparently subsidiary nature of the Italian theatre combined to depress. Desertions increased sharply. Survival looked more attractive than suffering, and the latter's value was questioned.

In these circumstances a successful push by Eighth Army in November up the Bologna road, driving the Germans from Forli and Faenza and across the Lamone River on 7th December, was achievement indeed. Northwards, parallel to the Adriatic coast, II Canadian Corps took Ravenna on 5th December. At considerable cost Eighth Army pushed onwards to the Senio River, reached by 1st Canadian Division and 56th Division on 4th January. Thereafter the armies dug in, rested, trained and prepared to go on in the spring. Large quantities of new equipment arrived, including assault engineer equipment; and the Engineers were as busy as ever, constructing huge numbers of bridges, repairing shattered lines of communication and generally starting to restore the ravages of war. And in the mountains in the west and centre of the Allied front men kept watch, froze, patrolled and endured.

The Battles for the Gothic Line in the late summer and autumn of 1944 should not be unduly overshadowed by other contests in other theatres, fought on very much more favourable terms. In eight weeks' incessant fighting, an Allied force, inferior to the enemy in number of divisions (an inexact measurement, but still yielding a different balance from that in any other theatre), penetrated a strong and prepared position in some of the most unpromising terrain in Europe in appalling weather. Conditions made it impossible for the Allied Armies to break finally into open country, clear of the mountains, across the rivers. Had they done so the Germans could not have stood south of the Alpine barrier. The enemy reaction proved once again that the campaign in Italy was playing its essential part in Allied strategy. German divisions were held there and drawn there because of the vigour with which the battle was pressed to within an inch of victory.

On 9th April 1945 the British Army began its last great offensive of the Italian campaign, which in less than three weeks led to the destruction of the German Army in Italy. The achievement was soon subsumed in a general triumph on all European fronts. Amid the turmoil of world events it is easy to forget that this was one of the most imaginative as well as most successful battles fought by Eighth Army, which now included all British and Imperial divisions (except 6th South African Armoured Division, fighting with a United States corps).[1]

The enemy, although desperately short of fuel and therefore of mobility, was by no means beaten. With Kesselring moved to the Western Front, Vietinghoff now commanded Army Group C, which had received some replacements and still numbered twenty-three divisions, including three Panzer or Panzer Grenadier divisions, against which the Allies deployed seventeen. The immensely superior equipment position and armoured strength of the Allies would inevitably be decisive, as would Allied air power, in anything like open country, but in a strong, natural defensive position Army Group C was still a hard nut to crack, and of higher quality than the Wehrmacht elsewhere.

And there was still some strength in the German position. From west to east of the front the Germans still hung on in the Apennines south of Bologna, facing Fifth Army. This constituted their right flank. Their centre, facing south-east astride Highway 9, rested on the River Senio, behind which a further sequence of rivers – the Santerno, the Sillaro, the Idice – all covered Bologna and ran northwards into the River Reno. The Germans had on their left flank the twenty-mile-long Lake Comacchio; and to the south-west of it a large expanse of land was flooded. Between these floods and the lake was only a narrow isthmus running north to Argenta from the bridge across the Reno at Bastia. If driven back towards Bologna, Vietinghoff could ultimately withdraw behind the Reno, pivoting on the flooded area and lake on the extreme left of the German line.

To do this, however, Vietinghoff needed some latitude. He knew

---

[1] 6th South African Armoured Division contained British as well as South African troops in the Italian campaign.

well how dangerous and laborious withdrawal would be if every line were held too long. He reckoned his only hope lay in having freedom to carry out such manoeuvres as Army Group C could still perform, to show still some of that agility at which German troops had long proved masters. Like all German Commanders in his position, he received no discretion. Hitler's orders were as inexorable as usual. Army Group C was to fight for every last yard of North Italian soil, while to its rear the Western powers were already across the Rhine, racing into Westphalia and the Palatinate.

Alexander, by now promoted Field Marshal, had been appointed Supreme Allied Commander, Mediterranean; and General Clark was in command of the Allied Armies. Fifth Army (General Truscott) was to carry out the main and final thrust of the army group, being directed to debouch from the mountains, fight his way down into the plain, move northwards, west of Bologna and west of the River Reno, and trap the German divisions before they could withdraw across the Po to their known final line on the River Adige. Four days earlier Eighth Army was to attack north-westwards – to attract the German reserves (in so far as they could move) and ultimately form the righthand pincer of a great encircling movement between the Reno and Po Rivers.

Clearly, Eighth Army's advance could, at worst, be yet another expensive move forwards from river to river. The ground on the right was constricted by the floods; and it was difficult to see how an orderly enemy withdrawal to the River Reno might be pre-empted. McCreery decided, nevertheless, to try. He planned to attack the Argenta Gap between lake and floods, using amphibious vehicles to carry troops and negotiate the water: large numbers of these (known as "Fantails") had reached Italy during the winter. The left hinge of the German position, including the bridge across the Reno at Bastia, would thus be attacked from an unexpected direction. Simultaneously Eighth Army's main attack would be made across the Senio River, north-west. The enemy would be assaulted from the front and have his left flank shattered and his fall-back position turned. Thereafter the whole weight of the army could be put behind the most promising thrust line.

For this operation McCreery had eight divisions and a number of independent brigades, including a parachute brigade, which it was hoped to use at the Argenta Gap. His British divisions were 56th, 78th (back with Eighth Army since the Gothic Line Battles) and 6th Armoured. The New Zealanders were in at the last, as they had been at the first. 8th and 10th Indian Divisions were both back in Eighth Army, as were Anders's two Polish divisions. I Canadian Corps had been withdrawn to North-West Europe after the autumn offensive, while

4th and 46th Divisions had been hurried to Greece to deal with the threat of civil war. McCreery's divisions were divided between three British corps, V, X and XIII; and II Polish Corps.

The Eighth Army plan was to use 56th Division on the remarkable right-flank operation, employing all the Fantails, supported by a Royal Marine Commando brigade and, if conditions permitted, an airborne assault by 2nd Parachute Brigade on a key bridge. For the main assault McCreery ordered V Corps with three divisions to cross the River Senio and attack north-west, while II Polish Corps on their left were to attack with one division immediately north of the highway, the Bologna road. McCreery kept 6th Armoured Division in army reserve and both X and XIII Corps Headquarters were held for use in subsequent stages of operations.

It proved impossible to drop the Parachute brigade because of German anti-aircraft defences, but otherwise the right-flank operation went admirably and achieved complete surprise. The brigades of 56th Division swung in from an unexpected direction at the Argenta Gap. The key bridge at Bastia, at which the Parachute brigade had been aimed, however, could not yet be taken. It would unlock the door for Eighth Army to the open country north of the Reno, and was closely invested.

On the main front the attack of V Corps across the Senio with two assaulting divisions was preceded by a remarkable bombardment. First, strategic bombers dropped 175,000 fragmentation bombs over the German gun areas. Some two hundred bombers followed, also targeted on German gun areas. Next five hundred fighter bombers came in to attack five separate times, alternating with five forty-minute artillery bombardment programmes. After the fifth artillery concentration the aircraft came in for the last time, but without attacking. That was the signal for the infantry to advance, supported by 1,000 pieces of field artillery. It was fitting that this final battle of Eighth Army was accompanied by massive use of the artillery arm. As the Second World War proceeded, the British Army became ever more adept at the use of concentrated artillery to minimise casualties and achieve results; and the artillery was perhaps the one Arm of the British Army professionally acknowledged by the German enemy as his superior.

8th Indian Division on the right and 2nd New Zealand Division on the left went forward together. Nothing could stop them. Three days later they had not only crossed the Senio but had bridgeheads across the next river, the Santerno, while the third division of V Corps, 78th Division, crossed the Senio behind them and swung north, making for the Bastia Bridge and the junction with 56th Division. On 16th April

360

Bastia fell and the Germans were driven back to the northern part of the Argenta Gap. Meanwhile, on the main front, McCreery brought forward XIII Corps with 10th Indian Division, and directed them, with the New Zealanders also under his command, from river to river towards Bologna, while V Corps's effort was directed northwards, towards Argenta.

West of Bologna the Fifth Army attack started on 14th April. To break clear of the mountains initially involved as hard fighting as ever. The German infantry, on both Fifth and Eighth Army fronts were performing with great valour but little hope, and the remaining mobile groups of Vietinghoff's four Panzer Grenadier divisions were intervening in the battle with their habitual energy and skill and with as much agility as their scarce fuel allowed. But the tide was now flowing strongly. The Fifth Army plan was to punch a hole in the German defences and pass through two armoured divisions. They succeeded and, by 20th April, cut Highway 9 between Bologna and Modena. Bologna fell to the Poles on 21st April. No defensive position could now be sustained south of the Po, and the last hope of the German Army lay in reaching it.

The hope was soon shattered. McCreery had moved 6th Armoured Division to the Argenta area under V Corps. This division now broke through at Argenta and turned north-west along the north bank of the Reno, towards the Po. The pincers were closing. No German resistance could possibly be patched up, no position organised, no flanks secured. No defiles or natural obstacles now helped the fleeing remnants of Tenth and Fourteenth Armies. The Allies could drive where they willed, sweeping up like a spring wind the storm-tossed leaves of a defeated enemy. At the village appropriately called Finale Fifth and Eighth Armies at last joined hands on 23rd April. On 25th April the leading troops of 6th Armoured Division crossed the Po. On 28th April German delegates arrived at Alexander's Headquarters. On 2nd May a cease-fire took effect throughout the Italian front. The German forces had surrendered unconditionally.

Thus ended the Italian campaign. Churchill, throughout the war, seldom failed to goad commanders in the field with exhortation, enquiry, criticism and often ill-judged operational advice. In victory, however, he was as warm and generous as he had been querulous along the way. On 29th April he sent his telegram of congratulations to Alexander. "I rejoice," it began, "in the magnificently planned and executed operations of the 15th Group of Armies which are resulting in the complete destruction or capture of all the enemy forces south of the Alps." And the telegram ended –

This great final battle in Italy will long stand out in history as one of the most famous episodes in this Second World War. Pray give my heartfelt congratulations to all your commanders and principal officers of all Services and above all to the valiant and ardent troops whom they have led with so much skill.

16

The Road to Mandalay

In South-East Asia Command not least of the triumphs of Fourteenth Army's last, brilliant campaign was that it was launched at all.

In his diary on 7th August 1944 Brooke noted: "We shall have to go on operating in Burma, it is . . . clear that the best way of doing so is to take the whole of Burma by an airborne attack on Rangoon." The jungle war was expensive in resources and, with its long casualty lists from tropical disease as well as battle, a mighty consumer of men. Nor did it seem likely to lead to quick Japanese collapse. When Mountbatten offered two alternative plans for SEAC: an air and seaborne operation against Rangoon christened DRACULA,[1] or an overland advance by Fourteenth Army to be named CAPITAL, the Chiefs of Staff had little difficulty in preferring DRACULA.

The problem, however, was that DRACULA required resources as yet unlikely to be available. Furthermore DRACULA held few attractions for the Americans. It was remote from the prime purpose of helping China and opening the Burma road. It made little use of the recent American and Chinese (and British) successes in taking Myitkina and Mogaung in the north. Furthermore it could not be undertaken before March 1945, when resources might be assembled in the Bay of Bengal. For the British the choice was disagreeable – a protracted campaign, peripheral to final victory over Japan (which all perceived would be attained not in Burma but in the Pacific): or a major effort for swift operational success, which could not possibly be undertaken for many months and which the Americans did not support.

A compromise emerged, in the hope of something of the best of both worlds. On 16th September Mountbatten received new orders from London. They were unambiguous. He was to recapture the whole of Burma, by means both of DRACULA, conceived as a final blow against an enemy whose strength had been bled elsewhere in Burma; and also of CAPITAL – defined by Mountbatten, in his proposals, as an advance across the Chindwin to a general line, Pakokku – Mandalay – Lashio,

[1] DRACULA, as a plan, had many vicissitudes before being finally ordered in attenuated form and as a revised concept.

and to be limited to "the stages . . . necessary to the security of the air route and the attainment of overland communications with China". DRACULA's target date was March 1945. CAPITAL was to be launched as soon as practicable.

The Burma road to China ran from Mandalay.

Whatever the strategic situation as seen in London and Washington, it was unthinkable to those in command in Burma that, at this moment of triumph, pursuit should slacken. In Europe the enemy was being chased towards the Po and the Rhine. In Burma he should be driven to the Irrawaddy. At Myitkina, Mogaung, Kohima and Imphal the Japanese had been beaten in the field. They were likely to have plenty of sting left, as their rearguards fought for time on the approaches to the Chindwin or in the valleys running south from Myitkina, but, for Slim, this was no time to relax the pressure. Despite the appalling conditions of the monsoon, XXXIII Corps was ordered to take up the running after Imphal was relieved and to use the 11th East African Division (now arrived in Fourteenth Army) to push down the Tamu road, the track to the Chindwin at Sittaung and the Kabaw Valley. 5th Division was struggling at the same time along the road to Tiddim against the Japanese 33rd Division, across torrential waterways, by roads and tracks swept away or converted to rivers of mud. The daily rate of advance averaged two miles. The Japanese in retreat were still capable of fierce and effective action. On the British side, for every man who fell to the enemy's fire five were victims of malaria, scrub typhus or other tropical disease. The rain fell without ceasing. It was a dreadful period. Slim, however, was determined that as little time as possible should be wasted at the start of the next season – a campaign which should finally clear Central Burma, and perhaps more. He had been ordered to seize a bridgehead across the Chindwin at Kalewa by mid-December 1944. He intended to better that.

At the end of August, General Kawabe, Commander of Burma Area Army, was replaced by General Kimura – judged by Slim to be the most able of his Japanese opponents. Kimura realised the Imperial Army's limitations: divisions were at very low strength, some only a handful of battalions, and even morale had been terribly affected by the drubbings received at Kohima and Imphal. Kimura assumed that the Allies would press forwards from north and west towards the Irrawaddy Valley, and southwards in Arakan towards the delta. He appreciated as well as any the impossibility of holding a "line" in Burma – and his was four hundred miles long. He decided to withdraw the main part of his forces east of the Irrawaddy, with covering positions west of it; and to draw back his left in Arakan, to concentrate on the defence of the Irrawaddy Delta, with forward positions on the Arakan coast at Ramree Island and Taungup to be held as long as possible.

The heart of Kimura's defence was to be the rail, road and river centre of Mandalay on the Irrawaddy. His positions were to run from the Kachin Hills, north of Lashio, through Mongmit to Mandalay. This sector was the responsibility of Thirty-Third Army, from North Burma (Lieutenant-General Honda), with two divisions. South-west from and including Mandalay, Kimura ordered the depleted Fifteenth Army (Lieutenant-General Katamura had replaced Mutaguchi) with four divisions to hold the Irrawaddy as far as Pakokku, with a strong reserve posted at the vital road and rail junction of Meiktila. On Katamura's left, Lieutenant-General Sakurai's Twenty-Eighth Army, with two divisions and two independent brigades, was responsible for the oil-fields at Yenangyaung and thence west into Arakan, covering the Irrawaddy Delta. All troops were to be in their new positions by 1st December.

Facing Kimura in Central Burma, Slim had four preoccupations. First, he had to push his men forwards, through the monsoon and after, and gain the Chindwin. Second, he had to rest his troops: divisions were withdrawn, flown out for recuperation after some particular objective was reached. Third, he needed to be sure that his next battles could be logistically supported. CAPITAL was a major operation. The enormous engineering effort already applied to roads, railways, waterways, pipelines and airfields in Assam needed also to be extended to and forwards of Imphal. The line of communication would need to support, it was reckoned, 10,500 tons per day by the beginning of 1945;[1] and 6,500 tons per day would be needed on the Arakan Line. Beyond Imphal a force of five divisions employed on CAPITAL would need a monthly total of 75,000 tons. This was the engineering requirement, second to none in the war. It was met.

Fourth, Slim had to decide how, at last, he would advance across the Chindwin and take Burma from the Japanese.

Slim first planned to combine the crossing of the Chindwin at Kalewa with an airborne operation in the area of Yeu and Shwebo. XXXIII Corps would advance from Kalewa with armour and artillery – with as much mechanised punch as Fourteenth Army could deploy, on the

---

[1] This assumed CAPITAL, and the build-up for DRACULA, as well as continued maximum assistance by air and later by road to China.

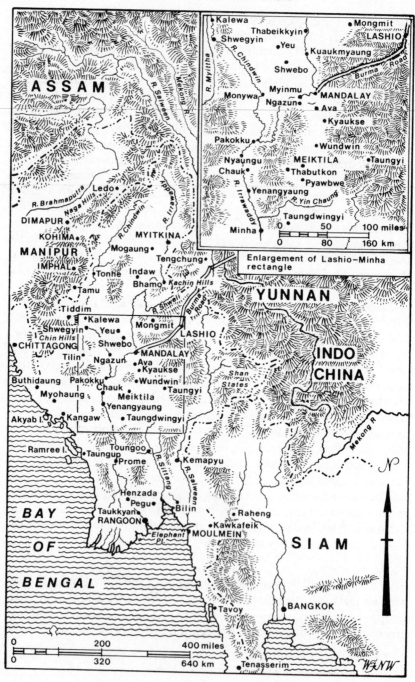

Burma

suitable terrain for mechanised operations between the Chindwin and Irrawaddy Valleys. To this hammer IV Corps was to be the anvil, deployed by air to the area of Shwebo with two divisions flown in to reinforce a parachute assault by 50th Parachute Brigade. Thus Slim hoped to concentrate his army north of Mandalay as a force of irresistible strength, and smash the enemy assumed to be attempting a defence of the Chindwin. Mountbatten's first CAPITAL directive to Giffard mirrored an appreciation by Slim and was based on this concept. The Japanese were to be destroyed between the two great rivers.

One difficulty, however, existed. The airborne operation could not take place before February, when the parachute brigade would be ready. But Slim was meanwhile making progress towards the Chindwin. By mid-November XXXIII Corps were in control of every road and track west of the river and by 2nd December had taken Kalewa and prepared for bridging. By then Slim had made up his mind. He decided on change. He could not wait until February and the airborne operation, suspecting anyway that all aircraft would be needed for supply rather than deployment. He believed that the Japanese beyond the Chindwin were in poor shape and must be given no respite. He ordered IV Corps, which had moved forwards after a brief rest, to cross the river at Sittang and Tonhe and start moving eastwards.

He had further reasons for haste. The Japanese had launched an offensive in China with the result that Chiang Kai-shek had asked for the recall of two Chinese divisions from Northern Combat Area Command. Lieutenant-General Sir Oliver Leese, who had taken over from Giffard as Commander of "Allied Land Forces South East Asia", now told Slim that his operations should, as soon as possible, aim to link up with the forces of NCAC, in the general area of Indaw. Accordingly, 19th Division of IV Corps set out across the Chindwin, with orders to take Pinlebu, forty miles west of Indaw, and exploit towards Wuntho, in the valley through which ran the railway to Mandalay.

Slim reckoned that contact could thus be made with 36th (British) Division (serving under NCAC); IV Corps could then move south, east of the Chindwin and astride the railway valley towards their objective of Shwebo. Accordingly, moving by tracks, without their artillery, since it could not yet be brought up to the Chindwin, delayed rather by terrain and a precipitous escarpment than by the scattered garrisons of the enemy, 19th Division took Pinlebu on 14th December and next day made contact with 36th Division. Northern and Central Fronts were united at last. On 10th December the bridge across the Chindwin at Kalewa was opened to traffic, and 2nd (British) Division took over from

11th East African Division on the east bank of the river. IV Corps could now be assembled in the north for their drive down towards Yeu and Shwebo,[1] while XXXIII Corps thrust east from Kalewa.

Throughout these operations, there had been suspiciously little effective interference from the enemy. Kimura, indeed, was slowly manoeuvring his army east of the Irrawaddy, so that by 1st December only covering forces (although of some strength) remained west of the river. The general import of this now became clear to Slim. His object was the destruction of the enemy's army, and if he continued with his present concept he would beat the air and waste time. With the flexibility of mind of the great commander he realised he must change his plan. He had now to smash the enemy not west but east of the Irrawaddy. He had to trap the Japanese by getting south of Mandalay and across their communications southwards by road, rail and river to Rangoon. On 18th December Slim gave out new orders.

XXXIII Corps (Stopford) was directed to take 19th Division under command, and to concentrate, with 2nd (British) and 20th Divisions, a tank brigade and an independent infantry brigade, in the area of Shwebo. At the same time IV Corps (Messervy), with 7th and 17th Divisions, a tank brigade and an independent East African brigade, was to move south with the greatest possible secrecy by the Myittha Valley from Kalemyo to Tilin, and thence via Sinthe to the Irrawaddy at Pakokku. There a bridgehead was to be gained across the mighty river.

In the second, and decisive phase of the operation Stopford was to seize bridgeheads north and south of Mandalay itself. At the same time Messervy was to debouch from the Pakokku bridgehead and race to Meiktila, fifty miles to the east. The second phase was to be complete by the end of February, and thereafter the two corps would advance southwards towards Rangoon, having, Slim hoped, destroyed the larger part of Kimura's army. This was EXTENDED CAPITAL.

Stopford's XXXIII Corps advanced on a broad front towards the Irrawaddy. On the right 20th Division was, by 14th January, tapping at the Japanese defences of Monywa, place of wretched memory for survivors of BURCORPS. In the centre 2nd Division entered Shwebo on 9th January. On the left 19th Division (Major-General Rees) was already moving south towards Shwebo astride the railway. Seizing what he rightly saw as a chance, Rees managed to cross the river and

---

[1] Command of IV Corps was taken over on 8th December by Lieutenant-General Messervy.

establish two bridgeheads – at Thabeikkyin and Kyaukmyaung – on the night of 11th January. Slim wanted Stopford's operation to be overt, threatening, forcing reactions from Kimura and his army commanders north and south of Mandalay, drawing their strength away from the area of that thrust across the river towards Meiktila for which IV Corps, having taken every possible measure of deception and security, began to advance down the Myittha Valley, far west of the Chindwin, on 15th January. In this concept Fourteenth Army was brilliantly successful. With Kimura believing that Rees's bridgeheads must represent the principal British attack, Honda, commanding Thirty-Third Army, launched a series of savage and unsuccessful counter-attacks against them in the last days of January, thus further depleting his forces.

Slim kept the timing of EXTENDED CAPITAL firmly in his own hands. This was an army battle. He did not wish 20th Division to cross the Irrawaddy and threaten Mandalay from the south – to threaten to pinch the place out between the two convergent thrusts of 20th and 19th Divisions – until, far to the south, IV Corps was ready to cross the river for the drive on Meiktila. The whole operation needed masterly orchestration; and Slim was the master. On the night of 12th February 20th Division crossed the Irrawaddy, established a bridgehead at Myinmu, due west of Mandalay, and was ordered to break out and drive to Kyaukse, cutting the enemy's communications to the south. Japanese reaction was immediate. This, at last, must be the British main thrust. Every reserve to hand was now launched against 20th rather than 19th Division. Meanwhile Rees, in the north, crossed the river with the rest of his division and began to move from his bridgeheads southwards on Mandalay on 22nd February. Mandalay was now desperately threatened from every direction by XXXIII Corps. On 25th February 2nd Division, in the centre, seized a bridgehead at Ngazun, immediately east of 20th Division.

On 14th February IV Corps crossed the 2,000 yard wide Irrawaddy at Nyaungu. The operation was brilliantly conceived and executed by 7th Division (Major-General Evans). Three "dummy" attempts were made at crossing in different places, supported by convincing fire plans and flank protection attacks. By 16th February the bridgehead was 4,000 yards deep. IV Corps had achieved near total surprise. Now the task was to exploit it. Messervy had no intention of losing time. His plan was to drive 17th Division (Major-General Cowan) as fast as possible towards Meiktila with two brigades mounted in transport, supported by a brigade of tanks, using the adequate roads east of the Irrawaddy. No attempt would be made to clear the road, which it was accurately presumed would be cut behind the advance when the Japanese reacted:

clearance would be undertaken by 7th Division, debouching from the bridgehead and following up. 17th Division would be supplied by air, having seized the airfield at Thabutkon, ten miles west of Meiktila. Evans would be reinforced by air – his third brigade was to fly in. The concept was bold, the emphasis on speed and risk wholly admirable.

By 26th February, Thabutkon airfield was in British hands and the fly-in began. On 2nd March, Cowan began his attack on Meiktila, held by three gallant but outnumbered Japanese battalions. Tanks and infantry fought their way through the streets. On 5th March, 17th Division were in control of the town. IV Corps was now standing south of Mandalay between the Irrawaddy and the Karen Hills. Fifteenth and Thirty-Third Japanese Armies were trapped; and within the larger trap the divisions of XXXIII Corps from north and west, fighting through or outflanking the Japanese rearguards, were moving ever nearer Mandalay.

The assault on Mandalay began on 8th March. While 19th Division attacked the city itself, 2nd and 20th Divisions worked their ways eastwards, with 2nd Division taking Ava and Tadau, and 20th Division directed on the road running south from Mandalay through Kyaukse and Wundwin to Meiktila. Mandalay was held by the Japanese 15th Division, and the heart of its defence was in Fort Dufferin, a great square enclosure with walls nearly two miles long on each face, brick walls twenty-three feet high, banked with earth ramps on the inner side and surrounded by a forty-foot moat. Every device of twentieth-century warfare was employed to reduce this noble and archaic structure, with little success. Heavy bombardment from the air did nothing to bring down the walls: and when they were breached by heavy artillery firing at point-blank range the attacking troops, like many of their forefathers, found that it was easier to make a breach than carry it by assault. The attempts went on for ten days, while the rest of the city was cleared in savage street fighting. The remnants of 15th Division managed to slip away to the south-east, including, astonishingly, on the night of 19th March, those members of the garrison of Fort Dufferin who had not been killed during the bombardment. The fort was eventually surrendered on 20th March by some Burmese who explained that all the Japanese had left. The British were, for a little, again masters of Mandalay.

At Meiktila, however, the struggle was far from over. Kimura had been as mystified as Slim intended over the direction of the British main thrust. The Japanese now, with justice, regarded the battle for Meiktila as the decisive issue of the rest of the campaign. With Meiktila and its road system in British hands they could have no options left but a retreat, whether slow or rapid, by the same invasion route they had trod three years before. Towards Meiktila Kimura hurried anything that could be spared from south or north.

It was not much. But in the north the Japanese had been helped by a fortunate circumstance. Chiang Kai-shek had decided to withdraw his Chinese divisions once Northern Combat Area Command (now under the American Lieutenant-General Sultan, who had replaced Stilwell) reached the Burma road. In consequence the Japanese Thirty-Third Army was relieved of some pressure – the only effort against it being by the British 36th Division,[1] marching south between the Irrawaddy and the Kachin Hills, crossing the Shweli River after a hard fight, and entering Mongmit on 7th March, two days after the fall of Meiktila. As a result Kimura was able to draw on Thirty-Third Army for the crucial battle at Meiktila, and on 14th March ordered Honda to make his way to Kalaw, east of Meiktila. Honda was to take under command his own 18th Division, already in the area having moved from the north and managed to bypass Mandalay, as well as 49th Division which had been brought up from the south. His orders were simple: to destroy the British defenders of Meiktila. At the same time a task force under Major-General Yamamoto attacked northwards on both banks of the Irrawaddy towards the IV Corps crossing places at Nyaungu.

The Japanese counter-attacks at Meiktila were first concentrated on the airfields. 17th Division had been reinforced by a brigade from 5th Division, the only reserve division, which Slim had now allotted to Messervy. The brigade had been brought in by air. All supply was by air. The airfield, so vital to the defence, was attacked and counter-attacked. For a short while from 18th March it was dominated by the Japanese and all supplies were air-dropped, while the reinforcing 5th Division brigade fought off attack after attack at point-blank range. But the airfield was not the only enemy objective. The Japanese attacked with all the strength they could muster, from all directions.

Cowan's way, in response, was to conduct an aggressive offensive-defensive. Leaving the minimum troops in position, he conducted a series of brilliant sweeps and spoiling attacks against the Japanese communications and bases. He never resigned the initiative. He knew that he only had to win a little time for the road from the Irrawaddy behind him to be cleared and the full weight of IV Corps to come to his support. To the north 20th Division of XXXIII Corps was now not far off at Wundwin. On 30th March a column of 17th Division made contact with 20th. On 31st March, 5th Division, from the IV Corps

---

[1] 36th Division was brought to the Mandalay area on 30th March.

bridgehead, came in from the west. On 1st April the airfield was reopened. Three days earlier Honda, his two divisions having suffered heavy losses, had received permission to break off the struggle. The Battle of Meiktila was over. The Japanese "Burma Area Army", remarked the British historian of the war, "had virtually ceased to exist as a fighting force".[1]

While these stirring events had been taking place in the valley of the Irrawaddy there had also been action in Arakan. Before the start of CAPITAL, XV Corps (Lieutenant-General Christison) was taken under direct command of Allied Land Forces Headquarters (Lieutenant-General Sir Oliver Leese) since its operations had, at least initially, no direct interaction with those of the rest of Fourteenth Army. Christison was ordered to undertake an offensive – Operation ROMULUS – in December 1944, to clear Northern Arakan of Japanese, to take Akyab (and, later, Ramree Island by amphibious assault) and thus provide air bases well to the south for the final attacks towards Rangoon. The removal of the Japanese threat in Arakan would liberate two divisions – Christison still commanded two Indian and two West African divisions – for operations elsewhere, notably for DRACULA.

ROMULUS was founded on the premise that the Japanese Twenty-Eighth Army would aim to hold their positions in Arakan, including Akyab, whereas they had, in fact, been directed only to impose delay while the main body withdrew to the Irrawaddy Delta. When ROMULUS began, therefore, both sides were more than ordinarily confused about their opponents' intentions. Akyab was taken peacefully by 25th Indian Division on 4th January, having already been evacuated. Astride the Mayu River north of Foul Point, on the other hand, fighting was hard, since the Japanese detachment there only received permission to withdraw on 26th December.

In the Kaladan Valley, east of the Mayu, another strong Japanese force opposed 81st West African Division in front of Myohaung. It appeared to Christison that this detachment might be cut off and destroyed with a shallow flanking movement by 82nd West African Division and with a deeper attempt at envelopment by 25th Division, advancing eastwards to Kangaw from Akyab. This was to be an amphibious movement. The Arakan coast is a network of river, creek and swamp and operations were dependent upon craft able to negotiate them.

[1] S. Woodman Kirby, *The War Against Japan*, HMSO, 1958.

The attempt failed. When the assault troops of 25th Division approached Kangaw on 22nd January, with a considerable convoy of craft, they occupied their first objective – some high ground dominating the beaches and the road running down the coast. Thereafter there was bitter fighting as the Japanese counter-attacked in strength. 25th Division were only secure at Kangaw by 8th February after a hard struggle during which the Japanese detachment withdrawing from Myohaung had moved south and east. Meanwhile Ramree Island was taken, after some more savage and courageous fighting by the small Japanese detachment left there to impose delay. Although a divisional assault took place on 21st January under heavy naval and air bombardment, a Japanese force of some five hundred were able to maintain themselves and inflict casualties until 17th February.

The fierce reaction to the British advance on Kangaw was not, or not primarily, an attempt at escape from Myohaung. The Japanese were sure that the main British object of operations in Arakan would be to break through, to move across the Arakan Yomas to the Irrawaddy Valley; there were two possible routes, the northernmost of which ran down the coast and through Kangaw. It was no part of the original British plan to move east as feared, and the fighting at Kangaw thus arose from misunderstanding rather than design. The British priority was to seize the airfields at Akyab and Ramree; and since the Japanese did not intend to hold them, this, too, was a case of mismatch between the plans of the two sides!

Thenceforth, however, the aims of the opposing forces came more directly into collision. Leese thought that after taking Ramree XV Corps might be able to move east by the southern of the two routes to the Irrawaddy Valley – from Taungup to Prome – as well as probing eastwards by the northern route which had already aroused so spirited a reaction at Kangaw. At the same time Slim told Christison that the best service his corps could render Fourteenth Army would be to stop any Japanese movement reinforcing their troops in the Irrawaddy Valley. Neither aim was achieved. Because of the claims of other operations Christison received no air supply after 7th March. The Japanese were thereafter able to hold Christison's limited attempts to advance. The terrain was admirably adapted to defence. Twenty-Eighth Army had little difficulty, therefore, in withdrawing troops to join their main body in the Irrawaddy Valley. But XV Corps could not follow. Though the Arakan campaign of 1945 enabled DRACULA to be mounted, it did not greatly affect the dispositions or plans of the Japanese. It did, however, secure forward airfields of great importance for the final act; the triumphant advance of Fourteenth Army to

Rangoon. Akyab, stocked by huge efforts during the preceding two months, came into operation on 20th March, and Ramree on 15th April. Without these the army could have slowed to a walk. Slim's men were now 500 miles from their railhead at Dimapur. Every device had been planned and used to support Fourteenth Army. Huge tonnages of timber had been felled and made into boats for river supply. Work on the roads forward of Imphal was ceaseless. But without air supply even a beaten enemy could not have been effectively pursued.

"Pursuit," said traditional Prussian doctrine, "should be to the last breath of man and beast." Slim might have added that it should be completed before the monsoon. There was also the question of DRACULA. This had originally been intended as the *coup de grâce*, the seizure of Rangoon in face of an enemy whose main strength had been weakened or destroyed in Central Burma. Now Slim fancied Fourteenth Army might itself reach Rangoon – overland. DRACULA was ordered to take place in early May – an airborne and amphibious operation by 26th Division and 50th Parachute Brigade – but it was conceived as administrative insurance. Fourteenth Army looked likely to take Rangoon – but perhaps later than hoped, and perhaps beyond the limits of supply until Rangoon was opened as a port. DRACULA would, at least, expedite this. After the Battle of Meiktila Slim set his two corps on the road south without delay – XXXIII Corps on the army's right, by the Irrawaddy Valley, by Prome and Henzada; IV Corps on the left, by the railway route, the Sittang Valley, through Toungoo and Pegu. These, too, were names with bitter memories for survivors of BURCORPS. The most durable as well as most resolute survivor was Slim.

The great advance to Rangoon began on 1st April. Kimura's Armies were in no condition to do other than delay and demolish and they did both with skill and courage. Japanese columns would be seen on the march, bombarded or shelled, and then observed continuing at half strength and in good order. Garrisons would be surrounded, few if any prisoners taken and the count of dead equate to the estimate of total enemy strength. Nevertheless the Japanese had been so reduced by the battles of Central Burma that their fighting capacity was completely inadequate to put up a sustained resistance.

Kimura ordered Thirty-Third Army to withdraw down the Sittang Valley through covering positions established by Fifteenth Army and to hold Toungoo – whose airfield was, as it happened, crucial to the DRACULA plan and a major objective for IV Corps (Messervy). Yet

Thirty-Third Army had a total strength of less than one division and was opposing a strong and mobile British corps of three divisions, with complete command of the air. Kimura ordered Twenty-Eighth Army to hold the Irrawaddy Valley, and to extricate all troops in Arakan – yet XXXIII Corps (Stopford) was already moving towards the points where the routes from Arakan ran across the Arakan Yomas to the Irrawaddy. The corps, with 7th and 20th Divisions, took Yenangyaung and its oil installations on 20th April. The limiting factor on Stopford's advance was logistic – his air supply was so reduced in order to concentrate on one main army thrust that when he took Prome (evacuated by the Japanese) on 3rd May only one brigade could be pushed forwards towards Rangoon.

On Fourteenth Army's left, Messervy's IV Corps, with 5th, 17th and 19th Divisions, had a hard fight at Pyawbwe, twenty miles south of Meiktila. Over 1,000 Japanese dead were found when the place fell. By 19th April, it was clear that Thirty-Third Army was no longer a coherent body of troops. Toungoo Airfield was taken on 22nd April. On 29th April, 17th Division attacked Pegu – the last major position before Rangoon, and itself on the escape route from Rangoon to the east. By 1st May, Pegu was clear of the Japanese task force defending it, and IV Corps began bridging the Pegu River: fifty miles to go to Rangoon.

On 2nd May, the monsoon broke, and Fourteenth Army's long advance from Imphal was over. That day Operation DRACULA took place. One parachute battalion emplaned at Akyab and dropped at Elephant Point, twenty miles south of Rangoon, without opposition. The assault troops of 26th Division transferred to landing craft thirty miles offshore in the early hours of the morning. A great air bombardment prepared the way. The first assault waves, reaching shore at 7 a.m., were unopposed. The Japanese had gone. Rangoon was occupied on 4th May. There were skirmishes to come and there were plans to be made for operations which would never be carried out; but in terms of major operations for the British Army, the war against Japan was over.

Fourteenth Army and all who fought in Burma had some reason for their sense of being forgotten. The war against Germany had overwhelming priority, whereas the war against Japan, as far as the British were concerned, had largely to be judged in terms of how few British resources it might need and yet be kept going. After the first alarms of 1942, once it was clear that the Japanese strategic offensive had spent its force and that India was not threatened, the war in South-East Asia did not preoccupy the British Government or Chiefs-of-Staff until 1944.

There was a second reason, contained within the first. The United States with her effort in the Pacific theatre was pre-eminent. The British – and the British Army's – role, a campaign in Burma, seemed to many, including many who took part, as peripheral to the defeat of Japan: laborious, expensive and unrewarding. Such a mood can be fatal to morale, and to overcome it and win reflects particular glory and requires leadership of transcendent quality. It is against this background that the achievement of the army should be seen. It was, very largely, an achievement of the Indian Army, under British command, but most Indian divisions contained British formations or units, and the British Army was involved from first to last. The first days, as elsewhere, were dreadful. Humiliating defeat led to painful withdrawal. The final days redeemed all. In Burma the Japanese Imperial Army suffered its greatest defeat in any land campaign.

The final campaign in Burma, following the heroic Battles of Imphal and Kohima, was a classic combination of operational brilliance with logistic skill. Like other campaigns, but most of all in South-East Asia, success was only attained because air superiority had been won, and air effort, on a huge scale, was available both for support and for supply. It is true to say that the campaign was not outshone by the British in the Second World War. The soldiers who made it possible fought and suffered in some of the most difficult terrain on earth. Their trials were painful, their discipline admirable. No army had a lower incidence of misbehaviour or inadequacy. They faced an enemy who hardly understood the term "surrender", whose fanatic courage made of every Japanese soldier a platoon and every company post a fortress. Against such foes victory was earned indeed.

17

"Forward on Wings of Flame"

In North-West Europe, by the end of September 1944, the Allied advance had reached the Vosges, the Moselle and, in the extreme north, the Rhine. In the far south of Eisenhower's command General Devers's 6th Army Group, consisting of Seventh (US) and First French Armies, had landed on the Mediterranean coast of France, marched up the valley of the Rhone, and now faced east on the historic military routes between France and Germany via Belfort. In the centre, Third (US) Army of Bradley's 12th Army Group had crossed the Moselle, and taken Nancy and Luneville; while on their left First (US) Army, had liberated Luxembourg, passed through the Ardennes, crossed the "Maastricht Appendix", and was investing Aachen.

In the north the British Second Army of Montgomery's 21st Army Group occupied a narrow salient reaching across the Waal, with German forces not only to the east, between Rhine and Meuse, but on their left flank in Western Holland from the Zuider Zee southwards to both banks of the Scheldt. For in 21st Army Group area there was also a German bridgehead south of the Scheldt, on the line of the Leopold Canal, running east from Zeebrugge and covering the port of Breskens and ferry sites to Walcheren and South Beveland. By this route considerable German forces had escaped from the debacle of the Battle of France. Between 5th and 22nd September 82,000 men, 530 guns, 4,600 vehicles and 4,000 horses crossed. This was no mean increment to the German forces in Holland on Second Army's western flank. And while the Germans still held positions on the banks of the Scheldt the use of the great port of Antwerp was denied to the Allies. Delay in this quarter carried a heavy penalty.

Otherwise, and with the exception of Zeebrugge at the west end of the German bridgehead and of Dunkirk where a German garrison held out, the Channel ports were clear of the enemy. They had been taken in succession, in each case with few casualties and after formidable bombing attacks which had inevitably caused much destruction, thereby delaying the reopening of the port after capture. Le Havre fell to I (British) Corps, attacked by 49th and 51st Divisions, on 12th

377

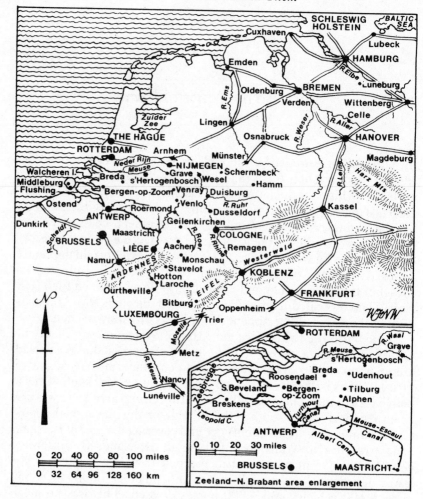

North-West Europe

September. On 22nd September, Boulogne was taken by II (Canadian) Corps, and on 30th Calais surrendered. Ostend was in Allied hands by the end of the month. These operations were carried out under orders of Crerar's First Canadian Army. But until the ports were usable – and Antwerp was most important of all – the Allied logistic chain ran back from all points on the great arc of the front, from North Holland, from the Moselle, from Alsace, to Cherbourg at the north-west tip of the Continent or to the beaches of Normandy. When Montgomery, there-

378

fore, issued new orders after the failure of MARKET GARDEN, he accepted the need for step by step operations; and the first step, tardily recognised by the High Command, must be the clearance of Antwerp and the Scheldt. The opportunity for a great strategic victory, for full exploitation of the destruction of the German Army in Normandy, had been fleeting and had passed. It may have already passed when MARKET GARDEN itself was launched. "By the end of *the first week in September*" – General Zimmermann (Chief Operations Officer, Army Group D) has written – "the Western Front was comparatively calm."[1]

Montgomery now ordered First Canadian Army to complete operations on the Scheldt, and to push north thereafter on the axis Tilburg – S'Hertogenbosch, on Second Army's left. Second Army was to "tap" eastwards against the North-Western Ruhr, that part of the great industrial complex which lay west of the Rhine. Meanwhile the Germans performed remarkable feats of organisation in the time unexpectedly given to them. They recovered their breath. The experienced Commanders and Staffs of the Wehrmacht formed and, at least in a rudimentary way, trained new formations of the young, the old and the sick. Rundstedt, to the relief of every German soldier, was once more recalled to assume the command in the West. By October, there was again something of a front, and weakly held though it was, it sufficed to check the enormous Allied Armies, suffering from logistic problems, "overstretched" and recovering from a sharp attack of euphoria. It promised to be a bleak winter.

Although the Scheldt was cleared by First Canadian Army, British troops also took part; 49th and 52nd (Lowland) Division were fighting as part of Canadian Corps in the Canadian Army, as was the whole I (British) Corps. The fighting took place in particularly disagreeable circumstances – among the marshes and flooded lowlands of South Beveland and Walcheren and the country hemmed by the Leopold Canal south of the river. North of the river South Beveland was free of Germans by the end of October. The south bank, the bridgehead covering Breskens, was cleared after a bitter struggle. That left the island of Walcheren, connected to South Beveland by a 1,200 yard straight causeway and occupied, with the port of Flushing, by a large German garrison. Virtually the whole island was flooded by bomber attacks on the dykes except for the towns of Middleburg and Flushing. A series of amphibious assaults from south and west were mounted, as well as a succession of desperate attempts on the causeway. Ultimately

[1] Author's italics. Zimmermann, *The Fatal Decisions*, Michael Joseph, 1956.

Walcheren's last strongpoint surrendered. The island was in Allied hands by 8th November. Antwerp could at last be brought into use.

On the right wing of First Canadian Army was I (British) Corps, and while their comrades to the west struggled across the floods, canals and dykes of the Scheldt Estuary and the adjoining lands, I Corps pushed up to and across the Turnhout Canal, east of Antwerp. I Corps was thus advancing towards Alphen and Tilburg, on the left of the Second Army salient. In Western Holland, south of the Meuse, seven German infantry divisions of Fifteenth Army still faced First Canadian Army, covering Tilburg and S'Hertogenbosch and also fronting eastwards towards Second Army (Dempsey) at Grave and Veghel. In the autumn of 1944 Dempsey had, therefore, the task of attacking both east and west – east towards the Ruhr and west towards the Waal Estuary in conjunction with the Canadians. He also had to hold off a number of unsuccessful counter-attacks against the British bridgehead on the island, the country between Nijmegen and Arnhem.

On the eastern flank Dempsey deployed VIII Corps and attacked towards Venlo with 11th Armoured and 3rd Divisions on 12th October, capturing Venray: but there was no further progress. In the north, XXX Corps was on the "island", with XII Corps on the western flank. On 22nd October XII Corps attacked westwards, with its right on the Meuse. Deploying 7th Armoured, 15th, 51st and 53rd Divisions, supported by two independent armoured and one tank brigade, XII Corps took S' Hertogenbosch, Udenhout and Tilburg by 27th October. By the end of the month, the Germans had been driven back to two small bridgeheads south of the Meuse, as the Canadians pushed northwards on Second Army's left, taking Breda, Roosendael and Bergen-op-Zoom. By 8th November, 21st Army Group had closed up to the Meuse almost throughout its length west of Grave: First Canadian and Second British Armies stood shoulder to shoulder once again. This tidying of the front, although necessary in order to produce a secure base for further operations eastwards, was something of an anti-climax. There was a sense of going in the wrong direction.

But the greatest change of mood was produced by fresh perceptions of the enemy. In August and at the beginning of September the German Army had seemed beaten and in full flight. In October, November and December it appeared to be fighting as skilfully as ever. The resistance of Fifteenth Army to Allied advances in Western Holland, and some spirited attacks from the German bridgehead west of the Meuse in the Venlo area, showed that there were, once again, no chances to be taken with the Wehrmacht. And some of the Panzer and

Panzer Grenadier divisions were receiving new equipment and becoming more formidable. Montgomery's operations for the rest of the year were designed to clear the enemy from the west bank of the Meuse, and – further south – its tributary, the Roer, which joins the Meuse at Roermond. For these operations 21st Army Group changed its dispositions. First Canadian Army took over the northern flank, including Nijmegen and the "island". Second Army was deployed facing east, its left near Grave, facing the Reichswald Forest into which new German divisions were known to have moved, its right wing next to the sector held by the Ninth (US) Army of Bradley's 12th Army Group, opposite Geilenkirchen and in the Dutch province of Limburg, the "Maastricht Appendix".

In mid-November VIII and XII Corps, in the north of Second Army's front, pushed forwards. The ground was sodden, every built-up area, canal line or embankment mined and converted into an obstacle. By 3rd December, the army was on the Meuse. Further south XXX Corps attacked, in conjunction with the Americans, and took Geilenkirchen. Except for a bridgehead west of the river around Heinsberg the army was also on the Roer. Twenty miles to the east ran the Rhine. In the far north, in the Canadian sector, the "island" was flooded by German destruction of the Arnhem-Nijmegen Dyke, and the two British divisions – 49th and 51st – fighting as part of the Canadian Army were withdrawn to a contracted Nijmegen bridgehead. Montgomery continued to plan with his usual thoroughness but found the going slow and laborious. It was, as he saw it, the inevitable consequence of not concentrating effort earlier, when the German Army was incapable of stopping any determined advance. Whether that was the cause, or overall logistic constraints, or lack of energy at the crucial moment in early September, it was now a depressing business and Montgomery thought – and said – that it boded ill for future operations. If the Allies could so falter when the ball had been at their feet, what assurance could there be that they would not show equal vacillation and suffer comparable setback at the great business of crossing the Rhine, surrounding the Ruhr and conquering Germany itself? In the British Army, too, there was uncertainty about what was meant to be happening, when, and for what long-term purpose? Eisenhower, however, by no means shared Montgomery's dissatisfaction. He thought it inevitable that there should be a pause while the Allies closed up to the Rhine and recovered their logistic balance. Unlike Montgomery, he had never believed that the war might have been won in the autumn. Montgomery, too, reiterated his view with increasing force that all forces north of the Ardennes should be under one command and that the only Allied main effort should be to encircle the Ruhr. Eisenhower, on the other hand, believed that a thrust north and south of the Ruhr would be complemented and not diminished by an advance – strong, albeit less strong – on the axis Frankfurt-Kassel once the Rhine was crossed. The Rhine, however, was not yet crossed, and on 13th December Montgomery issued his first orders for the battle which was to clear the enemy from the west bank: Operation VERITABLE, which he hoped to begin on 12th January.

As part of a complex pattern of regrouping and movement in preparation for VERITABLE, divisions of Second Army relieved each other in what was by now once again a line, with little but artillery and patrol activity. The fortunate were moved into Belgium for a Christmas break. Two divisions – 50th (at this time) and 59th (earlier) – were removed from the order of battle for manpower reasons. Reorganisation for a longer haul was the mood of the season. Meanwhile the Germans were known to have assembled again an armoured reserve – Sixth SS Panzer Army – presumably to help deal with the massive Allied onslaught to and across the Rhine which they must expect in the New Year.

Strong and sometimes bitter argument about future operations occupied the first weeks of December. Montgomery's views were known to and increasingly shared by the British Chiefs-of-Staff. The British Government was uneasy. Eisenhower was asked to London for consultation. The debate was interrupted on 17th by extraordinary news. The impossible had happened, the ghost was suddenly far from laid. Three German Armies, with twenty divisions including, with reserves, twelve Panzer divisions, were marching westwards through the Ardennes.

The German Ardennes offensive of December 1944, the last German offensive of the Second World War, was Hitler's brainchild. He laid down tactical details for the objectives of the armies to be employed, and brushed aside any suggestion that ends were disproportionate to means. The actual conduct of operations was competently executed under Rundstedt's remote and disapproving supervision: in the professional view of the German General Staff the attempt could never have the strength to succeed, whatever tactical gains might be won in the short term. Fuel was extremely short; air cover was minimal. There was no faith in the concept, and its disappointing progress was not unexpected. The offensive finally exhausted German strength, painfully recovered to some degree after the near-collapse of the summer.

382

It dissipated armoured reserves which might have made the Allies' subsequent advance to and across the Rhine far bloodier. Above all it drew forces which could otherwise have reinforced the Eastern Front. It certainly made Eisenhower's next task easier, and probably advanced the date of Allied victory. But when the blow fell these advantages were less apparent to the Allies than the dangers of the present situation. For the German attack fell on part of the front held thinly by only four American divisions, and soon achieved alarming local success.

Although the Battle of the Ardennes was almost entirely an American struggle – and certainly, in the end, an American victory – it greatly marked the winter for all the Allies, and it delayed the start of VERITABLE. It has its place, therefore, in the British Army's concluding chapter of the German war. British dispositions were altered to deal with it should matters get worse and the Germans reach the Meuse: they never did. British divisions took part in the ultimate counter-attacks which broke up and forced the withdrawal of the remnants of Army Group B. They succeeded.

The Battle of the Ardennes started on 16th December. Army Group B (Field Marshal Model) advanced with two Panzer Armies – Fifth and Sixth SS – with Seventh Army moving westwards on the left, protecting the Army Group's southern flank. On the main front Sixth SS Panzer Army (General Dietrich) was directed on the Meuse at Liège and thereafter on Antwerp. On Dietrich's left Fifth Panzer Army (General von Manteuffel) was to cross the Meuse around Namur and move on Brussels. The first encounters, therefore, were between four American divisions and the full strength of Fifth and Sixth Panzer Armies, amounting to some sixteen divisions, on a frontage of fifty miles between Monschau and Bitburg. The attack was intended to split the Allied front. Preliminary moves had all been made in darkness. German security over plans had been very strict. Bad weather inhibited Allied flying. In consequence complete surprise was achieved, and at first it appeared that, once again and incredibly, the German *schwerpunkt* might become another classic deep penetration. Units holding the front were overrun or sent flying in confusion. It was like a nightmare from which the Allies hoped somewhat desperately to awake.

The awakening came rapidly and was largely brought by the valiant fighting of American soldiers, often cut off and in some places disorganised, but managing to hold key points sufficiently long to enable the High Command to recover its balance. Early German tactical successes could not be or were not exploited. Rundstedt had instructed that the Meuse should be reached on the first day. In fact on 20th December – the fifth day of battle – Sixth SS Panzer Army

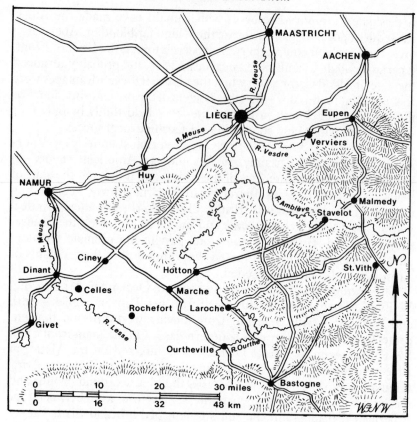

The Ardennes

reached Stavelot, still over twenty miles from the river, and made little progress thereafter. On the same day Fifth Panzer Army, on the centre of the front, reached the Ourthe River at Hotton, Laroche and Ourtheville but had not taken the important road junction of St. Vith (which was captured on the night of 21st) nor Bastogne (which was never captured). A further advance on Fifth Panzer Army Front brought 2nd Panzer Division to Celles on 23rd, and Panzer Lehr Division to Rochefort. The Meuse still lay five miles ahead. The weather improved on the same day and the Allied air forces began to take their toll. On 26th December, General Patton's Third (US) Army, advancing from the south, relieved Bastogne and made contact with the heroic defenders of 101st (US) Airborne Division. The German offensive was over. It was, exactly, a nine-day wonder.

There had been some disagreeable moments. Fifth Panzer Army's advance drove a wedge deep into Bradley's 12th Army Group area. Thereafter all American troops north of the German penetration were placed under Montgomery's command – in effect the American First Army (General Hodges) and Ninth Army (Lieutenant-General Simpson). Montgomery ordered the British Second Army to send XXX Corps – four divisions and four independent armoured brigades strong – to deploy behind the Meuse and to place strong detachments at the Meuse Bridges between Liège and Givet. 29th Armoured Brigade accordingly took station on the Meuse. Guards Armoured, 43rd, 51st and 53rd Divisions deployed from Maastricht to Givet. Montgomery told Brooke that he hoped and thought he would not have to use them to "sort out", as he put it, the Ardennes. Montgomery's contribution to the battle was, in the words of General von Manteuffel, commanding Fifth Panzer Army, "that he turned a series of isolated actions into a coherent battle fought according to a clear and definite plan".[1] He was perfectly confident that should the Germans reach the Meuse they would meet an even greater disaster. As usual his confidence was infectious. It was soon a question of the timing and direction of the counter-stroke.

Bradley's counter-attack from the south began on 30th December, fourteen days after Model's operation had started. Montgomery attacked from north and north-west four days later: on 3rd January, XXX Corps attacked as part of First (US) Army, eastwards near the tip of the German salient. 6th Airborne Division, brought from reserve in England, and 53rd Division, supported by three armoured or tank brigades reached Marche. On 11th January, 51st Division, having relieved 53rd, took Laroche. On 13th, the British made contact with Bradley's American divisions attacking from the south. Further to the east the Americans recaptured St. Vith on 23rd January. The Battle of the Ardennes was over. On 18th January, Montgomery signalled to Brooke his revised target date for the offensive which was to take 21st Army Group through the Reichswald Forest and up to the Rhine, and clear the enemy from the country between Rhine and Meuse. Operation VERITABLE: 8th February 1945.

The German defensive "Westwall Line" – the "Siegfried Line" – ran from the Swiss border up the east bank of the Rhine, then west of the river and through the Saar to Trier and thence to Aachen through the

---

[1] Jacobsen & Rohwer, *Decisive Battles of World War II*, André Deutsch, 1965. Almost the same words are used in Chester Wilmot, *Struggle for Europe*, Collins, 1965.

Eifel and Eastern Ardennes. Thereafter it extended north to the Waal, a few miles east of Nijmegen. Further south the "Westwall" in some cases had, and in others was intended to have, permanent and formidable fortifications, although these were largely neglected until September 1944. The northern extension had only a trench system; but the terrain, in winter, lent itself to defence. Near the great rivers there was considerable flooding, and movement off roads was generally impossible. Woods and forests covered much of the front, intersected by narrow rides, themselves quickly mud-bound. Roads were narrow and their surface nowhere resistant to the passage of a modern army with its mighty mass of tracked vehicles. The natural grimness of the country was underscored by the laying of large-scale minefields. Villages and small towns were prepared for defence, and their reduction to rubble by air attack did not lessen their defensibility. In the towns few civilians remained. In the north of this northern sector the most formidable barrier was the Reichswald Forest, four miles deep, through which ran the "Westwall" and through which must come any southward attack to clear the country between Rhine and Meuse.

Holding the northern part of the "Westwall" against which VERITABLE was to be launched, was the German First Parachute Army (General Schlemm), part of Army Group H (General Blaskowitz). Schlemm had five divisions, of differing quality; and some thirty-six self-propelled anti-tank guns in the area of the Reichswald. One Panzer and one Panzer Grenadier division were in army group reserve.

Montgomery planned two convergent operations. The United States Ninth Army (Simpson), placed for the time being under his command, was to attack north-east to the Rhine from the Roer. This was operation GRENADE, across low-lying, saturated fields and through sad, shattered towns. Two days earlier First Canadian Army (Crerar) was to attack south-east to the Rhine from the area immediately south of Nijmegen. This was VERITABLE. There had been an essential preliminary. While the Battle of the Ardennes was reaching its closing stages, during the counter-attacks which finally drove the Germans back behind their starting-line, Second Army had conducted a small and separate offensive. The Germans still held a shallow bridgehead west of the Roer River, south of Roermond. As a preliminary to GRENADE and VERITABLE, Montgomery ordered Dempsey to attack and eliminate this bridgehead – Operation BLACKCOCK, carried out by XII Corps with 7th Armoured and 52nd Divisions. They attacked in the familiar, sodden winter conditions on 16th January. Operations went slowly but by 26th January had achieved success. The Germans had been driven east of the Roer. Soon afterwards they destroyed the discharge valves on the Roer Dams and flooded the river, causing delay in launching GRENADE.

For VERITABLE First Canadian Army was given XXX (British) Corps (Horrocks) to carry out the first phase – the breaching of the "Westwall" and clearance of the Reichswald. Thereafter II Canadian Corps (including 49th British Division) was to come up level or pass through as the battle required. British and Canadian divisions were allocated to corps as the situation demanded and without distinction. XXX Corps had for the initial battle 15th, 51st and 53rd British Divisions, together with 2nd and 3rd Canadian Divisions, and in reserve Guards Armoured and 43rd Divisions. Eight British divisions took part in VERITABLE. Supporting each infantry division was an armoured or tank brigade. To reach the ultimate objective, the Geldern – Xanten area, would, with GRENADE, squeeze the enemy from the west bank of the Rhine. It was not a distant objective; nor was it extensive. It involved, however, the breaching of a position recognised by the enemy as the final defence of the Reich in front of the Rhine itself. It also involved fighting through country and in conditions as difficult and demanding as any yet encountered by 21st Army Group.

VERITABLE began with the most intense artillery programme yet fired by the British Army in the Second World War. Over 1,000 guns took part. Thereafter the attacking divisions moved forward at 10.30 a.m. on 8th February on a seven-mile front. The defenders were largely stunned by the artillery bombardment, and the first objectives were in most cases taken without great difficulty. On the right, 51st Division gained a lodgement in the southern corner of the Reichswald by midnight. In the centre, 53rd Division breached the "Westwall" during the night. On the left, 15th Division cleared the villages of Kranenburg and Frasselt, and started to attack the main position in the early hours of 9th February. On the extreme left, the Canadians cleared the enemy from the flooded lands between Reichswald and Rhine. German losses were severe and Schlemm brought up his only reserve, 7th Parachute Division, from his left near Geldern to the area of Cleve where there seemed most danger of an Allied breakthrough.

The breakthrough did not quickly come. Those familiar and related impediments to advance, mud and traffic chaos, intervened. Behind the front a large number of vehicles of different divisions were trying simultaneously to use very few roads. To exacerbate the matter, Horrocks received a misleading report about the situation near Cleve. He thought 15th Division had gained ground which would make

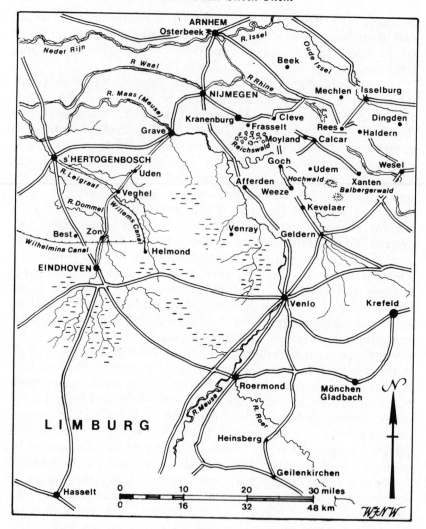

From Meuse to Rhine

it possible to get round and isolate the place: and he ordered up 43rd Division to "pass through" 15th, and drive forward, south of Cleve, to Goch and Udem. This had the unfortunate effect of superimposing one division upon another along one road, much of it under several feet of flood water. 43rd Division, so far from driving south on Goch, was soon enmeshed in fierce fighting in the ruins of Cleve. And in the rear the congestion became ever more appalling. Meanwhile the only German armoured reserve, XLVII Panzer Corps (General von Luttwitz) with two divisions, was hurried north towards the Reichswald Front.

Bitter fighting and the weight of Allied artillery prevailed. By 11th February, 15th and 43rd Division had managed to push east and south through Cleve and the place was ultimately cleared next day. But it took a further week to push forwards the next five miles, although the "Westwall" was formally "breached". The Germans improvised a switch line, from the Cleve forest to Moyland, and attempted to counter-attack northwards towards Cleve, without success. In the Reichswald itself these counter-attacks met head-on the advancing 53rd Division, in the centre of XXX Corps, with considerable losses to both sides. Ultimately the Reichswald was cleared after fierce battles in appalling conditions, where progress was measured by the rate a laden infantryman could move through deep mud and under fire. Three miles south of the southern tip of the Reichswald was the town and vital road junction of Goch. Crerar had now brought II Canadian Corps in on the left of the front, to push down the Calcar-Xanten axis, while XXX Corps was to drive for Goch, Weeze and Kevelaer.

Goch was well prepared for defence, garrisoned by 15th Panzer Grenadier Division, surrounded by anti-tank ditches and strongpoints. Horrocks used four divisions – 15th, 43rd, 51st and 53rd – and moved round the east, cutting the Goch-Calcar road and securing the high ground on that flank on 17th February. 15th Division fought their way into the town on 18th, and together with brigades of 51st and 53rd Divisions cleared it by 21st. At the same time, on the right, 52nd Division struggled down the eastern bank of the Meuse through Afferden; and the Canadians, on the left flank, after desperate fighting and heavy losses, took Moyland on 22nd February and attacked the enemy deployed on the Goch-Calcar road. Thus far, First Canadian Army had lost more than 6,000 men, over 4,500 of them British. But 11,000 prisoners had been taken and German casualties were known to be high.

The next phase was to be an attack on the high ground south of Calcar by II Canadian Corps, including 11th Armoured and 43rd British Divisions. XXX Corps, with Guards Armoured, 3rd, 15th, 51st, 52nd and 53rd British Divisions, was to attack on the Canadians' right, southwards along the Meuse, and eastwards in a convergent attack with II Canadian Corps. On 23rd February GRENADE could at last begin – the American Ninth Army attack from the south, north-eastwards to the Rhine between Dusseldorf and Wesel. The British and Canadians were now attacking the Germans' final position west of the Rhine, the Hochwald and Balbergerwald and the wooded hills to the south and west; named by the Germans the "Schlieffen position". In the last days of February XXX Corps fought their way southwards towards the advancing Americans: contact between the two armies was made on 3rd March. At the same time Horrocks swung two divisions north-eastwards towards Wesel. Every wood, village and farmstead was defended with energy in this last line screening the Rhine. General Schlemm shepherded his depleted forces back to the river with skill. There was no breakthrough. Every withdrawal was made in good order. German rearguards inflicted considerable casualties on their pursuers until the end.

On 10th March the Wesel Bridges were blown. North of the Ruhr the German Army no longer stood on the west bank of the Rhine. Nineteen German, twelve American, four Canadian and eight British divisions had taken part in VERITABLE and GRENADE, as well as a huge number of artillery and engineer groups and specialised units. British and Canadian casualties had totalled 15,500. Twenty-two thousand German prisoners had been taken. VERITABLE was over. It had been as hard fighting as any phase of the North-West European campaign, fought in the inhospitable winter of the lower Rhineland, on a narrow front where the only tactic was to apply massed artillery fire and batter at a stoutly defended door. VERITABLE held few surprises. It could not be assisted by mobility or manoeuvre. VERITABLE was a killing match; slow, deadly and predictable. It was the last of its kind.

While these bloody battles were going on in the north, the First and Third (US) Armies had started their own offensive movements in and south of the Ardennes. In theory, operations in 21st Army Group Area had, at this time, priority; but Eisenhower's operational concept, that which had led to considerable acrimony with Montgomery, was to close up to the Rhine throughout its length, and it was not consistent with the ardent temperament of Patton, Commander of Third Army, to lag behind the leaders in any race. In the second two weeks of March, First and Third Armies advanced to the Rhine on their own account, cleared the Saar, took over 100,000 prisoners and seized two bridges across the Rhine at Oppenheim and Remagen. Bradley's 12th Army Group had thus already punched a hole into the Palatinate by the time 21st Army Group crossed the Rhine north of the Ruhr; and the bridgehead at Remagen seized on 7th March was already eight miles deep.

Nevertheless the route to the North German Plain lay across the lower Rhine. The country further south was thought to present more difficulties to the advance of armies: and there was never question but that the assault crossing by 21st Army Group must take place. It may be

thought, in retrospect, supportive of Eisenhower's original concept –
to advance on a broad front – that so many armies were, in the event,
able to advance simultaneously and in rough alignment to the Rhine,
and cross it; whereas Montgomery, opposing the concept, had maintained that only concentration on one sector and one thrust would
produce sufficient power for success. The matter was by this stage
academic. The German Army in the West was still capable of brave
resistance by individual battalion or division but cohesion had largely
gone, lack of armour and fuel made manoeuvre impossible, and Allied
superiority of strength both on land and in the air was such that an
advance on one or on a hundred thrust lines would have been possible
without serious rebuff. Hitler's Ardennes offensive had fatally weakened a Wehrmacht already fought to a standstill on every war front.
From east, south and west it was time for the *coup de grâce*: time to bring
the whole dreadful and destructive business to an end. The part of the
British Army in this final act was to cross the Rhine and roll eastwards
into the heart of Germany.

North of the Ruhr the Rhine barrier was held by First Parachute Army,
its seven divisions weary, short of men and every munition of war after
the Battles of the Reichswald and the Roer. Troops were thinly spread.
Villages and farmsteads were well prepared for defence, and were in
many cases to hold out desperately. There were, however, few mobile
reserves and the ability to concentrate force against an Allied crossing
and bridgehead was minimal.

Montgomery planned that the Rhine crossing should be undertaken
by Second Army. As in VERITABLE both British and Canadian divisions – the same divisions – were to take part.

Second Army assault was to take place on a twelve-mile front
between Rees and Wesel. On the right, XII Corps (Lieutenant-
General N. M. Ritchie) had four divisions – 7th Armoured, 15th, 52nd
and 53rd – and four independent brigades: the actual assault crossing
was to be undertaken at Wesel by 1st Commando Brigade, and north of
Xanten by 15th Division. On the left, XXX Corps (Horrocks) had five
divisions – Guards Armoured, 3rd, 43rd, 51st and 3rd Canadian –
with one independent brigade: the assault crossing was to be made at
Rees, by 51st Division. Both corps were supported by a number of
artillery and engineer groups and by specialised armoured vehicles for
amphibious use ("Buffalos") as well as tanks equipped with flotation
gear for swimming ("DD" Tanks). These last had been developed, like
all specialised armour, by the resourceful 79th Division, General

Hobart's creation. II Canadian Corps, with two Canadian divisions and one independent brigade, was to follow up; and VIII Corps (Lieutenant-General E. H. Barker) was in army reserve with 11th Armoured Division and one independent armoured brigade. I Corps (Lieutenant-General J. T. Crocker) was to undertake administration in the rear areas once the Rhine was crossed. South of the Second Army, General Simpson's Ninth (US) Army was to cross on a two divisional front between Duisburg and Wesel, under 21st Army Group command. The crossing was to be accompanied by a massive airborne operation by XVIII (US) Airborne Corps, including 6th (British) Airborne Division. Two divisions were to be dropped on a five-mile front some five miles behind the Rhine north of Wesel, with orders to seize certain bridges and important ground for the subsequent advance of the army group across the Issel River and into Westphalia. The operation was to be launched on the night of 23rd March. As VERITABLE had inched forward, huge supply dumps had been built up as early as possible between Meuse and Rhine to support subsequent operations.

The assault troops crossed the river in "Buffalos" in the darkness of 23rd March. Not all objectives were taken by dawn – there was still plenty of sting and tactical vigour shown by the enemy when cornered – but there was no serious setback. Following waves came across in assault boats. At ten o'clock on the morning of 24th March the airborne operation took place – with no question, as heretofore, of difficulty in link-up with ground forces. By nightfall, after the first complete day of battle, 15th Division had joined hands with 6th Airborne, and by midnight the first light bridge across the Rhine was complete. By 26th March, twelve bridges for heavy vehicles were ready, and the bridgehead had been widely expanded. Next day the Second Army line ran through Mechlen to Isselburg, Haldern and Dingden Woods, ten miles from the Rhine; and Dempsey had eight divisions already on the east bank. Further south, Simpson, with six divisions already across, had reached Schermbeck, well on the way to Münster. Throughout Eisenhower's command the Allies were across the Rhine. Churchill visited Montgomery's Headquarters with Brooke to witness the operation. He wrote in Montgomery's autograph book before departure a message. It ended with the words, "Forward on Wings of Flame to final victory."

The final weeks of the German war saw the British Army advance deep into the shattered Reich. Individual towns and villages were fiercely defended; and this was particularly so if SS units were encountered, or, it must be said, the very young whom German manpower shortage had now impelled into the ranks and who often fought with a devotion and bravery which astonished their opponents. But these apart the spirit of fanaticism had all but died in the German Army. German soldiers knew that hope had gone. They knew what was happening on the Eastern Front, and to their compatriots overrun by or fleeing before the Red Army. German military discipline held, but where they could decently give up the fight they did so. For their part the Allies advanced with caution. It was inevitable, with the outcome so certain and so imminent, that men did not wish to court death if risk could be avoided. Operations, in many cases, were understandably sluggish. The challenge of earlier days, the exaltation of liberation of occupied territories, was past. The advancing columns would run on to the defences of a village. A few tanks would be hit, a few casualties would be inflicted. The place would be masked while the following echelons deployed to find a way round. A well placed anti-tank gun on the edge of a wood, probably using its last rounds of ammunition, would take toll from this manoeuvre and withdraw. An artillery programme would be fired, time would be spent, another unit be pushed through to take the lead. A few prisoners would come in, a few of our own dead be hastily buried, a few more miles advanced. Then some route would be found where few defenders were in evidence and a larger leap forward achieved. Acts of heroism in such circumstances – and there were many – are the more meritorious. Casualties – and they were not few – become a little more poignant. The final battles were seldom easy, but to fight them was to engage in a race where the result was already known. The necessity was clear but the stimulus flagged.

Montgomery had understood from Eisenhower that Simpson's Ninth Army was to remain under his command until the end. He planned that it should advance on Magdeburg, on the Elbe, and detach a right wing to encircle the Ruhr from the north. Meanwhile Second Army would advance to the Elbe between Hamburg and Wittenberg, and First Canadian Army would clear North Holland and the North Sea coast. It was urgent, Montgomery told his commanders on 27th March, that all should show the utmost energy, to give the enemy no pause. He well realised that there could be dangerous relaxation near the end. After crossing the Elbe, he intended 21st Army Group to move on the axis of Hanover-Berlin.

On 28th March, however, Eisenhower told Montgomery that, once 21st Army Group had united east of the Ruhr, Simpson's Ninth Army would revert to Bradley's command. 21st Army Group would, thereafter, protect the north flank of 12th Army Group's advance. Bradley's advance would be the main Allied effort, directed on Leipzig. As agreed by Eisenhower independently with Stalin, the Western Allies would not advance on Berlin.

This change of plan – for so it seemed to Montgomery and the British Chiefs-of-Staff – was unwelcome in London, appearing as it did to relegate the British Army to a subordinate function for the closing stages of the European drama. It had been agreed by the Combined Chiefs-of-Staff that the main thrust into Germany should be in the north, although there should be another parallel advance by Frankfurt and Kassel. This now appeared overridden. There was also indignation that Eisenhower had corresponded direct with Stalin. And there was growing concern, particularly on the part of Churchill, at Soviet actions and ambitions, which led to his suggestion that the gaining of Berlin by the Western Allies might be an excellent political move; that junction with the Red Army should be effected as far to the east as possible. Political and military factors were intertwined. The British protested to their Allies at both the political and the military level. Their protests were summarily rejected. By now the American Armies so greatly outnumbered the British that the United States could not fail to have the best of the argument. Furthermore the Americans had a strong case for defending Eisenhower. The Supreme Commander had never received a political directive – as he might have done – to place particular emphasis on Berlin or Prague or any other place which might have fallen without difficulty to his forces. Thus he had every reason to put military factors first, and by those factors his plan – to make the Allied *schwerpunkt* in the centre towards Leipzig – was not demonstrably wrong. He had earlier, it is true, written that all energies in the last stage should be concentrated on a rapid thrust to Berlin, but in the absence of directions from above he had every right to adjust his plans and change his mind. Berlin was of no great military significance. As to direct correspondence with Stalin, he could and did observe that no lesser Soviet authority appeared capable of making and keeping a high level strategic compact. Nor, in actual consequence, were the operations of 21st Army Group substantially altered. Nor was victory evidently delayed.

While to their south 12th Army Group enveloped the Ruhr, their armies from south and north of it uniting on 1st April with over 300,000 prisoners taken, Second Army advanced with three corps in parallel. On the right, VIII Corps (Barker), on 8th April, crossed the Leine River north of Hanover, which fell to Ninth (US) Army: while on their left XII Corps (Ritchie) reached the Weser at Verden on the same day.

Further north, XXX Corps (Horrocks) had seized a bridge and crossed the Ems at Lingen after stiff fighting, and was moving towards Bremen. Everywhere, however disconnected and isolated, there were German rearguards, individual anti-tank guns well deployed and taking toll of the leading British tanks, blown bridges and scattered mines. By 20th April the German Army in the north had been hemmed in on the north coast, in Oldenburg and in the Cuxhaven Peninsula; in the area east of the Elbe; and in Schleswig-Holstein. The British Army had advanced two hundred miles from the Rhine. Thereafter the tempo of advance slackened. On 27th April, Bremen was fully cleared. VIII Corps crossed the Elbe on 29th April. Hamburg was invested. In the south the American Third Army had already penetrated deep into Franconia and was within miles of the Czechoslovak border. The Red Army was already battering its way into Berlin. On 30th April Hitler committed suicide.

On 4th May 1945, Montgomery received a German delegation at his Headquarters on Lüneburg Heath. All German forces in Holland, Dunkirk, North-West Germany, Schleswig-Holstein, Denmark, Heligoland and the Frisian Islands surrendered unconditionally. Four days later a general instrument of capitulation was signed in Berlin. The German war was over.

The eleven month campaign in North-West Europe was the British Army's crowning achievement in the Second World War. It was not the most difficult achievement, nor the most costly in suffering, nor the most dramatic in terms of breath-catching shifts of fortune: but it set the crown on the long march from Dunkirk. The campaign, as far as the British Army was concerned, was dominated by Montgomery. His individual battles, decisions, or contentions may long be debated: GOODWOOD, MARKET GARDEN, the delay in opening the Scheldt after the fall of Antwerp, the acrimony with Eisenhower over the priority to be given to 21st Army Group's northern thrust. These matters remain speculative. In war no man can say how an untried alternative course of action would have gone, since in war nothing is certain until it is over.

But Montgomery's achievement – and it is right to reiterate it in the concluding chapter of this work – was to keep iron control of operations: to inspire with confidence all who served under his command; and to make sure that his soldiers were never puzzled, frustrated or unsure of victory. He radiated certainty that all would be well. He communicated energy. He was never at a loss. He enjoyed difficulties, and, a thoroughly experienced and thoughtful professional, he mastered them. His temperament was ideal for war. From the first days commanding 3rd Division on the retreat to Dunkirk, assured, cocky, in good spirits; through the time of arrival in North Africa, determined to change attitudes, to be impervious to the tired knowingness of the "old desert hands"; finally to his acceptance of the German surrender on Lüneburg Heath, Montgomery dominated the collective consciousness of the British Army. He was less imaginative and in some ways less gifted than Slim; and lacked his noble humility. He was less tactful, less gracious than Alexander; considerably less adroit with Allies. He antagonised the Americans with his insensitivity. But he mastered events. He made battle and enemy conform to his will: and his will was of steel. Clausewitz remarked that "determination proceeds from a special type of mind, from a strong rather than a brilliant one." Whether or not his mind was brilliant, Montgomery's was superbly strong.

The British Army that finished the war in 1945 – under Slim in Burma, under Alexander in Italy, under Montgomery in North-West Europe – was very different from that which went to war in 1939. It was not simply or even primarily a question of size, although expansion had been huge. It was not only a matter of equipment, although there is a shattering contrast between the paucity of resources, the lack of armour and anti-aircraft artillery, the general sense of ignorant poverty in 1939 or 1940 and the abundance of the later years and of the end. It was, most of all, a matter of professionalism. As the war went on, the army changed its character and became expert. Its officers and non-commissioned officers became, in the main, adept at their jobs. Staffs became skilful, their work smooth running. Organisation, from being bumbling and amateur, became rational and effective. None of this, however, would have sufficed for victory unless the soldiers themselves had become masters of their art.

They had done so. In the years of victory, a solid confidence in the British Army made its performance as different as is possible to imagine from the record of the early tragedies and defeats. Its early setbacks and disgraces – for so men felt them – had derived from the unpreparedness of the nation to face unpalatable facts or make uncomfortable assumptions; and in consequence the army was without purpose or support until too late. It was starved of resources, incompetently administered and too small. For years British Governments persuaded themselves, and a public ready to hear, that Britain could stand aside from Continental war on land and that the dangers, if they existed, could be dealt with by others: that the readiness of the army, or the preparing of the people to serve in it, were unnecessary for Britain.

For years British Governments had settled comfortably for the propositions that if war ever came it could not possibly last long, it could not involve a large national army, and it could not directly threaten the homeland except from the air. War, as before, harshly exploded illusion. And when the task at last was clear and urgent the British turned themselves into soldiers with skill and speed.

The British Army did not always behave impeccably, whether in battle or out of it. It was sometimes ponderous, lacking in élan. It rarely showed the "handiness" in mobile battle which was the hallmark of the Afrika Korps. It is difficult to imagine that a Rommel or a Patton on the Waal on 19th September 1944 could not have reached the Arnhem Bridge – somehow. The British Army did not always die in the last ditch with the fanaticism of the Japanese. But it came to know its business. And, without histrionics, it did it. Providence, the extraordinary course of events, and the mistakes of the enemy provided time for the army to make good its mistakes, repair and restart the machine and drive it to ultimate triumph. The men who composed the British Army of the Second World War learned their trade and became entirely professional. They came from an unmilitary and in some degree an anti-military generation. They were called to an army which had been neglected as to equipment, training, tactical doctrine and the provision of a cadre of sufficient officers and non-commissioned officers for expansion. They had never until 1939 been exposed to the beneficent effects of even a short period of national service. They suffered, in the early encounters, considerable blows to their confidence and their self-respect. They were, at the beginning, too often ineptly commanded and placed in situations where no soldier could win. They were, at the end, richly endowed with equipment, worthily led, confident, skilful and deservedly victorious. They had reached the same point, after many vicissitudes, as their fathers in November 1918. "Our story in this war," wrote Churchill to Brooke with dignity, after electoral defeat in 1945, "is a good one, and this will be recognised as time goes on." British soldiers could have used the same quiet words.

War is inseparable from grief, and the soldiers knew that the best of their number lay for ever where, as Pericles said, "on the far off shores there is an abiding memorial that no pen or chisel has traced". Of these the great Athenian's words to his own countrymen may suffice for ours – "Take these men, then, as your examples. Like them, remember that prosperity can be only for the free, that freedom is the pure possession of those alone who have the courage to defend it."

Appendix I

DIVISIONS OF THE BRITISH ARMY, 1939–45

Apart from Home Defence "County" Divisions, and excluding divisions of the Indian Army and Colonial Divisions, the British Army formed forty-eight divisions in the Second World War.

Armoured Divisions

An armoured division's organisation was frequently changed. Typically, it consisted of one or more armoured brigades, each consisting of three or four tank regiments: a total of some two hundred tanks, normally cruiser tanks. In addition, an armoured division had a support group, or lorried infantry brigade; and each armoured brigade had one or more "motor battalions" – infantry travelling in special vehicles designed for cross-country work and thus able to move with tanks. An armoured division had, normally, its own armoured-car regiment, for reconnaissance. The divisional artillery, typically, consisted of field artillery regiments of three batteries, each of eight guns; regiments on a scale of one to each brigade of the division. The divisional artillery also frequently included an anti-tank regiment and a light anti-aircraft regiment. The divisional engineers normally comprised a field squadron for the close support of each brigade, and a field park of heavy and specialised equipment. Divisional Signals were responsible for communications down to and including Regimental and Battalion Headquarters: within the regiment or battalion communications were a regimental matter. There was also, on occasions, an independent machine-gun company.

An armoured division's logistic troops included field ambulances and the ability to set up an advanced dressing station as well as support each brigade with posts for the immediate handling and clearing of casualties. There were a number of transport companies for the supply of the division forward of a distribution point which would be established and itself supplied by corps or army transport. There were Ordnance field parks – mobile distribution and supply centres handling the entire, huge business of spares replacement: and in an armoured division were field workshops, normally on a scale of one for each brigade, in addition to the fitters and detachments for "light aid" – immediate repair or preparation for backloading – attached to each unit. The division consisted of between 10,000 and 14,000 men and had a total of between 3,000 and 4,000 vehicles of all types. It needed about 140 miles of road for column movement. The British Army possessed or formed eleven armoured divisions during the Second World War, as listed below. In addition there were formed or deployed some fourteen independent armoured or tank brigades. In ordinary usage an "armoured" brigade was equipped with cruiser tanks, a "tank" or "army tank" brigade with "infantry" tanks (examples are the "Matilda" and the "Churchill" tanks), slow-moving, heavily armoured, designed for close support of infantry rather than for manoeuvre, and normally placed in support of a nominated infantry division. Some armoured brigades originally formed part of armoured divisions but were later made independent brigade groups and used as corps, army or army group reserves.

DIVISIONS	THEATRES OF ACTIVE SERVICE	COMMENT
Guards	North-West Europe	Formed from a number of Guards brigades in 1941, and engaged in the Battles of Normandy, the advance to the Nederrijn, the Rhineland, the crossing of the Rhine and the advance to the Elbe. All regiments of the Household Troops were represented.
1st	France 1940, Egypt and Libya Tunisia Italy	Formally the "Mobile Division", a Regular division in the United Kingdom, the division moved to France in incomplete form in 1940. In November 1941 it moved to Egypt, and engaged in the Battles of Gazala and Alamein, advancing with Eighth Army to Tunisia thereafter. In Italy the division fought as part of Eighth Army once again.
2nd	Egypt	Formed in 1939, the division was divided on reaching the Mediterranean, and its 1st Armoured Brigade sent to Greece. The Headquarters was overrun in Cyrenaica in Rommel's offensive of spring 1941 and the division was not re-formed thereafter.
6th	Tunisia Italy	Formed in 1940, 6th Armoured Division was among the first to reach Tunisia as part

Divisions	Theatres of Active Service	Comment
		of First Army, and fought at Bou Arada and Fondouk. In Italy the division fought under Eighth Army to the end.
7th	Egypt and Libya Tunisia Italy North-West Europe	The original Middle East "Mobile Division" (General Hobart) was redesignated 7th Armoured Division in February 1940. The original "Desert Rats", they fought in O'Connor's first offensive which ended with the destruction or capture of the Italian Army at Beda Fomm; in the Western Desert battles of 1941 and 1942, culminating in the victories of Alam El Halfa and Alamein; in the advance of Eighth Army to Tunisia; in the Salerno landings and the South Italian campaign; and were then transferred to England to take part in OVERLORD, the Battles of Normandy and the Low Countries, and the crossing of the Rhine.
8th	Egypt	The division was formed in England in 1940 and moved to Egypt in 1942: but never operated as a division and was disbanded in January 1943.
9th		Formed and disbanded in the United Kingdom.
10th	Egypt	Formed originally in Palestine from 1st Cavalry Division, was moved to Egypt and took part in the Battles of Alam El Halfa and Alamein, and thereafter moved to Syria. It was disbanded in Egypt in 1944.
11th	North-West Europe	Formed in England in 1941, 11th Armoured Division was, like Guards Armoured Division, retained in England for OVERLORD. The division took part in the Battles of Normandy, took Antwerp, advanced into the Low Countries and engaged in Operation VERITABLE.
42nd		Formed and disbanded in the United Kingdom, from 42nd (Infantry) Division, a first-line Territorial division from Lancashire (q.v.).

DIVISIONS	THEATRES OF ACTIVE SERVICE	COMMENT
79th	North-West Europe	Formed in the United Kingdom in 1942, in 1943 79th Armoured Division was given responsibility for the development of all "special armoured vehicles" – amphibious tanks, minefield and obstacle-clearing tanks and assault engineer vehicles, flame throwers et al. As such it did not operate as a division but individual brigades, regiments and squadrons supported particular formations in North-West Europe, dependent on the needs of the battle: and were crucial to its success.

Infantry Divisions

An infantry division normally consisted of three infantry brigades, each of three battalions, and with divisional artillery, engineers and communications on a scale comparable to an armoured division. Infantry divisions' transport was mechanical throughout the war, although in some theatres there was extensive reliance on mule-pack companies in support. There was no troop-carrying transport established within the division: the infantry marched, unless transport was specifically allocated. Logistic services were, again, on a comparable scale to those in armoured divisions, although tonnages to be carried, whether as spares or in re-supply, were, of course, much less.

As with the armoured division many changes took place during the war, in the size and shape of infantry divisions. The division's size increased as the war went on – at full strength it counted under 14,000 men in 1939 and over 18,000 in 1944. Vehicles increased from under 3,000 to over 4,000 (but including 1,000 motorcycles). There was little difference in vehicle count between an infantry and an armoured division. An anticipatory version of Parkinson's Law applied, however, and stores increased to fill the carrying capacity available. A British corps of four divisions moving on one road would extend from London to Inverness.

It may be regarded as curious that the British Army retained certain divisions at home, and disbanded some during the war. The reason was shortage of manpower, and particularly of specialist power. It was more economic to reinforce existing formations even at the cost of breaking up others.

The British Army possessed or formed thirty-five infantry divisions in the Second World War, as listed below. In addition, there were formed nine County divisions, for coastal defence, each commanding a number of brigades but without the divisional troops which formed part of the establishment of field force divisions. The list of the field force given below does not include divisions of the Indian Army, nor the Colonial divisions. Nor are listed independent Guards and infantry brigade groups, which formed part of the field force and were placed in divisions as the need arose. Finally there was a large number of more or less static brigades for Home Defence, for the defence of Malta and other garrisons; numbering over forty in sum.

Division	THEATRES OF ACTIVE SERVICE	COMMENT
1st	France and Belgium 1940 Tunisia Italy	The division, one of the original Regular divisions of the army, was part of the BEF. Evacuated at Dunkirk, it later took part in the expedition of First Army to Tunisia, and thereafter, in Italy, took part in the fighting at Anzio, the advance to Rome and the Battles of the Gothic Line. Like *all* infantry divisions its battalions, as the war went on, were a mixture of Regular and Territorial or wartime battalions.
2nd	France and Belgium 1940 Burma	An original Regular division and part of the BEF. The division moved from England to India in 1942, and was brought into the Battle of Kohima, taking part thereafter in CAPITAL in 1944.
3rd	France and Belgium 1940 North-West Europe	An original Regular division and part of the BEF. The division took part in OVERLORD, the Battles of Normandy, the advance into the Low Countries, VERITABLE and the crossing of the Rhine.
4th	France and Belgium 1940 Tunisia Italy	An original Regular division and part of the BEF. The division took part in the Tunisian campaign in First Army, and in the Italian campaign as part of Eighth Army; and was moved to Greece in the crisis of December 1944.
5th	France and Belgium 1940 Sicily Italy	An original Regular division and part of the BEF. Two brigades took part in the expedition to and fighting in Madagascar in 1942. In 1942 the division was sent to India, and thence to Persia, Iraq, Syria and thence took part in the landings in Sicily – HUSKY – and in the advance up the east

DIVISIONS	THEATRES OF ACTIVE SERVICE	COMMENT
		flank of Italy to the Battles of the Sangro in 1943. In 1944 the division was engaged on the West Italian flank, in the crossing of the Garigliano, and the Anzio landings; and in the advance to Rome in summer 1944.
8th	Palestine	A Regular division before the war, the division was disbanded in Palestine in 1940
12th	France and Belgium 1940	A Territorial division, with regiments mainly recruited in the Home Counties, the division moved to France for "labour duties" and was caught up, without supporting artillery, logistic or communications, in the campaign which began in May 1940. Disbanded in England in July 1940.
15th	North-West Europe	A Territorial division, 15th was a Scottish division, formed in the main from Scottish regiments. An OVERLORD division it took part in the Battles of Normandy, the advance in the Low Countries, VERITABLE, and the Rhine crossing.
18th	Malaya and Singapore	A Territorial division, drawn from East Anglia, 18th was sent to India at the end of 1941 and immediately diverted to Singapore, where part of the division was deployed forwards to the mainland. The division was largely destroyed or taken prisoner in the fighting on Singapore Island.
23rd	France and Belgium 1940	A Territorial division, with North Country regiments from Durham and Yorkshire, 23rd Division suffered the same fate as 12th (q.v.). It was disbanded.
36th	Burma	Originally an Indian division, 36th became a British division in 1944 and took part in the march south from the Northern Combat Area Command, joining Fourteenth Army in the Battles for Mandalay.
38th		A Territorial division, formed in 1939 and disbanded in England in 1944.
42nd	France and Belgium 1940	A Territorial division, almost entirely composed of Lancashire and Manchester regi-

Appendix I

DIVISIONS	THEATRES OF ACTIVE SERVICE	COMMENT

ments, 42nd Division served in the BEF, and in November 1941 was converted into an armoured division (q.v.).

43rd — North-West Europe

A Territorial division, composed of regiments from the Wessex Counties, 43rd Division took part in OVERLORD, the Normandy battles, the advance in the Low Countries, VERITABLE, and the Rhine crossing.

44th — France and Belgium 1940 / Egypt

A Territorial division, and part of the BEF in 1940, the division was composed of regiments from the Home and Southern Counties. In 1942 the division was sent to Egypt, arriving for the Battles of Alam El Halfa and Alamein. It was disbanded in January 1943.

45th

A Territorial division, disbanded in England in 1944.

46th — France and Belgium 1940 / Tunisia / Italy

Composed of regiments from the Midlands and Yorkshire, 46th Division, a Territorial division, was part of the BEF, and then took part in the Tunisian campaign as part of First Army. The division landed at Salerno, and advanced up the west coast of Italy; and after the fall of Rome took part in the Battles of the Gothic Line.

47th

Originally the 2nd (London) Territorial Division, 47th Division was so designated in November 1940. It originally consisted primarily of London regiments but at some time also included battalions from Scotland, Ireland and the West Country. It was disbanded in 1944.

48th — France and Belgium 1940

With regiments from Oxfordshire, Buckinghamshire, Northamptonshire, Warwickshire, Staffordshire, Worcestershire and Gloucestershire, as well as Irish and Scottish battalions at various times, 48th Division, a Territorial division, was highly representative and its designation of "South Midland", applicable to its origins rather than its ultimate character. The division was part of the BEF and ceased to be a first-line division in 1942.

DIVISIONS	THEATRES OF ACTIVE SERVICE	COMMENT
49th	Norway 1940 North-West Europe	49th Division, a Territorial division, was nominally a Yorkshire division but included battalions from Welsh and Midland regiments as well. Although not fighting as a division, its brigades fought individually in the Norwegian Expedition of 1940. Thereafter it became an OVERLORD division, fought in the Battles of Normandy, and as part of I Corps in the operations to clear the Scheldt.
50th	France and Belgium 1940 Egypt Libya Tunisia Sicily North-West Europe	50th Division, a Territorial division, was rooted in the north. Its regiments were largely from Northumberland, Durham and Yorkshire. It had, however, as the war continued, brigades with London, Midland and Home Counties regiments as well. Originally part of the BEF, 50th Division went to the Middle East in the spring of 1941 and was first sent to Iraq and Syria. Deployed then to Egypt it took part in the Western Desert battles of 1942, culminating in Alamein; advanced with Eighth Army to Tunisia; landed in Sicily; was withdrawn to England for OVERLORD, and took part in the Battles of Normandy, and the advance in the Low Countries.
51st	France 1940 Egypt Libya Tunisia Sicily North-West Europe	51st (Highland) Division, a Territorial division composed of Highland regiments, was surrounded and forced to surrender at St. Valéry-en-Caux in June 1940. Reconstituted in England by the renaming, in August 1940, of 9th (Highland) Division, it moved to Egypt in August 1942 in time for the Battle of Alamein. Thereafter it advanced with Eighth Army to Tunisia, landed in Sicily, and was withdrawn to England for OVERLORD. The division took part in the Battles of Normandy, in Operation VERITABLE and in the Rhine crossing.
52nd	France 1940 North-West Europe	52nd Division, a Territorial division composed in the main of Lowland Scots and Glasgow regiments, was sent to France to "start a new BEF" in 1940 and evacuated from western French ports in June. Thereafter the division was deployed to North-West Europe in October 1944, took part in

DIVISIONS	THEATRES OF ACTIVE SERVICE	COMMENT
		the clearance of the Scheldt, in Operation VERITABLE and in the Rhine crossing.
53rd	North-West Europe	A Welsh Territorial division, composed of Welsh regiments, 53rd Division crossed to Normandy in June 1944 and took part in the Battles of Normandy, the advance in the Low Countries, VERITABLE and the Rhine crossing.
54th		A Territorial division, based in West Lancashire, 54th Division remained in the United Kingdom.
56th	France and Belgium 1940 Burma	Originally 1st (London) Territorial Division, 56th Division was largely composed of London and Home Counties regiments although commanding also, at various times, Scottish battalions and a Guards brigade. Part of the BEF in 1940, the division was sent to India in 1942, and thence to the Kohima Battle in 1944, followed by CAPITAL and the campaign for Mandalay in 1945.
59th	North-West Europe	A Territorial division, primarily of Staffordshire but also of Lancashire regiments, the division took part in OVERLORD and the Battles of Normandy, and was disbanded in October 1944.
61st		A Territorial division, formed in September 1939, and retained in the United Kingdom.
66th		A Territorial division, formed in September 1939 and disbanded in the United Kingdom in June 1940.
70th	Egypt Libya India	Originally a Regular division – 7th Division – in Egypt, and then redesignated 6th Division until October 1941. 70th Division formed part of the garrison of Tobruk, and took part in the CRUSADER battle when Tobruk was relieved. Thereafter the division was sent to India and formed the basis of "Special Force", the Chindit Long Range Penetration force. The division was disbanded as such in November 1943.

DIVISIONS	THEATRES OF ACTIVE SERVICE	COMMENT
76th		Formed in England in 1941 and disbanded in 1944.
77th		A career exactly parallel to that of 76th Division (q.v.). These divisions were re-designated from the "County" division formed to act as immediate defence on the coast, against invasion in 1940; and, like several other divisions, were ultimately disbanded in order to provide reinforcements for other formations.
78th	Tunisia Sicily Italy	78th Division was formed in England in 1942, with regiments from several parts of the United Kingdom, with a Guards brigade, and no clear Territorial affiliation. The division took part in the Tunisian campaign as part of First Army, in the landings in Sicily, and in the Italian campaign as part of Eighth Army, until the final act.
80th		Formed in 1943 and disbanded in 1944 in the United Kingdom.

Airborne Divisions

The airborne division, an innovation of the Second World War, was the outcome of extensive experiment during the war and in battle itself. The general pattern was that of parachute troops dropping – or, at least, trained and equipped to drop – by parachute, and airlanded troops arriving by glider or by (later) transport aircraft. The establishment provided for two parachute and one airlanding brigades.

Supporting arms and logistic services were based on a comparable scale to other divisions – a field squadron or company of engineers, a field ambulance, supporting each brigade for instance; and those supporting the parachute brigades were themselves parachute troops. The armoured reconnaissance and artillery regiments (including anti-tank artillery) were airlanded. An airborne division consisted of 12,000 men: 1,000 scout cars (lightly protected); 3,000 bicycles; 1,000 motorcycles; about six hundred "soft skinned" vehicles; and twenty-two light tanks.

The British Army formed two airborne divisions in the Second World War. They are listed below. Parachute brigades were switched between divisions, or fought as infantry in other, non-airborne, divisions.

Division	Theatre of Active Service	Comments
1st	Tunisia Sicily Italy North-West Europe	1st Airborne Division was formed in 1941. Brigades took part in the North African landings as part of First Army: the Sicilian landings as part of Eighth Army: the Italian landings (from the sea) and the Italian campaign until the spring of 1944. The division was reassembled in England as Part of I (Airborne) Corps and took part in MARKET GARDEN, being dropped at Arnhem. Thereafter, after heavy casualties, the remainder were withdrawn to England.
6th	North-West Europe	6th Airborne Division was formed in 1943. It took part in OVERLORD, attacking ahead of the seaborne assault on D Day. After the early Normandy battles, the division was withdrawn to England, and again deployed to North-West Europe in reserve during the Ardennes offensive of Christmas 1944. Withdrawn again to England in February 1945, the division took part in the Rhine crossing, as a division and in the airborne role.

Appendix II

CODEWORDS USED IN THE TEXT

ABERDEEN	Chindit base in Burma, 1944
AVALANCHE	Allied landings at Salerno, September 1943
BARBAROSSA	German invasion of Russia, June 1941
BATTLEAXE	British offensive in the Western Desert, June 1941
BLACKCOCK	British offensive on the Roer, January 1945
BLACKPOOL	Chindit base in Burma, 1944
BLUECOAT	British offensive at Caumont, August 1944
CAPITAL	British offensive in Burma, December 1944
COMPASS	British offensive in the Western Desert, December 1940
CRUSADER	British offensive in the Western Desert, November 1941
DIADEM	Allied offensive in Italy, May 1944
DRACULA	British air and seaborne assault on Rangoon, May 1945
DRAGOON	Allied landings in Southern France, August 1944
DYNAMO	Evacuation of British Expeditionary Force from Dunkirk, May–June 1940.
EXTENDED CAPITAL	Further British offensive in Burma, to take Mandalay, Meiktila and advance on Rangoon, winter and spring 1945
GRENADE	American offensive between Meuse and Rhine, February 1945
GOODWOOD	British and Canadian offensive at Caen, July 1944
HA-GO	Japanese offensive in Arakan, February 1944
HAMMER	British operation against Trondheim, April 1940 (cancelled)
HUSKY	Allied invasion of Sicily, July 1943
LIGHTFOOT	Battle of Alamein, October 1942
MARKET GARDEN	Anglo-American Airborne and Second (British) Army offensive to cross the Meuse, Waal and Nederrijn Rivers, September 1944
MARITA	German invasion of Greece, April 1941
MAURICEFORCE	British force operating from Namsos, Norway, April 1940
MERKUR	German invasion of Crete, May 1941
MULBERRY	Prefabricated harbour for Operation OVERLORD
OCHSENKOPF	German offensive in Tunisia, February 1943
OVERLORD	Allied invasion of France, June 1944
ROMULUS	British offensive in Arakan, December 1944

Appendix II

RUPERTFORCE	Allied force operating at and from Narvik, Norway, April 1940
SEELÖWE	Intended German invasion of England, 1940
SHINGLE	Anglo-American landings at Anzio, January 1944
SICHELSCHNITT	German offensive in France, Belgium, Holland and Luxembourg, May 1940
SICKLEFORCE	British force operating from Aandalsnes, Norway, April 1940
SUPERCHARGE	Final phase of Battle of Alamein, November 1942
TORCH	Allied landings in North Africa, November 1942
U-GO	Japanese offensive at Imphal and Kohima, March 1944
ULTRA	Intelligence material derived from intercepted and decyphered German signals
VERITABLE	British and Canadian offensive between Meuse and Rhine, February 1945
VULCAN	British offensive in Tunisia, April 1943
WESERUBUNG	German invasion of Norway, April 1940
WHITE CITY	Chindit base in Burma, 1944

Sources and Bibliography

Apart from published works, of which a bibliography is given below, I have had access to the "Alanbrooke Personal Files", which have for the last twenty-seven years represented a separate section of the Alanbrooke Papers at the Liddell Hart Centre, King's College, London. This section, originally loaned to Sir Arthur Bryant for work on *Triumph in the West* and *Turn of the Tide* (Collins), has now been reunited with the main collection of Alanbrooke Papers to which I have also had access. It contains, among other documents, personal correspondence between Lord Alanbrooke and his contemporaries: and quotations in the text from, or reference to, correspondence and signals between Alanbrooke and Generals Alexander, Auchinleck, Montgomery et al are taken therefrom or from the Alanbrooke Papers themselves.

In 1949 and 1950 an excellent series of monographs was produced under the aegis of the War Office, to record and distil the lessons of the Second World War. These were produced for each Arm of the Service, for training, manpower problems, etc., and can be seen in the Ministry of Defence Library. The Statistical Digest produced by the Central Statistical Office as part of the History of the Second World War has also been invaluable.

I have drawn on personal papers of my own, and where attribution of quotation is appropriate have referred to them as "Fraser Papers".

I have been helped by regimental histories of regiments involved in particular battles. Unless a quotation has been made, however, I have not specified these.

The following bibliography is selective. The literature of the Second World War and of the British Army's part in it is immense. To each of the authors listed, whether I have agreed with all their conclusions or not, and to many others whose insights or recollections have helped me, I owe a debt of gratitude.

Angus, Tom, *Men at Arnhem*, Leo Cooper, 1976.
Barnett, Correlli, *Britian and Her Army*, Allen Lane, 1970.
    The Desert Generals, William Kimber, 1960.
Bayerlein, Lieutenant-General Fritz, *El Alamein*, published in *The Fatal Decisions*, Michael Joseph, 1950 (henceforth *The Fatal Decisions*).

Sources and Bibliography

Bidwell, Shelford, *Gunners at War*, Arms and Armour Press, 1970.
    The Chindit War, Hodder and Stoughton, 1979.
Blumenson, Martin, *General Lucas at Anzio*
    General Bradley's Decision at Argentan published by Harcourt and Brace, 1959, in *Command Decisions* (henceforth *Command Decisions*).
    Rommel's Last Victory, George Allen and Unwin, 1968.
Bond, Brian, *Chief of Staff, The Diaries of Sir Henry Pownall*, Leo Cooper, 1974.
    France and Belgium, 1939–1940, Davis Poynter, 1975.
    Liddell Hart – A Study of his Military Thought, Cassell, 1977.
    British Military Policy between the Two World Wars, Clarendon Press, 1980.
Carver, Michael, *Tobruk*, B. F. Batsford Ltd, 1964.
    El Alamein, B. F. Batsford Ltd, 1962.
Chalfont, Alun, *Montgomery of Alamein*, Weidenfeld and Nicolson, 1976.
Churchill, Winston, *The Second World War*, Cassell, 1949.
Collier, Richard, *The Sands of Dunkirk*, Collins, 1961.
Colville, J. R., *Man of Valour*, Collins, 1972.
Connell, John, *Wavell*, Collins, 1964.
Cooper, Matthew, *The German Army*, Macdonald and Janes, 1978.
Davin, D. M., *Crete*, War History Branch, Department of Internal Affairs, New Zealand, 1953.
De Guingand, Sir Francis, *Operation Victory*, Hodder and Stoughton, 1947.
Deny, T. K., *The Campaign in Norway*, HMSO, 1952.
Ellis, L. F., *The War in France and Flanders, 1939–40*, HMSO, 1953.
    Victory in the West, HMSO, 1968.
Falk, Stanley L., *Seventy Days to Singapore*, Robert Hale and Co, 1975.
Farrar-Hockley, Anthony, *Infantry Tactics, 1939–45*, Almark, 1976.
Fergusson, Bernard, *The Watery Maze*, Collins, 1961.
Frost, Major-General John, *A Drop Too Many*, Cassell, 1980.
Gibbs, Norman, *Grand Strategy, Volume I, History of the Second World War*, HMSO, 1976.
Guderian, Heinz, *Panzer Leader* (Tr), Michael Joseph, 1952.
Hamilton, Nigel, *Monty*, Hamish Hamilton, 1981.
Hinsley, F. H., *British Intelligence in the Second World War*, HMSO, 1979.
Horne, Alistair, *To Lose a Battle*, Macmillan, 1969.
Howard, Michael, *The Continental Commitment*, Temple Smith, 1972.
Jackson, Robert, *Dunkirk*, Arthur Barker Ltd, 1976.
Jackson, W. G. F., *The Battle for Italy*, B. T. Batsford Ltd, 1976.
    The Battle for Rome, B. T. Batsford Ltd, 1969.
Jacobsen, Hans Adolf and Rohwer, Jurgen, *Decisive Battles of World War II – The German View*, André Deutsch, 1965.
Lewin, Ronald, *Montgomery as Military Commander*, B. T. Batsford, 1971.
    Slim, Leo Cooper, 1976.
    The Chief, Hutchinson, 1980.
Liddell Hart, Basil, *The Rommel Papers*, Collins, 1953.
    The Tanks, Cassell, 1970.
    Memoirs, Cassell, 1965.
    History of the Second World War, Cassell, 1970.
Macdonald, Charles, *The Decision to Launch Operation Market Garden, Command Decisions*.
Mackesy, Piers, *Churchill and Narvik*, RUSI Journal, 1970.

McIntyre, Donald, *Narvik*, Fontana/Collins, 1970.
Matloff, Maurice, *The Anvil Decision, Command Decisions.*
Mathews, Sidney T., *General Clark's Decision to Drive on Rome, Command Decisions.*
Molony, C. J. C., *The Mediterranean and the Middle East*, HMSO, 1973.
Montgomery of Alamein, *Memoirs*, Collins, 1958.
Nicolson, Nigel, *Alex*, Weidenfeld and Nicolson, 1973.
Parkinson, R., *The Auk*, Hart Davis, Macgibbon, 1977.
Percival, A. E., *The War in Malaya*, Eyre and Spottiswoode, 1949.
Pitt, Barrie, *Crucible of War*, Jonathan Cape, 1980.
Playfair, I. S. O., *The Mediterranean and the Middle East*, HMSO, 1954.
Pogue, Forrest, *The Decision to Halt at the Elbe, Command Decisions.*
Ruppenthal, Roland G., *Logistics and the Broad-Front Strategy, Command Decisions.*
Ryan, Cornelius, *A Bridge Too Far*, Hamish Hamilton, 1974.
Shepperd, G. A., *The Italian Campaign, 1943–54*, Arthur Barker Ltd, 1968.
Sixsmith, Major-General E. K. G., *British Generalship in the Twentieth Century*, Arms and Armour Press, 1970.
Slim, Viscount, *Defeat into Victory*, Cassell, 1956.
Smith, E. D., *Battle of Burma*, B. T. Batsford Ltd, 1979.
Stewart, J. McD. G., *The Struggle for Crete*, OUP, 1966.
Strawson, John, *The Battle of North Africa*, B. T. Batsford, 1969.
Trevor-Roper, H. R. (ed.), *Hitler's War Directives*, Sidgwick and Jackson, 1964.
Von Manteuffel, General Hasso, *The Ardennes*
    The Fatal Decisions
Von Mellenthin, Major-General F. W., *Panzer Battles, 1939–1945*, Cassell, 1955.
Von Senger und Etterlin, F., *Neither Fear nor Hope* (Tr), Macdonald, 1963.
Wilmot, Chester, *Struggle for Europe*, Collins, 1952.
Wilson, Field Marshal Lord, *Eight Years Overseas*, Hutchinson, 1948.
Woodman Kirby, S., *The War Against Japan*, HMSO, 1958.
Zimmermann. Lieutenant-General Bodo, *The Fatal Decisions*, Michael Joseph, 1956.

Index

Index

British Expeditionary Force: formed, 24, 26; deployment, 26–9; and 1940 German offensive, 54–7, 59–63, 77; withdrawal, 57, 60, 63–5, 68–72, 77–8; remnants, 73; assessed, 78–80
Brooke, Field Marshal Sir Alan: commands BEF II Corps, 24, 56, 69; and BEF withdrawal, 65–6, 76–7; as C. in C. Home Forces, 84–5, 87; as CIGS, 84; character, 84, 87; supports airborne troops, 94; and Commandos, 95; on indiscipline, 108; and Wavell, 114; and Ritchie, 176–7; and defence of Burma, 203; and Anderson, 251; Montgomery writes to, 253–4, 265–6, 331–2, 335, 347, 385; and Sicily operations, 264–6; and Salerno, 272; and Anzio, 282; and Cassino, 286; on Wingate, 316*n*; and Normandy operations, 331–2, 335; and Montgomery's advance, 347; and invasion of Southern France, 351; and Alexander's Vienna strategy, 357; on final Burma campaign, 363; and Ardennes battle, 385; and Rhine crossing, 392; and British achievement, 397
Brooke-Popham, Air Marshal Sir Robert, 181
Browning, Lt.-Gen. F. A. M., 94, 343
Bruce-Scott, Major-Gen. J., 198
Bruneval: 1942 raid, 96, 247*n*
Bucknall, Lt.-Gen. G. C., 328, 338
Bulgaria, 132–3
Burcorps, 208–9, 211, 304
Burma: defence, 192, 198–9, 207; Japanese invasion and occupation, 198–211; and India, 199; indiscipline in, 210; British retreat from, 211; logistical difficulties, 293; Wavell's offensive, 293–8; disparate Allied views on, 301–2; operations in, 306–15; final campaign and victory, 363–76
Burma Area Army (Japanese), 364, 372
Burnett-Stuart, Gen. Sir John, 16

Caen, 327, 328, 330–7

Caesar Line (Italy), 287, 290–1
Calais: in 1940 campaign, 67–8, 78; 1944 surrender, 378
Cambrai, Battle of, 7
Campbell, Brig. J. C., 180
Capital, Operation, 363, 365
Carton de Wiart, Major-Gen. Sir Adrian, 36, 40, 45
Casablanca, 247, 251
Cassino (Italy), 278–80, 282, 285–9
Cauldron, Battle of the (1942), 219–20, 226
Caumont (Normandy), 337–8
Chamberlain, Neville, 15, 17–21, 30, 50
Chappell, Brig. B. H., 141
Cherbourg, 326, 331, 340, 378
Chiang Kai-shek, 203*n*, 209, 302, 367, 371
China: Concession areas, 11; and defence of Burma, 203, 205, 208–9; and Allied operations in Burma, 293–4, 298, 301–4, 319, 363, 371; and Allied strategy, 302–3; Japanese offensive against, 367
Chindits, 299–302, 305–6, 309, 315–20
Chindwin River, 210, 293–4, 304–5, 309, 311, 364–7
Christison, Lt.-Gen. A. F. P., 303, 305–8, 315, 372–3
Churchill, (Sir) Winston: on unpreparedness for war, 5; on offensive fighting, 8; supports Finland, 30; and Norwegian campaign, 32–3, 48, 52; succeeds as Prime Minister, 50; and BEF 1940 campaign, 63; orders Gort to leave, 71; and Dunkirk evacuation, 71; Brooke advises against Brittany redoubt, 77; relations with military chiefs, 86–7, 361; and Wavell, 114, 140, 160; and Crete, 140; and Middle East supplies, 155; and Auchinleck, 161; and defence of Burma, 201; and invasion of Southern France, 351; and Alexander's Vienna strategy, 357; on Alexander's Italy victory, 361; and Rhine crossing, 392; suspicion of

419